AF712844

Knowledge Management and Leadership in the AI Era

Harnessing Technology for Innovative Organizations

Artificial Intelligence in Organizations: Transformative Technologies, Applications, and Impacts

Print ISSN: 2979-0700
Online ISSN: 2979-0719

Series Editor: Tereza Raquel Merlo *(University of North Texas, USA)*

AI-adoption is becoming increasingly widespread. It is a transformative force reshaping countless fields and industries, revolutionizing the way organizations create and capture value. In this new world, a clear understanding of AI's implications has become indispensable for both business leaders and academic researchers. This series was developed to serve as a bridge between theory and practice, offering a holistic view of AI in business from foundational knowledge to advanced applications and future directions.

Designed to guide executives, managers, and professionals, the series explores how organizations can strategically leverage AI for innovation, sustainable growth, and competitive advantage. At the same time, the books of this series provide scholars and students with a deeper understanding of current trends, opportunities, and challenges, including ethical considerations, regulatory shifts, and workforce transformation. By integrating academic rigor with practical relevance, this series equips its readers with the knowledge, strategies, and foresight necessary to successfully navigate and lead in an AI-powered future.

Published

Vol. 4 *Knowledge Management and Leadership in the AI Era: Harnessing Technology for Innovative Organizations*
edited by Tereza Raquel Merlo and Patrícia de Sá Freire

Vol. 3 *AI Unleashed: Industry Use Cases and Innovations*
by Marc Helmold, Ayse Kucuk Yilmaz, Tracy Dathe and Florian Hummel

Vol. 2 *Navigating Inequities and Social Justice in the Age of Artificial Intelligence*
edited by Kendra Albright, Tereza Raquel Merlo and Naresh Kumar Agarwal

Vol. 1 *AI-Driven Revolution: Transforming the Business Landscape*
edited by Tereza Raquel Merlo

Volume 4

Artificial Intelligence in Organizations: Transformative Technologies, Applications, and Impacts

Knowledge Management and Leadership in the AI Era

Harnessing Technology for Innovative Organizations

editors

Tereza Raquel Merlo

University of North Texas, USA

Patrícia de Sá Freire

Federal University of Santa Catarina, Brazil

World Scientific

NEW JERSEY • LONDON • SINGAPORE • BEIJING • SHANGHAI • HONG KONG • TAIPEI • CHENNAI • TOKYO

Published by

World Scientific Publishing Europe Ltd.
57 Shelton Street, Covent Garden, London WC2H 9HE
Head office: 5 Toh Tuck Link, Singapore 596224
USA office: 27 Warren Street, Suite 401-402, Hackensack, NJ 07601

Library of Congress Cataloging-in-Publication Data
Names: Merlo, Tereza Raquel, 1972– editor | Sá Freire, Patrícia de editor
Title: Knowledge management and leadership in the AI era : harnessing technology for innovative organizations / editors, Tereza Raquel Merlo, University of North Texas, USA, Patrícia de Sá Freire, Federal University of Santa Catarina, Brazil.
Description: New Jersey : World Scientific, [2026] | Series: Artificial intelligence in organizations: transformative technologies, applications, and impacts ; vol. 4 | Includes bibliographical references and index.
Identifiers: LCCN 2025047259 | ISBN 9781800617407 hardcover | ISBN 9781800617414 ebook | ISBN 9781800617421 ebook other
Subjects: LCSH: Knowledge management | Leadership | Technological innovations--Management | Artificial intelligence--Business applications
Classification: LCC HD30.2 .K636845 2026 | DDC 658.4/038--dc23/eng/20260204
LC record available at https://lccn.loc.gov/2025047259

British Library Cataloguing-in-Publication Data
A catalogue record for this book is available from the British Library.

Copyright © 2026 by World Scientific Publishing Europe Ltd.

All rights reserved. This book, or parts thereof, may not be reproduced in any form or by any means, electronic or mechanical, including photocopying, recording or any information storage and retrieval system now known or to be invented, without written permission from the Publisher.

For photocopying of material in this volume, please pay a copying fee through the Copyright Clearance Center, Inc., 222 Rosewood Drive, Danvers, MA 01923, USA. In this case permission to photocopy is not required from the publisher.

For any available supplementary material, please visit
https://www.worldscientific.com/worldscibooks/10.1142/Q0512#t=suppl

Desk Editors: Murali Appadurai/Srinidhi Murugan

Typeset by Stallion Press
Email: enquiries@stallionpress.com

Printed in Singapore

We dedicate this volume, Knowledge Management and Leadership in the AI Era: Harnessing Technology for Innovative Organizations, to all visionary leaders, knowledge professionals, and scholars who are committed to shaping organizations that balance technological advancement with human values, to the pioneers who dare to explore the synergies between artificial intelligence and knowledge management, leadership, and education, whose courage and curiosity inspire progress, and to our families and friends, whose unwavering support, patience, and encouragement made this work possible.

© 2026 World Scientific Publishing Europe Ltd.
https://doi.org/10.1142/9781800617414_fmatter

Foreword

In an era characterized by rapid technological advances, exponential data proliferation, and the accelerating pace of digital transformation across industries and societies, organizations, both small and large, and individuals alike are navigating unprecedented changes in how information is created, processed, managed, shared, and utilized. The convergence of knowledge management (KM) and artificial intelligence (AI) is defining how knowledge is generated, distributed, and applied across diverse organizational and institutional contexts. *Knowledge Management and Leadership in the AI Era: Harnessing Technology for Innovative Organizations* is a timely and critical contribution to this ongoing digital transformation and evolution. The edited book encapsulates cutting-edge scholarly contributions from a diverse group of academics and practitioners.

The book is divided into three sections. The first section, "Reimagining Knowledge Management Through Artificial Intelligence," presents theoretical frameworks and applied studies exploring how AI maps, preserves, and amplifies organizational knowledge while addressing issues such as ethical, cultural, and practical implications. The second section, "Rethinking Education and Learning Through AI and KM," focuses on education and professional learning environments. The chapters discuss the roles of AI in academic integrity and its impact on knowledge creation by humans and machines. It emphasizes the importance of educational leadership in the age of AI. The third section, "Leadership, Organizational Transformation, and the Human Factor," brings to the discussion the human dimension and the complex challenges ranging from digital transformation to sustainability. This section highlights the importance of collaborative intelligence and entrepreneurial thinking.

The contributions made in this book reflect the increased recognition that the integration of AI into KM is not merely a technical endeavor but also a profoundly human and social issue. Leadership in the age of AI requires more than technical skills; it also necessitates deeper systems thinking, ethical awareness, and unwavering commitment to science and innovation.

I commend the editors, Dr. Tereza Raquel Merlo and Dr. Patrícia de Sá Freire, for putting these book chapters together in a timely manner, which reflect a rich and diverse collection. I invite readers to engage deeply with the chapters in the book and not only view AI and KM through a technical lens, but also explore the rich human, social, and cultural dimensions.

Dr. Suliman Hawamdeh
Regents Professor,
University of North Texas, USA

© 2026 World Scientific Publishing Europe Ltd.
https://doi.org/10.1142/9781800617414_fmatter

Preface

The intersection of knowledge management (KM) and artificial intelligence (AI) marks a critical juncture in the transformation of contemporary organizations. In this rapidly shifting landscape, the ability to generate, share, and apply knowledge is being profoundly reshaped by intelligent technologies. These innovations challenge and expand traditional models of leadership and organizational learning. This book, *Knowledge Management and Leadership in the AI Era: Harnessing Technology for Innovative Organizations*, responds to this context by proposing a multifaceted and ethically grounded reflection on how individuals and organizations can manage knowledge and lead with purpose in times of technological acceleration.

The conceptual foundations that orient this book stem from the principles of *transhuman co-production* – an emerging and ethically committed lens for understanding the interaction between humans and AI. Unlike the predominant techno-optimist discourses, this view emphasizes not only the disruptive potential of AI but also the non-delegable responsibility of humans in shaping and steering its application. The capital "H" in *transHuman* signals the irreplaceable role of human discernment, values, and context in this relationship. As editors, we adopt this perspective as a guiding principle: innovation, to be transformative, must be co-produced with intentionality, care, and a clear commitment to the common good. This paradigm permeates the various contributions in this volume, linking ethics, education, technology, and the critical role of leadership in a cohesive and human-centered narrative.

Organized in three thematic sections, the volume brings together researchers and practitioners from diverse institutions, cultural backgrounds, and areas of expertise, creating a plural and polyphonic dialogue that mirrors the complexity of the subject.

The first section, dedicated to reimagining KM through AI, explores how intelligent systems can support knowledge creation, mapping, and governance, enhancing processes while also surfacing ethical and operational dilemmas. Cases and models presented in this section reveal how AI, when thoughtfully applied, can become an ally in structuring and strengthening organizational intelligence.

The second section addresses the transformations in educational ecosystems, highlighting the convergence of KM, digital technologies, and new roles for educators in the era of AI. Discussions on neolearning, academic integrity, and the evolution of leadership in learning environments emphasize the need for more adaptive, human-centered, and responsible pedagogical strategies. From corporate universities to public institutions, authors investigate how innovation in learning methodologies aligns with leadership development and knowledge democratization.

The third section expands the debate to organizational transformation and human agency. Here, the role of collaborative and transformative leadership, algorithmic decision-making, and the importance of resilience and ethical discernment are brought into focus. Contributors examine how inner development goals, transhuman co-production, new forms of teamwork, and leadership strategy are not mere responses to change but catalysts for more sustainable and reflective modes of organizing and, ultimately, organizational competitiveness.

Throughout the book, a set of transversal themes stands out: the ethical integration of AI, the preservation of critical human judgment, the institutionalization of inclusive knowledge practices, and the design of future-oriented leadership models. These themes unify the contributions and also point to key research and action agendas for scholars, organizational leaders, and policymakers alike.

The authors featured in this work come from a range of organizational contexts, from universities to corporate environments and governmental sectors, and they contribute theoretical insights, applied research, and innovative practices. Their diversity strengthens the book's mission: to illuminate the paths by which technology, knowledge, and leadership can be rethought in a more collaborative, ethical, and transformative way.

Beyond the richness of ideas, the book presents a repertoire of methodological approaches, frameworks, and applied models, which, by themselves, already constitute a valuable resource for scholars and practitioners. Whether through diagnostic instruments for knowledge maturity, experimental designs for leadership development, or models of collaborative intelligence and neolearning, the tools presented herein provide robust foundations for further academic inquiry and practical experimentation. These contributions advance not only our understanding but also our capacity to transform organizations responsibly and innovatively. This includes comprehensive frameworks for AI-driven business process optimization, with practical insights into tools such as process mining and robotic process automation. These contributions bridge theory and implementation, equipping readers with actionable pathways to align technological innovation with operational excellence.

We, as editors, hope the book serves as a space for reflection and inspiration. In inviting readers to navigate these pages, we also invite them to imagine and enact new ways of leading and learning – ways that honor human complexity while embracing the potential of technological augmentation.

This book is more than a compilation of academic contributions – it is a collective call to rethink the foundations of organizational existence in the AI era. Let these pages inspire action, provoke dialogue, and cultivate futures anchored in knowledge, ethics, and shared responsibility.

True leadership arises not from power or position, but from the courage to serve with wisdom (Plato, 427–347 BCE), the strength to act with virtue (Aristotle, 384–322 BCE), the humility to lead by example (Confucius, 551–479 BCE), the duty to uphold justice (Cicero, 106–43 BCE), the commitment to the common good (John Locke, 1632–1704), and the vision to inspire transformation (James MacGregor Burns, 1918–2014), all within a framework of legitimate and ethical authority (Max Weber, 1864–1920).

Tereza Raquel Merlo
Patrícia de Sá Freire

© 2026 World Scientific Publishing Europe Ltd.
https://doi.org/10.1142/9781800617414_fmatter

About the Editors

Tereza Raquel Merlo is a postdoctoral researcher at the Federal University of Rio de Janeiro (UFRJ), affiliated with the Brazilian Institute of Information in Science and Technology (IBICT). She is a researcher, professor, and practitioner. At the University of North Texas (UNT), she instructs courses in knowledge management tools and technologies. Dr. Merlo is also the CEO of Merlo Management Consulting, where she delivers global business solutions.

Her research focuses on knowledge management systems and their impact on organizational strategies and operations. Her professional interests span business strategies, process improvement, sales strategies, business intelligence, machine learning, artificial intelligence, and leadership.

Dr. Merlo earned her Ph.D. in organizational management with a minor in information technologies, complemented by two master's degrees in information sciences from the Federal University of Bahia (UFBA) and UNT. She has been recognized with numerous awards for leadership, data and project management, information literacy, diversity and inclusion, and business development. Her academic journey includes prestigious scholarships such as Coordenação de Aperfeiçoamento de Pessoal de Nível Superior (CAPES) and Fundação de Amparo à Pesquisa do Estado da Bahia (FAPESB).

She plays an active role in scientific committees for international journals such as *Knowledge and Performance Management, Knowledge-Based*

Systems, Journal of Information and Knowledge Management, Glossary of Innovation, Organizational Knowledge, and *Scientific and Technological Information*, published by IBICT.

Dr. Merlo serves on the international advisory board of the International Conference on Knowledge Management (ICKM) and has chaired several of its annual conferences. Previously, Dr. Merlo built a significant career in library management, including roles at the City of Austin, Texas, where she led various projects within information sciences and chaired the Culture and Diversity Committee. She was also actively involved with the Texas Library Association, serving as its chair.

Dr. Merlo has authored and edited the book *Understanding, Implementing, and Evaluating Knowledge Management in Business Settings* and *AI and Data Analytics Applications in Organizational Management* published by IGI Global. Additionally, she is the chief editor of the book series *Artificial Intelligence in Organizations: Transformative Technologies, Applications, and Impacts* and has edited four volumes within this series, published by World Scientific. Most recently, Dr. Merlo published a book with Taylor & Francis, focusing on artificial intelligence and ethics, titled *Ethical AI and Data Science: Building Trustworthy and Transparent Systems*.

Dr. Merlo's extensive professional experience encompasses engagements with multiple Fortune 100 companies, leading projects and teams focused on deal management, cloud computing, data analytics, business intelligence, and sales operations and strategies. She has been invited as a speaker or keynote speaker to numerous international conferences.

Patrícia de Sá Freire is a distinguished professor at the Federal University of Santa Catarina (UFSC), specializing in knowledge management and digital learning. She is also a permanent researcher in the Graduate Programs in Knowledge Engineering and Management, as well as in Administration, at the same institution. She leads the ENGIN Laboratory – Engineering for the Integration and Governance of Knowledge and Organizational Learning. She holds a Ph.D. and a master's degree in knowledge engineering and management from UFSC.

With extensive experience in educational technology integration and faculty development, her research focuses on leveraging artificial intelligence to enhance teaching methodologies and student engagement. Dr. de Sá Freire has authored numerous publications, shaping the dialogue on education's future in Latin America. She is a sought-after speaker at international conferences, bridging innovation and practical application in academia. Dr. Sá has authored 18 books and published over 300 articles in conferences, journals, and books, establishing her reputation in Brazil's **organizational innovation ecosystem**. She holds rights to six organizational innovation frameworks and was recognized as the Most Innovative Professor of 2024 by the Federal University of Santa Catarina, Brazil.

© 2026 World Scientific Publishing Europe Ltd.
https://doi.org/10.1142/9781800617414_fmatter

About the Contributors

Mariya Gavrilova Aguilar is a clinical assistant professor in the Department of Management at the G. Brint Ryan College of Business at the University of North Texas (UNT). She also serves as the Director of Student Experience at UNT's The People Center. She teaches both graduate and undergraduate courses in human resource management, strategic rewards, talent management and development, and leadership. Mariya has expertise in performance improvement, curriculum development, leave administration, and career exploration. Her research interests include creating a career identity, evaluating mentoring effectiveness, and enhancing learning outcomes in management and higher education.

Jeff M. Allen is a regents professor at the University of North Texas and a leading voice in organizational wisdom, evidence-based decision-making, and workforce transformation. With over three decades of experience, he helps leaders and teams bridge individual insights with collective wisdom. As the founding director of the Center for Knowledge Solutions, Dr. Allen has worked globally to advance knowledge-sharing in organizations. His latest book, *Fostering Wisdom at Work*, offers strategies for thriving in today's dynamic workplace. A longtime editor and mentor, he continues to shape how professionals lead with purpose, insight, and innovation.

Pamela Scott Bracey currently serves as a clinical professor and chair of the Department of Multidisciplinary Innovation at the University of North Texas. She has been awarded multiple prestigious awards for excellence in teaching, technology integration, and providing stellar community-engaged project-based learning experiences for her students. Dr. Bracey has published a textbook entitled *Administrative Management & Procedures* (2021) and currently serves as president of the National Business Education Association. Dr. Bracey holds a Ph.D. in applied technology and performance improvement, with a minor in gifted and talented education, an M.S. degree in higher education administration, and a B.S. in business technology education.

Graziela Grando Bresolin holds a Ph.D. and a master's degree in knowledge engineering and management from the Federal University of Santa Catarina (UFSC), with a doctoral research period at the Department of Engineering for Innovation at the University of Salento, Italy. She also holds a bachelor's degree in business administration. She is a researcher at the Laboratory of Knowledge Integration Engineering and Multilevel Governance (ENGIN/UFSC). She is a co-creator of the Neolearning and MindBuilders Experience methodologies, focused on accelerating learning curves and talent development. Her research interests include experiential and expansive learning, andragogy and heutagogy, active and agile learning methodologies, neolearning, networked corporate universities, the university of the future, and neoteacher competencies.

Kamilla Lima Viveiros Cardoso is a Ph.D. student in the Graduate Program in Information Science at the Federal University of Santa Catarina (since 2024). She holds a master's degree in information science from UFSC (2024) and a bachelor's degree in library science from the same university (2017). She also completed a postgraduate specialization in fashion, art, and technology at the Metropolitan Faculty of the State of São Paulo (FAMEESP; 2023). Her research focuses on sustainable fashion, open innovation, and fashion information, with an emphasis on strategic information management in collaborative environments. She has experience in extension projects, the organization of scientific and cultural events, and the use of technology in applied research in the fields of fashion and information science.

Arturo Cavalcanti Catunda holds a Ph.D. in education from the Federal University of Bahia and has a solid academic background that includes a master's in administration, specializations in business intelligence and management, and an M.B.A. in marketing; he is also currently pursuing a law degree. He works as an administrator at Petrobras University as part of the knowledge management team. In this role as the project owner of an agile HR team, he leads the development of technological solutions for knowledge management, including the application of artificial intelligence. As an administrator at Petrobras, he has experience in several areas, such as procurement, human resources, and finance. He is a collaborating professor at Petrobras University and has taught at other higher education institutions, including the Federal University of Alagoas and the National Industrial Apprenticeship Service (SENAI-BA). His professional career includes academic coordination and work on educational management projects financed by the World Bank. He has also authored several fiction books.

Solange Maria da Silva is a professor at the Federal University of Santa Catarina (UFSC), affiliated with the Department of Administrative Sciences (CAD). She is a permanent faculty member in the Graduate Program in Engineering and Knowledge Management (PPGEGC), focusing on the knowledge management research area, and in the Graduate Program in Administration (PPGAdm), conducting research in the field of leadership. She holds a postdoctoral degree (2018) from the Pontifical Catholic University (PUC), a Ph.D. (2007) and a master's degree (1999) in production and systems engineering from UFSC (Florianópolis Campus), and a bachelor's degree in business administration from the School of Business and Management (ESAG/UDESC, 1995). She is the coordinator of Lead(H)er (Research Laboratory on Leadership and the Development of Women Leaders) and a member of the UFSC research groups LGR (Laboratory of Leadership and Responsible Management) and IGTI (Research Center on Intelligence, Management, and Technology for Innovation). She also has experience as a consultant in research and extension projects with public and private organizations, focusing on the corporate–university network model (UCR), knowledge management, leadership, and the development of women leaders.

Marcos Baptista Lopez Dalmau holds a bachelor's degree in business administration from the Federal University of Santa Catarina (1999) and a master's degree (2001) and a Ph.D. (2003) in production engineering from the same institution. He currently serves as a full professor at the Federal University of Santa Catarina and a faculty member of the Graduate Program in Business Administration (PPGA) at the master's and doctoral levels at UFSC, as well as the Professional Master's Program in University Administration (PPGAU/UFSC). He is also a coordinator at NUPERH (Center for Research and Studies in Human Resources). He has experience in the field of business administration, with an emphasis on human resources, focusing mainly on the following topics: employer branding, competency-based management, and distance education.

Ieda Pelógia Martins Damian is a professor in the Undergraduate Program in Information Science and Documentation, Department of Education, Communication and Information, Faculty of Philosophy, Sciences and Letters (FFCLRP) at the University of São Paulo (USP). She is also a professor in the Graduate Program in Information Science at Universidade Estadual Paulista (UNESP), Marília campus, São Paulo. She completed her postdoctoral degree from the University of Salamanca (USAL), Spain, in 2020. She holds a Ph.D. in organizational management from the School of Economics, Business and Accounting of Ribeirão Preto, University of São Paulo (FEA-RP/USP), 2012; a master's degree in organizational management from FEA-RP/USP, 2009; and a bachelor's degree in systems analysis from the Pontifical Catholic University of Campinas, 1994. Since 2019, she has served as a member of the Fiscal Council of the Brazilian Association for Education in Information Science (ABECIN). Her research areas include knowledge management, information management, competitive intelligence, and reference services.

Fabiana Edier Dassoler is a Ph.D. student in engineering and knowledge management at the Federal University of Santa Catarina (UFSC). She holds a master's degree in Methods and Management in Evaluation, is a specialist in business management, and has a bachelor's degree in philosophy.

Cristiano José Castro de Almeida Cunha has a Ph.D. (1988) in business administration from Rheinisch-Westfälische Technische Hochschule Aachen, a master's degree (1981) in production engineering from the Federal University of Santa Catarina (UFSC), and a bachelor's degree (1977) in geological engineering from the School of Mines and Metallurgy in Ouro Preto. He was previously a visiting professor at IGIA, France (1991). He was also a former faculty member of the Graduate Program in Administration at UFSC. Currently, he is a professor in the Graduate

Program in Engineering and Knowledge Management at UFSC. He serves as the coordinator of the Laboratory of Leadership and Responsible Management (LGR) at UFSC. He has extensive experience as a consultant in the field of management, working primarily in the areas of leadership, executive learning, organizational restructuring, and strategic management.

Neri dos Santos is a senior professor in the Graduate Program in Engineering and Knowledge Management at the Federal University of Santa Catarina (EGC/UFSC). He holds a B.Sc. degree in mechanical engineering from the Federal University of Santa Catarina (1976), an M.Sc. degree in ergonomics from the University of Paris, France (1982); a Ph.D. in ergonomics from the Conservatoire National des Arts et Métiers, France (1985); and a postdoctoral fellowship in cognitive engineering from the Polytechnic School of Montreal, Canada. Previously, he served as the dean of the Polytechnic School of the Pontifical Catholic University of Paraná (PUCPR) from 2015 to 2018. He serves on the editorial boards of the following journals: *American Journal of Industrial Engineering*, *International Journal of Knowledge Engineering and Management*, *Ergonomic Action and Production*, and the *Journal of Science & Technology*. His fields of research and teaching are centered around engineering and knowledge management.

Richard Heininger works as a senior lecturer at the Institute of Information Systems – Communications Engineering at the Johannes Kepler University (JKU) Linz. His research interests lie in the broad field of cyber-physical systems. He wrote his doctoral thesis on the negotiation of agent autonomy with the help of digital process twins. His teaching and research activities at the JKU allow him to share his practical experience with students and work on concepts for autonomous business process participants.

Kris S. Helge holds a J.D. from South Texas College of Law Houston, a Ph.D. in Information Science, an M.L.S. from the University of North Texas, and a B.A. from Baylor University. He has published books, book chapters, and articles and has presented on various topics in information governance. Kris serves as an adjunct faculty member at Texas A&M University School of Law and Rutgers University. He also leads an information governance program at the Colorado Judicial Branch.

Selvi Kannan is a researcher in human capital theory, knowledge management, and leadership studies, with a particular focus on the socio-technical dynamics of organizational change in the artificial intelligence (AI) era. She holds a Ph.D. in human capital and knowledge management from Victoria University, Australia. Her research is situated at the intersection of leadership resilience, digital transformation, and systems thinking, examining how institutions and individuals adapt to technological complexity through grounded, human-centered strategies.

Dr. Kannan's scholarly contributions draw on qualitative, relational, and narrative methodologies to investigate emergent models of leadership and knowledge flows within innovation-intensive environments. Her recent work explores how AI reshapes decision-making, organizational identity, and learning systems. Her studies contribute to evolving discourses in leadership scholarship, particularly around the development of adaptive capacity, ethical foresight, and institutional resilience in digitally disrupted contexts.

She has led and contributed to interdisciplinary research projects across higher education, government, and industry sectors, with an emphasis on practice-based inquiry and co-designed interventions. She has served on national task forces related to AI and future skills, and her academic leadership includes supervision of higher degree research students and curriculum design in digital capability, entrepreneurship, and innovation.

Dr. Kannan is currently the Lead of Industry and Community Partnerships at the University of Tasmania's School of Information and Communication Technology and a member of the Australian Computer Society (ACS) Tasmania Branch Executive Committee. Her chapter in this volume introduces a ground-up model for resilient leadership, offering empirical insights into the balance between technological acceleration and human agency.

Alessandro Margherita is an associate professor at the Department of Engineering for Innovation of the University of Salento (Italy) and a research partner at UFSC (Brazil). He teaches business and project management and start-up creation. His research activity is focused on digital transformation, HRM and analytics, and emergency management. He is the author of more than 100 research works and manuals for practitioners, and he serves on the editorial board of *Business Horizons*. He was a visiting scholar at the Center for Digital Business of MIT Sloan (USA), a research affiliate at the Center for Collective Intelligence of MIT Sloan, and a visiting researcher at Peking University (China). He is a member of the Scientific Committee and Board of AICE (Italian Association of Cost Engineering), the innovation manager at the Italian Ministry of Economic Development (MISE), and the scientific coordinator of research projects and international research networks on HR analytics and emergency management.

Demis Marques holds a Ph.D. in knowledge engineering and management. He conducts research in the areas of knowledge management, knowledge auditing, and the application of knowledge to technological innovation. He has experience in scientific and technological projects and works as a professor in undergraduate and graduate programs, teaching courses on management, innovation, and emerging technologies. He is the co-author of the book *Transhuman Co-production: A Manual for the Ethical Use of Artificial Intelligence in Academic Writing*.

Alex Marson has over 35 years of experience in leadership and business transformation. He is the creator of Neoliderança®, an innovative approach that drives the evolution of leaders, organizations, and ecosystems toward a more prosperous and regenerative future. As the former CEO of an industrial holding, he led a large-scale cultural and business transformation, significantly increasing stakeholder value.

With an M.B.A. in business management and specializations in leadership and innovation, Alex has worked as a consultant and mentor, supporting leadership succession, governance, and strategic business transformations. Since March 2024, he has been advising the Business Academy of the Federation of Industries of Santa Catarina (FIESC) on aligning leadership development with the vision of neoindustrialization. He is the founder of Neoliderança Ltd. and remains committed to fostering business ecosystems that integrate economic value with social and environmental responsibility.

Paloma Martinez-Hague holds a Ph.D. in strategic management from the Consortium of Universities of Peru. She is a researcher in human resource management and management education, as well as an associate professor in the Department of Management Sciences at the Pontificia Universidad Católica del Perú (PUCP). She coordinates the Alumni Network within the School of Management at PUCP.

She serves as a researcher and thesis advisor specializing in management topics and lectures nationally and internationally on human resource management, managerial skills, and business administration. Prior to completing her Ph.D. summa cum laude, she earned her master of arts in human resource development and knowledge management from Lancaster University, United Kingdom. She also holds a master of philosophy degree from the Maastricht School of Management in the Netherlands and a bachelor's degree in business administration from PUCP.

Tayane Cristina Mattera Souza has a master's degree in information science from the Federal University of Bahia, is a specialist in competitive intelligence, and holds a DEA (Diplôme d'Études Approfondies) in scientific and technological information from Université Aix-Marseille. She has received training in group development from the Brazilian Society for Group Dynamics (SBDG) and holds a bachelor's degree in library science.

A specialist in knowledge and competency management in the HR field, Tayane has gained extensive experience working at Petrobras since 2003. She has served as a KM manager, leading teams to meet the needs of the company's business areas. She has developed and implemented customized projects to promote the sharing and preservation of critical knowledge. She also has significant experience in teaching, both in undergraduate and postgraduate programs, in synchronous and asynchronous formats.

She possesses solid knowledge in people, process, and business management, project management, customer service technologies, management and information technologies, conflict management, and group dynamics.

Monica Scoz Mendes is a doctoral student in administration at the Postgraduate Program in Administration (PPGAdm) at the Federal University of Santa Catarina (UFSC). She holds a master's degree (2017) in university administration from the Postgraduate Program in University Administration (PPGAU) and a bachelor's degree (2008) in business administration, both from UFSC. She also holds a specialization (2011) in business management from the Getúlio Vargas Foundation (FGV). Currently, she works as an administrator at the Department of Personnel Administration (DAP) within the Pro-Rectory for People Development and Management (PRODEGESP) at UFSC.

Gonzalo Rafael Merino Braga holds a degree in business administration from the University of Lima (1995) and an M.B.A. from the City

University of London (1999), specializing in marketing. He is currently pursuing his Ph.D. at the University of Minho, working on ethical and sustainable marketing. He also serves as a professor at the Pontificia Universidad Católica del Perú (PUCP) in the area of marketing and business and has supervised several theses. He is a research member of the GEMA study groups at PUCP and NUPERH at the Federal University of Santa Catarina (UFSC). His teaching and research are mainly concerned with sustainable and ethical marketing, team leadership, and employer branding. He has more than 30 years of work experience in international companies in the commercial area, industrial marketing, and regional sales in Latin America.

Ricardo Pereira is a university professor, researcher, and consultant in technology and innovation. He holds a Ph.D. in engineering and knowledge management (PPGEGC) from the Federal University of Santa Catarina. He also earned a master's degree in production engineering, with a focus on organizational intelligence, from the Federal University of Santa Catarina (2009). He holds bachelor's degrees in business administration (2002) and law (2013), both from the Federal University of Santa Catarina, and a specialization/M.B.A. in global management from the Independent University of Lisbon (2004). With experience in integrating artificial intelligence and innovative methodologies in educational and organizational settings, Ricardo develops strategies to drive competitiveness and innovation in companies, bridging the gap between academia and industry practice. He is the series editor and a member of the scientific committee at Editora Arquétipos, having edited dozens of books on a wide variety of topics. He is the founder of @mentor.I.A., a project aimed at democratizing the use of generative artificial intelligence in research, through which he has mentored dozens of professors and graduate students from higher education institutions across the country (profiles on Instagram and YouTube). He is a reviewer for the scientific journals *Pretexto*, *Revista Brasileira de Gestão e Inovação*, *América Latina Hoy*, and *Administração Pública e Gestão Social*. His research focuses on artificial intelligence applied to education and in organizational contexts, Industry 5.0, the metaverse, mass personalization in industry, digital transformation, and knowledge and innovation management.

Alexandra Augusta Pereira Klen is a mechanical engineer and Ph.D. in manufacturing automation from the Federal University of Santa Catarina (UFSC), Brazil, with over 35 years of experience spanning academia, research, industry, and the arts. Her expertise lies in innovation management, collaborative networks, sustainable value chains, and the circular economy. In 2025, she was appointed as a member of the Global Future Council (GFC) on Advanced Manufacturing and Value Chains of the World Economic Forum (WEF).

Throughout her career, Alexandra has collaborated with institutions such as the Bremen Institute of Production and Logistics (BIBA, Germany) and the European Commission, serving as an evaluator, reviewer, and rapporteur for international R&D&I initiatives.

Beyond science and industry, Alexandra integrates an artistic lens into her professional journey as a dancer, choreographer, and cultural producer – weaving together the arts, systems thinking, and human development.

Karla Cristina Rocha Botão is currently a master's student in the Graduate Program in Knowledge Engineering and Management at the Federal University of Santa Catarina (UFSC). She holds a bachelor's degree in international relations from the University of Brasília (1999) and an M.B.A. in planning, budgeting, and public management from Fundação Getúlio Vargas (2012). She is a career public servant at the Brazilian Federal Highway Police, where she has worked since 2006 under a full-time work arrangement. Her professional trajectory encompasses extensive experience in the field of public administration, with emphasis on institutional integrity, internal affairs, internal control, and public security. She is a co-author of the book *Glossary of PRF Terminology: Traffic and Traffic Accidents* (2023) and participated in the organization of an international scientific event in 2023. She served as a coordinator and lecturer in the Specialization Course in Police Sciences (2022) and participated in examination committees for graduate programs. In the academic field, her interests include leadership, public governance, knowledge management, and institutional ethics, with active involvement in research and scientific development sectors.

Amy Rosellini is a distinguished human resources consultant specializing in organizational learning and human capital strategy. She is an adjunct professor at SMU Cox School of Business. Since 2013, Amy has led RLT Impact, a consulting firm offering fractional chief human resources officer (CHRO) and learning services. With over two decades of experience spanning manufacturing, retail, construction, and real estate, Amy designs impactful knowledge management strategies to enhance corporate learning. Dr. Rosellini's research has been featured in numerous refereed articles and books. She is a sought-after keynote speaker at conferences nationwide, delivering compelling talks on learning methodologies and innovative human capital strategies.

Denilson Sell is a professor in the Graduate Programs in Business Administration at the Santa Catarina State University (ESAG/UDESC) and in Knowledge Engineering and Management at the Federal University of Santa Catarina (UFSC), Brazil. He also serves as director and senior researcher at Instituto Stela, where he leads innovative research and development initiatives.

With extensive expertise in knowledge management, digital transformation, analytics, big data, and artificial intelligence (AI), Denilson has coordinated numerous projects and consultancies across various sectors. His experience encompasses the development of knowledge management and analytical solutions in industries such as oil and gas (e.g., integrated risk management), electricity (e.g., fraud detection, network management, and load forecasting), financial services (e.g., ethics and integrity management), healthcare (e.g., knowledge management and expertise location), and education (e.g., AI applications for research management and student retention).

His recent research interests include organizational resilience, digital platforms, and the integration of generative AI in knowledge governance processes. Denilson is actively involved in academic and professional communities internationally, regularly contributing to knowledge management and innovation through publications, consulting activities, and participation in prestigious international conferences and awards.

Callie D. Shaw holds a J.D. from Loyola College of Law and an LL.M. in energy and environmental law from Tulane Law School in New Orleans, Louisiana. She earned a Ph.D. in criminal justice from Texas State University, an M.S. in sociology, and a B.S. in criminology from Texas A&M University – Kingsville. Dr. Shaw has authored numerous book chapters, journal articles, and editorials and has delivered presentations on topics ranging from law enforcement mental health to her legal work during the 2010 BP oil spill.

She currently serves as an assistant professor of criminal justice at Texas A&M University – Corpus Christi and as an adjunct course manager at Texas A&M University School of Law. Additionally, she is a member of the Nueces County Public Defenders Oversight Board.

Luciana Poli Silva, a human potential enthusiast, has been working in the field of knowledge management, development, and organizational learning for over 30 years. She holds M.B.A. degrees in positive psychology, advanced business management, human resources management, and educational psychology, as well as a B.A. degree from the Federal University of Rio de Janeiro (UFRJ).

She is a speaker, has presented papers in Brazil and abroad, and is the author of national and international articles.

She has been working at Petrobras for over two decades, where she has served as a knowledge management consultant for Petrobras University, Upstream, and HSE for 20 years. She is currently a doctoral candidate in knowledge engineering and management in the Graduate Program in Engineering, Knowledge Management, and Media at the Federal University of Santa Catarina (UFSC).

She has extensive experience in the development and implementation of projects in large multinational companies such as Petrobras, Shell, Zara, and Souza Cruz. She is also the mother of a teenager, her most challenging and rewarding mission.

Christian Stary is a full professor at the Institute of Business Informatics – Communications Engineering and also leads the Competence Centre on Knowledge Management at the Johannes Kepler University Linz. He earned his Ph.D. in conceptual modeling of human–computer interaction at the Vienna University of Technology in 1988, was promoted to associate professor there in 1993, and became a full professor in 1995. His research interests include usability engineering, knowledge management, learning support, socio-technical system design, and process management.

Graziela Simone Tonin serves as an associate dean of computer engineering and a professor at Insper. She holds a Ph.D. in computer science from the University of São Paulo (2018), with a research internship at UMBC (USA), a master's degree from the Federal University of Pernambuco (2011), and a bachelor's degree from Integrated Regional University of the High Uruguay and Missions (URI; 2008). She received the IBM Fellowship Award (2012) and completed a venture finance program at the University of Oxford. She leads gender-related research at the Gender Studies Center within Insper's Center for Public Policy and coordinates the São Paulo School of Advanced Science in Sustainability and Complex Systems. Graziela serves on scientific committees of conferences in agile methodologies, technical debt, and software engineering and is a guest reviewer for several international journals. She mentors startups in programs such as Inovativa Brazil and Inovativa de Impacto and evaluates entrepreneurship initiatives such as the Centelha program. She has been invited to speak and lead workshops in a number of countries. For over a decade, she has led social projects at the Grupo Mulheres do Brazil, focusing on gender equity and empowerment.

Kelly Cristina Benetti Tonani Tosta is an associate professor at the Federal University of Fronteira Sul (UFFS). She earned her Ph.D. (2012) in knowledge engineering and management from the Federal University of Santa Catarina (UFSC) and her master's (2008) and bachelor's (2005) degrees in business administration, also from UFSC. She has professional experience in the field of people management, having served as Director of People Management at UFFS (2010–2011) and as Chief of Staff (2011–2016). Currently, she teaches in the Professional Master's Program in Public Administration (PROFIAP) and, through an academic partnership, also teaches in the Graduate Program in University Administration at UFSC. She has coordinated several research and extension projects funded by internal and external sources. She has published over 40 articles in academic journals and more than 113 full papers in conference proceedings, in addition to book chapters and edited volumes. She has extensive experience in projects related to competency-based management and entrepreneurial and innovation competencies. She is the mother of Alice, Bento, and Lucas.

Humberto Tonani Tosta is a professor at the Federal University of Fronteira Sul (UFFS), where he teaches, conducts research, and engages in outreach activities in the fields of entrepreneurship, innovation, and management. He holds a Ph.D. in business administration from the Federal University of Santa Catarina (UFSC), serving as the coordinator of EMPREENDE UFFS (the entrepreneurship program of the Federal University of Fronteira Sul) and the Business Incubator – INNE (Center for Innovation and Business). He is also a permanent faculty member of the Professional Master's Program in Public Administration (PROFIAP) and a researcher at the Institute for Research and Studies in University Administration (INPEAU). He has extensive experience training entrepreneurs, developing innovation ecosystems, and supporting the creation of innovative businesses, with a strong focus on fostering connections between universities, government, and society.

Andréa Cristina Trierweiller is the secretary of planning and budget and an associate professor at the Federal University of Santa Catarina (UFSC). She teaches in the Graduate Programs in Information and Communication Technologies (PPGTIC) and Methods and Management in Evaluation (PPGMGA). She coordinates the Innovation and Sustainability Management Laboratory (LABeGIS) and is a member of NUGEN, a center recognized for its interdisciplinary approach. Her research focuses on ESG, innovation, entrepreneurship, public management, and sustainability. She also completed a postdoctoral internship focusing on management assessment, using Item Response Theory (IRT) applied to topics such as sustainability and innovation. Dr. Trierweiller holds a Ph.D., a master's, and a specialization in production engineering and a bachelor's in business administration, all from UFSC.

Nilara Izabel Von Fruauff Pavan holds a master's degree in university administration from the Federal University of Santa Catarina (UFSC), a specialization in data science and analytics from University of São Paulo (USP), and a bachelor's degree in administration from the Federal University of Fronteira Sul (UFFS) and in marketing from the Community University of the Chapecó Region (Unochapecó). Currently, she participates as a volunteer in the research and extension group in entrepreneurship at UFFS. Her research areas include entrepreneurship, entrepreneurial education, and entrepreneurial skills.

Thomas Weißenbacher completed his bachelor's degree in business informatics at Johannes Kepler University Linz and is currently employed at a globally operating corporation. In his bachelor's thesis, he examined the potential of artificial intelligence (AI) for companies in the context of integration into existing business processes. His academic interests include the application of AI and digital business strategies.

Tara L. Whitson earned her M.S. in information systems from Tarleton State University in 2007 and is currently pursuing a Ph.D. in information science at the University of North Texas. She began her career in 2008 as a systems engineer, later advancing to manager of online instructional support at Tarleton State University. Since 2020, she has been an instructor of computer information systems at Tarleton State University, where she teaches courses in computer concepts and applications, database theory and applications, management information systems, and systems analysis and design. Her research interests include artificial intelligence, digital citizenship, digital literacy, human-computer interaction, and technology integration.

© 2026 World Scientific Publishing Europe Ltd.
https://doi.org/10.1142/9781800617414_fmatter

Acknowledgments

We wish to convey our profound gratitude to Gláucia Milanez Fujimoto, whose legal acumen and steadfast support were indispensable to the successful completion of this work.

Additionally, we extend our appreciation to our colleagues, collaborators, institutions, and practitioners, including corporate partners and professionals engaged in applied projects, whose support, expertise, and practical insights greatly contributed to shaping and strengthening this work.

© 2026 World Scientific Publishing Europe Ltd.
https://doi.org/10.1142/9781800617414_fmatter

Contents

Section 1

Reimagining Knowledge Management Through Artificial Intelligence

© 2026 World Scientific Publishing Europe Ltd.
https://doi.org/10.1142/9781800617414_0001

Chapter 1

Artificial Intelligence and Knowledge Management: Moving Toward Intelligent Organizations

Neri dos Santos

Federal University of Santa Catarina, Brazil

nerisantos@gmail.com

Abstract

The rise of artificial intelligence (AI) is transforming organizational knowledge management (OKM), driving the evolution toward intelligent organizations. This chapter explores the intersection of AI and OKM, highlighting how advanced algorithms, machine learning, and cognitive systems can optimize the creation, organization, dissemination, and application of knowledge within organizations. Therefore, the objective of this chapter is to critically examine and discuss the impact of AI on OKM, exploring the opportunities and challenges inherent in implementing these technologies in organizational contexts. To achieve this, the methodology is based on a robust literature review, analyzing contemporary theories and studies on the subject to provide an updated overview of AI's role in enhancing OKM. The study's main findings indicate that AI expands organizations' cognitive capabilities by capturing and interpreting large volumes of data, automating OKM processes, and improving insight-driven decision-making, ultimately increasing organizational productivity. Technologies such as predictive models, natural language processing, and recommendation systems have the potential to structure both tacit and explicit knowledge, facilitating information access and enhancing team collaboration. Furthermore, AI is reshaping OKM processes by significantly impacting knowledge creation, storage, retrieval, sharing, and application. In terms of creation, AI enables the discovery of hidden patterns and the generation of new insights from vast datasets. Regarding storage and retrieval, AI enhances the organization of explicit knowledge by integrating multiple information channels. In sharing, AI fosters collaboration by connecting experts and creating dynamic knowledge networks. In applications, AI facilitates the retrieval of relevant knowledge and reduces barriers to accessing strategic information. The study's primary contribution lies in advocating for human–AI collaboration as a critical factor for successful OKM. While AI provides specialized and analytical intelligence, humans play an essential role in bringing judgment, contextualization, and strategic vision. Therefore, building an effective symbiosis between humans and AI is crucial for organizations seeking to enhance their learning and innovation capabilities. By adopting learning-centered approaches and fostering collaborative intelligence between humans and AI, organizations can unlock the strategic value of these technologies, promoting more efficient knowledge management and creating a sustainable competitive advantage.

Keywords: Artificial intelligence, knowledge management, organizational knowledge management, organizational intelligence.

1.1 Introduction

The rise of artificial intelligence (AI) represents one of the most transformative forces of our time, especially in the context of organizational knowledge management (OKM). In a world increasingly driven by knowledge, the ability to identify, create, store, share, and apply knowledge efficiently has become a key strategic differentiator. With the evident technological acceleration and the advent of generative AI, we are currently witnessing digital transformation taking place in organizations.

To fully understand the concept of digital transformation, we must first define and differentiate the terms "digitization," "digitalization," and "digital transformation," as the use of these terms has generated some ambiguity within the scientific community. Most researchers use these terms interchangeably, while in reality, there is a significant difference between them. In an excellent systematic literature review on digital transformation, Mahraz *et al.* (2019) emphasized the need to distinguish among these three terms. According to the authors, "digitization" refers to the conversion of data and information from analog to digital formats and the resulting changes (e.g., in workflows, communication, or interconnected units). In contrast, "digitalization" is a vaguely used expression, ranging from any use of social media by an organization to more specific definitions, such as the use of data and digital technologies by individuals or organizations to automate data handling, optimize organizational processes, and change business models from a factory-based pipeline to a digital platform format.

Finally, "digital transformation" is a new concept used by researchers, consulting professionals, and executives, which frequently changes in form and content depending on the context in which it is applied. It highlights the cultural transition from the industrial era to the digital era. Fundamentally, we can point out that digital transformation represents a paradigm shift – a cultural change – from an analog industrial era fading into a digital industrial era that is currently unfolding.

In academic literature, the term digital transformation is often used imprecisely, as there are no formal definitions. Many authors have attempted to define and discuss this concept (Liu *et al.*, 2011; Berman, 2012; Bharadwaj *et al.*, 2013; Fitzgerald *et al.*, 2013; Luna-Reyes and Gil-Garcia, 2014; Henriette *et al.*, 2015; Matt *et al.*, 2015; Hess *et al.*, 2016; Westerman, 2016; Horlach *et al.*, 2017; Karagiannaki *et al.*, 2017; Liere-Netheler *et al.*, 2018; Mergel *et al.*, 2019), but in fact, there is no consensus on its definition. Although the term "digital transformation" has been in use for some time – first mentioned in 2000 (Patel and McCarthy, 2000), originally associated with digitalization – its concept is more recent. Today, it refers to a phenomenon linked to new uses by citizens and unique objects that directly impact business models based on digital platforms.

The first conceptual definition of the term appeared in the book *Information Systems Research: Relevant Theory and Informed Practice,* published by Springer (Stolterman and Fors, 2004). According to the authors, "digital transformation can be understood as the changes that digital technology causes or influences in all aspects of human life."

However, in this chapter, we will use the concept proposed by Pacheco *et al.* (2020), who define digital transformation as the fundamental change in the economy, organizations, and society in general, caused by the comprehensive application of digital technologies and disruptive digital business models. In this context, there has been accelerated adoption of AI, particularly driven by generative AI, which is redefining production logic, the role of workers, and the very concept of professional competencies. In fact, the incorporation of AI is not merely a technological response but a structural transformation.

Therefore, this chapter aims to critically investigate how AI is reshaping OKM processes and fostering the emergence of intelligent organizations. Its objective is to discuss the opportunities and challenges of applying AI in OKM, examining how these technologies enhance organizational learning, innovation, and sustainable competitive advantage.

It is emphasized that knowledge theory underpins research concerned with science, nature, and the conditions and/or first principles of organizational knowledge; according to some authors (Shieber, 2019; Bastien *et al.*, 2020; Henly and Sprague, 2020; Sprague, 2020), it also addresses the truth value or reliability of knowledge in general.

From this perspective, as shown in Table 1.1, the main terms addressed in this chapter are presented, along with their definitions and key concepts.

Table 1.1. Definitions and key-concept terms in artificial intelligence and knowledge management.

Term	Definition/Key Concepts
Artificial intelligence (AI)	A field of computer science focused on creating systems capable of tasks that usually require human intelligence, such as perception, reasoning, learning, decision-making, and interaction. AI includes speech and image recognition, natural language processing, and problem-solving and has broad transformative potential across sectors.
Machine learning (ML)	A subfield of AI that develops algorithms capable of identifying patterns in large datasets and improving performance over time without explicit programming. Includes supervised, unsupervised, and reinforcement learning. Applications in KM include classifying and grouping knowledge, behavior prediction, recommendation personalization, and analysis automation.
Cognitive systems	Advanced computing systems simulating human cognition (e.g., perception, reasoning, and learning). Combine AI, ML, and natural language processing (NLP) to interact with humans intuitively. Examples include intelligent assistants and medical decision-support systems, Language, Reasoning, and learning. They combine AI, machine learning, and Natural Language Processing to interact with humans in a more intuitive and intelligent way.

Table 1.1. (*Continued*)

Term	Definition/Key Concepts
Deep learning	An advanced ML technique using multi-layered neural networks to recognize complex patterns in large, unstructured datasets (e.g., images, audio, text). Applications: facial recognition, language generation, medical diagnostics, etc.
Intelligent agents	Autonomous programs that perceive their environment, make decisions, and act independently to achieve goals. They support knowledge retrieval, monitor information flow, suggest content, and facilitate collaboration.
Expert systems	Rule-based AI systems simulating expert decision-making in narrow domains. Include a knowledge base, inference engine, and user interface. Limitations include difficulty handling uncertainty and maintaining knowledge currency.
Knowledge representation	Formalizing human knowledge for computational interpretation, storage, and inference. Techniques include ontologies, logic, and semantic graphs. Good representation supports complex reasoning and problem-solving.
Automated reasoning	Computational ability to derive logical conclusions from a set of premises, simulating human reasoning. Core in expert systems and rule-based platforms.
Organizational knowledge	Organizational knowledge can be defined as the collective capacity of an organization to create, share, and apply knowledge in order to achieve its strategic objectives. It emerges from the interaction between individual knowledge (tacit and explicit), within a specific organizational context, being shaped by historically evolved collective understandings and supported by organizational processes and cultures.
Organizational knowledge management (OKM)	Organizational knowledge management is a structured process of identifying, capturing, storing, and applying knowledge within an organization to improve performance and business continuity. It involves transforming data and information into actionable insights, making them easily accessible to employees, and fostering a culture of continuous learning and improvement.

Source: National Academies (2025); Jarrahi *et al.* (2022); Birzniece (2011); Santos and Varvakis (2020).

1.2 Methodology: AI-Assisted Systematic Literature Review Using ELICIT

To understand how AI contributes to OKM in the context of intelligent organizations, we employed a systematic literature review supported by the AI research assistant platform **ELICIT®**. This tool allowed us to screen, extract, and synthesize insights from academic studies retrieved from the Semantic Scholar corpus, comprising over 126 million papers.

1. **Research question**
   How can AI contribute to OKM in the context of intelligent organizations?
2. **Screening criteria**
   We applied the following inclusion criteria to ensure relevance and rigor:
   - **AI-OKM focus**: Studies must involve the use of AI in OKM.
   - **Empirical or systematic**: Only empirical studies or systematic reviews were included.
   - **Organizational setting**: Research had to focus on business, corporate, or institutional contexts.
   - **OKM processes**: Studies must address at least one core OKM process (identification, creation, storage, sharing, or application).
   - **Organizational learning**: Required consideration beyond purely technical implementations.
   - **Organizational level**: Focused on organizational, not just individual, knowledge processes.
3. **Data extraction and analysis**
   We extracted data from 10 key studies regarding:
   - research design and AI integration strategies,
   - knowledge management processes addressed,
   - AI technologies applied,
   - organizational context and challenges,
   - key findings and benefits,
   - success and implementation factors.

Next, the thematic analysis was organized into two main analytical tables: summarizing mechanisms (Table 1.2) and success factors (Table 1.3).

Table 1.2. Thematic analysis of artificial intelligence-enabled knowledge management mechanisms.

Study	OKM Process	AI Technology	Implementation Approach	Reported Benefits
Pai *et al.* (2022)	Extraction, curation, transfer, creation	ML, neural networks, hybrid systems	AI integrated into KM systems; human–AI collaboration	Efficiency, improved retrieval, competitive advantage
Harfouche *et al.* (2017)	Extraction, curation, training, prediction	Multi-agent AI	Multi-agent system for knowledge creation	Dialogue, knowledge consolidation
Sira (2024)	Creation, transfer	Digital assistants, AI decision support	Balanced technical/organizational approach	Breaking silos, strategic alignment
Murad and Kurdy (2020)	Extraction, curation, creation, analysis	Semantic techniques, NLP, ontologies, Latent Dirichlet Allocation (LDA)	Multi-level AI system (auto, chat, email)	86% accuracy, instant answers
Anumba and Khallaf (2022)	Capture, storage, sharing, retirement	Data mining, ML, computer vision, NLP, knowledge base systems	AI-enhanced KM subprocesses	Better decision-making, increased intellectual capital
Olan *et al.* (2022)	Analysis, curation, transfer	Data analytics, fuzzy set-theoretic AI	Complementary AI–KM sharing system	Process optimization, resource use
Alstete and Meyer (2020)	Extraction, curation, transfer	Intelligent agents	Conceptual integration in organizational memory	Extended cognition, enhanced retrieval
O'Leary (1998)	Creation (implied)	Knowledge bases, ontologies	Case study in professional services	Not specified
Nestian *et al.* (2020)	SECI: socialization, externalization, combination, internalization	ML, expert systems, intelligent agents	AI as partner in SECI KM model	Innovation, real-time metrics
Abecker *et al.* (1998)	Identification, acquisition, development, use, preservation	Knowledge discovery, data mining, thesaurus generation	Three-layered hybrid AI–human model	Improved problem-solving, human knowledge amplification

Table 1.3. Thematic analysis: organizational implementation factors.

Study	Success Factor	Description	Evidence	Impact Level
Pai *et al.* (2022)	Leadership, structure, incentives	Leadership traits, organizational arrangements, rewards	Systematic review	High
Harfouche *et al.* (2017)	Dialogue, recursive relations	Linking individual and organizational knowledge	Multi-agent AI framework	Moderate
Sira (2024)	Data governance, leadership, engagement	Governance, executive sponsorship, training	Mixed-methods	High
Murad and Kurdy (2020)	Cultural change, automation	Overcoming knowledge-as-power culture	Case study in a humanitarian agency	Moderate
Anumba and Khallaf (2022)	System integration, flexibility	Overcoming system fragmentation	Construction sector review	High
Olan *et al.* (2022)	Knowledge integration	Combining new and existing knowledge	Theoretical framework	Moderate
Alstete and Meyer (2020)	Human–machine cognition	Enhancing organizational memory formation	Conceptual exploration	Moderate
O'Leary (1998)	Technological integration	Adapting knowledge bases and ontologies to organizational needs	Case study	Moderate
Nestian *et al.* (2020)	Human–AI partnership	Emphasizing AI as complement to human actors	Systematic review	High
Abecker *et al.* (1998)	Hybrid approach, user feedback	Blending AI systems with human feedback for continuous refinement	Three-layered hybrid model	High

1.2.1 *Synthesis of key insights*

- AI augments all OKM processes, including identification, creation, curation, sharing, and application, through technologies such as machine learning, ontologies, and intelligent agents.
- AI contributes to OKM by automating core processes and supporting knowledge operations, requiring hybrid human–AI approaches and clear leadership for effective implementation.
- Reported benefits include greater efficiency, enhanced retrieval, improved decision-making, innovation, and organizational learning.
- Key implementation factors for success are strong leadership, organizational readiness, cultural change, hybrid AI–human collaboration, robust data governance, and continuous learning.

This methodologically structured review enables a theoretically grounded and evidence-based understanding of how AI fosters the evolution of OKM toward intelligent organizations.

1.3 Artificial Intelligence in the Knowledge Era

We are living in an era marked by the predominance of knowledge as the main strategic asset for organizations and societies. In this context, AI emerges not only as a disruptive technology but as a structuring element of the new logic for knowledge creation, dissemination, and application.

AI is radically transforming OKM by expanding human capabilities to observe, interpret, and act upon complex information in real time. According to Jarrahi *et al.* (2022), AI represents a new foundation for OKM, especially through deep learning techniques that simulate human capabilities such as seeing, hearing, interpreting, and deciding. In this model, AI does not replace the human being but works in partnership, enhancing the cognitive and operational capabilities of professionals, especially in knowledge-intensive activities.

Birzniece (2011) complements this view by highlighting that AI techniques – such as neural networks, intelligent agents, and genetic algorithms – have been successfully applied to a number of tasks, including text mining, pattern recognition, and the representation of tacit knowledge. This enables the development of intelligent KM systems that not only store knowledge but also learn, evolve, and adapt to changes in organizational and social contexts.

Beyond its direct impact on OKM, AI is recognized as a general-purpose technology with profound implications for the future of work. According to the National Academies report (2025), AI has the potential to double the growth rate of the United States' GDP over the next decade, thanks to its ability to increase productivity across various sectors. However, its impacts are not limited to the economy; it transforms the very concept of expertise, creating new types of competencies and demanding continuous reskilling of the workforce. AI can both replace routine tasks and augment human activity in complex domains such as healthcare, education, and design.

However, the benefits of AI are not automatic. For the knowledge era to be inclusive and promote collective well-being, complementary investments in education, infrastructure, and ethical governance are essential. This includes ensuring that AI is used to enhance – rather than diminish – human capacity to learn, decide, and innovate.

AI, therefore, is not merely a technological tool. It is a strategic ally in building more intelligent, adaptive, and just organizations and societies in the knowledge era.

1.4 The Transformation of OKM with AI

1.4.1 *Overview of OKM and its processes*

OKM is a strategic approach focused on the identification, creation, storage, sharing, and application of knowledge within organizations. Its objective is to promote continuous organizational learning, generate innovation, and improve decision-making, as illustrated in Figure 1.1.

The main OKM processes are as follows:

- **Knowledge identification**: Involves finding, mapping, and understanding the knowledge an organization or individual possesses, whether explicit or tacit. It includes identifying skills, experiences, key information, and areas where knowledge needs to be improved or developed.
- **Knowledge creation**: Involves generating new knowledge from experiences, interactions, data, and insights, both internal and external.
- **Storage**: Refers to the systematization and documentation of knowledge in accessible repositories, such as databases, manuals, and

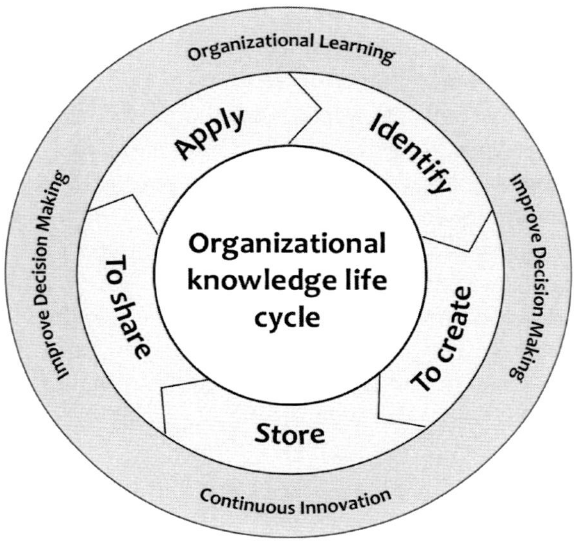

Figure 1.1. Organizational knowledge management life cycle.

Source: Young, R., APO Knowledge Management Facilitator's Guide. Asian Productivity Organization, Tokyo, 2020.

digital platforms, which can be quickly located and accessed when needed.

- **Sharing**: Pertains to the dissemination of knowledge among members of the organization, fostering collaboration and avoiding redundancy of effort.
- **Application**: Involves the use of knowledge at the appropriate time to guide decisions, solve problems, and improve processes.

1.4.2 *The impacts of AI on OKM processes*

AI is transforming each of these processes by enabling organizations to operate with greater intelligence, speed, and precision:

- **Knowledge identification: recognition, mapping, and classification**
  In the knowledge identification process, recognition, mapping, and classification must be considered. Recognition consists of identifying

potential knowledge sources (Ale *et al.*, 2014), while classification allows each type of knowledge to be better utilized. AI algorithms can be programmed to automatically recognize, map, and classify files, extract relevant data, and even detect anomalies in documents. This change not only reduces the time spent on manual tasks but also minimizes human error, improving the overall quality of document management processes.

- **Knowledge creation: pattern discovery and insight generation**
  Using techniques such as machine learning, deep learning, and data mining, AI enables the analysis of large volumes of data and the identification of previously unseen correlations and patterns. This promotes the creation of new knowledge from both structured and unstructured data, such as text, images, videos, and customer interactions (Jarrahi *et al.*, 2022; Waykar, 2022). AI-based tools also enable content synthesis, aiding in the production of automated reports and summaries based on multiple knowledge sources (Kudryavtsev *et al.*, 2024).
- **Storage and retrieval: multichannel organization and integration**
  AI optimizes knowledge storage by automatically classifying information, suggesting metadata, and integrating multiple sources (such as documents, emails, chats, and videos) into smart repositories. Additionally, semantic search algorithms and intelligent agents enable contextualized and precise retrieval of relevant information using natural language (Birzniece, 2011; Kudryavtsev *et al.*, 2024).
- **Sharing: dynamic networks and expert connection**
  AI facilitates connections between employees through recommendation systems, internal expert mapping, and the creation of knowledge networks. Virtual assistants and intelligent bots also support real-time sharing by answering frequently asked questions and guiding employees to the best sources of knowledge (Waykar, 2022; Kovačić, 2022).
- **Application: contextualized use of knowledge for strategic decisions**
  AI-based solutions support contextualized decision-making by providing predictive analytics, simulations, and action suggestions based on historical data and future trends. These systems can function as copilots for managers, offering scenario-based decisions and empirical evidence to promote greater agility and accuracy in knowledge application (Jarrahi *et al.*, 2022; Kudryavtsev *et al.*, 2024).

1.5 Artificial Intelligence Technologies Facilitating OKM

As previously discussed, OKM has been deeply transformed by the advancement of AI technologies. These technologies enhance organizations' ability to identify, create, store, share, and apply knowledge more efficiently and strategically. The following are some of the main AI technologies that act as OKM enablers, along with examples of their use in organizational contexts:

Natural Language Processing (NLP)
Natural language processing is a technology that enables machines to understand, interpret, and generate human language. In the context of OKM, NLP facilitates the extraction and organization of tacit knowledge contained in unstructured texts, such as emails, reports, and internal forums (Zaoui Seghroucheni *et al.*, 2025).

Organizational example:
Companies use NLP tools to analyze large volumes of customer feedback and internal documents, extracting recurring themes and strategic insights.

Tools like IBM's Watson Discovery can identify linguistic patterns and generate automatic answers to frequently asked questions, promoting knowledge dissemination.

Predictive Models
Predictive models are algorithms that use historical data to forecast future behaviors. They support knowledge-based decision-making by anticipating scenarios and suggesting proactive actions (Jamarani *et al.*, 2024).

Organizational example:
In human resources, predictive models are used to forecast employee turnover risk, enabling companies to adopt retention strategies based on knowledge.

In innovative environments, these models help predict the performance of new products based on data from previous projects.

Recommendation Systems
Recommendation systems personalize the delivery of content, documents, and connections among people within the organization, based on individual interests and history (Isinkaye *et al.*, 2015).

Organizational example:
Internal knowledge platforms use recommendation systems to suggest technical articles, courses, or internal experts based on an employee's profile.

Companies like Google and Microsoft already implement systems that automatically suggest relevant documents related to users' ongoing tasks.

Cognitive Agents and Knowledge Bots
Cognitive agents and bots are AI-based interactive systems that answer questions, automate repetitive tasks, and facilitate access to institutional knowledge (Karyotaki *et al.*, 2022).

Organizational example:
Knowledge bots are used to train new employees by answering questions about internal processes, policies, or systems.

More advanced cognitive agents can act as virtual project assistants, offering insights and recommendations based on organizational data.

The incorporation of these AI technologies into OKM not only automates processes but also enhances the collective intelligence of organizations. The integrated use of NLP, predictive models, recommendation systems, and knowledge bots contributes to creating more agile, innovative, and data-driven organizational environments.

1.6 Benefits and Challenges of Implementing AI in OKM

The adoption of AI technologies in OKM has the potential to profoundly transform how knowledge is identified, created, stored, shared, and applied within organizations. However, successful implementation requires not only technological investment but also attention to human, cultural, ethical, and strategic factors. The following are the main benefits and challenges associated with this transformation (Novalin *et al.*, 2024):

1.6.1 *Identified benefits*

- **Increased organizational productivity:** AI automates repetitive and data-intensive tasks such as document classification, information extraction, and FAQ responses. This frees up time for employees to focus on more strategic and creative activities.
  Example: Internal chatbots and cognitive assistants answer operational and procedural questions, reducing the burden on support departments.
- **Improved knowledge-based decision-making:** AI-powered solutions, such as predictive models and big data analytics, provide real-time insights grounded in historical and current data. This strengthens informed decision-making, reducing uncertainty and risk.
  Example: Recommendation systems and predictive analytics help leaders identify market trends, operational bottlenecks, or innovation opportunities.
- **Promotion of continuous innovation:** By enabling quicker and smarter access to strategic data and knowledge, AI fosters a culture of experimentation, continuous learning, and ongoing improvement.
  Example: AI-powered ideation platforms help assess the feasibility and impact of new ideas submitted by employees, promoting open and collaborative innovation.

1.6.2 *Challenges and limitations*

- **Technical and cultural barriers:** Integrating AI into KM processes can be hindered by outdated infrastructure, a lack of qualified personnel, and resistance to change among employees.
  Example: Lack of interoperability between systems or unfamiliarity with intelligent tools may lead to rejection or underuse of the solutions.
- **Ethical and algorithmic bias issues:** Algorithms may reproduce or amplify biases present in training data. Moreover, heavy use of data raises concerns about privacy and transparency in automated decisions.

Example: A biased candidate recommendation system may perpetuate gender or racial inequalities if not ethically monitored and controlled.

- **Need for data governance and strategic alignment:** The success of AI depends on the availability of high-quality, well-governed, up-to-date data aligned with the organization's strategic goals. The absence of clear policies can undermine the reliability of intelligent systems.
  Example: Without a taxonomy and content curation policy, semantic search and analysis systems may return irrelevant or outdated information.

Implementing AI in OKM represents a significant opportunity to generate strategic value through organizational intelligence. However, its effectiveness depends on overcoming technical, cultural, and ethical challenges, along with establishing strong governance aligned with institutional strategy.

1.7 Human–AI Collaboration as a Strategic Element in OKM

The integration of humans and AI systems has become an essential strategic factor for organizations seeking innovation, efficiency, and competitive advantage in the digital era. In OKM, this collaboration does not aim to replace humans with machines but rather to enhance their capabilities through a model of collaborative intelligence. In the following, the main aspects of this symbiosis are discussed, focusing on the complementarity between AI's analytical intelligence and human contextual judgment (Akinnagbe, 2024):

Analytical Intelligence vs. Contextual Intelligence
AI operates with excellence in analytical intelligence – that is, the ability to identify patterns, process large volumes of data, recognize correlations, and predict scenarios. However, it still lacks contextual intelligence, which is typical of human beings – such as judgment, intuition, cultural understanding, and the interpretation of ambiguity (Kutz, 2008).

Organizational example:
An algorithm might suggest replacing a supplier based on performance metrics. However, the manager may consider contextual factors such as

long-term business relationships or reputational impacts that are not represented in structured data.

Human–Machine Symbiosis for OKM

- **Strategic role of human judgment:** Even in highly automated environments, final decisions on sensitive matters – such as innovation, ethics, or cultural change – still rely on human judgment. The human role shifts from executor to knowledge curator, responsible for validating, adapting, and applying the insights provided by AI (Zhou *et al.*, 2021).
- **Complementarity between AI and human capabilities:** AI expands logical reasoning and data processing capacity, while humans contribute critical thinking, empathy, and creativity. This complementarity creates a hybrid system for decision-making and knowledge generation (Inga *et al.*, 2023).

Organizational example:
In R&D project recommendation systems, AI classifies and prioritizes ideas based on historical data and technological trends. Then, specialists assess strategic, ethical, and cultural feasibility aspects, refining the final choices.

Use Cases of Collaborative Intelligence

- **Collaborative diagnostics in engineering and healthcare:** AI suggests hypotheses based on case histories, and specialists confirm or adjust them based on their experience.
- **Corporate learning support bots:** Systems interact with users by suggesting personalized content, while human mentors guide strategic learning.
- **Strategic planning with AI:** Platforms like IBM Watson and Salesforce Einstein provide analyses and forecasts, but it is human leaders who define action priorities.

Collaboration between humans and AI is not merely a matter of technological efficiency – it represents a new paradigm in knowledge management. The collaborative intelligence model allows AI to act as a strategic partner, while humans remain central to meaning-making and critical judgment. This symbiotic relationship offers a promising path toward more adaptive, intelligent, and resilient organizations (Zhou *et al.*, 2021).

1.8 Pathways to Intelligent Organizations

In an era of intensive information and accelerated digital transformation, the concept of intelligent organizations is becoming increasingly relevant. These organizations are capable of continuous learning, adapting to dynamic contexts, and systematically generating innovation. When AI is integrated with OKM, it opens new pathways to make companies more resilient, adaptive, and future-oriented. The following are three strategic pillars for building truly intelligent organizations (Schwaninger, 2009):

1. *Organizational Learning Models with AI*

Traditional organizational learning relies on collecting past experiences, critical reflection, and transforming practices. With AI, this learning becomes more dynamic, scalable, and accurate. Systems based on machine learning, NLP, and knowledge mining enable real-time capture of lessons learned, identification of hidden patterns, and the suggestion of new courses of action.

Example: Platforms like Microsoft Viva or IBM Watson Studio identify competency gaps, suggest personalized learning paths, and monitor the effectiveness of applied knowledge within teams, fostering continuous learning based on data.

2. *KM Centered on Continuous Learning*

Intelligent KM is not limited to document storage or cataloging best practices. It has been repositioned as a living system centered on continuous learning, integrating data, people, and processes. AI acts as a catalyst, connecting diverse knowledge sources (formal and informal) and offering automated, contextualized, and personalized curation.

Example: Organizations using AI to feed communities of practice, suggest internal experts, or anticipate training needs based on new projects demonstrate a mature use of KM focused on learning.

This process enables the creation of knowledge feedback loops, where the knowledge generated is tested, validated, and reintegrated into the organizational system, generating an upward spiral of innovation and adaptation (Nonaka and Takeuchi, 1995).

3. *Sustainable Competitive Advantage Through Intelligent OKM*
The competitive advantage of intelligent organizations lies not only in their products or services but also in their ability to learn faster and better than their competitors (De Geus, 1988). AI-mediated OKM provides insights that accelerate decision-making, improve operational efficiency, and anticipate market movements.

Moreover, this collective and augmented intelligence enables the organization to:

- react quickly to changes in the external environment,
- create new data- and knowledge-based business models,
- engage employees as co-producers of strategic knowledge.

Example: Startups and large corporations that use AI to map consumer behavior trends and quickly adapt their products exemplify how OKM can drive continuous innovation and sustainable value.

Becoming an intelligent organization is a continuous process that requires a learning culture, knowledge governance, and the strategic adoption of AI technologies. More than just digitizing processes, it involves reconfiguring the logic of management by placing dynamic, personalized, and applied knowledge at the center of decision-making. In this scenario, OKM – with the support of AI – ceases to be a support function and becomes a strategic asset essential for the future of organizations.

1.9 Final Considerations

The incorporation of AI into OKM represents a profound strategic transformation, with direct implications for organizational productivity, innovation, and sustainability. Throughout this chapter, we discussed enabling technologies such as NLP, predictive models, recommendation systems, and cognitive agents, as well as their impacts on the processes of identifying, creating, storing, sharing, and applying knowledge.

It was demonstrated that although AI offers substantial benefits – such as intelligent process automation, enhanced analytical capabilities, and the promotion of continuous organizational learning – its implementation faces technical, cultural, ethical, and governance-related challenges. Human–AI collaboration emerges as a critical factor, establishing a collaborative intelligence model in which AI's analytical capacity complements human contextual and strategic judgment.

The adoption of AI-mediated OKM, when well structured, can generate sustainable competitive advantages by enabling organizations to learn faster, innovate continuously, and build resilience in the face of change.

1.9.1 *Recommendations for managers and organizational policymakers*

- Foster a culture of continuous and adaptive learning, encouraging the strategic use of AI to support knowledge-based decision-making.
- Develop data and knowledge governance structures that ensure quality, security, ethics, and alignment with organizational goals.
- Invest in leadership and team training, promoting digital fluency and the effective integration of human competencies with algorithmic capabilities.
- Establish clear institutional policies on AI use, with transparent guidelines regarding privacy, accountability, and the explainability of automated decisions.

1.9.2 *Suggestions for future research*

- Design AI-based models and tools to identify, create, store, share, and use organizational knowledge.
- Develop continuous learning models for the development of human capital in organizations, based on AI.
- Investigate hybrid models of AI-augmented organizational learning, focusing on effectiveness metrics and strategic impact.
- Explore the interaction between human cognition and AI in organizational contexts.
- Analyze the effects of AI on the dynamics of tacit and relational knowledge, often invisible in traditional OKM systems.
- Research the role of AI in the innovation process of products, services, and business models.
- Conduct studies on the integration of diverse fields of knowledge to solve complex organizational challenges.

- Develop adaptive governance frameworks that integrate AI, OKM, and open innovation in complex ecosystems.
- Apply AI to model, strengthen, and measure social capital and relationship networks within organizations.
- Develop AI-integrated OKM practices aimed at organizational and environmental sustainability.
- Investigate how AI-based media transform the production, dissemination, and use of organizational knowledge.
- Explore the ethical and epistemological boundaries of AI in decision-making, especially in sensitive contexts such as healthcare, education, and public safety.

References

Abecker, A., S. Sintek, L. Hovy, and A. Abebe. 'Toward a Technology for Organizational Memories.' *IEEE Intelligent Systems*, 13, no. 3 (1998): 40–48.

Akinnagbe, O. B. 'Human-AI Collaboration: Enhancing Productivity and Decision-Making.' *International Journal of Education, Management, and Technology*, 2, no. 3 (2024): 387–417, https://doi.org/10.58578/ijemt.v2i3.4209.

Ale, M. A., G. H. Torti, P. D. Turco, L. M. T. Aranda, and G. I. D. T. Reyes. 'A Conceptual Model and Technological Support for Organizational Knowledge Management.' *Science of Computer Programming*, 95 (2014): 73–92.

Alstete, J. W. and J. P. Meyer. 'Intelligent Agent-Assisted Organizational Memory in Knowledge Management Systems.' In *Knowledge Management and Organizational Learning*, edited by W. R. King. Springer, Cham, 2020, 199–215.

Anumba, C. and R. Khallaf. 'Use of Artificial Intelligence to Improve Knowledge Management in Construction.' In *IOP Conference Series: Earth and Environmental Science*, Vol. 1101. IOP Publishing, 2022, 062001.

Bastien, S., J. Kitching, and R. Sims. *Theory of Knowledge*. 3rd ed. Pearson: London, 2020.

Berman, S. J. 'Digital Transformation: Opportunities to Create New Business Models.' *Strategy & Leadership*, 40, no. 2 (2012): 16–24.

Bharadwaj, A., O. A. El Sawy, P. A. Pavlou, and N. Venkatraman. 'Digital Business Strategy: Toward a Next Generation of Insights.' *MIS Quarterly*, 37, no. 2 (2013): 471–482.

Birzniece, I. 'Artificial Intelligence in Knowledge Management: Overview and Trends.' *Scientific Journal of Riga Technical University, Computer Science. Applied Computer Systems*, 44, no. 1 (2011): 57–63.

De Geus, A. 'Planning as Learning.' *Harvard Business Review*, 66, no. 2 (1988): 70–74.

Fitzgerald, M., N. Kruschwitz, D. Bonnet, and M. Welch. 'Embracing Digital Technology: A New Strategic Imperative.' *MIT Sloan Management Review*, 55, no. 2 (2013): 1–12.

Gasik, S. 'A Model or Project Knowledge Management.' *Project Management Journal*, 42, no. 3 (2011): 23–44.

Harfouche, A., B. Quinio, S. Rouis Skandrani, and R. Marciniak. 'A Framework for Artificial Knowledge Creation in Organizations.' In *Proceedings of the Thirty-Eighth International Conference on Information Systems (ICIS 2017)*. 2017, 11–15. Association for Information Systems, Seoul, South Korea.

Henly, C. P. and J. Sprague. *Theory of Knowledge*. 5th ed. Hodder Education: London, 2020.

Henriette, E., M. Feki, and I. Boughzala. 'The Shape of Digital Transformation: A Systematic Literature Review.' In *MCIS 2015 Proceedings*. 2015, 10.

Hess, T. 'Options for Formulating a Digital Transformation Strategy.' *MIS Quarterly Executive*, 15, no. 2 (2016): 123–139.

Horlach, B., P. Drews, I. Schirmer, and T. Böhmann. 'Increasing the Agility of IT Delivery: Five Types of Bimodal IT Organization.' In *Proceedings of the 50th Hawaii International Conference on System Sciences*. 2017, 5420–5429.

Inga, J., M. Ruess, J. H. Robens, T. Nelius, S. Rothfuß, S. Kille, P. Dahlinger, A. Lindenmann, R. Thomaschke, G. Neumann, S. Matthiesen, S. Hohmann, and A. Kiesel. 'Human-Machine Symbiosis: A Multivariate Perspective for Physically Coupled Human-Machine Systems.' *International Journal of Human-Computer Studies*, 170 (2023): 1–15. Article 102926, https://doi.org/10.1016/j.ijhcs.2022.102926.

Isinkaye, F. O., Y. O. Folajimi, and B. A. Ojokoh. 'Recommendation Systems: Principles, Methods and Evaluation.' *Egyptian Informatics Journal*, 16, no. 3 (2015): 261–273.

Jamarani, A., S. Mohammadi, M. Kashani, M. Albari, and S. Moradi. 'Big Data and Predictive Analytics: A Systematic Review of Applications.' *Artificial Intelligence Review*, 57, no. 176 (2024), https://doi.org/10.1007/s10462-024-10811-5.

Jarrahi, M. H., G. Westerman, T. Dahlberg, and A. Sidorova. 'Artificial Intelligence and Knowledge Management: A Partnership Between Human and AI.' *Business Horizons*, 65, no. 2 (2022): 129–139, https://doi.org/10.1016/j.bushor.2022.03.002.

Karagiannaki, A., G. Vergados, and K. Fouskas. 'The Impact of Digital Transformation in the Financial Services Industry: Insights From an Open Innovation Initiative in Fintech in Greece.' In *MCIS 2017 Proceedings*. 2017, 15.

Karyotaki, M., D. Athanasios, and S. Charalabos. 'Chatbots as Cognitive, Educational, Advisory & Coaching Systems.' *Technium Social Sciences Journal*, 30 (2022): 109–126.

Karyotaki, M., D. Athanasios, and S. Charalabos. 'The Implementation of Artificial Intelligence in Knowledge Management: A Systematic Literature Review.' In *2024 IEEE International Conference on Interdisciplinary Approaches in Technology and Management for Social Innovation (IATMSI)*. IEEE, 2024.

Kovačić, M., B. Babić, and C. Krajnović. 'Using Artificial Intelligence for Creating and Managing Organizational Knowledge.' *Technical Gazette*, 29, no. 4 (2022): 1413–1418.

Kudryavtsev, D., U. A. Khan, and J. Kauttonen. 'Transforming Knowledge Management Using Generative AI: From Theory to Practice.' In *Proceedings of the 16th International Joint Conference on Knowledge Discovery, Knowledge Engineering and Knowledge Management (IC3K 2024) – Volume 3: KMIS*. 2024, 362–370.

Kutz, M. R. 'Toward a Conceptual Model of Contextual Intelligence: A Transferable Leadership Construct.' *Leadership Review*, 8 (2008): 18–31.

Liere-Netheler, K., S. Packmohr, and K. Vogelsang. 'Drivers of Digital Transformation in Manufacturing.' In *Proceedings of the 51st Hawaii International Conference on System Sciences*. 2018, 4216–4225.

Liu, D., O. Shenkar, and G. Zhang. 'Resource Fit in Digital Transformation – Lessons Learned From The CBC Bank Global E-Banking Project.' *Management Decision*, 49, no. 10 (2011): 1728–1742.

Luna-Reyes, L. F., and J. R. Gil-Garcia. 'Digital Government Transformation and Internet Portals: The Co-Evolution of Technology, Organizations and Institutions.' *Government Information Quarterly*, 31, no. 4 (2014): 545–555.

Mahraz, M.-I., A. Benabbou, and N. Cheikhrouhou. 'A Systematic Literature Review of Digital Transformation.' In *Proceedings of the International Conference on Industrial Engineering and Operations Management*. Toronto, Canada, 2019, 23–25.

Matt, C., T. Hess, and A. Benlian. 'Digital Transformation Strategies.' *Business and Information Systems Engineering*, 57, no. 5 (2015): 339–343, https://doi.org/10.1007/s12599-015-0401-5.

Mergel, I., N. Edelmann, and N. Haug. 'Defining Digital Transformation: Results from Expert Interviews.' *Government Information Quarterly*, 36, no. 4 (2019): 101385.

Murad, B. M. and M.-B. Kurdy. 'Knowledge Management Referral System Using Artificial Intelligent Techniques.' In *2020 21st International Arab Conference on Information Technology (ACIT)*. IEEE, 2020, 1–7.

National Academies of Sciences, Engineering, and Medicine. *Artificial Intelligence and the Future of Work*. The National Academies Press: Washington, DC, 2025, https://doi.org/10.17226/27644.

Nestian, A., S. Tiță, and A. L. Guță. 'Incorporating Artificial Intelligence in Knowledge Creation Processes in Organizations.' In *Proceedings of the International Conference on Business Excellence*, Vol. 14. 2020, 1119–1129.

Nonaka, I. and H. Takeuchi. *The Knowledge-Creating Company: How Japanese Companies Create the Dynamics of Innovation*. Oxford University Press, 1995.

Novalin, A., A. Gunawan, and Prihandoko, B. 'The Implementation of Artificial Intelligence in Knowledge Management: A Systematic Literature Review.' In *2024 IEEE International Conference on Interdisciplinary Approaches in Technology and Management for Social Innovation (IATMSI)*. IEEE, 2024, https://doi.org/10.1109/IATMSI60426.2024.10502986.

O'Leary, D. E. 'Using AI in Knowledge Management: Knowledge Bases and Ontologies.' *IEEE Intelligent Systems*, 13, no. 3 (1998): 34–39.

Olan, F., J. Olanrewaju, E. Eze, and R. Dada. 'Artificial Intelligence and Knowledge Sharing: Contributing Factors to Organizational Performance.' *Journal of Business Research*, 145 (2022): 605–618.

Pacheco, R. C. S., N. Santos, and R. Wahrhaftig. 'Transformação digital na Educação Superior: modos e impactos na universidade.' *Revista NUPEM*, 12, no. 27 (2020): 94–128.

Pai, R. Y., S. Alathur, L. D'Souza, G. Thomas, and A. Joseph. 'Integrating Artificial Intelligence for Knowledge Management Systems – Synergy Among People and Technology: A Systematic Review of the Evidence.' *Economic Research-Ekonomska Istraživanja*, 35, no. 1 (2022): 5154–5186.

Patel, K. and M. P. McCarthy. *Digital Transformation: The Essentials of e-Business Leadership*. McGraw-Hill: New York, 2000.

Santos, N. and G. R. Varvakis. *Fundamentos teóricos de gestão do conhecimento*. Pandion: Florianópolis, 2020.

Schwaninger, M. *Intelligent Organizations: Powerful Models for Systemic Management*. 2nd ed. Springer: Berlin, Heidelberg, 2009.

Shieber, J. H. *Theories of Knowledge: How to Think about What You Know*. The Teaching Company: Chantilly, 2019.

Sira, M. 'Artificial Intelligence in Knowledge Capture and Transfer: Breaking Down Organizational Silos.' *System Safety: Human – Technical Facility – Environment*, 6, no. 1 (2024): 312–321.

Sprague, J. *Theory of Knowledge for IB Diploma: Skills for Success*. 2nd ed. Hodder Education: London, 2020.

Stolterman, E. and A. C. Fors. 'Information Technology and the Good Life.' In *Information Systems Research*, edited by B. Kaplan, D. P. Truex, D. Wastell, A. T. Wood-Harper, and J. I. DeGross. IFIP International Federation for Information Processing, vol. 143. Springer: Boston, MA, 2004, 687–692.

Waykar, Y. A. 'The Role of Artificial Intelligence in Knowledge Management.' *International Journal of Scientific Research in Engineering and Management*, 6, no. 6 (2022): 1–4.

Westerman, G. 'Why Digital Transformation Needs a Heart.' *MIT Sloan Management Review*, 58, no. 1 (2016): 19–21.

Young, R. *Knowledge Management Tools and Techniques Manual*. Asian Productivity Organization: Tokyo, 2020.

Zaoui Seghroucheni, O., M. Lazaar, and M. Al Achhab. 'Using AI and NLP for Tacit Knowledge Conversion in Knowledge Management Systems: A Comparative Analysis.' *Technologies*, 13, no. 2 (2025): 87, https://doi.org/10.3390/technologies13020087.

Zhou, L., S. Paul, H. Demirkan, L. Yuan, J. Spohrer, M. Zhou, and J. Basu. 'Intelligence Augmentation: Towards Building Human-Machine Symbiotic Relationship.' *AIS Transactions on Human-Computer Interaction*, 13, no. 2 (2021): 243–264, https://doi.org/10.17705/1thci.00149.

© 2026 World Scientific Publishing Europe Ltd.
https://doi.org/10.1142/9781800617414_0002

Chapter 2

Knowledge Management Focused on Organizational Memory: A Comparative Study Between Spanish and Brazilian Organizations

Ieda Pelógia Martins Damian

University of São Paulo, Brazil

iedapm@usp.br

Abstract

Based on the assumption that knowledge management and organizational memory complement each other to help organizations achieve their strategic objectives, Damian and Moro-Cabero (2020) developed a knowledge management model focused on the characteristics of organizational memory, and its applicability was verified in Spanish and Brazilian organizations. The objective of this study is to carry out a comparative analysis of the results found in Spanish and Brazilian organizations to identify aspects that can contribute to the successful implementation of knowledge management in organizations. In terms of methodological approach, this study utilized a bibliographical survey based on the concepts involved in the research and interviews conducted with the managers of the Spanish and Brazilian organizations. Findings indicate that Spanish and Brazilian organizations were still in an incipient state regarding knowledge management and lacked organizational memory, indicating that there is significant work to be done in both areas. Beyond the differences and similarities between Spanish and Brazilian organizations, the use of a model for implementing knowledge management focused on organizational memory is fundamental. The originality of the study lies in the development of comparative analyses between Brazilian and Spanish organizations to adapt a knowledge management model that considers organizational memory. Its practical implications are to adapt a knowledge management implementation model that considers the characteristics of organizational memory so that more organizations are successful in this implementation and can, therefore, enjoy the benefits arising from knowledge.

Keywords: Knowledge management, organizational memory, spain, brazil, comparative study, model.

2.1 Introduction

As the raw material for innovation and the development of sustainable competitive advantages, knowledge occupies a prominent place in organizations and is considered a strategic resource in any organizational context that includes competitiveness, globalization, and technological progress. In this scenario, according to Santos *et al.* (2019), knowledge has become the main driver of organizational development and innovation, as the implementation of its management is a key topic for all types of organizations concerned with continuous improvement and obtaining a competitive advantage.

According to Alvarenga Neto (2008), to add value to an organization, knowledge must be managed effectively, which involves establishing a strategic vision for the use of knowledge so that its acquisition, creation, and dissemination promote creativity, innovation, learning, and training. For the author, knowledge management (KM) also includes the competence to provide an appropriate organizational context where the essential role of organizational culture and people is recognized, in an environment where information and knowledge are considered the only elements capable of strengthening essential organizational characteristics and contributing to sustainable competitive advantages, which are fundamental to the survival of organizations in increasingly competitive scenarios.

Despite the benefits of KM, many organizations fail to implement it due to its complexity and comprehensiveness. As stated by Shahabadi *et al.* (2018), KM consists of behavioral, cultural, technological, and strategic elements. To achieve more successful outcomes with the implementation of KM, it is recommended to use models that guide organizations along the way. A KM model, because it is logical, allows people to understand how organizations produce, share, and use knowledge (Silva and Valentim, 2008). This understanding leads to people's involvement in KM, which is essential for its successful implementation.

According to Santos and Valentim (2021, p. 6):

> The materialization of a knowledge management model can be considered a tool that allows the planning and development of better actions aimed at the tacit and explicit knowledge existing in a given organization, as well as an important mechanism for identifying and highlighting some aspects that deserve attention for organizations when implementing this management model.

Even if the literature includes a considerable number of KM models, Damian and Moro-Cabero (2020) identified that these do not highlight the interrelationship between KM and organizational memory (OM). By analyzing the characteristics of knowledge and the processes involved in its management, the authors state that the characteristics of OM are fundamental to the implementation of KM in organizations. According to Jarrahi *et al.* (2023), the creation and maintenance of an OM is one of the basic functions of KM, so that knowledge resources can be tracked.

OM, according to Antunes and Pinheiro (2020), is concerned with storing organizational knowledge for future use and is related to the processes of acquiring, retaining, and retrieving that knowledge. As it helps to prevent knowledge loss, the authors conclude that OM helps the organization achieve its desired results. "[...] OM captures, organizes and disseminates the knowledge generated in the environment, so that the organizational subject, based on the interrelations established, can generate 'new' knowledge and intelligence for the organization" (Santos *et al.*, 2016, p. 1153).

The complementary relationship between KM and OM is highlighted by Freire *et al.* (2012, p. 49) when they state that:

> [...] organizations, to maintain and expand their competitive advantages over their competitors, must manage the knowledge of their intellectual active capital, which is the result of the sum of the knowledge of

> everyone in the organization. This means using knowledge management tools to create new knowledge, based on the renewal of information and the use of the structure of their organizational memory.

Given the close relationship between KM and OM, as well as the gap identified in the literature regarding KM models that consider OM, Damian and Moro-Cabero (2020) developed a KM model that incorporates the characteristics of OM, whose application was verified in Spanish and Brazilian organizations. Based on these verifications, the following research question arises: Can a comparative analysis of the results found in Spanish and Brazilian organizations identify aspects that can contribute to the successful implementation of KM within organizations? The objective of this study is to carry out a comparative analysis of the results found in Spanish and Brazilian organizations to identify aspects that can contribute to the successful implementation of KM in organizations.

As methodological procedures, a bibliographical survey was conducted on the concepts involved in the research, and interviews were conducted with the managers of the Spanish and Brazilian organizations. The research is qualitative in nature, characterized as descriptive and exploratory, and encompasses organizations within the service sector of Ribeirão Preto, state of São Paulo, Brazil, and the meat sector of Salamanca, Spain. The qualitative technique of content analysis was used as the research methodology.

2.2 Theoretical Reference

Knowledge, according to Wilson (2006), can be understood as what people know, including their understanding and the mental processes of understanding and learning that occur in the human mind. Based on personal experience, knowledge, according to De Sordi (2015), is that conceived by individuals through analysis and reflection based on a set of information.

From a more organizational perspective, Pérez-Montoro Gutiérrez (2008) states that knowledge comprises all the information a person internalizes or assimilates, directed toward action, and represents the mental state of the organization, which, based on the assimilation of information, guides the actions of its stakeholders. Takeuchi and Nonaka (2008) state that knowledge is a resource derived from people's cognitive processes and is generally associated with organizational activities.

In the same sense, Duarte *et al.* (2014) state that knowledge is the product of interpreting a set of information used to solve problems and make decisions. Given its applicability, it is possible to verify its importance for organizations. As Cerdá (2013) points out, knowledge has become the most important raw material of the 21st century, with the ability to contribute to increasing organizational competitiveness. Supporting these statements, Damian (2020) states that knowledge adds value to organizations by enabling them to build sustainable competitive advantages and providing benefits to all those involved in this management, such as organizations, employees, collaborators, partners, customers, governments, and citizens.

All organizations possess knowledge; therefore, as Damian and Moro-Cabero (2021) point out, mere possession of knowledge is not a differentiator. The difference, according to the authors, lies not in possession but in how organizations use it to drive action and generate benefits. For knowledge to be used efficiently, adequate management of this resource is necessary.

KM, according to Stefano and Sartori (2016), is considered an orderly process for the acquisition, organization, and communication of knowledge, both tacit and explicit, with the aim of contributing to the achievement of more effective results through better decision-making and strategic definition. To this end, KM proposes "[...] the construction of a learning environment that fills the information gaps of a post-industrial society [...] from the creation, identification, integration, recovery, sharing, and use of knowledge in different environments" (Silva *et al.*, 2016, p. 31).

By integrating organizational strategy, KM, according to Hoffmann (2016), can be understood as a management model that encourages individuals to use resources already available in the organization with the aim of developing better operational practices without necessarily incurring the cost of obtaining new resources. According to Antunes and Pinheiro (2020), KM should be understood as the management of the processes of creating, storing, accessing, and disseminating an organization's intellectual resources. For Damian (2020, p. 4), KM:

> [...] can be understood as a comprehensive management model centered on organizational strategy and aimed at the success of organizational goals and objectives, made possible by efficient processes and management techniques aimed at generating value, creating, managing, disseminating and reusing knowledge in a spiral of tacit and explicit, individual, group and organizational knowledge. Its results have an impact on the competitiveness of the organization and prevent corporate amnesia, being a significant and intangible resource that exceeds the value of capital.

According to Santos and Damian (2018), the purpose of KM is to ensure that knowledge is utilized across diverse organizational activities, especially those involved in decision-making processes. Manuti and Monachino (2020) state that KM takes care of the acquisition and management of knowledge found in individuals, with the aim of reducing redundancies and cognitive gaps.

For KM to achieve the desired results, Antunes and Pinheiro (2020) state that organizations must be committed to increasing the capacity of individuals and knowledge enhancers, as they constitute the source that generates an organization's intellectual resources, which, being valuable, rare, inimitable, and irreplaceable, contribute to the generation of sustainable competitive advantage.

Another precaution to ensure that KM achieves its expected objectives is to align it with the vision and mission of the organization since this management influences decision-making by obtaining and interpreting relevant information and contributing to increased innovation and competitiveness (Mohamad *et al.*, 2017).

Still, in relation to its benefits, Oliveira-Del-Massa *et al.* (2018) point out that KM allows for more assertive planning and decision-making processes, even in volatile economic and/or political scenarios, since KM provides the necessary support to make decisions from logical and consistent perspectives. The authors also state that KM helps to increase quality, creativity, and innovation within organizations. Silva (2022) points out that knowledge is present at all organizational levels and that its management is fundamental to increasing its added value, both individual knowledge and the collective knowledge that constitutes the organization.

As benefits of KM for organizations, Lousada *et al.* (2011) point out that KM as a competitive tool helps to increase the ability to generate ideas, increase the value of the organization, and provide support for decision-making. According to Leonardi *et al.* (2011), KM helps to maximize efficiency and return on an organization's knowledge assets. Villasana Arreguín *et al.* (2021) add that KM helps to increase creativity, innovation, and organizational performance. For the authors, it is through KM that organizations acquire the competitive capacity necessary to guarantee their survival and create competitive advantages.

Despite the numerous benefits of KM, its implementation is often not easy. Therefore, it is recommended to use models designed for this purpose.

Villasana Arreguín *et al.* (2021) claim that KM models demonstrate the importance of knowledge for an organization, as well as other important aspects such as its dynamics, complexity, and strategic nature.

Through an extensive review of the literature, Damian and Moro-Cabero (2020) found that the structures of KM models are made up of KM processes, namely creation, storage, sharing, and use of organizational knowledge. For the authors, the use of a KM model is an essential condition for implementing this management and achieving the desired results.

KM models, for Pizzaia *et al.* (2018, p. 65), "open new paths for the systemic structuring of knowledge so that organizations can achieve innovation and sustainability." KM models promote the establishment of processes aimed at codification and knowledge sharing, with the aim of increasing competitiveness and innovation (Dalkir, 2011).

Due to the importance of KM implementation models and the need for these models to consider OM, Damian and Moro-Cabero (2020) developed a KM implementation model focused on the characteristics of OM, whose applicability was verified in Spanish and Brazilian organizations. The model in question was developed based on the main KM processes identified by the authors, namely identify, create/obtain, store, disseminate/share, use, and evaluate. All these processes consider the characteristics of OM.

OM refers to the "ability of organizations to save, retain and use information from the past in current activities. It is a key element that allows organizations to learn from past mistakes and successes" (Melgar-Sasieta *et al.*, 2011, p. 1). According to Pereira *et al.* (2016), OM should be viewed as the explicit representation of knowledge and information relevant to the organizational context, with the aim of facilitating access, sharing, and reuse of these resources among organizational subjects.

Boghossian *et al.* (2019, p. 102) consider OM to be "a natural foundation for decision-making and knowledge management." For Feitoza and

Duarte (2021), OM facilitates the process of managing, sharing, and creating knowledge.

In relation to the interrelationship between KM and OM, Damian (2020, p. 13) states that both serve the same purpose, which is:

> [...] taking care of organizational knowledge so that it is not lost and is used to support organizational activities, decision-making processes, and the preservation of intellectual capital, to contribute to the development of sustainable competitive advantages.

Nascimento and Vitoriano (2017) state that OM contributes to the successful implementation of KM in organizations by handling the registration and dissemination of tacit knowledge within them. The authors emphasize that one of the functions of OM is to support KM processes since OM is linked to KM through the transformation of its repositories into knowledge repertoires, which contribute to decision-making and enable organizations to obtain a competitive advantage.

2.3 Materials and Methods

The research is qualitative in nature, characterized as descriptive and exploratory. The research universe consisted of companies in the meat sector in Salamanca, Spain, and companies in the service sector in Ribeirão Preto, São Paulo state, Brazil.

A bibliographic survey of the main works and authors in information science on KM and the KM implementation model was conducted. Semi-structured interviews with managers of the companies described above were carried out – nine with managers of Spanish companies and nine with managers of Brazilian companies.

To qualitatively analyze the specific characteristics of the contexts studied and thus contribute to the successful implementation of KM focused on the characteristics of OM, interviews were conducted with managers from companies in the manufacturing sector in Salamanca, Spain, and the services sector in Ribeirão Preto, São Paulo state, Brazil.

Bardin's (2011) content analysis was used to construct the qualitative research, using categorical analysis with categories defined *a priori* and comprising the stages of Damian and Moro-Cabero's (2020) KM implementation model.

Categorical analysis, which involves developing categories *a priori*, i.e., prior to data collection, was chosen because, according to Bardin (2011), when categories are defined *a priori*, the researcher enters the data collection phase focused on what needs to be analyzed. This alternative is suitable for the purpose of this research, which is based on the stages of the model for implementing KM focused on the characteristics of OM by Damian and Moro-Cabero (2020).

Content analysis involves various types of analysis to understand the manifest and latent meanings of the material collected. Among these types, thematic or categorical analysis, which involves breaking down the text into categories according to analogical regrouping, was used in this research. The categories were defined *a priori* and are based on the stages of the KM model proposed by Damian and Moro-Cabero (2020). Nine interviews were conducted with managers of companies in the manufacturing sector in the province of Salamanca, Spain, and nine interviews were conducted with managers of companies in the service sector in the city of Ribeirão Preto, state of São Paulo, Brazil. These sectors were chosen due to their relevance.

According to the Asociación Nacional de Industrias de la Carne de España (ANICE), the meat sector is the fourth most representative industrial sector in Spain and the leading producer in the Spanish food and beverage industry, providing 24.3% of food industry jobs in Spain (ANICE, 2024). According to data from the Junta de Castilla y León (JCyL), the meat sector in the Comunidad de Castilla y León, where Salamanca is located, serves as a benchmark, ranking first in terms of production and consumption and accounting for 26% of the agri-food industry, which is crucial to the local economy (JCyL, 2024).

Data from the Ministry of Labor and Social Security (2024) reveal that the service sector is responsible for 44.1% of the jobs created in the first half of 2021. This percentage is even higher, at 50.63%, when analyzing the state of São Paulo and increases to 55.9% in the city of Ribeirão Preto, which justifies the relevance of studies that consider the sector in the city. The importance of the service sector can also be seen in Brazil's gross domestic product (GDP), where the sector has experienced consecutive increases, reaching 74% in 2020, according to the National Confederation of Trade in Goods, Services and Tourism (2020). When compared to the same period in the previous year, in January 2020, the services sector in the state of São Paulo grew by 22.2% (Folha de São Paulo, 2024). These figures are more meritorious due to the fact that the state is responsible for the largest share of Brazil's GDP – 31.6% in 2020 (CENSO 2022, 2024).

The results were analyzed and interpreted by revisiting the objectives related to the theoretical-methodological framework underpinning this research. At this point, the aspects related to the contexts analyzed that can influence the successful implementation of KM are highlighted. To this end, a table was developed that highlights the implications and guidelines related to KM focused on the characteristics of OM in relation to those presented by the surveyed companies.

2.4 Results and Discussion

Of the companies that participated in this research, the Spanish companies had an average of 15 years of existence, and the Brazilian companies had an average of 21 years, making them well-established in their respective markets. The Spanish companies were smaller, had fewer employees, and were mostly family-owned in comparison, with companies managed by the second or third generation of the family. In the Brazilian context, the size of the companies surveyed was more variable, and there was less family management. In contrast to the Spanish companies, there were Brazilian companies managed by their founders, who were around 40 years old.

A key characteristic of Spanish companies was the fact that they had a seal of designation of origin. The quest to obtain and maintain this seal contributes to the implementation of KM, particularly the provision of training by external institutions responsible for awarding these seals and the conduct of ongoing evaluations.

All the companies surveyed had managers who were experienced in their sectors and had been with the companies for a considerable amount of time. Most of the Spanish managers had family ties to the founders of the companies, and the Brazilian managers were either owners themselves or came from the market. The family-oriented nature of the Spanish companies was reflected in the high level of commitment from top management, as they were running a family business that "my grandfather passed on to my father and my father passed on to me." In addition to the family aspect, Spanish managers were clear about the importance and need for qualified professionals to increase their competitive potential.

Among the Brazilian companies, managers were more often the founders and tended to be around 40 years old. In these cases, there was greater agility and availability in relation to the changes needed to implement KM focused on the characteristics of OM, as they were very attentive to market demands and committed to seeking competitive advantages for their companies. Moreover, they had the advantage of having the autonomy to implement the necessary changes.

All interviewees considered KM to be important, although they sometimes showed a lack of clarity regarding the concept.

A common characteristic of all the surveyed companies was the existence of long-serving employees with considerable knowledge and experience. Although this characteristic is very advantageous for KM, it was not properly utilized for this purpose because the companies did not implement formal KM processes and activities. To ensure that the knowledge of the organizational subjects is not lost, KM makes use of OM, which the managers recognized as relevant during the research but which had not been implemented in any of the companies they represented.

The lack of management focus on knowledge needs meant that companies generated a large volume of data, information, and knowledge that could be lost or misused. This situation was also aggravated by the lack of OM.

In the Spanish companies, there was a greater lack of formal job definitions or career plans, and it was common to find cases of employees "doing a bit of everything."

As the companies surveyed lacked formal practices for identifying the knowledge needed to carry out their activities, it was found, in both the Spanish and Brazilian contexts, that the most common way of seeking knowledge was to consult more experienced employees. There was unanimous agreement that employees knew where to turn for the knowledge they needed and that there were no difficulties in accessing this knowledge. As they had well-experienced employees who were considered great sources of knowledge, the companies had not yet woken up to the need to implement formal KM initiatives aimed at identifying knowledge needs. In the same way that it is positive to have experienced employees, it is worrying how dependent organizations are on them in terms of knowledge: If they leave the company for any reason, there would be a significant loss of knowledge that could even make it impossible to carry out several organizational activities.

Performance indicators, internal and external benchmarking, process mapping, normalization, and standardization were the most recurring practices in Spanish companies, driven by the acquisition of the designation of origin seal and the intention to operate in international markets.

Implementing KM through a pilot project, as suggested by Damian and Moro-Cabero's (2020) KM model, is the most appropriate alternative for the companies surveyed since no formal KM activities were identified. In addition, as mentioned above, KM is complex and comprehensive, so implementing it all at once across an entire organization that does not yet have formal knowledge initiatives is not the most appropriate course of action.

Training and capacity building were carried out by the surveyed companies, although often without adequate planning or frequency. Motivational and reward policies were more frequently observed in Brazilian companies. These themes are positive for KM, but none of the companies had implemented the above-mentioned KM-related activities. This situation appears favorable to the implementation of KM, strengthening the need to create OM because no activities to retain organizational knowledge were detected. In this regard, it is essential to strengthen the need for activities that convert individual knowledge into organizational knowledge.

Teamwork and an environment of trust were cited as key elements in most of the companies surveyed, facilitating knowledge sharing, which is one of the most important processes in KM. For knowledge sharing to occur, companies need to provide an environment geared toward this purpose, which includes, among other things, trust, respect, recognition, and motivation. This environment was found in the Spanish and Brazilian companies that participated in this research, which shows that they offer the necessary conditions for the implementation of KM.

Another enabler of knowledge sharing is information and communication technologies (ICT), which were present in the companies participating in the study but were not used for this purpose. It is worth noting that ICT brings together a set of tools that facilitate knowledge sharing and should therefore be used.

A situation resembling that of implementing ICT was found in relation to the external environment, representing an important source of knowledge acquisition and sharing that the surveyed companies had not sufficiently exploited. An improvement was reported in the mediation of relationships with customers, suppliers, competitors, and partners of Spanish companies, previously conducted traditionally and with little added value for all parties involved; this has significantly improved with the intervention of the organizations certifying the designation of origin.

Another common point between the Spanish and Brazilian companies was the lack of systematic and orderly storage of knowledge. When knowledge was stored, the process occurred without adequate criteria, which made it impossible to use it later. It was possible to observe certain accommodations in relation to the lack of proper knowledge storage due to the presence of experienced employees and the family-oriented nature of many companies, where knowledge was passed down from "father to son" to prevent the loss of knowledge. This highlights the urgent need to implement KM and OM to prevent important knowledge from being lost, especially when employees leave.

Dissemination of knowledge did not seem to occur in the Spanish context; and in the Brazilian context, it happened in a tentative and informal manner, primarily through meetings. When knowledge is not disseminated, its use is compromised. To avoid this, the implementation of KM is essential. In addition, it was possible to observe a certain confusion in the understanding of this process, as the managers interviewed conflated it with the process of searching for knowledge. For example, when asked about the activities related to the dissemination of knowledge, the response included that the employees know where to find the knowledge they need, they seek knowledge from a more experienced employee, or they search for information on the internet. The lack of proper understanding of the process hinders the implementation of knowledge dissemination, as well as KM.

An alternative to reversing the above situation could be the use of motivational and reward policies that encourage collective work, which were not found in any of the companies surveyed.

No formal procedures were identified for the use of skills and knowledge assets, but managers pointed out that knowledge was used in a wide range of organizational activities. In the case of the Spanish companies, a greater concern was identified with the use of knowledge in activities directly related to production, which was related to the designation of origin label. Furthermore, due to the characteristics of Spanish organizations (small or medium-sized, family-owned, and with employees performing diverse functions), their managers stated that skills and knowledge were frequently utilized. In Brazilian companies, the use of knowledge reported by managers was related to legislation and inspections. Despite the different approaches presented, it can be said that in all these cases, the development of formal procedures significantly contributes to the use of organizational knowledge, highlighting the importance of implementing KM.

Not only was it not carried out, but managers also did not have a clear and correct concept of evaluating and discarding unnecessary knowledge, which was sometimes confused with discarding documents or cleaning up data in the system or database. Regarding the knowledge assessment process, none of the contexts surveyed identified any activities that assessed or measured knowledge resources. Without measuring results, the expansion of KM and resource allocation is limited.

Table 2.1 presents the main aspects found in the research, as well as the implications and guidelines related to KM, focusing on the proposed characteristics of OM.

By analyzing the data collected, it was possible to see that the companies surveyed lacked formal activities and processes aimed at KM and OM. Another important aspect to be addressed is the fact that the breadth and depth of the main concepts involved in KM and OM were sometimes unclear to the managers who took part in the interviews, which is a significant issue.

2.5 Final Considerations

Although the importance of KM, focused on OM, was recognized and the companies surveyed had suitable environments for implementing KM, it was found that ICT, which is essential for KM focused on OM, was underused. The fact that they are consolidated in their markets, have low turnover, and employ professionals who have been with the organizations for a long time are positive aspects that the companies surveyed presented and which should be explored in relation to the implementation of KM.

Considering the analysis carried out and answering the question that guides the research, as well as its objective, it is clear that Damian and Moro Cabero's (2020) KM model is not only appropriate but also the most suitable way to implement KM, both in the Spanish and Brazilian contexts.

The main contributions of this research to the academic field are the development of studies on KM and OM, with an emphasis on implementation models, to strengthen research in the field of information science.

The main limitations of this research include the fact that it involved only two sectors (services and meat) and only two countries (Brazil and Spain).

Table 2.1. Implications and guidelines related to knowledge management focused on the characteristics of organizational memory in relation to the characteristics presented by the companies surveyed.

Features	Context	Implications and Guidelines Related to Knowledge Management (KM) Focused on the Characteristics of Organizational Memory (OM)
Companies consolidated in their markets.	Brazil and Spain	Consolidation in their markets adds stability, experience, and knowledge that must be exploited through KM to build sustainable competitive advantages.
Smaller companies, with fewer employees and more family-owned, run by the second or third generation of the family.	Spain	In smaller environments, employees are more likely to meet and share knowledge. The family culture found showed great appreciation for the knowledge of past generations. These aspects are very positive for KM.
More companies are run by their founders, who are around 40 years old.	Brazil	Managers with appropriate and up-to-date academic backgrounds, with the autonomy to be the "owners of the business," who are young and eager to make their businesses thrive, are of great value to the success of KM.
Have a seal of designation of origin.	Spain	The seal of designation of origin represented a major competitive advantage for the Spanish companies surveyed, which adjusted their operations to obtain it; most of them focused on quality. These adjustments are in line with the context suggested for the implementation of KM, making these companies more prepared for such an implementation.
Companies with managers who were experienced in their sectors and had been with the companies for a long time.	Brazil and Spain	The knowledge and experience of managers are relevant conditions, as it is they who determine the paths and conditions for implementing KM.
Managers consider KM to be important but are unclear about the concepts involved.	Brazil and Spain	Recognizing the importance of KM is fundamental to its implementation, as is a correct understanding of its concepts, which needs to be worked on with managers as one of the first activities in implementing KM.

(*Continued*)

Table 2.1. (*Continued*)

Features	**Context**	**Implications and Guidelines Related to Knowledge Management (KM) Focused on the Characteristics of Organizational Memory (OM)**
There were employees who had been with the company for a long time and who had considerable knowledge and experience.	Brazil and Spain	KM is the best way to ensure that the knowledge of these employees is used for the organization and that it is not lost, which can happen through OM.
Lack of activities focused on knowledge needs.	Brazil and Spain	Without a clear idea of what is needed, companies run the risk of generating a large volume of knowledge that can be lost and misused. Implementing KM, with an emphasis on the process of identifying knowledge needs and creating OM, is the appropriate way to reverse this situation.
A major lack of formal job definitions or career plans.	Spain	The formal definition of functions and career plans is fundamental to identifying the knowledge that the company needs to carry out its activities and build sustainable competitive advantages.
More recurrent use of performance indicators, internal and external benchmarking, process mapping, normalization, and standardization.	Spain	These are important practices that help to identify the knowledge needed and which should be used by companies seeking to implement and use KM.
Recommendation for implementing KM through a pilot project.	Brazil and Spain	As it involves complex and comprehensive management, it is recommended that KM be implemented through a pilot project, especially when management initiatives are still in their infancy.
Training is carried out without adequate planning or frequency.	Brazil and Spain	Training and capacity-building are significant for gaining knowledge, but they need to be carried out in accordance with the knowledge needs of the organization, and this needs to be done in a planned way.
Existence of motivational and reward policies.	Brazil	Motivational and reward policies are highly favorable to KM if they are directly related to this goal.

Teamwork and an atmosphere of trust.	Brazil and Spain	Teamwork and an atmosphere of trust are important enablers of knowledge sharing and therefore need to be exploited in favor of KM.
Availability of information and communication technologies (ICT).	Brazil and Spain	ICT is an enabler of knowledge sharing and should be used for this purpose.
Using relationships with customers, suppliers, competitors, and partners as a source of knowledge.	Spain	The external environment is a relevant source of knowledge that companies should exploit.
Lack of systematic and orderly storage of knowledge.	Brazil and Spain	The storage of knowledge is one of the stages in the implementation of KM, which aims to minimize the loss of organizational knowledge as well as ensure that knowledge is available whenever it is needed since its existence is fundamental. The use of OM is suggested.
Lack of formal actions for the dissemination of knowledge.	Brazil and Spain	Knowledge dissemination is one of the stages in the implementation of knowledge as a way of ensuring that knowledge is used and adds value to organizations. Therefore, the implementation of formal actions aimed at disseminating knowledge is mandatory for organizations wishing to implement KM.
Lack of formal procedures for using skills and knowledge assets.	Brazil and Spain	KM activities are aimed at using knowledge to create a competitive advantage for those who use it. To ensure that knowledge is being used appropriately, formal actions must be implemented for this purpose.
Lack of a clear and correct concept of evaluation and discarding unnecessary knowledge.	Brazil and Spain	For actions to be put into practice properly, they must first be understood.
Lack of activities aimed at discarding unnecessary knowledge.	Brazil and Spain	Unnecessary knowledge should not be retained and needs to be discarded.
Lack of activities to evaluate or measure knowledge resources.	Brazil and Spain	Although not mathematically exact, measuring the results of KM activities is fundamental to expanding KM and allocating the necessary resources.

In view of these limitations, it is suggested that future research encompass other sectors and other countries in order to explore new scenarios whose characteristics may contribute to improving the considered KM model and increasing the success of KM implementation within organizations.

References

Alvarenga Neto, R. C. D. de. *Gestão do Conhecimento em Organizações*. Saraiva: São Paulo, SP, 2008.

Antunes, H. de J. G. and P. G. Pinheiro. 'Linking Knowledge Management, Organizational Learning and Memory.' *Journal of Innovation & Knowledge*, 5, no. 2 (2020): 140–149.

Asociación Nacional de Industrias de la Carne de España (ANICE). 2024, http://www.anice.es (accessed 10 January 2024).

Bardin, L. *Análise de conteúdo*. Edições 70: Lisboa, 2011.

Boghossian, R. G., E. F. Barbosa, and L. A. Gomes. 'A Memória Organizacional e os Sistemas de Informação Suportando a Tomada de Decisão.' *Prisma.com*, no. 38 (2019): 102–125.

CENSO 2022. 'Quinze Estados Têm PIB Acima da Média Nacional em 2018; Sergipe é o Único com Queda.' 2024, https://censo2022.ibge.gov.br/2012-agencia-de-noticias/noticias/29447-quinze-estados-tem-pib-acima-da-media-nacional-em-2018-sergipe-e-o-unico-com-queda.html?start=80 (accessed 20 January 2024).

Cerdá, J. D. 'Gestión Documental y Gobierno Abierto: El Archivo en la República de los Dados.' *Tábula: Estudios Archivísticos de Castilla y León*, no. 16 (2013): 123–137.

Confederação Nacional do Comércio de Bens, Serviços e Turismo. 2024, https://www.portaldocomercio.org.br (accessed 20 January 2024).

Dalkir, K. *Knowledge Management in Theory and Practice*. Elsevier: Burlington, MA, 2011.

Damian, I. P. M. 'Inter-relações Entre Gestão do Conhecimento e Memória Organizacional.' *Palabra Clave*, 10, no. 1 (2020).

Damian, I. P. M. and M. M. Moro-Cabero. 'Modelos de Gestão do Conhecimento Voltado às Características da Memória Organizacional.' *Informação & Informação*, 26, no. 3 (2021): 157–180.

Damian, I. P. M. and M. M. Moro-Cabero. 'Proposição de um Modelo de Gestão do Conhecimento Voltado às Características da Memória Organizacional.' *Encontros Bibli: Revista Eletrônica de Biblioteconomia e Ciência da Informação*, 25 (2020): 1–21.

De Sordi, J. O. *Administração da Informação: Fundamentos e Práticas para uma Nova Gestão do Conhecimento*. Saraiva: São Paulo, SP, 2015.

Duarte, E. N., R. A. da S. Lharena, and S. de L. Lira. 'Gestão do Conhecimento: Origem, Evolução, Conceitos e Ações.' In *Da Informação a Auditoria de Conhecimento: A Base para a Inteligência Organizacional*, edited by E. N. Duarte, R. A. da S. Lharena, and S. de L. Lira. Editora da UFPB: João Pessoa, 2014.

Feitoza, R. A. B. and E. N. Duarte. 'Interface Entre a Memória Organizacional e a Gestão do Conhecimento: Observações no Arquivo do Sebrae – PB.' *Revista Brasileira de Educação em Ciência da Informação*, 8 (2021): 1–13.

Folha de São Paulo. 2024, https://saopaulo.folha.uol.com.br/o-melhor-de-saopaulo/2020/servicos/04/setor-de-servicos-cresceu-222-no-estado-de-sp-em-janeiro.shtml (accessed 23 January 2024).

Freire, P. de S., M. M. Moro, and F. R. M. Rocha. 'Memória Organizacional e seu Papel na Gestão do Conhecimento.' *Revista de Ciências da Administração*, 14, no. 33 (2012): 41–51.

Hoffmann, W. A. M. 'Gestão do Conhecimento e da Informação em Organizações Baseados em Inteligência Competitiva.' *Ciência da Informação*, 45, no. 3 (2016): 31–43.

Jarrahi, M. H., G. Askay, A. Eshraghi, and P. Smith. 'Artificial Intelligence and Knowledge Management: A Partnership Between Human and AI.' *Business Horizons*, 66, no. 1 (2023): 87–99.

Junta de Castilla Y León (JCyL). *Estudio del Sector Cárnico en Castilla y León*. 2024, http://www.castillayleon.ccoo.es/7f9e3b8194b39f8a841a3628fee032f8000054.pdf (accessed 20 January 2024).

Leonardi, J., M. M. Moro, and M. L. P. Valentim. 'Estrutura Organizacional Sob a Ótica de um Sistema de Representações Simbólico.' *Perspectivas em Gestão & Conhecimento*, 1, no. 1 (2011): 40–58.

Lousada, M., M. L. P. Valentim, and N. M. S. Goudard. 'Políticas de Indexação no Âmbito da Gestão do Conhecimento Organizacional.' *Informação & Sociedade: Estudos*, 21, no. 1 (2011): 191–202.

Manuti, A. and D. Monachino. 'Managing Knowledge at the Time of Artificial Intelligence: An Explorative Study with Knowledge Workers.' *East European Journal of Psycholinguistics*, 7, no. 2 (2020): 179–190.

Melgar-Sasieta, H. A. M., M. L. P. Valentim, and M. M. Moro. 'A Memória Organizacional no Contexto da Engenharia do Conhecimento.' *DataGramaZero*, 12, no. 3 (2011): 1–21.

Ministério do Trabalho e Previdência. *Painel de Informações do Novo CAGED*. 2024, https://www.gov.br/trabalho-e-previdencia/pt-br (accessed 24 January 2024).

Mohamad, A. A., M. N. M. Noh, and M. H. M. Ali. 'Knowledge Management in MSC Malaysia: The Role of Information Technology Capability.' *International Journal of Business and Society*, 18, no. S4 (2017): 651–660.

Nascimento, N. M. and M. C. C. P. Vitoriano. 'O Estudo da Produção Documental e a Memória Organizacional em Ambientes Empresariais.' *Em Questão*, 23, no. 1 (2017): 202–227.

Oliveira-Del-Massa, H. C., M. L. P. Valentim, and M. M. Moro. 'Competência em Informação no Apoio à Gestão do Conhecimento.' *Informação & Sociedade: Estudos*, 28, no. 1 (2018): 257–267.

Pereira, M. O. F., M. M. Moro, and M. L. P. Valentim. 'A Memória Organizacional nos Processos de Gestão do Conhecimento: Um Estudo na Universidade Federal do Paraná.' *Informação & Informação*, 21, no. 1 (2016): 348–374.

Pérez-Montoro Gutiérrez, M. *Gestión del Conocimiento en las Organizaciones: Fundamentos, Metodología y Praxis*. Trea: Gijón, 2008.

Pizzaia, A., M. L. P. Valentim, and M. M. Moro. 'O Papel da Comunicação na Gestão do Conhecimento: Aspectos Relevantes e Estímulo a Novas Pesquisas.' *Perspectivas em Gestão & Conhecimento*, 8, no. 2 (2018): 62–81.

Santos, B. R. P. and I. P. M. Damian. 'O Mapeamento do Conhecimento por Meio da Análise SWOT: Estudo em uma Organização Pública de Saúde.' *Em Questão*, 24, no. 3 (2018): 253–274.

Santos, C. D. and M. L. P. Valentim. 'Modelos de Gestão do Conhecimento e as Inter-relações com a Cultura Organizacional.' *Revista Brasileira de Educação em Ciência da Informação*, 8 (2021): 01–11.

Santos, J. C. dos, M. M. Moro, and M. L. P. Valentim. 'A Memória Organizacional Como Diferencial Competitivo em Ambientes Organizacionais.' In *Anais do XI Seminário de Pesquisa em Ciências Humanas*. Londrina, 2016.

Santos, V. C. B. D., M. L. P. Valentim, and M. M. Moro. 'A Cultura Organizacional Como Fator Crítico de Sucesso à Implantação da Gestão do Conhecimento em Organizações.' *Informação & Sociedade: Estudos*, 29, no. 1 (2019): 51–66.

Shahabadi, A., M. Nemati, and M. S. S. Hosseini. 'The Evaluation of Impacts of Knowledge-Based Economy Factors on the Improvement of Total Factor Productivity (A Comparative Study of Emerging and G7 Economies).' *Journal of the Knowledge Economy*, 9, no. 3 (2018): 896–907.

Silva, E. A. 'Transformação Digital e a Gestão do Conhecimento: Relações na Produção Cientifica.' In *Informação, Dados e Tecnologia*, edited by T. M. R. Dias. Advanced Notes in Information Science, Vol. 2. ColNes Publishing: Tallinn, Estonia, 2022, 43–52.

Silva, H. M. da and M. L. P. Valentim. 'Modelos de Gestão do Conhecimento Aplicados à Ambientes Empresariais.' In *Gestão da Informação e do Conhecimento no Âmbito da Ciência da Informação*, edited by M. L. P. Valentim. Polis: Cultura Acadêmica, São Paulo, 2008.

Silva, L. C., M. L. P. Valentim, and M. M. Moro. 'Melhores Práticas para Aplicação de Projetos de Gestão do Conhecimento: Instituindo Ambientes Colaborativos.' *Biblos: Revista do Instituto de Ciências Humanas e da Informação*, 30, no. 1 (2016).

Stefano, N. M. and S. Sartori. 'A Gestão do Conhecimento e o Capital Intelectual: Enfoque Teórico para Discussão.' *Revista Ingeniería Industrial*, 15, no. 2 (2016): 179–192.

Takeuchi, H. and I. Nonaka. *Gestão do Conhecimento*. Bookman: Porto Alegre, 2008.

Villasana Arreguín, L. M., E. L. Martínez, and R. V. Martínez. 'La Gestión del Conocimiento, Pasado, Presente y Futuro. Una Revisión de la Literatura.' *Trascender, Contabilidad y Gestión*, 6, no. 18 (2021): 53–78.

Wilson, T. D. 'A Problemática da Gestão do Conhecimento.' In *Inteligência, Informação e Conhecimento*, edited by K. Tarapanoff. IBICT; UNESCO: Brasília, 2006.

© 2026 World Scientific Publishing Europe Ltd.
https://doi.org/10.1142/9781800617414_0003

Chapter 3

Application of Generative Artificial Intelligence in the Mapping and Analysis of Critical Knowledge: A Case Study in the Oil and Gas Sector

Denilson Sell[*,§], Luciana Poli Silva[†], Arturo Cavalcanti Catunda[‡], and Tayane Cristina Mattera Souza[‡]

[*]*Federal University of Santa Catarina, Brazil*

[†]*Federal University of Rio de Janeiro, Brazil*

[‡]*Federal University of Bahia, Brazil*

[§]*denilsonsell@gmail.com*

Abstract

Organizations face increasing challenges in managing their most valuable asset: knowledge. The complexity of identifying and analyzing critical knowledge, ensuring assertiveness in investments, and maximizing value creation motivates this study. In response, a method was created to guide the mapping and analysis of an organization's critical knowledge, aiming to better direct knowledge management programs and ensure an effective contribution to strategy and institutional deliverables. The method was developed based on design science research, through a literature review of knowledge audit approaches, an analysis of proven practices, and experimentation with generative artificial intelligence (GenAI) in various tasks related to planning, mapping, and knowledge analysis, as well as the development of knowledge management strategies. This chapter aims to demonstrate, through a case study conducted at Universidade Petrobras – the corporate university of Petrobras, one of the world's largest energy companies and an international reference in deepwater oil exploration – how GenAI can integrally support the different stages of a knowledge audit based on the established method. The initial results show significant efficiency gains in identifying organizational needs, greater accuracy in categorizing knowledge assets, and agility in generating strategic recommendations, confirming the potential of GenAI to expand the reach and effectiveness of knowledge audits in large organizations.

Keywords: Critical knowledge, knowledge audit, generative artificial intelligence, knowledge mapping, knowledge engineering.

3.1 Introduction

In the current scenario of constant changes in society and business, organizations must always be able to understand the environment and adapt to new realities; otherwise, they face the risk of perishing before better-positioned and higher-performing competitors (private sector) or the obsolescence of their relevance to society (public institutions). Knowledge management (KM) is a central element for organizational sustainability in dynamic environments, where knowledge is recognized as a critical intangible asset for strategic adaptation (Fraga, 2019; Sveiby, 2003; Nieves *et al.*, 2014). Its relevance lies in the ability to transform tacit and explicit knowledge into inputs for innovation, decision-making, and the generation of competitive value (Dalkir, 2017).

However, literature highlights persistent challenges: studies indicate that 40–60% of KM initiatives fail due to misalignments between organizational strategies and knowledge management practices (Pour, 2019; Curado, 2017), as well as deficiencies in the articulation of local objectives, employee engagement, and change management (Martinsons *et al.*, 2017; Vold and Haave, 2019). Such findings reflect the inherent complexity of KM and the importance of an assertive approach that directs investments and supports organizations in overcoming challenges.

Within the field of KM, knowledge mapping and analysis are fundamental activities in the knowledge audit process, a qualitative assessment technique that deeply examines the health of an organization in terms of knowledge. The knowledge audit aims to identify, evaluate, and direct the effective management of critical knowledge, ensuring that these intellectual assets are used to achieve strategic objectives and generate organizational value (Dalkir, 2017; Marques, 2017, 2022). This process enables organizations to identify knowledge gaps, assess information flows, optimize processes, mitigate risks associated with strategy, foster innovation, and set priorities for the KM agenda (Suo *et al.*, 2009; Gourova *et al.*, 2009; Burnett *et al.*, 2013; Dalkir, 2017; Sell *et al.*, 2020).

To guide the audit process at Petrobras, a method was established that adopts best practices described in the literature, combining various tools, including generative artificial intelligence (GenAI) as a foundational instrument in all stages. This method, called the "Method for Mapping and Analyzing Critical Knowledge" (Sell *et al.*, 2024), comprises four main stages: pre-mapping, planning, mapping, and post-mapping. During the pre-mapping phase, opportunities and knowledge gaps are identified to define the mapping scope. Planning involves the development of detailed plans and awareness programs. The mapping itself covers the identification, organization, and analysis of critical knowledge. Finally, post-mapping includes the definition and prioritization of strategic actions in KM.

Throughout these stages, various knowledge-intensive tasks are performed, such as handling large volumes of heterogeneous content, producing strategic analyses, organizing and representing knowledge, and prospecting scenarios and trends. In this context, knowledge engineering (KE) plays a crucial role, providing methods and techniques to support the analysis of organizational strategy, the elicitation and modeling of knowledge, and the development of knowledge systems (Schreiber *et al.*, 2000; Sell *et al.*, 2020; Dos Anjos and Sell, 2024).

The method proposed by Sell *et al.* (2024) is contextualized with the recent evolution of KM, with the integration of large language models (LLMs) within GenAI. This integration offers new possibilities to meet the demands of content processing and knowledge-intensive activities (Allen *et al.*, 2023; Corchado *et al.*, 2023; Dos Anjos and Sell, 2024; Pan *et al.*, 2023). It promotes greater efficiency and effectiveness in mapping and analyzing critical knowledge (Sell *et al.*, 2024), especially in complex environments with large data volumes, such as those faced during the process of KM at Universidade Petrobras (UP).

UP plays a crucial role as a strategic catalyst for Petrobras, one of the largest energy companies in the world, through systematic knowledge management. Collaborating closely with business areas, UP is responsible for identifying and developing critical knowledge aligned with the company's strategic planning. Its challenges include establishing processes to detect emerging demands and innovation opportunities, as well as implementing analytical tools to inventory, map, and prioritize knowledge. These actions aim to ensure continuous alignment between intellectual assets and corporate objectives, reinforcing Petrobras's ability to navigate complex business environments and transform knowledge into a sustainable competitive advantage.

Based on this context, the research question was established: "How can the potential of GenAI be leveraged in the process of mapping and analyzing critical knowledge?" This article aims to describe how the Method for Mapping and Analyzing Critical Knowledge, integrated with GenAI, has been applied by UP within Petrobras. To this end, in addition to this introduction, the article covers the subject of AI and its impact on KM, as well as presents ChatPetrobras, Petrobras's corporate GenAI; the details of the Method for Mapping and Analyzing Critical Knowledge; the case study of the method's application in the context of UP; and final considerations.

3.2 Artificial Intelligence, Knowledge Management, and ChatPetrobras

Currently, we are witnessing the popularization of AI, most likely triggered by the emergence of GenAI, notably present in the system that popularized this technique: ChatGPT. GenAI is characterized by producing original responses from provided data patterns, creating new content similar to what would be produced by humans. Behind the code of this revolution lie large language models (LLMs).

LLMs are fundamental elements of GenAI and represent a remarkable advance in AI. Because they can recognize user input, they demonstrate high performance in various natural language processing tasks (Corchado *et al.*, 2023). These models, trained on vast corporate content, operate as probabilistic natural language models, predicting likely token sequences based on learned probability distributions to form the most accurate and relevant response to the user's input, commonly called a "prompt" (Allen *et al.*, 2023).

Apparently, 2024 marked the consolidation of GenAI in the organizational work environment. At least, this is what the 2024 Annual Work Trend Index Report points out. The report highlights the rapid and extensive adoption of GenAI by knowledge professionals: 75% are using it, and almost half (46%) began using it within the past six months. The report provides quantitative data on the perceived benefits of AI by users, such as time savings (90%), greater focus on important work (85%), increased creativity (84%), and greater job satisfaction (83%). This large-scale, short-term dissemination demonstrates a significant change in how work is performed and knowledge is accessed and used. This scenario implies an urgent need for KM strategies that consider this new reality (MICROSOFT; LINKEDIN, 2024).

Unsurprisingly, in the 2024 annual survey conducted by KMWORLD on the 100 companies that matter most to KM, these companies were attentive to the potential of AI. In this report, GenAI increasingly appears as a technology that significantly contributes to KM. Machine learning, semantic search, natural language processing, knowledge graphs, chatbots, and many other features drive advances in KM in numerous ways: They enhance the extraction, organization, and dissemination of knowledge; discover probable user questions; create and curate knowledge content; deliver relevant answers in less time; personalize digital experiences; provide contextual insights; automate critical business processes; and help knowledge workers overcome information overload, among others (Ojala, 2025).

Aware of this technological and cultural transformation, Petrobras, for information security reasons, makes its own GenAI, ChatPetrobras, available to its employees. ChatPetrobras is a virtual assistant based on LLMs, developed internally by Petrobras on the company's private cloud infrastructure, allowing only its employees to use the functionalities similar to those offered in OpenAI's ChatGPT. Its main function is to assist the company's employees in their activities, answering questions and helping with various tasks. As with the utilities available in ChatGPT, ChatPetrobras enables users to obtain answers to general questions, help with analyses, provide support for code programming, offer information about the company, and help with writing and reviewing texts (PETROBRAS, 2023).

In a recent literature review, Marra and Júnior (2025) agree that GenAI has been exerting a transformative influence on KM, significantly impacting the processes of socialization, externalization, combination, and internalization (SECI). GenAI enhances the generation and flow of knowledge within organizations through task automation and the handling of large volumes of data. According to the authors, tools such as ChatGPT have the potential to considerably improve four processes – creation, capture, organization, and dissemination of information – and offer innovative insights based on extensive datasets. This technology can also assist in the transfer of tacit knowledge, overcome communication barriers, and evolve KM from a process facilitator into a "wisdom" provider capable of offering strategic insights, predicting outcomes, and identifying patterns, contributing to innovation and efficiency. Successful integration of GenAI with KM requires essential collaboration between humans and technology, as well as an organizational culture that promotes learning and innovation. For the authors (op. cit.), it is essential to balance the use of GenAI with human interactions to avoid reducing cognitive engagement and team cohesion.

This article focuses on Petrobras' experience in applying GenAI in knowledge audits. A knowledge audit is a critical stage of any KM initiative. Initially conceived as a simple mapping of knowledge (Liebowitz *et al.*, 2000; Hylton, 2002), its mission has come to encompass a thorough analysis of the relationship between knowledge, strategic objectives, and institutional deliverables (Marques, 2017, 2022; Gretsch *et al.*, 2012). This process, which includes pre-mapping, planning, inventory, and post-mapping phases (Perez-Soltero *et al.*, 2006; Cheung *et al.*, 2007; Shek, 2007; Mohd Drus *et al.*, 2017; Sell *et al.*, 2024), generates tangible results such as exposing critical gaps, opportunities for cost and risk reduction, and guidelines to improve the coordination and protection of knowledge (Dalkir, 2017).

Knowledge audits involve knowledge-intensive activities, such as context analysis, elicitation, organization, and evaluation of critical assets, that benefit from consolidated methods of KE, such as CommonKADS, with its process, agent, and strategic flow modeling artifacts (Schreiber *et al.*, 2000; Sell *et al.*, 2020; Sell *et al.*, 2024). The rise of GenAI creates unprecedented opportunities to scale and deepen these stages, as such models can automate the screening and categorization of large textual corpora, support the elicitation and refinement of knowledge bases, and generate personalized analytical reports (Dos Anjos and Sell, 2024; Corchado *et al.*, 2023; Allen *et al.*, 2023).

Indeed, several studies highlight the potential of GenAI to fill gaps in KM processes but also warn of ethical and governance challenges (Pan *et al.*, 2023; Alavi, 2024; Taherdoost and Madanchian, 2023; Kitsios and Kamariotou, 2025). To turn this potential into reliable results, it becomes essential to articulate GenAI within a structured audit method that integrates KE practices (modeling, validation, and maintenance of knowledge) with prompt engineering and quality and traceability controls (Allen *et al.*, 2023; Schreiber *et al.*, 2000). Thus, the convergence between KE and GenAI promises substantial gains in scale, accuracy, and strategic value in knowledge audits, provided it is governed by a methodologically sound approach aligned with organizational needs (Sell *et al.*, 2024), an approach explored in the next section.

3.3 Method for Mapping and Analyzing Critical Knowledge

The Method for Mapping and Analyzing Critical Knowledge was conceived following the methodological principles of Design Science Research (DSR), as proposed by Peffers *et al.* (2006). This approach, characterized by its cyclical and pragmatic nature, aims to develop artifacts that solve real problems through systematic construction and validation processes (Sell *et al.*, 2024).

The proposed Method for Mapping and Analyzing Critical Knowledge at UP is based on models established by Marques (2022) and Sell *et al.* (2024), comprising four sequential stages (Figure 3.1): pre-mapping, planning, mapping, and post-mapping. Each of these stages is presented in this section.

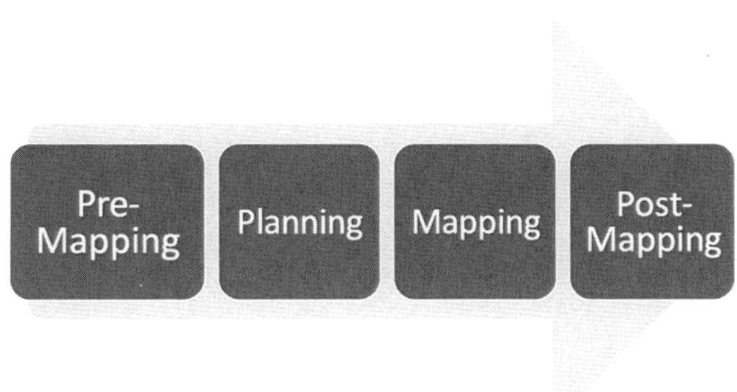

Figure 3.1. Stages of the method for mapping and analyzing critical knowledge.

3.3.1 *Pre-mapping*

The pre-mapping stage is the initial stage of the method and aims to establish the scope for subsequent phases. It is a critical stage, as it underpins the identification and prioritization of institutional development opportunities and knowledge gaps, which will be the subject of detailed analysis in the subsequent mapping. Activities carried out during pre-mapping include: (i) the identification of strategic and local drivers; (ii) the analysis of emerging needs; (iii) the analysis of future opportunities; (iv) the analysis of points of attention for knowledge management; and (v) prioritization for scope definition.

The scope delimitation should consider the dynamic nature of organizational knowledge needs, taking into account multiple variables, such as: (i) changes in strategic planning; (ii) operational performance indicators; (iii) emerging demands from various hierarchical levels and functional areas; (iv) requirements from the interorganizational network and external stakeholders; and (v) prospective trends that may impact current knowledge paradigms (Cheung *et al.*, 2007; Loxton, 2014).

To carry out these activities, the literature suggests using instruments to guide interviews, conduct collaborative groups, and organize brainstorming. These instruments systematically guide the identification of strategic and local drivers, critical success factors associated with the objectives of the strategic plan or at the local level, and areas for performance improvement, in collaboration with managers (Sell *et al.*, 2024). Along with each instrument, the model provides guidance on how GenAI can be applied to guide the execution of activities and configure the scope of the knowledge audit.

Activities related to KM diagnosis can be used as guidance for a knowledge audit. In this sense, as input in pre-mapping, the results of the KM maturity and corporate education system analysis are used. These analyses should be carried out periodically to identify internal conditions, formal and institutionalized practices, and the results of the current KM strategy. Such analyses seek to reveal points of attention that should be addressed in the KM and learning strategy together with critical knowledge, thus guiding the preparation of a knowledge development and retention plan, carried out in the final stage of the model.

3.3.2 *Planning*

The planning stage aims to develop a detailed mapping plan based on the scope and priorities established in the pre-mapping stage, as well as feedback and insights collected from internal and external stakeholders from the previous stage. This stage also seeks to mobilize and allocate the necessary resources and establish an awareness program to ensure the effectiveness and alignment of the audit process with the organization's strategic objectives. In this stage, GenAI tools authorized for corporate use can be used to support the prospecting of elements to compose the planning and awareness program (Sell *et al.*, 2024).

3.3.3 *Mapping*

The knowledge mapping stage aims to inventory, represent, analyze, and classify knowledge (Liebowitz, 2000; Hylton, 2002; Shek, 2007; Burnett *et al.*, 2013; Marques, 2017, 2022; Sell, 2020) according to the scope defined in the pre-mapping phase. This process is essential to ensure that all relevant knowledge – tacit, implicit, and explicit – is properly inventoried and cataloged. Thus, it is possible to obtain a comprehensive and structured view of the knowledge necessary to execute the organizational strategy and institutional deliverables, as well as to guide the survey of the organization's existing knowledge repertoire.

Also, in this stage, GenAI can play a fundamental role, for example, when used to:

- explore critical success factors and identify knowledge aligned with prioritized objectives and strategies;
- support classical knowledge engineering methodological approaches, such as laddering (Schreiber *et al.*, 2000), concept classification, and repertory grids (Schreiber *et al.*, 2000; Shadbolt and Smart, 2005);
- support the classification of knowledge into subcategories or further refine definitions and propose taxonomies, such as Bloom's taxonomy or domain classifications;
- coherently structure knowledge, using natural language, to facilitate understanding and incorporation into organizational routines.

The categorized knowledge can be represented through different models, such as knowledge maps, taxonomies, thesauri, and ontologies. The choice of the ideal model requires careful analysis of the questions it should answer. For simpler demands, it is possible to use basic structures, such as controlled vocabularies, glossaries, mind maps, or conceptual maps. In situations requiring computational support, such as content organization or knowledge systems, it is recommended to opt for more advanced models, such as taxonomies, thesauri, or ontologies (Sell *et al.*, 2024).

The mapping of knowledge should be followed by prioritizing those to be addressed by the organization's knowledge development and retention plan, which will be developed in the next stage due to their criticality. Knowledge can be considered critical due to the importance and vulnerability of knowledge identified within intra- and interorganizational networks, processes, strategic areas, or roles, and their relationship with organizational strategic objectives. The adapted proposal by Fraga (2019) is suggested, drawing on studies by, among others, Ricciardi (2009) and Formanski (2018). Table 3.1 identifies possible criteria for analyzing the criticality of mapped and categorized knowledge.

Table 3.1. Knowledge criticality factors.

Relevance	Innovative content	Characteristic of knowledge from the standpoint of state of the art, enabling the innovation of the organization's products and services.
	Technical content	Characteristic of knowledge from the standpoint of the quality, extent, and complexity of its technical content.
	Alignment with strategy	Positioning of knowledge from the strategic perspective of the organization or its contribution to the accomplishment of its tasks.
Vulnerability	Difficulties in acquisition and training	Criterion related to the issue of training and acquisition of skilled human resources in knowledge.
	Difficulties in capturing and transferring in context	Difficulty in capturing and transmitting knowledge as a function of its context: the way it is structured and the internal environment of the organization.
	Scarcity or rarity	Criterion that qualifies the risk of knowledge loss, that is, assessing the availability of that knowledge, both within the organization and in the market.

Source: Adapted from Fraga (2018).

3.3.4 *Post-mapping*

The post-mapping stage is an opportune moment for a strategic review of the company's KM. Critical knowledge, KM maturity diagnosis, and insights obtained throughout the mapping stage will serve as input to realign the knowledge development and retention plan.

At this stage, based on recommendations for strategic KM routes, actions are planned that should comprise the knowledge development and retention plan. Therefore, the results of this review are the updated plan itself, along with strategic recommendations and detailed actions, the Resource Allocation Matrix, and the KPIs linked to KM.

Table 3.2 summarizes all four stages of the Model for Mapping and Analyzing Critical Knowledge. This model can be explored in greater depth by referring to Sell *et al.* (2024).

Table 3.2. Stages of the model for mapping and analyzing critical knowledge.

Stage	Main Activities	Products / Results
1 – Pre-mapping	• Identify the strategic and local drivers. • Analyze the emerging needs. • Analyze future opportunities. • Analyze the points of attention for the knowledge management (KM). • Prioritize and define the scope.	• Diagnosis of the maturity of KM and the Corporate University Network (CUN). • Scope of mapping critical knowledge.
2 – Planning	• Develop and establish a mapping plan. • Establish an awareness program. • Mobilize and allocate resources.	• Mapping plan. • Mobilized team. • Awareness program implemented.
3 – Mapping	• Inventory knowledge. • Organize the knowledge. • Analyze the knowledge and knowledge processes. • Validate critical knowledge.	• Knowledge inventoried, represented, analyzed, and classified. • Critical knowledge.
4 – Post-mapping	• Recommend strategic actions. • Plan actions.	• Updated knowledge development and retention plan with strategic recommendations and detailed action plans. • Resource allocation matrix. • Defined KPIs.

Source: Sell *et al.* (2024).

3.4 Case Study: Universidade Petrobras

Petrobras is a mixed-capital company and one of the largest oil and gas producers in the world, headquartered in Brazil. It operates in exploration and production, refining, energy generation, and commercialization. As of December 31, 2023, its workforce comprised approximately 46,700 people, including subsidiaries in Brazil and abroad (Petrobras, 2024).

The company is recognized for its technical capacity and innovation in deep- and ultradeep-water oil exploration, and to support the training of its technical staff, it has UP, which is responsible for the corporate education of Petrobras employees and collaborators. In addition to supporting training and development initiatives, UP is also responsible for guiding and implementing KM, in partnership with the organization's various business areas.

According to ISO 30401 (2018), which addresses knowledge management systems, it is essential for the organization to identify relevant external and internal issues impacting its ability to achieve desired results. In this sense, UP coordinates Petrobras's Knowledge System and involves decision-makers from business areas in actions that impact the retention, access, registration, sharing, and application of knowledge.

The Petrobras Knowledge System consists of a set of academies, knowledge technical committees (KTCs), and professionals dedicated to KM and establishing policies and guidelines for this area throughout the company. It is important to clarify that Petrobras (2025) defines knowledge as "the dimension of knowing that corresponds to a series of information assimilated and structured by the individual, which allows them to organize reality and apply it in activities that generate scientific, technical, economic, social or cultural value," and the area of knowledge as "the delimitation of a certain field of knowledge, a conceptual structure that brings together a set of associated knowledge about a certain specialty or process."

The academies are tactical administrative structures provided for in the organizational chart. They are responsible for proposing and operationalizing educational solutions for the areas of knowledge under their responsibility. To define the scope of each academy, UP defined a taxonomy containing the areas of knowledge and related knowledge, which organizes the training offerings in the human resources system. The academies coordinate the KTCs.

The KTCs comprise professionals from various business areas and play the role of directing and deciding on each area of knowledge under their influence. Thus, the KTCs identify training needs within areas of knowledge aligned with business interests and seek to ensure that development actions promoted at UP are connected to the company's needs. Currently, there are 13 academies and 51 KTCs linked to 87 areas of knowledge that cover all of the company's businesses.

UP also has a KM department within its organizational structure, dedicated to forming KM policies, specifically in modeling, implementing, and guiding knowledge management practices, such as mentoring, tutoring, on-the-job training, technical and managerial rotations, communities of practice, and others. This department also fosters the knowledge ambassadors forum, comprised of KM enthusiasts who help disseminate best practices among Petrobras's various business areas.

UP promotes cycles for updating areas of knowledge and their respective domains, which serve as a reference base for composing the portfolios of its educational actions. Its objective is to identify and analyze the critical knowledge emerging and necessary to enable the company's strategies and processes, aiming to plan actions for the development and management of its knowledge assets.

In this context, seeking a methodology to systematically, consistently, and standardly map the areas of knowledge and knowledge necessary for the company's businesses, UP sought consultancy from researchers in KE and management at the Federal University of Santa Catarina (UFSC), who presented the Method for Mapping and Analyzing Critical Knowledge, previously reported in this chapter.

The purpose of using this method was, in addition to promoting a systematic, consistent, and standardized mapping of knowledge, to support the Petrobras Knowledge System and its respective development solutions portfolio, without losing sight of the objective of offering Petrobras's technical staff the knowledge necessary to address business challenges.

The first application cycle of the method took place in 2025, and, given the work context of UP, it was necessary to adapt the activities of the methodological proposal, which consisted of the stages defined in Table 3.3.

The following sections will detail each stage, its activities, and the results achieved.

Table 3.3. Application of the stages of the method for mapping and analyzing critical knowledge at Petrobras.

Stages	Activities	Product/Output
1 – Pre-mapping Responsible: UP knowledge management department	• Identify strategic and local drivers. • Apply AI prompts to: o analyze emerging needs; o analyze future opportunities; o analyze key attention points for Knowledge Management (KM). • Suggest revisions of knowledge areas and specific knowledge items.	• Scope of suggested revisions for knowledge areas and specific knowledge for each academy.
2 – Planning Responsible: UP knowledge management department and academies	• Develop and establish a mapping plan. • Establish an awareness program. • Mobilize and allocate resources.	• Mapping plan. • Mobilized team. • Awareness program implemented.
3 – Mapping Responsible: Academies and KTCs	• Inventory knowledge. • Organize knowledge into knowledge areas. • Assess the criticality of the knowledge.	• Knowledge inventoried, represented, analyzed, and classified. • Critical knowledge identified.
4 – Post-mapping Responsible: Academies	• Recommend strategic actions. • Plan knowledge management and development actions.	• Revisions of the academies' development solutions portfolios.

Source: Adapted from Sell *et al.* (2024).

3.4.1 *Pre-mapping*

In the case presented, during pre-mapping, the UP KM Department identified strategic and local drivers, considering a set of documents relevant to the process, including: the Petrobras 2050 Strategic Plan, the Petrobras 2025–2029 Business Plan, and the Basic Organization Plan – which describes the responsibilities of all areas and respective management – as well as other documents related to human capital trends in the energy industry and beyond.

To carry out analyses of emerging needs, future opportunities, and points of attention for KM, the UP KM Department used the ChatPetrobras GenAI, as previously described. It was used with prompts suggested by the Method for Mapping and Analyzing Critical Knowledge and adapted to Petrobras's reality to assist in identifying knowledge, pointing out trends, compiling information, and providing input for identifying relevant knowledge.

Using ChatPetrobras, it was necessary to create a specific context with the documents for use in the analysis. Contexts are based on Retrieval-Augmented Generation (RAG), a technique that combines a GenAI model with an information retrieval system to generate more diverse and higher-quality responses. The generative model creates search instructions from the user's prompt, and the retrieval system searches for relevant texts in a knowledge database. These texts are used by the generative model as context to choose the best response. RAG allows language models to access external information that may not be present in their training data or the user's prompt (Petrobras, 2023).

Once the context was built, the analysis began with the following prompt:

> *[We are in the context of mapping critical knowledge for the company. Understand critical knowledge as that which guides the company's strategies and has the potential to impact the business. Based on the following document, explore and enumerate possible objectives <OB> and business drivers <DB> that can best guide knowledge mapping].*

The first result provided an overview of how GenAI interpreted the context documents and related objectives and business drivers. However, the result was considered too brief, requiring more detailed analysis and a response.

A new prompt was then applied to improve ChatPetrobras's response:

> *[Perform a thematic analysis of the documents and list the keywords].*

In response to the prompt, the tool presented themes and related terms. For greater assertiveness, the tool was asked to justify how it generated each theme, with the following prompt inserted:

> *[Justify with which information you created each knowledge topic listed in your first answer].*

The tool was also asked to indicate on which pages of the documents each term was located. This made it possible to identify what had not been considered by the tool:

[Please redo this list indicating the page where these knowledge topics appear in the documents].

Next, the tool was asked to perform a comparative analysis between the identified themes and terms and the taxonomy used by UP, with the following prompt inserted:

[Perform a comparative analysis between the Taxonomy Document, where the areas of knowledge and the knowledge linked to them are listed, with the listed themes and terms, identifying the knowledge not included in the first document].

Based on these results, the UP KM Department specialists analyzed the themes and terms, seeking to classify what constituted "areas of knowledge" and "knowledge," based on the expertise of an information science professional and reference instruments such as glossaries from the oil and gas industry. Following this classification, a revision of the taxonomy was proposed.

As a result of this stage, the scope of critical knowledge mapping was completed, with a suggestion to review the areas of knowledge and knowledge for each academy. Compared to the original taxonomy, the analyses carried out with the help of the GenAI ChatPetrobras and the perspective of the professionals involved led to the identification of four new areas of knowledge and 20 new knowledge topics, as well as complementary observations regarding the scope of what was contained in already existing areas of knowledge.

At this point in the cycle of updating the areas of knowledge, it was decided not to carry out the KM maturity diagnosis and the Corporate University in Network (CUN), which may be carried out at a future opportunity.

3.4.2 *Planning*

The mapping plan developed by the UP KM Department was designed to cover stages involving 13 academies. The stages were to analyze the scope of the suggestions, validate them with the 51 KTCs, and perform a criticality analysis of the knowledge. This plan was validated in a UP senior leadership meeting, and the communication and awareness strategy involved sending messages to academy leaders and holding periodic meetings with their teams.

As a result of this stage, a mapping plan was obtained, along with a breakdown of the plan among the 13 academies, the mobilization of academy teams and KTCs, and the implementation of communication and awareness to execute the plan and achieve the objective of updating knowledge areas.

3.4.3 *Mapping*

With input from the pre-mapping stage, the UP KM Department assisted the academies and KTCs in understanding the activities of this stage: inventory knowledge, organize knowledge, analyze knowledge and knowledge processes, and validate critical knowledge. For this last activity, the academies were asked to assess the criticality of knowledge.

At Petrobras, the criterion used was adapted from Fraga (2018), as described in Table 3.1 and explained to the members of the academies. After an initial criticality analysis and assessment, these members took the refined list of knowledge to the KTCs, who then performed their analyses, considering perspectives at a strategic level.

A model table was used for criticality assessments, where values were defined for each criterion of relevance and vulnerability of knowledge. Greater weight was given to vulnerability criteria, considered more concerning at Petrobras in the current scenario. The average results generated a heat map visualization, highlighting the criticality of each knowledge item, as shown in Table 3.4.

Given the scope of suggestions and the opportunity to review areas of knowledge, the academies took this moment to internally deepen their evaluation of pre-existing areas of knowledge. Therefore, some academies conducted a complete review of their taxonomies. As a result of this stage, 99 areas of knowledge were confirmed, 16 new areas were introduced, and 24 areas were identified as obsolete, some of which were replaced to broaden the scope of knowledge.

As a second product of the update cycle, the results of the criticality assessment became an important instrument for guiding resource allocation to enable development actions oriented toward the organization's strategic objectives and the maintenance of key process know-how.

Table 3.4. Model table for defining knowledge criticality.

				Relevance			Vulnerability			
Academy	**KTC**	**Knowledge Area**	**Knowledge**	**Innovative Content**	**Technical Content**	**Strategy Alignment**	**Acquisition and Training**	**Difficulties in Capturing and Transferring in Context**	**Scarcity or Rarity**	**Criticality Evaluation**
Project management, digital transformation, and innovation	Data governance		Data architecture	5	5	5	3	5	5	4,6
Project management, digital transformation, and innovation	IA & analytics	Analytics	Dimensional modeling	3	5	5	3	3	3	3,4
Project management, digital transformation, and innovation	Industrial IOT	Industrial IOT	Industrial automation	3	3	3	3	3	3	3

Source: Adapted from Sell *et al.* (2024).

3.4.4 *Post-mapping*

The post-mapping stage focused on the UP KM Department's recommendation to the academies to review their development solutions portfolios, based on the conclusion of the cycle of updating the areas of knowledge and their respective knowledge, aiming to implement strategic actions for the development of Petrobras employees.

Thus, even if not explicitly stated in specific and individualized documents, the products of this stage – such as the knowledge development and retention plan, the resource allocation matrix, and the defined KPIs – are implicit in the reviews of the academies' development solutions portfolios, elements of the business plan, and indicators of UP. The effort to review these portfolios, due to updates in areas of knowledge, serves as the contributory link of the Method for Mapping and Analyzing Critical Knowledge.

3.5 Final Considerations and Implications

The Method for Mapping and Analyzing Critical Knowledge, originally proposed by researchers at the UFSC, found fertile ground for its application and adaptation at UP. The implementation of the method at UP demonstrated its flexibility and ability to adapt to the specific needs of a large corporation while maintaining its fundamental structure across four stages: pre-mapping, planning, mapping, and post-mapping.

A significant contribution of this experience was the systematic integration of GenAI, specifically through ChatPetrobras, especially in the pre-mapping stage. The use of GenAI proved particularly effective in the initial analysis of strategic documents, identification of patterns, and the suggestion of emerging knowledge. However, it is essential to emphasize that the success of this integration depended directly on human expertise at various points: in the proper formulation of prompts, in the critical analysis of generated responses, in validation by information science specialists, and, above all, in contextualizing the results with organizational realities.

A critical aspect observed during the application of the method at UP was the direct influence of the quality of documents used to create the GenAI analysis context. The experience showed that well-structured documents, with clear and consistent language, allowed ChatPetrobras to generate more accurate and relevant analyses. On the other hand, documents with terminological inconsistencies, redundancies, or a lack of standardization required more effort in prompt refinement and more rigorous critical analysis of generated responses. This finding highlights the importance of efficient document management as a prerequisite for the effective use of GenAI in knowledge mapping processes. Moreover, it underscores the need for organizations to maintain an up-to-date and well-structured document base, not only for recording and compliance purposes but also as a source of quality data for AI-based analyses, which are increasingly present in the organizational context.

The experience at UP showed that GenAI, although a powerful tool, acts as a facilitator of the process, not its protagonist. The final identification of new areas of knowledge and emerging knowledge, as well as the assessment of their criticality, remained essentially human activities, requiring the active participation of the academies and KTCs.

As a practical implication, the case analysis demonstrates that modernizing KM processes through GenAI is possible and desirable, provided the balance between automation and human analysis is maintained. For future research, it is suggested to investigate specific metrics to assess the effectiveness of integrating GenAI and knowledge mapping processes, as well as to explore other possible applications of this technology in other stages of the method.

Regarding the Method for Mapping and Analyzing Critical Knowledge, the implementation experience at UP highlighted the need and feasibility of adapting it to the specific organizational context without compromising its fundamental structure. At Petrobras, significant adaptations were observed, mainly in the pre-mapping stage, where it was not possible to rely on the results of the KM maturity diagnosis and the UCR as inputs for the other stages. Another notable adaptation occurred in the post-mapping stage, where, instead of generating specific and individualized documents such as the knowledge development and retention plan, the resource allocation matrix, and defined KPIs, it was decided to incorporate these elements into reviews of the academies' development solutions portfolios. This decision proved to be aligned with the organizational culture and practices already established in the company, maintaining coherence with the central objectives of the method – identifying, analyzing, and directing the management of critical knowledge – while adapting to Petrobras's existing processes and structures.

It is important to note that the experience of applying the method at UP does not end with this first cycle since the mapping and analysis of critical knowledge constitute a cyclical process, aligned with the company's strategic planning. This iterative nature of the process, in line with the methodological principles of design science research, suggests that new adjustments to the method will be necessary and welcome, considering the dynamic evolution of the organizational context. Factors such as the maturation of the KM culture within the academies and KTCs, the implementation of new information technology tools, and especially the accelerated development of AI will require a flexible and adaptive approach to applying the method.

References

Alavi, M., D. E. Leidner, R. Mousavi. A 'Knowledge Management Perspective of Generative Artificial Intelligence.' *Journal of the Association for Information Systems*, 1, no. 25 (2024): 1–12.

Allen, B. P., L. Stork, and P. Groth. 'Knowledge Engineering Using Large Language Models.' *arXiv* preprint arXiv:2310.00637, 2023.

Burnett, S., D. Williams, and A. Grinnall. 'The Strategic Role of Knowledge Auditing and Mapping: An Organizational Case Study.' *Knowledge and Process Management*, 20, no. 3 (2013): 161–176.

Cheung, C. F., W. M. Wang, V. Lo, and K. L. Choy. 'A Systematic Approach for Knowledge Auditing: A Case Study in Transportation Sector.' *Journal of Knowledge Management*, 11, no. 4 (2007): 140–158.

Corchado, J. M., F. S. López, V. J. M. Núñez, S. R. Garcia, and P. Chamoso. 'Generative Artificial Intelligence: Fundamentals.' *Advances in Distributed Computing and Artificial Intelligence Journal*, 12, no. 1 (2023): e31704. https://doi.org/10.14201/adcaij.31704.

Curado, C. 'The Review of "Successes and Failures of Knowledge Management" edited by Jay Liebowitz, Elsevier, Cambridge, MA 2016, pp. 221.' *Journal of Economics and Management*, no. 27 (2017): 150–155.

Dalkir, K. *Knowledge Management in Theory and Practice*. 3rd ed. MIT Press: London, 2017.

dos Anjos, A. and D. Sell. 'Advancing Expertise Locator Systems through Large Language Models: Insights from an Integrative Literature Review.' In *IFKAD (International Forum on Knowledge Asset Dynamics)*, 12 June 2024.

Formanski, J. G. 'A Estrutura da Rede Social Organizacional e sua Influência no Fluxo de Conhecimento Inovador.' PhD thesis, Universidade Federal de Santa Catarina, Florianópolis, 2018.

Fraga, B. D. 'Framework de Análise dos Conhecimentos Críticos Relacionados às Capacidades de Resiliência Organizacional.' PhD thesis, Universidade Federal de Santa Catarina, Florianópolis, 2019.

Freire, P. S., J. A. Souza, G. A. Dandolini, and A. Valdati. *Diagnóstico de Maturidade de Gestão da Informação e Conhecimento*. UFSC, 2016.

Gourova, E., A. Antonova, and Y. Todorova. 'Knowledge Audit Concepts, Processes and Practice.' *WSEAS Transactions on Business and Economics*, 6, no. 12 (2009): 605–619.

Gretsch, S., H. Mandl, and R. Schätz. 'Implementation Process of a Knowledge Management Initiative: Yellow Pages.' *New Research on Knowledge Management Models and Methods*, 14, no. 1 (2012): 311–332.

Hylton, A. *Measuring and Assessing Knowledge-Value and the Pivotal Role of the Knowledge Audit*. Hylton Associates: London, 2002.

Kitsios, F., and M. Kamariotou. 'Artificial Intelligence and Business Strategy towards Digital Transformation: A Research Agenda.' *Sustainability*, 13, no. 4 (2025), https://doi.org/10.3390/su13042025.

Liebowitz, J., B. Rubenstein-Montano, D. McCaw, J. Buchwalter, C. Browning, B. Newman, and K. Rebeck. 'The Knowledge Audit.' *Knowledge and Process Management*, 7, no. 1 (2000): 3–10.

Loxton, M. H. 'A Simplified Integrated Critical Activity-Based Knowledge Audit Template.' *Knowledge Management Research & Practice*, 12, no. 2 (2014): 236–238.

Marra, F. W. and D. Santiago Júnior. 'A Influência da IA Generativa nos Processos de Gestão do Conhecimento.' *Revista Delos*, 2025, https://ojs.revistadelos.com/ojs/index.php/delos/article/view/4453 (accessed 9 April 2025).

Marques, D. 'Modelo de Auditoria do Conhecimento em Gerenciamento de Projetos.' Master's thesis, Universidade Federal de Santa Catarina, 2017.

Marques, D. 'Framework para Auditoria do Conhecimento em Projetos Inter-organizacionais.' PhD thesis, Universidade Federal de Santa Catarina, 2022.

Martinsons, M. G., R. M. Davison, and Q. Huang. 'Strategic Knowledge Management Failures in Small Professional Service Firms in China.' *International Journal of Information Management*, 37, no. 4 (2017): 327–338.

Microsoft and LinkedIn. *Relatório Anual Índice de Tendência de Trabalho de 2024 da Microsoft e LinkedIn*. Slides, 8 May 2024.

Mohd Drus, S., O. Mohamed S., and M. Othman. 'Knowledge Audit Framework: A Case Study of the Malaysian Electricity Supply Industry.' *Journal of Information and Communication Technology (JICT)*, 16, no. 1 (2017): 103–120.

Nieves, J., A. Quintana, and J. Osorio. 'Knowledge-Based Resources and Innovation in the Hotel Industry.' *International Journal of Hospitality Management*, 38 (2014): 65–73.

Ojala, M. 'KMWorld 100 Companies That Matter in Knowledge Management 2025.' *KMWorld*. https://www.kmworld.com/Articles/Editorial/Features/KMWorld-100-Companies-That-Matter-in-Knowledge-Management-2025-167500.aspx (accessed 10 March 2025).

Pan, J. Z., S. Razniewski, J. C. Kalo, S. Singhania, J. Chen, S. Dietze, ... and D. Graux. 'Large Language Models and Knowledge Graphs: Opportunities and Challenges.' *arXiv* preprint arXiv:2308.06374, 2023.

Peffers, K., T. Tuunanen, M. A. Rothenberger, and S. Chatterjee. 'A Design Science Research Methodology for Information Systems Research.' *Journal of Management Information Systems*, 24, no. 3 (2006): 45–77.

Perez-Soltero, A., M. Barcelo-Valenzuela, G. Sanchez-Schmitz, F. Martin-Rubio, and J. T. Palma-Mendez. 'Knowledge Audit Methodology with Emphasis on Core Processes.' In *European and Mediterranean Conference on Information Systems*. 2006, 1–10.

Petrobras. *ChatPetrobras – FAQ*. PDF, Rio de Janeiro, 2023, https://petrobrasbr-my.sharepoint.com/personal/crotman_petrobras_com_br/_layouts/15/onedrive.aspx?id=%2Fpersonal%2Fcrotman%5Fpetrobras%5Fcom%5Fbr%2FDocuments%2FChatPetrobras%20%2D%20FAQ%2Epdf&parent=%2Fpersonal%2Fcrotman%5Fpetrobras%5Fcom%5Fbr%2FDocuments&ga=1 (accessed 14 April 2025).

Petrobras. *Relatório Anual e Form 20-F 2023*. 2023, https://petrobras.com.br/ (accessed 14 March 2024).

Pour, M. J., H. Z. Matin, H. R. Yazdani, and Z. K. Zadeh. 'A Comprehensive Investigation of the Critical Factors Influencing Knowledge Management Strategic Alignment.' *Knowledge Management & E-Learning*, 11, no. 2 (2019): 215–232.

Ricciardi, R. I. 'Gestão Estratégica do Conhecimento: Uma Metodologia de Estruturação e Análise dos Recursos de Conhecimento.' PhD thesis, Universidade de São Paulo, São Paulo, 2009.

Schreiber, G., H. Akkermans, A. Anjewierden, R. de Hoog, N. R. Shadbolt, W. van de Velde, and B. Wielinga. *Knowledge Engineering and Management: The CommonKADS Methodology*. MIT Press: Cambridge, Massachusetts, 2000.

Sell, D., L. P. da Silva, and P. de Sá Freire. 'Modelo de Gestão do Conhecimento. Implantação do Modelo UCR na Universidade da Polícia Rodoviária Federal.' Relatório Técnico, 2020.

Sell, D., L. P. da Silva, and P. de Sá Freire. 'Método de Mapeamento e Análise do Conhecimento da Petrobras.' Relatório Técnico, 2024.

Sell, D., L. P. da Silva, and P. de Sá. Freire. 'Método de Mapeamento e Análise dos Conhecimentos Críticos com Suporte de Inteligência Artificial Generativa.' In *KM Brasil 2024 – 19 Congresso Brasileiro de Gestão do Conhecimento*. Brasília, 2024.

Shadbolt, N. and P. R. Smart. 'Knowledge Elicitation: Methods, Tools and Techniques.' In *Evaluation of Human Work*, edited by J. R. Wilson and S. Sharples. CRC Press: Boca Raton, Florida, 2005, 163–200.

Shek, W. Y., K. L. C., and M. N. N. 'Systematic Knowledge Auditing: A Case Study in a Power Utility Company.' *Journal of Information & Knowledge Management*, 6, no. 4 (2007): 231–239.

Suo, B. M., J. B. Wang, and H. B. Zhang. 'Notice of Retraction: Primarily Research on Knowledge Audit for Evaluating Enterprise Knowledge Management Capability.' In *2009 International Conference on Management and Service Science*. IEEE, 2009, 1–5.

Sveiby, K. E. *A Nova Riqueza das Organizações: Gerenciando e Avaliando Patrimônios de Conhecimento*. 7th ed. Campus: Rio de Janeiro, 2003.

Taherdoost, H. and M. Madanchian. 'Artificial Intelligence and Knowledge Management: Impacts, Benefits, and Implementation.' *Computers*, 12, no. 4 (2023): 72.

Vold, T. and H. M. Haave. 'The Emergence-and Collapse-of Results From Knowledge Management Initiatives: A Case Study From Norway.' In *European Conference on Knowledge Management*. 2019, 882–890.

© 2026 World Scientific Publishing Europe Ltd.
https://doi.org/10.1142/9781800617414_0004

Chapter 4

Knowledge Management Maturity in Relation to Alumni and AI-Based Functionalities: An Applied Study at UFSC

Fabiana Edier Dassoler* **and Patrícia de Sá Freire**

Federal University of Santa Catarina, Brazil

**fabiana.dassoler@gmail.com*

Abstract

This article presents a case study on the maturity of knowledge management (KM) at a Brazilian public university, focusing on institutional relationships with graduate alumni. The research was conducted at the Federal University of Santa Catarina (UFSC) and is based on the hypothesis that alumni are strategic sources of organizational intelligence whose value requires consolidated KM practices and mediating technologies, such as artificial intelligence (AI). Utilizing a qualitative and exploratory approach, the study combined an integrative literature review with a diagnosis applied to institutional managers, employing an adapted KM maturity assessment tool. The results indicate that the average KM maturity level in relation UFSC alumni is 1.27, classified as “reaction” according to the Asian Productivity Organization model, reflecting a low level of institutionalization of the topic, with deficiencies in the technology, processes, and people dimensions. Based on these findings, five AI-based functionalities were proposed, namely a semantic engine, intelligent segmentation, engagement prediction, analytical dashboards, and an explainable chatbot, grounded in principles of transhuman co-production and algorithmic ethics. This study significantly contributes by proposing an analytical and functional model that not only strengthens the university–alumni relationships but also guides responsible digital transformation in public higher education institutions through a critical and ethical valorization of institutional knowledge, mediated by AI.

Keywords: Knowledge management, artificial intelligence, alumni, maturity diagnosis, public higher education.

4.1 Introduction

Amid the advance of digital transformation, higher education institutions (HEIs) face the challenge of maintaining active ties with their graduates, recognizing them as strategic assets for educational innovation, institutional assessment, and knowledge governance. However, the relationship with graduates is still managed in a fragmented manner. It often lacks a systematic feedback structure, resulting in missed opportunities for co-producing value following academic training (Garzón Castrillon, 2018).

In this context, knowledge management (KM) emerges as an integrative approach to recognize, systematize, and enhance the experiences and career trajectories of graduates. The adoption of KM enables the university to view knowledge as a distributed and dynamic organizational resource that relies on institutional relationships. However, the effectiveness of this management depends on the maturity of its processes, technologies, and strategies – dimensions that remain largely underexplored in the context of Brazilian HEIs, particularly at the postgraduate level (Nuss, 2024).

At the same time, artificial intelligence (AI) technologies have expanded the scope of KM, offering possibilities for predictive analysis of engagement, identification of institutional feedback patterns, and the generation of large-scale insights. Even so, the use of AI in educational and institutional management processes necessitates ethical and epistemological considerations, particularly concerning algorithmic transparency, human autonomy in decision-making, and respect for the co-production of knowledge through transhuman collaboration (Freire and Marques, 2024).

Despite the growing literature on KM and AI in organizational settings, a scientific gap remains in articulating the relationship between assessing KM maturity and proposing AI-based solutions for institutional alumni engagement. Few studies propose models that combine internal diagnostics with viable technological functionalities, particularly in Brazilian public universities (Ranthun and dos Santos Junior, 2024).

In this context, the general objective of this study is to evaluate the level of maturity in KM at the Federal University of Santa Catarina (UFSC) regarding its institutional capacity to interact with former graduate students and propose functionalities based on AI, including models that compare internal diagnostics with viable technological functionalities, especially in Brazilian public universities.

4.2 Theoretical Framework

KM has become a strategic area in the public sector, particularly in the university context, by recognizing knowledge as an essential organizational asset for innovation, institutional effectiveness, and continuous learning. Classic authors such as Wiig (1994), Nonaka and Takeuchi (1997), and Davenport and Prusak (1998) have established the fundamental theoretical foundations for understanding KM as a structured process of creation, conversion, sharing, and application of knowledge, aiming to improve organizational decisions.

However, the reality of Brazilian public universities reveals barriers to the institutionalization of KM, such as data fragmentation, the absence of integrated knowledge policies, and the low systematization of tacit KM practices. The complexity of academic structures and the epistemological plurality present in HEIs require approaches adapted to their public missions and the democratic values that govern these organizations (Calmeto and Cribb, 2022).

In this context, the concept of KM maturity becomes relevant, understood as the degree of development of organizational practices focused on KM across dimensions such as processes, people, technologies, leadership, and strategy. This maturity can also be viewed as critical institutional readiness, associated with the ability to consider, articulate, and mobilize distributed knowledge for innovation in complex contexts, as proposed by Freire *et al.* (2021).

Models such as the Asian Productivity Organization (APO, 2020) and the Knowledge Management Model for Brazilian Public Administration – MGCAPB (Batista, 2013) offer diagnostic tools that allow identifying the stage of evolution of KM in an organization. When applied in universities, these models require methodological adaptations that consider the particularities of scientific production, academic autonomy, and the diversity of knowledge.

Studies revisited in the literature review indicate that many HEIs operate at initial levels of maturity with informal, undocumented, and poor data-based practices. Regarding alumni connections, particularly in postgraduate studies, this maturity is often even more limited due to the lack of systematic initiatives that incorporate alumni into institutional KM strategies (Damián Simón, 2020).

Recognizing alumni as co-producers of knowledge and sources of organizational intelligence implies valuing their professional trajectories, collaboration networks, and applied experiences, which can enhance academic and institutional processes. Alumni should be regarded not only as active collaborators in the ongoing improvement of their courses and careers but also as individuals who require the support of the university to enhance their professional performance through continuing education (Garzón Castrillón, 2018).

The integration of AI into KM processes offers valuable opportunities to transform the management of relationships with alumni. Technologies such as predictive analytics, semantic engines, customer service chatbots, and recommendation systems enable a responsive, personalized, and strategic approach to institutional communication and engagement. However, as Freire and Marques (2024) warn, the use of AI must be guided by ethical and epistemological principles, ensuring that these technologies serve as mediators, not substitutes, for the co-production of knowledge.

The perspective of transhuman co-production proposed by the authors challenges the instrumental use of AI and presents a critical model in which human subjects and intelligent systems collaborate to create institutional meaning. This approach necessitates algorithmic transparency, data governance, and active institutional involvement in curating AI-mediated processes. For alumni, the relationship with the university extends beyond registration data or engagement metrics; it encompasses historical, emotional, and epistemological connections that must be honored and ethically activated. By viewing alumni as strategic assets of the university and suggesting the use of AI as an ally in KM, this research aims to offer a practical model that integrates maturity diagnostics, a critical foundation, and innovative functionality proposals. This approach seeks to enhance the responsible digital transformation of public universities, emphasizing the importance of valuing distributed institutional knowledge and expanding the social impact of higher education.

4.3 Methodology

This study is characterized as applied research with a qualitative approach, guided by an exploratory case-study strategy. The choice of this strategy is based on the need to understand, in depth, a complex institutional phenomenon: the maturity of KM in a public university, situated in its real and specific context, with a focus on the relationship with graduate students. According to Yin (2009) and Gil (2002), the case study is particularly appropriate when the researcher seeks to investigate contemporary events over which they have little or no control and that involve multiple sources of evidence.

The research was conducted at the UFSC, a public HEI with a well-established track record in research and graduate studies. The empirical focus was on analyzing institutional maturity in KM in terms of its ability to engage with graduate program alumni. This delimitation facilitated the integration of organizational, technological, and relational dimensions within the same analytical protocol. The investigation was carried out in two major, interdependent stages.

The first part was an integrative literature review aimed at mapping theoretical and empirical approaches that connect KM, alumni, and AI in the context of higher education in Latin America. The methodological strategy follows the Systematic Search Flow method (Ferenhof and Fernandes, 2015), which includes defining the research protocol, consulting databases, organizing bibliographic references, establishing inclusion and exclusion criteria, using combined descriptors, and conducting qualitative analyses of the selected studies. A systematic review of literature covering Latin American countries from the past five years was conducted using the Scielo.org database via the CAPES Periodical Portal. This database was selected because it focuses on evaluating studies in Spanish and Portuguese that represent the geographic scope. This stage aimed to provide theoretical support for both the institutional diagnosis and the functional proposition based on AI.

The second stage involved applying a diagnostic instrument adapted from consolidated models for assessing maturity in KM (Batista, 2013; APO, 2020) and the Knowledge Management Model of the Federal Highway Police – MGCPRF, developed by Sell *et al.* (2020). The instrument was redesigned for the university context in alumni management and organized into eight dimensions: institutional strategy, leadership, processes, people, technology, knowledge processes, learning and innovation, and results. Each dimension was broken down into indicators and questions previously validated by academic peers with expertise in KM and university management.

Data collection was conducted through a structured survey administered to managers of 85 graduate programs at UFSC, yielding 26 responses, which represented 21% of the institution's programs. The respondents are directly involved in graduate management and include representatives from the Office of the Vice Rector for Graduate Studies, program coordinators, and technical staff from strategic areas. The survey instrument was made available electronically, ensuring the confidentiality and anonymity of responses. Their expertise and institutional positioning justified the intentional selection of respondents.

Data analysis was conducted on two levels:

(1) Quantitative analysis of response frequencies and patterns by maturity dimension: respondents were asked to indicate their perceptions on a scale of 0–5, based on the Likert scale: 0 – "I don't know how to answer"; 1 – "Very poor performance or nothing being done"; 2 – "Poor performance"; 3 – "Adequate performance"; 4 – "Good performance"; and 5 – "Very good performance." Responses were tabulated, considering the means and modes for each question related to the dimensions answered by the participants. A Microsoft Excel spreadsheet was used as a tool, where the mean (or arithmetic mean) represents the "center" of the data, adding all values and dividing by the number of responses, using the formula =AVERAGE (range), and the mode is the value that appears most frequently in the responses, calculated using the formula =MODE.UNIT(range).

(2) Interpretative analysis of open comments and perceived inconsistencies based on categories previously defined in the literature. This analytical triangulation aimed to improve the validity of the diagnosis and accurately identify the main bottlenecks, opportunities, and areas for the development of institutional KM with a focus on alumni. As an analytical development, the results of the diagnosis were used as input for proposing institutional functionalities based on AI, consistent with the identified maturity levels. This stage was configured as a proactive action, as recommended by Deslandes and Iriart (2012), by transforming empirical data into recommendations based on theory and in line with the context.

The study adhered to all ethical principles of scientific research, including obtaining free and informed consent from participants, maintaining the confidentiality of the collected information, and refraining from disclosing institutional data in public reports. Since this survey focused on public servants in institutional roles rather than users in vulnerable situations, the research was deemed to pose minimal risk in accordance with the guidelines of CNS Resolution 510/2016. Nevertheless, the data were handled with the utmost caution, in alignment with the guidelines of the LGPD (Law No. 13,709/2018). Among the study's limitations, we acknowledge the small number of respondents and the restricted scope of the context – a single university. Such limitations, however, do not compromise the internal validity of the diagnosis; instead, they recommend caution when generalizing the results to other institutional contexts.

4.4 Presentation and Analysis of Results

This section presents the main results of the research, structured in three axes: (i) results of the integrative literature review, which theoretically support the study; (ii) a diagnosis of maturity in KM at the UFSC; and (iii) a critical synthesis that links the collected data to the propositions of basic functionalities in AI.

4.4.1 *Overview of the integrative and narrative review*

The literature review was conducted to identify approaches, methodologies, and gaps in scientific research at the intersection of KM, alumni relations, and the application of AI in HEIs. Initially, a search was conducted on Scielo.org over the past 10 years. The choice of this database was strategic to ensure coverage of relevant literature published in Portuguese and Spanish, the predominant languages in Latin America, with the purpose of assessing the maturity of KM in HEIs within this geographic context, where UFSC is located. The search strategy used was the terms "graduates" AND "artificial intelligence" AND "university" AND "institutional maturity" and "knowledge management." This specific topic in the databases, although comprehensive, did not result in published articles with an exact focus on that theme, region, and period. With this, we tested a set of keywords for each of the following three focuses: (1) graduate management by Latin American universities, (2) the level of maturity in KM in Latin American universities, and (3) technology/AI in universities. The idea is to combine them to increase relevance.

Focus 1: Integrative review based on Scielo.org – search strategy ("graduate students" OR "alumni" OR "graduate") AND ("information systems") OR ("monitoring systems") – The qualitative analysis of the articles selected in the integrative review followed the principles of thematic content analysis, allowing the systematic identification of patterns and categories emerging from the textual data. Initially, each article was read in an exploratory manner to gain a global understanding. Afterward, open coding was applied, identifying key excerpts and phrases that explained successes and weaknesses related to KM, relationships with alumni, and the application of AI technologies. The final portfolio consisted of 10 articles, six of which were Brazilian, two Mexican, one Ecuadorian, and one Colombian.

Some successes, highlighted as results of monitoring actions, included the creation of forums with alumni (Aguilar and Ramírez, 2024), the creation of a link between the institution and its alumni, progressive dialogue between actors (Garzón Castrillón, 2018; Demetrio *et al.*, 2020), a management tool and subsidies (Simon and Pacheco, 2017; Senger and Castro, 2024), the identification of demographic and social characteristics (da Silva *et al.*, 2022), a critical-reflective analysis of pedagogical projects (Aguiar *et al.*, 2021; Araújo *et al.*, 2022), and an analysis of the labor market (Hidalgo Villota, 2022; Damián Simón, 2020).

In the literature, significant gaps and weaknesses related to the monitoring of alumni were identified. In terms of programs and relationships, there is a need to implement mentoring and establish alumni associations (Aguilar and Ramírez, 2024). Curricular aspects require urgent alignment of the curriculum with students' needs (Senger and Castro, 2024). Digital tools and engagement represent weaknesses, characterized by low response rates to questionnaires and unattractive portals, making it difficult for users to participate and update data (da Silva *et al.*, 2022; Simon and Pacheco, 2017; Demetrio *et al.*, 2020). The difficulty in establishing and maintaining a bond with alumni is also a challenge (Garzón Castrillon, 2018). Finally, the literature points to the need to strengthen relationships between training institutions and employers (Aguiar *et al.*, 2021) and acknowledges the limitations of research due to the absence of a standardized system for comparison and monitoring and the use of single-case studies (Hidalgo Villota, 2022; Damián Simón, 2020).

Focus 2: Narrative review with a search on the topic of KM maturity levels in Latin American universities in the Scielo.org and Google Scholar databases. The final portfolio consisted of 10 articles, with seven Brazilian, one Mexican, and two Colombian case studies. It was possible to identify that the level of KM maturity in the universities studied, regardless of the theme, is at level 2 or 3 (on a scale of 1–5), positioning itself in the initial or introductory stage.

The literature presented several studies on KM maturity in the academic environment across various themes: distance education systems (Calmeto and Cribb, 2022), corporate education systems (Kraemer, 2018), startups (Loth *et al.*, 2019), public educational institutions with a general approach (Nuss, 2024; de Souza *et al.*, 2018), the human resources department of a federal university (Miranda Filho and da Costa Filho, 2023), educational innovation in universities (Vázquez González *et al.*, 2020; Vázquez González *et al.*, 2023), perception of teachers and administrative technicians in a public HEI (Marques *et al.*, 2020), research groups (Mejía Corrêa *et al.*, 2018), and strategic areas of the university (Carrillo and Gutiérrez, 2016).

Comparing the findings becomes challenging as they employ different methods and scales across various contexts and areas, corroborating the findings of previous studies (Kraemer *et al.*, 2017; Corrêa *et al.*, 2022). However, in the Brazilian cases, the majority used the MGCAPB maturity model by Batista (2013), an adaptation of the APO, and in the Colombian cases, the C-KMMM model was employed.

Focus 3: Narrative review with the theme of alumni monitoring using technology/AI in universities; seven articles from Scielo.org, Scopus, and Google Scholar were analyzed. While Scielo.org ensured a focus on Latin American contexts, the inclusion of Scopus and Google Scholar aimed to broaden the scope for relevant literature, even if not exclusively from the region, given the initial search limitations. Although few focused specifically on alumni, the selected works contributed to the understanding of AI applications in university contexts for strategic and KM purposes.

Benefits identified include efficient IT problem resolution, improved decision-making, resource optimization, proactive detection, and process automation (Funda and Francke, 2024); centralization of alumni data and automated extraction from Lattes, ORCID, and LinkedIn (Ranthun and dos Santos Junior, 2024); intelligent automation and personalized stakeholder engagement (Marcinkevage and Kumar, 2025); the use of algorithmically generated personas (AGPs) for insights and data-driven decision-making (Jansen *et al.*, 2025); the automation of administrative processes and pedagogical innovation (Montalván *et al.*, 2024); interactive dashboards and impact indicators (Cristina Da Silva and Favaretto, 2023); and cognitive engagement tools such as chatbots (Davenport and Ronanki, 2018).

Some weaknesses and challenges (with a focus on AI/technology) were identified, such as: poor data quality and availability (due to inadequate mechanisms and data silos), compatibility and integration with existing systems, resource constraints (investment), resistance to change, the need for training and staff skills development, ethical considerations (transparency and accountability) (Funda and Francke, 2024); decentralized and outdated information in existing portals, the explicit absence of advanced AI components (machine learning, ML, and predictive analytics) (Ranthun and dos Santos Junior, 2024); high costs of generative AI technologies and expertise, resistance to adoption by staff (driven by fear of replacement and distrust), the "black box" problem (understanding AI decisions) (Marcinkevage and Kumar, 2025); data complexity and methodology for creating AGPs, the need for investment in technology and training, the challenge of adapting to local cultural contexts (Jansen *et al.*, 2025); ethical concerns regarding the use of personal information, the digital divide (unequal access to technology), and a lack of formal scientific production on specific practical applications (Montalván *et al.*, 2024).

The literature review on the intersection of KM, alumni, and AI in Latin American HEIs reveals a promising, yet still maturing, field. Although the initial search on Scielo.org did not yield studies addressing all three elements simultaneously, expanding the search across three focal areas led to the identification of relevant findings. Regarding alumni management, good institutional practices were observed alongside persistent weaknesses. Regarding KM, institutions were generally found to be in low maturity stages, with methodological variation. Finally, in AI, innovation opportunities emerged alongside ethical, structural, and technological challenges.

4.4.2 *KM maturity diagnosis at UFSC*

The diagnostic instrument, although adapted from consolidated models (Batista, 2013; APO, 2020; Sell *et al.*, 2020), underwent a content validation process to ensure its relevance to the university context and alumni management. This stage involved consulting three academic peers and experts in the area of KM and university management, who reviewed the eight dimensions and their indicators to ensure clarity, relevance, and comprehensiveness in the UFSC scenario.

Based on the adapted instrument, the KM maturity diagnosis was applied to 26 institutional managers at UFSC, with strategic or transversal work focused on their relationships with graduate students. The eight dimensions evaluated were institutional strategy, leadership, processes, people, technology, knowledge processes, learning and innovation, and results.

The total assessment score is then compared to the KM maturity model. There are five levels in the maturity structure: reaction, initiation, introduction, refinement, and maturity.

Table 4.1. presents the knowledge management maturity levels and their respective score ranges (P), based on the classification levels of the APO framework (2020), with adaptations according to the model proposed by de Medeiros and Sell (2024), as follows: Level 1 – Reaction: The organization is unaware of what KM is and its importance for improving productivity and competitiveness; Level 2 – Initiation: The organization is beginning to recognize the need to manage knowledge or may already be starting a KM pilot project; Level 3 – Introduction: KM is fully implemented and deployed; Level 4: KM implementation is

Table 4.1. Knowledge management maturity levels and their score ranges (P).

Maturity Level	P Value Range
Reaction	$1.0 \leq P < 2.0$
Initiation	$2.0 \leq P < 3.0$
Introduction (expansion)	$3.0 \leq P < 3.5$
Refinement	$3.5 \leq P < 4.5$
Maturity	$4.5 \leq P \leq 5.0$

Source: Adapted from APO framework (2020) and de Medeiros and Sell (2024).

continually evaluated for continuous improvement; and Level 5: KM is fully integrated into the organization.

Descriptive analysis of response frequencies and patterns by maturity dimension: The responses, measured on a Likert scale from 0 to 5, were analyzed using the arithmetic mean and mode in a Microsoft Excel spreadsheet. The results are presented in Table 4.2.

Data analysis revealed a general level of institutional maturity, classified as reactive, with variations across different dimensions. Strategy and leadership presented more advanced levels, approaching level 2, reflecting institutional guidelines and values favorable to the valorization of knowledge, which were close to the initial level. On the other hand, the processes, people, and technology dimensions presented greater fragility, indicating a lack of incentive mechanisms, training, and technological infrastructure appropriate to the corporate governance (GC) cycle with alumni.

Interpretative analysis of open comments and perceived inconsistencies – Based on the descriptive responses of UFSC managers, it was possible to identify the following findings about the weaknesses and strengths in alumni management and monitoring, as well as their implications for GC and AI:

(i) Weaknesses identified:

Disarticulation and Lack of Systems Integration: There is a clear perception of "disarticulated systems... that do not communicate with each other,

Table 4.2. Summary of UFSC average and mode results by dimension.

Dimension	Average	Mode
Criterion 0.0: Strategy	1.89	1
Criterion 1.0: Leadership in information and knowledge management	1.39	2
Criterion 2.0: Process	1.22	1
Criterion 3.0: People	1.05	0
Criterion 4.0: Technology	1.65	0
Criterion 5.0: Knowledge processes	0.91	1
Criterion 6.0: Learning and innovation	1.44	0
Criterion 7.0: Results of information and KM	0.64	0
Total	**1.27**	**0**

such as the sites Estácios.ufsc.br and Egressos.sistemas.ufsc.br," in addition to the need for "tools that facilitate the daily lives of teachers, staff and students and to make the various systems at UFSC communicate digitally."

Lack of Defined Processes and Systems: Managers point out the "lack of centralized management" and the lack of "defined systems and processes for alumni management."

Limited Information Sharing: The difficulty in "sharing information" is an explicit weakness.

Lack of Coordinated Strategic Planning: The lack of "strategic, participatory and coordinated planning with all postgraduate programs, both to define what is desired and to create guidelines for greater monitoring of graduates" is a critical point.

(ii) Identified strengths:

Engaged and Willing Human Capital: One of the greatest strengths is the "individualized willingness of management and staff" and the fact that "Teachers, staff, and students, for the most part, defend and make UFSC work, even with all the adversities."

UFSC Brand Recognition (Alma Mater): The "public image of UFSC, the affection for the alma mater," generates an emotional bond that can be capitalized on to engage graduates.

Isolated Initiatives and Potential for Collaboration: There are "isolated initiatives within UFSC," which, although not yet articulated, show a beginning and a potential to be united in a coordinated effort.

Availability of Staff and a Large Number of Graduates: There are "staff who could work on this" and a "large number of graduates," which represents a significant body of work and an alumni base to be explored.

The application of the instrument to managers with strategic or cross-functional roles in their relationships with graduate students at UFSC ensured that the collected perceptions stemmed from individuals with in-depth knowledge of internal dynamics and challenges, thereby increasing the validity and relevance of the diagnostic data. This validation and adaptation process was essential to ensure that the managers' perceptions faithfully reflected the reality of KM maturity at UFSC, serving as a solid basis for interpreting the diagnostic results and for proposing AI functionalities.

4.4.3 *Critical synthesis and support for the proposal of AI functionalities*

The consolidation of data in a critical analysis matrix allowed us to identify the main institutional limitations and potentialities by dimension, which serves as a basis for the functional proposal in strategic dimensions with AI.

Technology: The diagnosis of KM maturity at UFSC revealed a marked weakness in the technology dimension (average of 1.65, mode 0), evidenced by the managers' perceptions of disjointed systems and a lack of tools to facilitate day-to-day activities.

To mitigate this deficiency, the implementation of a semantic search engine and document analysis is proposed. This AI-based functionality would act as an integrating layer, capable of digitally dialoguing with the various UFSC systems, such as estagios.ufsc.br and egressos.sistemas.ufsc.br, overcoming information silos. According to Davenport and Ronanki (2018), AI can perform data curation using ML, identifying probabilistic matches across disparate data formats and sources, which is essential for unifying dispersed knowledge about alumni. By centralizing and unifying knowledge about alumni, this functionality raises the level of maturity in the technology dimension, moving from a reactive stage to an initiation stage regarding KM infrastructure.

Processes: This dimension received an average of 1.22 and a mode of 1. The low maturity in the processes dimension, reflected by the absence of defined processes for alumni management and the difficulty in sharing information, is directly addressed by the proposal of intelligent segmentation and engagement prediction systems. By automating the analysis and classification of alumni profiles using clustering algorithms, AI allows for the standardization and targeting of communication and reintegration actions, overcoming the current informality of processes. The ability to predict the propensity for collaboration, according to Marcinkevage and Kumar (2025), transforms management from a reactive process into a proactive and strategic one.

People: The people dimension exhibited a mean of 1.05 and a mode of 0. The fragility of this dimension, which may be linked to the absence of adequate incentives and training mechanisms for alumni KM, is mitigated by the proposition of integrated analytical panels (dashboards) and an ethical and explainable conversational agent (chatbot). Although AI does not replace engaged human capital (a strength of UFSC), it can help by freeing employees from repetitive tasks to focus on high-value interactions. The chatbot, for example, can respond to frequent questions from alumni, while dashboards empower managers with management information for decision-making.

The implementation of AI is not isolated but contributes as a technical-organizational mediating solution for KM, respecting institutional autonomy and privacy. Improvements in one dimension (e.g., technology) can drive others (e.g., processes and results). The AI-based functional proposal, therefore, aims not only to solve specific problems but also to create a virtuous cycle of improving GC maturity. By integrating systems, automating data collection and analysis, and empowering stakeholders with insights, UFSC can move from a reactive level to one of initiation and, progressively, the introduction of GC, where practices are more implemented and continuously evaluated.

4.5 Proposing AI-Based Features

Based on a critical analysis of the maturity of KM at UFSC, particularly in relation to its impact on graduate students, this section proposes a set of institutional functionalities that leverage AI. The proposals presented here were constructed based on empirical data identified in the research and guided by epistemological and ethical principles anchored in the co-production of knowledge (Freire and Marques, 2024).

The logic underlying the proposal recognizes AI not as an autonomous solution but as a technical-organizational mediator of KM. In this sense, the functionalities must be articulated with human processes, respecting institutional autonomy, data privacy, and the role of individuals in building relationships with the university.

The first proposed functionality is the implementation of a semantic search and document analysis engine fed by curricular bases, academic productions, graduate data, and institutional information. This engine would allow the identification of thematic patterns in student production and connections between graduate programs and the areas of activity of alumni, and suggest potential areas of collaboration and curricular feedback.

Secondly, the use of intelligent segmentation systems for alumni profiles is proposed based on supervised clustering algorithms. This segmentation would allow alumni to be grouped by areas of training, field of professional activity, previous institutional engagement, and relational profile, enabling more targeted communication actions, specific thematic events, and qualified reintegration strategies.

Another strategic functionality is the adoption of institutional engagement prediction systems based on analysis of digital behavior, interaction history, and cross-referencing with academic and social data. These models could support decisions related to the offering of continuing education courses, invitations to panels or events, participation in evaluation forums, and specialized consultancy based on the identification of profiles with a greater propensity for collaboration.

The fourth proposal consists of implementing an integrated institutional analytical panel with interactive dashboards guided by AI to support the management of relationships with alumni. These panels would allow real-time monitoring of indicators such as communication reach, feedback on actions, alumni perceptions, and incidence of demands, organized by programs, teaching centers, and strategic areas.

Finally, it is proposed to create an ethical and explainable conversational agent (chatbot) with the capacity to automatically respond to frequent questions from alumni, while also incorporating algorithmic explanation mechanisms and institutional registration. This tool would function as a channel for welcoming, listening, and providing initial guidance while also feeding back into KM systems with data on the interests and recurring demands of alumni.

It is important to highlight that the adoption of these functionalities requires not only technological investment but also adequate levels of institutional maturity, especially within the processes and technology dimensions. The diagnostic analysis showed that these are critical areas at UFSC, thus requiring a phased implementation plan with a clear definition of those responsible, validation protocols, transparency of models, and ongoing training for the teams involved.

In addition, the need for an institutional committee focused on algorithmic ethics and AI governance, with representation from faculty, technical staff, students, and alumni, is reinforced. This committee will be

Table 4.3. AI functional complexity gradient in alumni relations: from automated response to strategic engagement.

Level of Proactivity/ Reactivity	AI Feature	Description
Reactive	Chatbot	Answers common queries, provides initial support
	Semantic search	Identifies patterns, connections, collaboration opportunities
	Segmentation system	Groups alumni for targeted communication and reintegration
	Prediction system	Predicts engagement, informs offers for ongoing involvement
Proactive	Integrated dashboard	Monitors indicators, supports alumni relationship management

Source: The authors, based on Davenport and Ronanki (2018) and Freire and Marques (2024).

responsible for monitoring implementation, assessing impacts, and proposing adjustments to the systems in line with the principles of the General Data Protection Law (LGPD) and considerations of epistemic justice in the university field.

Thus, the functionalities proposed here seek to translate the diagnosis into institutional action, supported by qualified GC, critical AI, and public commitment. This is a strategic transition path that articulates knowledge, technology, and institutional ties in an ethical, innovative, and social value-oriented way.

Table 4.3 illustrates the gradient of AI functional complexity in alumni relations, ranging from more reactive functionalities (such as chatbots) to more proactive ones (such as integrated dashboards), with intermediate stages demonstrating increasing sophistication.

4.6 Final Considerations

The research, of a qualitative nature and applied approach, combined a narrative review with a focus on Latin America to identify successes and weaknesses in other universities on the continent regarding alumni management and KM maturity levels, with the purpose of seeking an overview and identifying successes. However, comparison becomes difficult as researchers use different methods and scales across various contexts and areas. The diagnosis integrated the perspectives of institutional managers and a critical analysis of organizational conditions.

The results revealed that, although the university presents strategic intentionality and values favorable to KM, especially with regard to the valorization of knowledge and the role of graduates, an initial level of institutional maturity persists. Other studies identified in the literature review also indicated that other Latin American universities are at an early stage in terms of CG. In the case of UFSC, the most critical dimensions relate to operational processes and technological infrastructure, highlighting the fragmentation of practices and the absence of integrated, data-driven systems.

Based on this diagnosis, five AI-based functionalities were proposed, aligned with the identified maturity level: (i) a semantic document analysis engine, (ii) intelligent segmentation of alumni profiles, (iii) prediction of institutional engagement, (iv) interactive analysis panels, and (v) an ethical chatbot for welcoming and active listening.

These functionalities were conceived not as autonomous technological solutions but as instruments of technical-organizational mediation, guided by the principles of knowledge co-production and epistemic justice. The research contributes to the field of CG by offering an applied diagnostic model and functional proposal, with an emphasis on the institutional link with alumni as a strategic axis.

Furthermore, it raises concerns about the use of AI in public contexts, advocating for a critical, ethical, and explainable adoption anchored in institutional governance and the valorization of organizational authorship.

As a limitation, the institutional scope is restricted to UFSC, and the small number of respondents stands out. Such limitations, however, do not compromise the internal validity of the study but underscore the exploratory nature of the findings and emphasize the need for new comparative research in other public HEIs to enhance generalizability.

Finally, we reaffirm that strengthening the relationship between universities and alumni, supported by a mature and technologically mediated KM, constitutes a promising path to expand the social impact of public higher education, strengthen collaboration networks, and ethically leverage knowledge that goes beyond institutional walls.

References

Aguiar, K. L. D. A., M. A. Vieira, and E. B. L. de Domenico. 'Avaliação de Egressos de Cursos de Graduação em Enfermagem: Estudo Brasileiro Multicêntrico.' *Revista da Escola de Enfermagem da USP*, 55 (2021): e20200084.

Aguilar Hernández, E. A. and N. J. Ramírez Herrejón. 'La Formación del Arquitecto Nicolaíta en los Primeros Años del Siglo XXI.' *RIDE. Revista Iberoamericana para la Investigación y el Desarrollo Educativo*, 15, no. 29 (2024): e696, https://doi.org/10.23913/ride.v15i29.2009.

Araújo, F. R. D., C. E. D. S. Fontoura, W. R. P. Conti, F. R. Martins, R. E. Scachetti, and N. R. D. Oliveira-Monteiro. 'Autovaloração de Competências Genéricas em Egressos de um Bacharelado Interdisciplinar Brasileiro.' *Educação em Revista*, 38 (2022): e234741.

Asian Productivity Organization (APO). *Knowledge Management: Tools and Techniques Manual*. APO: Tokyo, 2020, https://www.apo-tokyo.org/ (accessed 15 June 2024).

Batista, F. F. *Modelo de Gestão do Conhecimento para a Administração Pública Brasileira (MGCAPB): O que sua Organização Precisa Saber Antes de Implantar*. 2013.

Calmeto, T. L. L. and A. Y. Cribb. 'Maturidade em Gestão do Conhecimento: Um Diagnóstico Sobre o Sistema de Educação a Distância de uma Instituição Federal de Ensino no Sul Fluminense.' *Revista Conhecimento Online*, 1 (2022): 161–188.

Carrillo, L. M. and J. P. L. Gutiérrez. 'Medindo a Maturidade da Gestão do Conhecimento na Faculdade de Ciências Básicas, Tecnologia e Engenharia da UNAD.' *Publicações e Pesquisa*, 10 (2016): 177–191.

Corrêa, F., C. P. A. D. Paula, F. Ziviani, and V. F. D. Faria. 'Maturidade em Gestão do Conhecimento: Aplicação Prática de um Método.' *Transinformação*, 34 (2022): e220002.

Cristina Da Silva, E. and F. Favaretto. 'Proposta de uma Ferramenta de Business Intelligence para o Acompanhamento dos Egressos dos Programas de Iniciação Científica do IFSULDEMINAS.' *Revista de Educação, Ciência e Tecnologia*, 12, no. 2 (2023): 1–23.

Da Silva, L. F. O. A., A. Ferreira, P. T. Lacerda, and Y. V. da Silva. 'Acciones Afirmativas en la Educación Superior y en la Movilidad Social: Un Estudio de Campo.' *Actualidades Investigativas en Educación*, 22, no. 2 (2022): 11.

Damián Simón, J. 'Empleabilidad y Situación Laboral de los Egresados de Contaduría en México: Periodo 2005-2018.' *Diálogos Sobre Educación. Temas Actuales en Investigación Educativa*, 11, no. 21 (2020): 1–30.

Davenport, T. and L. Prusak. 'Learn How Valuable Knowledge is Acquired, Created, Bought and Bartered.' *The Australian Library Journal*, 47, no. 3 (1998): 268–272: 268–272.

Davenport, T. H. and R. Ronanki. 'Artificial Intelligence for the Real World.' *Harvard Business Review*, 96, no. 1 (2018): 108–116.

De Medeiros, M. R. and D. Sell. 'Análise de Nível de Maturidade em Gestão de Conhecimento: Diagnóstico do Tribunal de Contas do Estado de Santa Catarina.' Technical Report, 2024.

De Souza, A. L. F., A. R. H. A. Helou, and A. P. L. Sohn. 'Identificação do Grau de Maturidade em Gestão do Conhecimento no Setor de Ensino: Um Estudo no Instituto Federal Catarinense Câmpus Araquari.' *Ciência da Informação*, 47, no. 2 (2018): 171–186.

Demetrio, R., R. D. F. Pellizzon, F. E. Hirai, and D. D. Freitas. 'Database of the alumni performance of the Ophthalmology Stricto sensu Postgraduate Program at Escola Paulista de Medicina, UNIFESP.' *Acta Cirurgica Brasileira*, 35, no. 2 (2020): e202000207.

Deslandes, S. F. and J. A. B. Iriart. 'Usos Teórico-Metodológicos das Pesquisas na Área de Ciências Sociais e Humanas em Saúde.' *Cadernos de Saúde Pública*, 28 (2012): 2380–2386.

Ferenhof, H. A. and R. F. Fernandes. 'Passo a Passo para Construção da Revisão Sistemática e Bibliometria.' In *Anais do Encontro Nacional de Engenharia de Produção (ENEGEP)*. 2015.

Freire, P. S., A. M. Alvares, and J. R. Silva. 'Conhecimentos Críticos para a Prontidão Tecnológica da Inovação.' In *Orienta: Prontidão para a Inovação Pública*, edited by P. S. Freire. UFSC, Programa de Pós-Graduação em Engenharia e Gestão do Conhecimento, 2021, 52–75.

Freire, P. S. and D. Marques. *Coprodução Transhumana: Manual de Uso Ético de Inteligência Artificial na Escrita Acadêmica*. Editora Arquétipos, 2024.

Funda, V. and E. Francke. 'Benefits and Challenges of AIOps Adoption and Usage in HEIs in Developing Countries.' *South African Journal of Higher Education*, 38, no. 6 (2024): 56–78.

Garzón Castrillón, A. 'Modelo para el Seguimiento y Acompañamiento a Graduados (SAG), una Visión Holística de la Gestión de la Calidad de la Educación Superior.' *Educación*, 27, no. 52 (2018): 201–218.

Gil, A. C. *Como Elaborar Projetos de Pesquisa*. Vol. 4. Atlas: São Paulo, 2002.

Hidalgo Villota, M. E. 'Condiciones Ocupacionales de los Graduados del Programa de Economía en la Universidad de Nariño, Colombia.' *Tendencias*, 23, no. 1 (2022): 277–314.

Jansen, B. J., S. Jung, A. Farooq, J. Salminen, K. Aldous, P. S. Msefula, A. Alabed, S. M. Khan, and R. O'Kennedy. 'Human-Centred Artificial Intelligence in Progressive Education: Unravelling the Benefits and Challenges in Qatar's HEIS.' In *The Future of Education Policy in the State of Qatar*, edited by E. Zaidan. Gulf Studies 21, 2025, 105–126.

Kraemer, R., P. de Sá Freire, J. A. de Souza, and G. A. Dandolini. 'Maturidade de Gestão do Conhecimento: Uma Revisão Sistemática da Literatura para Apoiar o Desenvolvimento de Novos Modelos de Avaliação.' *Perspectivas em Gestão & Conhecimento*, 7 (2017): 66–79.

Kraemer, R. 'Modelo de Maturidade do Sistema de Educação Corporativa.' PhD thesis, Universidade Federal de Santa Catarina, 2018.

Loth, A. F., F. G. Ferreira, G. T. Martins, and N. dos Santos. 'Aplicação do Framework de Gestão do Conhecimento APO: O Caso da Startup T5 Tecnologia.' In *Anais do Congresso Internacional de Conhecimento e Inovação (CIKI)*. 2019.

Marcinkevage, C. and A. Kumar. 'Generative AI in Higher Education Constituent Relationship Management (CRM): Opportunities, Challenges, and Implementation Strategies.' *Computers*, 14, no. 3 (2025): 101.

Marques, J. M. R., J. L. La Falce, F. M. F. R. Marques, C. F. De Muylder, and J. T. M. Silva. 'A Maturidade da Gestão do Conhecimento: Uma Comparação Entre a Percepção de Docentes e Técnicos Administrativos de uma Instituição Pública de Ensino Superior.' *Revista Conhecimento Online*, 1 (2020): 27–48.

Mejía Correa, A. M., A. Vesga Vinchira, and M. M. Gaviria Velásquez. 'Gestión del Conocimiento Científico en la Universidad de Antioquia: Integración de Herramientas para la Formulación de una Estrategia.' *Innovar*, 28, no. 69 (2018): 71–84.

Miranda Filho, D. E. and C. G. da Costa Filho. 'Avaliação do Nível de Maturidade em Gestão do Conhecimento: Estudo em uma Universidade Pública Federal.' *Revista Economia & Gestão*, 23, no. 65 (2023).

Montalván, B. K. C., A. B. C., and C. D. E. 'The Influence of Artificial Intelligence in Higher Education Based on Four Thematic Axes: A Bibliometric Study.' *Sapienza: International Journal of Interdisciplinary Studies*, 5, no. 2 (2024): e24035–e24035.

Nonaka, I. and H. Takeuchi. *Criação de Conhecimento na Empresa*. Campus: Rio de Janeiro, 1997.

Nuss, D. 'Avaliação do Nível de Maturidade em Gestão do Conhecimento em uma Instituição Pública de Ensino Superior.' Master's thesis, Universidade Tecnológica Federal do Paraná, 2024.

Ranthun, G. and G. dos Santos Junior. 'Plataforma Tecnológica para Apoio à Gestão de Egressos de Programas de Pós-Graduação Stricto Sensu.' *Revista Brasileira da Educação Profissional e Tecnológica*, 2, no. 24 (2024): e15503.

Sell, D., P. S. Freire, and J. L. Todesco. *Modelo de Gestão do Conhecimento: Elaboração do Modelo de Gestão do Conhecimento da PRF*. Ministério da Justiça e Segurança Pública. Universidade Federal de Santa Catarina, 2020.

Senger, M. H. and J. C. M. D. Castro. 'Contribuições de Egressos de Medicina para a Avaliação do Curso.' *Revista Brasileira de Educação Médica*, 48, no. 3 (2024): e067.

Simon, L. W. and A. S. V. Pacheco. 'Ações de Acompanhamento de Egressos: Um Estudo das Universidades Públicas do Sul do Brasil.' *Revista Brasileira de Ensino Superior*, 3, no. 2 (2017): 94–113.

Vázquez-González, G. C., I. U. Jiménez-Macías, and L. G. Juárez-Hernández. 'Construcción-Validación del Cuestionario: Madurez de Gestión do Conhecimento para Innovación Educativa en Universidades.' *Apertura*, 12, no. 1 (2020): 132–151, https://doi.org/10.32870/Ap.v12n1.1767.

Vázquez-González, G. C., I. U. Jiménez-Macías, L. G. Juárez-Hernández, and E. Bracamontes-Ceballos. 'Level of Maturity of Knowledge Management for Educational Innovation at the University of Colima, México.' *Nivel de Madurez de la Gestión del Conocimiento para la Innovación Educativa en la Universidad de Colima, México*, 2023.

Wiig, K. M. *Knowledge Management Foundations: Thinking About Thinking-How People and Organizations Represent, Create, and Use Knowledge.* Schema Press, Limited, 1994.

Yin, R. K. *Case Study Research: Design and Methods*. Vol. 5. Sage, 2009. This is a book, ISBN 978-1-4129-6099-1, published by Sage, pp. 1-126. Access link: https://books.google.com.br/books?id=FzawIAdilHkC&lpg=PR1&ots=l-3V4ckV-r&dq=Yin%2C%20R.%20K.%20Case%20Study%20Research%3A%20Design%20and%20Methods.%20Vol.%205.%20Sage%2C%202009.&lr&hl=pt-BR&pg=PA126#v=onepage&q&f=false.

© 2026 World Scientific Publishing Europe Ltd.
https://doi.org/10.1142/9781800617414_0005

Chapter 5

Potential and Impact of Integrating AI in Managing and Optimizing Business Processes

Thomas Weißenbacher, Richard Heininger, and Christian Stary*

Department of Business Informatics-Communications Engineering, Business School, Johannes Kepler University Linz, Austria

**christian.stary@jku.at*

Abstract

In this review study, we analyze the potential of Artificial Intelligence (AI) for organizations when embedding AI applications in existing business processes. While such an integration enables significant efficiency improvements, particularly in the automation, analysis, and monitoring of processes, successful AI implementations depend heavily on the conditions under which companies operate, the industry sector, and the technological maturity of the company. When reviewing AI applications in the context of business process management, we looked for approaches to identify inefficiencies in business processes. The analysis shows that data-driven methods such as process mining with process discovery algorithms and machine learning offer effective ways to identify bottlenecks and inefficient business process steps at an early stage. We also examined the criteria companies can use to evaluate whether AI is suitable for process optimization. Such a decision is highly context-dependent and influenced by several factors, including technological aspects, the industry sector, the economic benefits, and the company's strategic objectives. Overall, the successful implementation of AI requires not only technological adaptations but also significant investments in infrastructure, employee training, and change management processes.

Keywords: Artificial intelligence, artificial agents, business process management, process mining, machine learning, process discovery, process optimization, digital transformation, impact assessment.

5.1 Introduction

In recent years, rapid advances in the field of Artificial Intelligence (AI) have led to a transformative era for businesses across industries. Integrating AI into existing business processes is a critical step that promises unprecedented efficiency, innovation, and strategic advantage (Ilieva and Nikolov, 2019; Abuzaid, 2024; Waite *et al.*, 2025). The use of AI technologies seems critical for companies that want to remain competitive in an increasingly digital landscape. However, multiple dimensions of AI integration need to be taken into account to leverage its potential impact on operational workflows, decision-making processes, and overall business strategies (Prasanth *et al.*, 2023). The dimensions concern the digital transformation challenges of organizations, including automation, optimization, and the redesign of existing business processes.

This chapter focuses on the integration of AI techniques and technologies into existing business processes, with emphasis on increasing efficiency. The objective of the study is to answer the question of how AI techniques and technologies can be used to optimize existing business processes within a company without sacrificing their effectiveness. Emphasis is placed on the role of AI techniques and technologies, the acceptance of AI by organizations, and possible areas of application. A key issue is the lack of standardization of AI implementations in business processes. In addition, the successful integration of AI often requires significant infrastructure and expertise, which is a particular hurdle for small- and medium-sized companies when managing their business processes (Dumas *et al.*, 2018).

In this chapter, we analyze the intricacies of the transformative journey of AI integration into business processes, identifying challenges and opportunities, along with the overarching impact and potential for embedding AI in existing business processes. We examine how AI techniques and technologies along the various phases of the business process management (BPM) lifecycle (Dumas *et al.*, 2018) can increase efficiency and generate competitive advantage.

To address these issues, we review existing findings with respect to:

- analyzing which AI methods and AI technologies can be used to identify inefficiencies in business processes;
- the ability to systematically identify weak points as the basis for targeted use of AI techniques;
- enabling optimization of business processes, including prior problem analysis;
- identifying key criteria when assessing possible benefits of AI in specific business processes;
- the acceptance of AI approaches and solutions in organizations.

The following section summarizes opportunities and challenges when considering AI techniques to improve business operations. It turns out that AI readiness in the context of business process improvements requires ensuring technology acceptance and a performant infrastructure. We demonstrate through reviewing sample applications in the subsequent section how AI-supported solutions can contribute to increasing the efficiency of business processes. We provide corresponding results and key performance indicators (KPIs) from practical cases.

5.2 Opportunities and Challenges

This section reviews the recognized potential and application contexts that have been addressed in use cases and best practices to illustrate how AI techniques and technologies can be integrated into existing business processes. We also discuss the relevance of AI readiness in an organizational context. The insights gained serve as a basis for a systematic classification of specific AI technologies along the various phases in BPM, which we address subsequently.

5.2.1 *The role of AI technologies in business processes and their development*

In general, the integration of AI into business processes marks a revolutionary change in the way organizations operate and gain competitive advantage. Particularly, adopting AI technologies enables organizations to increase their efficiency and productivity, improve decision-making processes, and personalize customer experiences by automating repetitive and time-consuming tasks. In addition, AI applications enable the analysis of vast amounts of data in real time and provide insights and recommendations that support business decisions, thus improving decision-making (Svetlana *et al.*, 2022). AI-driven chatbots and virtual assistants can support customers around the clock, improve their experience, and ultimately allow for better understanding of user needs and increase brand loyalty. Customer data are thereby analyzed to identify patterns and preferences (Nigmatov and Pradeep, 2023).

Moreover, AI systems can help organizations mitigate risks by identifying potential risks and fraud and facilitating compliance with regulations. The latter helps to avoid costly fines and reputational damage. Finally, AI techniques mostly require access to new and innovative technologies. Applying novel technologies enables organizations to differentiate themselves from their competitors and thus gain a competitive advantage (Makar, 2023).

With respect to BPM, AI techniques and technologies have the capability to collect data, make predictions, and analyze behavioral trends. The integration of cloud technology, network devices, and digital content allows organizations to:

- streamline their processes,
- reduce their costs,
- increase their productivity,
- develop future marketing strategies (Prasanth *et al.*, 2023).

In addition, AI is considered a key driver of intelligent process automation, both creating a virtual workforce and enabling existing workers to take on more creative tasks (Svetlana *et al.*, 2022). Implementation in that respect leads to intelligent assistants such as Siri, self-driving cars, and advanced learning systems for video games. Virtual assistants are also used to identify data trends, reduce market risks, improve customer service through virtual guides, and identify compliance violations by analyzing large data sets. These capabilities strengthen the role of AI technologies in business operations and thus business process development (Makar, 2023).

The benefits of utilizing AI have become particularly evident when failures and error rates could be minimized through consistent, rule-based programming. Both continuous improvements in this way and effective process documentation have led to economic growth. Hence, AI techniques and technologies, including robotics, computer vision, speech recognition, machine learning (ML), and natural language processing (NLP), have the capability to increase the efficiency of processes and open up new economic opportunities. Once these changes are measured in a structured way, corporate management can rely on data-driven decision-making from a strategic perspective (Prasanth *et al.*, 2023).

5.2.2 *AI-readiness and acceptance in organizations*

The AI readiness of organizations describes the ability to strategically integrate AI in order to achieve a transformation of business processes and thereby generate competitive advantages. Svetlana *et al.* (2022) discuss the assessment of AI readiness in several dimensions, including technological infrastructure, organizational competencies, and strategic investments. It concerns several pillars as detailed in the following list:

1. A robust IT infrastructure, which includes cloud technologies and big data, forms the basis for the use of AI techniques.
2. At the same time, expertise in ML and data analytics, as well as training initiatives, is crucial to prepare employees for the demands of digital transformation.
3. In addition, a corporate culture that promotes innovation, investments in AI projects, and ethically responsible governance are crucial.

However, the acceptance of AI techniques and technologies is not equally distributed across business and industry sectors. According to Makar (2023), AI capabilities are used in the following domains:

- retail, with 40% of respondents believing that this domain has mature AI practices;
- financial services, with 38% believing;

- telecommunications, with 37% believing;
- computers, electronics and technology, with 35% believing;
- education, with only 10% of respondents sharing that belief;
- government, with also only 16% believing;
- media, with 29% believing;
- healthcare and life sciences, with 28% believing;
- defense, with 26% believing;
- manufacturing, with 25% of respondents sharing the belief of mature sectoral AI practices.

The organizations' awareness of AI concepts in the digital space had increased significantly between 2010 and 2019, particularly in ML and business intelligence (Prasanth *et al.*, 2023). Thus, most of the common AI applications that have evolved concern the:

- optimization of service operations,
- development of new AI-based products,
- improvement of existing products through AI.

Therefore, the analysis of customer service, segmentation, and acquisition plays a central role alongside customer service automation, product feature optimization, risk modeling, risk analysis, predictive service (maintenance), and targeted interventions (Makar, 2023).

The analysis of AI readiness in organizations raises the question of how the insights gained can be used strategically to integrate AI techniques and technologies into existing business processes in a targeted manner. Strategic process identification is therefore an essential factor when determining the areas in which the integration of AI can generate the greatest added value. The following section is dedicated to the strategic approaches organizations should pursue when integrating AI into business processes, e.g., along the phases of the BPM lifecycle (Dumas *et al.*, 2018).

5.2.3 *Strategic integration of AI into existing business processes*

The quality of an AI system's learning capabilities in a business context correlates with the quantity of available data. The availability of large amounts of data enables effective learning and the adaptability of AI

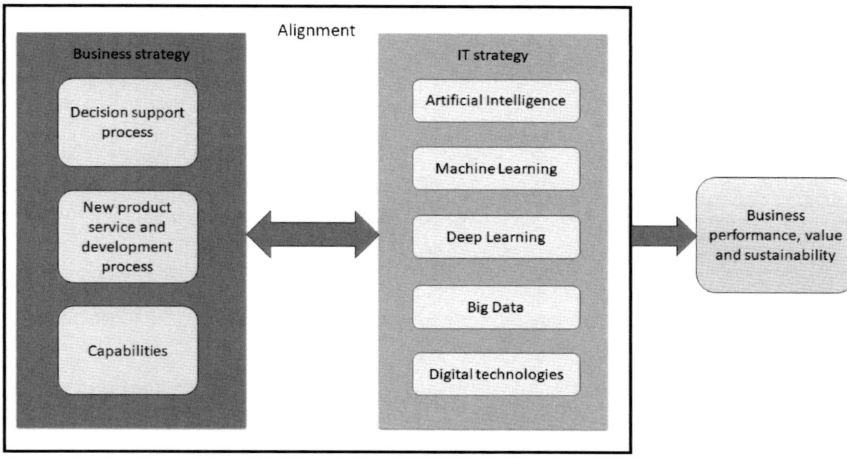

Figure 5.1. Conceptual framework according to Prasanth *et al.* (2023, p. 3).

systems. The daily production of data allows organizations to optimize their data collection using AI, so that predictions can be made about future developments, and real-time data processing can be used for problem-solving and innovation. However, the importance of a robust data infrastructure needs to be emphasized in that context, as the quality of the results directly depends on the quality of the underlying data (the "garbage in – garbage out" phenomenon) (Reim *et al.*, 2020).

The use of AI technologies has a significant impact on the way decisions are made in organizations, as AI applications can create a decisive competitive advantage. Therefore, the focus is on using social and cognitive capabilities to innovate products and services. Organizations that have a clearly defined business plan for the age of connectivity and integrate the latest AI technologies can generate a competitive advantage, as illustrated in the conceptual framework introduced by Prasanth *et al.* (2023) and depicted in Figure 5.1.

The left-hand side of Figure 5.1 shows the business strategy. It contains the decision support process, the development of new products and services, and the business capabilities. These elements are connected to the IT strategy of an organization. It specifically includes AI, ML, deep learning, big data, and digital technologies. Their alignment with the business strategy features improved business performance, value creation, and

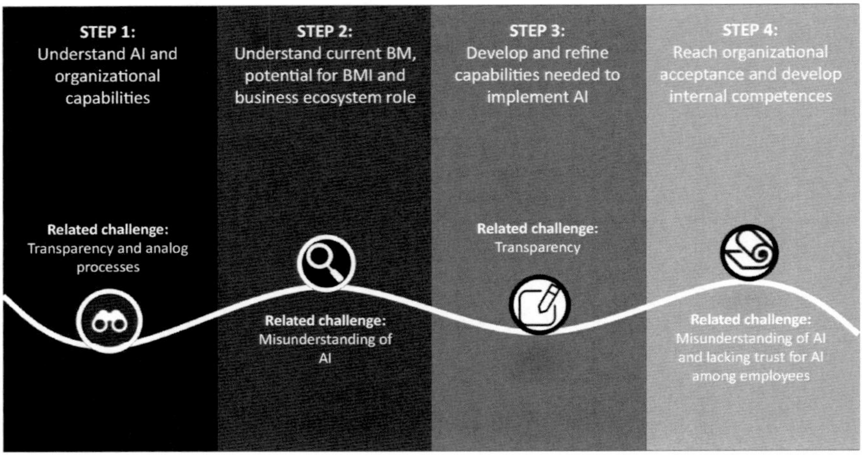

Figure 5.2. Conceptual framework and roadmap, including major challenges, according to Reim *et al.* (2020, p. 8).

Notes: BM: Business Model, BMI: Business Model Innovation.

sustainability, as depicted on the right-hand side of Figure 5.1 (Prasanth *et al.*, 2023).

Reim *et al.* (2020) have developed a roadmap that provides organizations with a structured approach to integrating AI into their business models. They refer to organizational capabilities as enablers. The roadmap itself is based on four central steps, which are designed as iterative processes, and emphasizes key challenges and strategies. Figure 5.2 illustrates the roadmap and the corresponding steps for operation:

Step 1: Understanding AI and organizational capabilities

Analyzing potential risks and opportunities forms the basis for implementing AI. The authors emphasize the need for a solid data infrastructure and overcoming transparency issues in order to build trust in the technology.

Step 2: Analysis of the current business model and role in the ecosystem

Companies should conduct an analysis of their existing business models in terms of value creation, value delivery, and value capture. Evaluating their position in the business environment enables the identification of innovation potential and its strategic use.

Step 3: Developing and refining capabilities
This step involves adapting technical, strategic, and organizational skills. These skills concern the transformation of core processes and the decision on strategic positioning, for example, as a "first mover" or "follower".

Step 4: Promoting organizational acceptance and skills development
The focus here is on engaging employees through training, pilot projects, and feedback loops. The roadmap emphasizes that acceptance within the organization is a decisive factor for the success of AI integration.

The strategic integration of AI can play a decisive role in several phases of the BPM lifecycle. Especially during the process redesign and process implementation phases, a clear strategy is required to ensure that AI technologies are effectively integrated into business processes. The assignment of phases enables a structured and practice-oriented classification of the content described above (Reim *et al.*, 2020).

5.3 AI and Business Processes

We first detail some benefits through the targeted use of AI technologies in organizations before structuring our results from two perspectives: (i) the business perspective, focusing on economic effects and operational optimization potential, and (ii) the AI perspective, which focuses on technological aspects, methodological approaches, and challenges of AI integration. This two-pronged approach enables a comprehensive analysis of the potential and limitations of AI use along the phases of the BPM lifecycle.

At the same time, it becomes clear that the BPM lifecycle, according to Dumas *et al.* (2018), cannot fully capture all the specific challenges of AI integration. Aspects such as ethical issues, the fairness of AI systems, or data protection represent overarching topics that cannot always be clearly assigned to a single phase. The BPM lifecycle should therefore be understood as a structuring framework that can be supplemented by other methodological approaches in order to take a holistic view of AI integration in business organizations.

5.3.1 *Efficiency gains through the targeted use of AI*

Dohmen and Moormann (2010) have already focused on the identification of inefficiency drivers in business processes. Their approach is based on a methodology that combines data envelopment analysis and data mining to enable more precise identification of inefficiency drivers than traditional methods. In particular, the use of process data to identify systematic patterns provides companies with a sound basis for deriving targeted optimization measures. The use of AI expands this potential by not only identifying inefficient patterns but also predicting and optimizing them in real time (*ibid.*).

While the classic data envelopment analysis approach is primarily based on the retrospective analysis of process data, AI enables adaptive and dynamic control of business processes. This opens up new opportunities for companies to address inefficiencies at an early stage and achieve sustainable process optimization in the long term (*ibid.*).

When AI is considered a key factor in the design of business models, its implementation requires an investment in the necessary infrastructure to ensure the system functions smoothly (Prasanth *et al.*, 2023). The accompanying digital transformation affects the way organizational units operate and requires the conversion of the traditional business model into a virtual representation (Svetlana *et al.*, 2022).

Analyzing the impact of AI on the functioning of organizations facilitates decision-making and thus the efficiency of transformation processes (Prasanth *et al.*, 2023). This study showed a decrease in effort spent on person-hours for activities such as reasoning, decision-making, management and coordination, and communication. Accordingly, hours spent with AI issues increased, as this effort was spent on data processing, job-related data exchange, and the execution of complex activities. This shift indicates that AI technologies are increasingly taking over tasks previously performed by humans, especially those associated with data and information-intensive processes (Prasanth *et al.*, 2023).

When applying AI technologies to increase productivity and efficiency in business administration, the respective management processes help companies reduce costs, improve decision-making quality and accuracy, and increase productivity and customer satisfaction. To optimize business processes, organizations are increasingly relying on intelligent information systems. These are able to adapt their parameters to changing conditions independently, i.e., without human intervention (Kovshova *et al.*, 2023).

The standardization of business processes creates a positive corporate image and is instrumental in significantly increasing the number of loyal customers and fostering long-term business relationships. When striving to uncover the link between human and machine intelligence, depending on the entrepreneurial process, research related to the intellectualization of business management systems and their efficiency has shown that AI can significantly improve business efficiency. Nevertheless, the introduction of AI technologies into business management systems requires significant investment in IT infrastructure and staff training. The effectiveness of the implementation of AI systems in organizations depends largely on the type of implementation and the specific business objectives (*ibid.*).

5.3.2 *The business (process management) perspective*

The following tables examine the use of AI techniques in BPM from a business perspective and show how organizations can achieve significant efficiency improvements, cost reductions, and process optimizations through AI applications. We follow the phases of the BPM lifecycle in order to structure the existing findings according to the objectives of the study. According to Dumas *et al.* (2018), the BPM lifecycle is a process that encompasses the phases of process identification, modeling, analysis, redesign, implementation, monitoring, and optimization.

The results show that the targeted use of techniques and technologies such as ML, NLP, process mining (PM) (Van der Aalst *et al.*, 2022), robotic process automation (RPA), and digital twins (DTs) not only support various process management phases but also enable creating direct economic benefits for companies.

In the following, for each BPM phase, applications of specific AI techniques are exemplified, and their impact is detailed in terms of concerned KPIs and results (Table 5.1).

Badakhshan *et al.* (2022) analyze a key business effect of AI in increasing the efficiency of operational processes. Companies that use PM algorithms for automated process identification benefit from significantly faster and more accurate detection of inefficient process steps. This enables optimization potential to be identified early on and replaces manual, time-consuming analyses. For example, the use of process discovery methods helped reduce manual data preparation in business processes from five hours per week to zero, resulting in a direct increase in productivity.

AI-supported conformance checks also demonstrate added operational value in process modeling (Table 5.2). These checks enable companies to

Table 5.1. Process identification.

Sample Application	AI Technique	Concerned KPI	Result
Recognition of ineffective processes	Process mining, process discovery algorithms	Time required	Reduction of manual effort to prepare data (from 5 to 0 hours per week)
Identification of process variants, erroneous sequences, missing steps, and bottlenecks	Process mining, process discovery algorithms	Lead time, number of process deviations	Possible causes of delayed orders with respect to certain plants or suppliers

Table 5.2. Process modeling.

Sample Application	AI Technique	Concerned KPI	Result
Reduction of reworking time and elimination of overhead activities to reduce costs	Process mining, conformity check	Number of process steps, process costs	Cost reduction by targeted adaptation of business rules and process steps
Optimized production planning of timely production	Intelligent digital twin, machine learning for predictive scheduling	Production time per order, machine capacity utilization	Increase in planning efficiency, reduction of bottlenecks
Smart factory asset management	Intelligent digital twin, predictive maintenance with anomaly detection	Downtimes, maintenance costs	Reduction of downtimes, optimized maintenance
Redesign of order-to-cash process	Process mining, conformity check	Process lead time	Efficiency increase of financial processes by system adaptations

compare actual and target processes and thus identify deviations at an early stage. Especially in production management, predictive analytics helps optimize machine utilization and reduce downtime, which in turn leads to improved resource utilization and lower operating costs (West *et al.*, 2021).

Table 5.3. Process analysis.

Sample Application	AI Technique	Concerned KPI	Result
Identification of inefficient credit freezes and their root cause	Process mining, predictive analyses, and clustering	Number of blocked orders	Reduction of unnecessary credit freezes
Combining descriptive (past) and predictive (future) analysis to better understand process behavior	Process mining, machine learning, predictive analyses, and clustering	Accuracy of prediction, process stability	Potential to predict the likelihood of problems and take early action

Table 5.4. Process redesign of currently running processes.

Sample Application	AI Technique	Concerned KPI	Result
Amazon: increasing sales through purchase recommendations	Machine learning, collaborative filtering	Number of sales	Increase in sales
Starbucks: optimizing store layout	Machine learning, AI analytics, cluster analysis of customer behavior	Number of sales, customer satisfaction	Increase in sales, increase in customer satisfaction
Automation of manual activities in office processes	Robotic process automation	Working hours, costs	Working time reduction in full-time equivalents, cost reduction

In process analysis, companies use ML-supported predictive models to proactively identify bottlenecks and risks (Table 5.3). This enables more precise planning of business processes and provides a better basis for management decision-making. Particularly in the financial sector, this leads to more precise credit risk assessment, which can prevent unnecessary credit freezes and improve both financial stability and customer satisfaction (Badakhshan *et al.*, 2022).

Process redesign is particularly relevant for companies that are fundamentally transforming their workflows through AI technologies (Table 5.4). RPA reduces the effort required for standardized, repetitive office processes and enables significant cost reductions (Axmann and Harmoko, 2020). Furthermore, AI-powered recommendation systems in e-commerce have been proven to increase sales by analyzing customer purchasing behavior and generating personalized product recommendations. For instance, a leading online retailer was able to increase sales by 35% by using ML algorithms, as more precise product recommendations led to higher conversion rates (Nigmatov and Pradeep, 2023).

Process implementation is a crucial step in integrating technological innovations into operational processes (Table 5.5). Companies are increasingly relying on NLP-powered voice and chatbot systems to automate customer interactions and optimize service processes (Nigmatov and Pradeep, 2023). One example is McDonald's, which implemented an NLP-based speech recognition system to shorten order times in the drive-thru, thus increasing customer satisfaction (*ibid.*).

Further studies show that the use of RPA can reduce operating costs in standardized financial processes by up to 50% (Kovshova *et al.*, 2023). Furthermore, AI technologies are being used to automate ordering processes, enabling greater accuracy and significantly reducing labor costs (Nigmatov and Pradeep, 2023). Companies that systematically deploy AI solutions such as RPA and PM have achieved productivity gains of up to 86%, a 90% improvement in quality, and a 92% increase in compliance (Axmann and Harmoko, 2020).

Another key application area of AI is in process monitoring, where predictive analytics and ML are used for error detection and quality assurance (Table 5.6). This is particularly important in healthcare, where ML-based fraud detection systems identify erroneous or fraudulent billing with over 90% accuracy and minimize financial losses (Makar, 2023). In logistics, predictive analytics optimizes supply chains by using ML for route optimization (Nigmatov and Pradeep, 2023). Companies such as UPS have been able to shorten delivery times and reduce transportation costs through the use of AI-supported fleet management systems (*ibid.*).

Process optimization, the final phase of the BPM lifecycle, demonstrates that companies are using AI technologies not only to automate existing processes but also for continuous process and business improvement (Table 5.7). The combined use of RPA and ML enables rule-based automation to be integrated with intelligent, learning systems, ultimately leading to dynamic adaptation and optimization of business processes (Badakhshan *et al.*, 2022).

Table 5.5. Process implementation.

Sample Application	AI Technique	Concerned KPI	Result
Automation of finance and accounting processes	Robotic process automation	Costs	Reduction of operating costs
McDonald's: speech recognition in drive-thru	Natural language processing, automated speech recognition	Order time, customer satisfaction	Reduction of order time, increase in customer satisfaction
BMW: chatbot for customer inquiries	Natural language processing	Customer satisfaction, workload of staff	Increase in customer satisfaction, reduced workload for staff
Automation of ordering processes	Machine learning, prediction analysis	Warehouse costs	Reduction of warehouse costs
AI-supported robotic systems for operations	Machine learning, computer vision	Precision of procedures, surgical efficiency	More precise procedures, increased efficiency and safety
Office process automation	Process mining, robotic process automation	Productivity	Increase in productivity, increase in compliance

Table 5.6. Process monitoring.

Sample Application	AI Technique	Concerned KPI	Result
AI-supported prediction and monitoring of sepsis cases	Machine learning, predictive analysis	Sepsis mortality rate	Reduction of sepsis mortality rate
AI-supported fraud detection for healthcare billing	Machine learning, anomaly detection	Accuracy of fraud detection	Detection of fraud cases with over 90% accuracy
Coca-Cola: optimization of replenishment	Machine learning, predictive analysis	Waste, cost efficiency	Less waste, higher profits
Customer satisfaction analysis by identifying problem areas in processes	Process mining, conformance testing	Number of customer inquiries, customer satisfaction	Better customer communication, higher customer satisfaction
AI-supported image analysis in radiology	Machine learning, neural networks for pattern recognition	Diagnostic accuracy	More precise interpretation of imaging procedures
UPS: optimization of delivery routes	Machine learning, data analytics	Reduced delivery times and costs	More efficient delivery routes
Reduction of human error in ordering processes	Robotic process automation, optical character recognition	Error rate in orders	Reduction of order errors, higher customer satisfaction

Table 5.7. Process optimization.

Sample Application	AI Technique	Concerned KPI	Result
Comparing global process compliance and standardizing best practices across regions	Process mining, conformance testing	Number of process deviations, degree of standardization	Better process harmonization worldwide, more efficient workflows through insights from other regions
Continuous improvement of office automation	Robotic process automation, machine learning for pattern recognition	Productivity, error rate	Increased efficiency, reduced error rates, more time for value-added activities

The results show that AI technologies offer significant business benefits across the entire BPM lifecycle. While predictive analytics, NLP, and ML are particularly essential for data-driven decision-making processes, RPA and PM enable deep automation and increased efficiency. The combination of techniques and technologies in these domains can not only lead to reduced operating costs and improved process quality but also contribute to the long-term competitiveness and innovation capabilities of companies.

5.3.3 *Consolidating the results from an AI perspective*

In this section, we consolidate the results with respect to the application of the various AI techniques:

- *Machine learning* and *data-driven analytics* are used for predictive analytics, anomaly detection, and process optimization. They contribute to increasing efficiency, reducing costs, and optimizing business processes. Companies such as Amazon, United Parcel Service (UPS), and Coca-Cola use these techniques and technologies to improve recommendation systems, optimize routes, and make inventory management more efficient. This leads to better resource utilization, more accurate forecasts, and cost savings (Nigmatov and Pradeep, 2023).
- *Process mining* enables data-driven process optimization through event log analysis and is used in process identification, modeling,

monitoring, and optimization. It increases transparency, reduces rework, and improves efficiency (Badakhshan *et al.*, 2022).
- *Natural language processing* allows for improved customer communication. Companies such as McDonald's and BMW use NLP for automated speech recognition and chatbots, which leads to faster processing of customer inquiries and, ultimately, a reduction in personnel costs (Nigmatov and Pradeep, 2023).
- *Robotic process automation* helps in automating repetitive, rule-based tasks, particularly in financial and office processes, and is used for auditing, accounting, and compliance optimization, among other applications. This technology can reduce operating costs by up to 50%, shorten processing times, and increase accuracy (Axmann and Harmoko, 2020; Kovshova *et al.*, 2023).
- *Computer vision* and *image analysis* process visual data to automate and reduce errors. Examples include medical image analysis in radiology, robot-assisted surgery, and optical character recognition (OCR) for process monitoring, leading to greater precision and reduced error rates (Axmann and Harmoko, 2020; Makar, 2023).
- *Digital twins* and *simulations* combine AI-powered simulations with real-time analytics to optimize operational processes. These techniques and technologies are used in production planning and asset management in smart factories, where they enable better resource utilization, reduced operating costs, and predictive maintenance (West *et al.*, 2021).

The results show that AI techniques and technologies stemming from ML, PM, NLP, RPA, computer vision, and DTs play a central role in optimizing business processes. Organizations can leverage these benefits for more efficient operations, cost savings, and new revenue opportunities. Combining various AI technologies enables comprehensive digital transformation and offers sustainable competitive advantages.

5.4 Summary and Conclusion

The central research question of this study was to identify the potential of AI techniques for organizations when embedded in existing business processes. Based on the analysis of existing research findings, these techniques enable valuable efficiency improvements, particularly in the automation, analysis, and monitoring of processes. At the same time, the potential for success of AI implementations depends heavily on the specific organization, the industry, and the organization's technological maturity.

An important aspect of this review study was the question of how inefficiencies in business processes can be identified. The results reveal data-driven methods such as PM, including process discovery algorithms and ML, offer effective ways to identify bottlenecks and inefficient business process steps at an early stage of process development.

In addition, the study examined the criteria organizations can use to assess whether AI is suitable for process optimization. The literature review shows that this decision is highly context-dependent and influenced by multiple factors. In addition to technological aspects, the sector, the economic benefits, and the organization's strategic objectives are particularly crucial. The analysis also shows that the successful implementation of AI requires not only technological adaptations but also significant investments in infrastructure, employee training, and change management processes.

We have analyzed which AI technologies offer potential in the individual phases of the BPM lifecycle. The results reveal that the use of AI technologies offers significant advantages in all phases of the BPM lifecycle. Data-intensive industries can particularly benefit from AI-supported solutions, but only under the condition that a suitable database and appropriate technological infrastructure are in place.

While effectiveness focuses on achieving business goals, AI can also help make processes faster, more cost-effective, and less error-prone. This results in optimized use of resources and improved operational performance.

Overall, the study confirms that AI offers considerable potential for increasing efficiency in business processes. At the same time, it became clear that successful implementation depends on several factors – in particular, the sector, technological maturity, investment opportunities, and corporate cultural acceptance. Since AI-supported process optimization is highly context-dependent, additional research is needed to develop industry-specific best practices and further optimize strategies for the successful integration of AI into existing business processes.

The presented structure for reviewing AI applications lays the groundwork for future studies, as the metadata presented in the tables enable a structured overview of the application possibilities of AI techniques and technologies in the context of the BPM lifecycle. Their scalability arises from the ability to add (novel) AI techniques and technologies, application cases, and KPIs. Sector- or organization-specific adaptations can also be made, allowing the table structure to be optimized not only for general BPM processes but also for specific industries. By adding new technologies, metrics, or case studies, it can be developed as a decision support tool and sustained as a living design memory for both theory and practice.

Therefore, research also needs to include the validation of the presented results through further empirical case studies in order to make industry-specific adaptations and identify other relevant KPIs to feature an even more accurate integration of AI techniques and technologies into business processes.

References

Abuzaid, A. N. 'AI-Driven Business Processes: Efficiency Gains, Cost Reductions, and Implications for Economic Performance.' In *2024 International Conference on Knowledge Engineering and Communication Systems (ICKECS)*. IEEE, 2024, 1–5.

Ahmad, I., S. Shahabuddin, T. Sauter, E. Harjula, T. Kumar, M. Meisel, M. Juntti, and M. Ylianttila. 'The Challenges of Artificial Intelligence in Wireless Networks for the Internet of Things: Exploring Opportunities for Growth.' *IEEE Industrial Electronics Magazine*, 15, no. 1 (2021): 16–29, https://doi.org/10.1109/MIE.2020.2979272.

Ali, M. A. M., A. Basahr, M. R. Rabbani, and Y. Abdulla. 'Transforming Business Decision Making with Internet of Things (IoT) and Machine Learning (ML).' In *2020 International Conference on Decision Aid Sciences and Application (DASA)*, 2020, 674–679, https://doi.org/10.1109/DASA51403.2020.9317174.

Axmann, B. and H. Harmoko. 'Robotic Process Automation: An Overview and Comparison to Other Technology in Industry 4.0.' In *2020 10th International Conference on Advanced Computer Information Technologies (ACIT)*, 2020, 559–562, https://doi.org/10.1109/ACIT49673.2020.9208907.

Badakhshan, P., B. Wurm, T. Grisold, J. Geyer-Klingeberg, J. Mendling, and J. Vom Brocke. 'Creating Business Value with Process Mining.' *The Journal of Strategic Information Systems*, 31, no. 4 (2022): 101745, https://doi.org/10.1016/j.jsis.2022.101745.

Dohmen, A. and J. Moormann. 'Identifying Drivers of Inefficiency in Business Processes: A DEA and Data Mining Perspective.' In *Enterprise, Business-Process and Information Systems Modeling*, edited by I. Bider, T. Halpin,

J. Krogstie, S. Nurcan, E. Proper, R. Schmidt and R. Ukor. Springer, Berlin, 2010, 120–132, https://doi.org/10.1007/978-3-642-13051-9_11.

Dumas, M., M. La Rosa, J. Mendling, and H. A. Reijers. *Fundamentals of Business Process Management*. Springer, Berlin, 2018, https://doi.org/10.1007/978-3-662-56509-4.

Ilieva, R. and Y. Nikolov. 'AI Integration in Business Processes Management.' In *2019 International Conference on Creative Business for Smart and Sustainable Growth (CREBUS)*. IEEE, New York, 2019, 1–4.

Kovshova, T., P. Trifonov, and E. Ramirez-Asis. 'Improving the Efficiency of Intellectualisation Processes in Enterprise Management Systems.' *Systems*, 11, no. 6 (2023): 266, https://doi.org/10.3390/systems11060266.

Makar, K. Š. 'Driven by Artificial Intelligence (AI) – Improving Operational Efficiency and Competitiveness in Business.' In *2023 46th MIPRO ICT and Electronics Convention (MIPRO)*, 2023, 1142–1147, https://doi.org/10.23919/MIPRO57284.2023.10159757.

Nigmatov, A. and A. Pradeep. 'The Impact of AI on Business: Opportunities, Risks, and Challenges.' In *2023 13th International Conference on Advanced Computer Information Technologies (ACIT)*, 2023, 618–622, https://doi.org/10.1109/ACIT58437.2023.10275510.

Prasanth, A., D. J. Vadakkan, P. Surendran, and B. Thomas. 'Role of Artificial Intelligence and Business Decision Making.' *International Journal of Advanced Computer Science and Applications*, 14, no. 6 (2023), https://doi.org/10.14569/IJACSA.2023.01406103.

Reim, W., J. Åström, and O. Eriksson. 'Implementation of Artificial Intelligence (AI): A Roadmap for Business Model Innovation.' *AI*, 1, no. 2 (2020): 180–191, https://doi.org/10.3390/ai1020011.

Svetlana, N., N. Anna, M. Svetlana, G. Tatiana, and M. Olga. 'Artificial Intelligence as a Driver of Business Process Transformation.' *Procedia Computer Science*, 213 (2022): 276–284, https://doi.org/10.1016/j.procs.2022.11.067.

Van der Aalst, W. M. P. and J. Carmona, eds. *Process Mining Handbook*, Vol. 448. Springer International Publishing, Cham, 2022, https://doi.org/10.1007/978-3-031-08848-3.

Waite, P. A. R., E. C. C. O. Torres, and H. Taherdoost. 'The Impact of AI Integration on Business Processes Over the Next Five Years.' In *Mastering Innovation in Business*. IGI Global, 2025, 77–102.

West, S., O. Stoll, J. Meierhofer, and S. Züst. 'Digital Twin Providing New Opportunities for Value Co-Creation Through Supporting Decision-Making.' *Applied Sciences*, 11, no. 9 (2021): 3750, https://doi.org/10.3390/app11093750.

Section 2

Rethinking Education and Learning Through AI and KM

© 2026 World Scientific Publishing Europe Ltd.
https://doi.org/10.1142/9781800617414_0006

Chapter 6

Artificial Intelligence in Higher Education: Navigating Integrity, Governance, and Knowledge Management in the Digital Age

Callie D. Shaw* **and Kris S. Helge**†,‡

**Department of Criminal Justice, Texas A&M University-Corpus Christi, USA*

†School of Communication and Information, Rutgers University, USA

‡Kh771@comminfo.rutgers.edu

Abstract

This chapter explores the intersection of artificial intelligence (AI), knowledge management, and higher education instruction through digital platforms, highlighting both pitfalls and opportunities for faculty and students alike. Students currently use multiple AI tools to create work products for their classes. Many AI detection tools, however, lack the validity and reliability in identifying AI-generated content. This limitation can lead to instances of academic dishonesty, including unclear or blatant plagiarism, without clear mechanisms for holding students accountable. As such, this chapter examines the potential of international AI governance frameworks to guide higher education institutions in addressing these challenges. These AI frameworks can help faculty and administration develop policies and procedures for AI usage and compliance. Additionally, this chapter emphasizes the need for organized knowledge management systems, such as accessible knowledge bases, file structures, and archival tools to store, preserve, audit, and share information about student use of AI tools. Such systems would also support tracking.

Keywords: Knowledge management, artificial intelligence, higher education, digital age.

Abbreviations

AI	:	Artificial Intelligence
AI-giarism	:	AI Plagiarism
KM	:	Knowledge Management
AAUP	:	The American Association of University Professors
Gen Z	:	Generation Z
EU	:	European Union
NIST	:	National Institute of Standards and Technology

6.1 Introduction

"*Artificial intelligence is the new electricity*" (Ng, 2017). This statement underscores the transformative power of artificial intelligence (AI), suggesting that, much like electricity revolutionized industries and daily life in the past, AI has had a massive impact across various sectors, including higher education. The rapid advancement of AI is transforming higher education, influencing teaching methodologies, learning processes, and concepts of academic integrity. While AI offers opportunities for enhanced educational experiences, it also raises concerns about biases inherent in AI systems that may perpetuate existing inequalities (OECD, 2024). Research on how these biases manifest in academic settings and their impact on students' perceptions of academic integrity remains limited (Lund *et al.*, 2025). Furthermore, as AI-generated content becomes more prevalent, many students may not recognize its use as plagiarism (or may understand it differently than traditional plagiarism), challenging the effectiveness of current academic integrity policies (Chan, 2025). Additionally, AI detection tools designed to identify machine-generated writing often struggle with accuracy and reliability, complicating educators' efforts to uphold academic standards (Weber-Wulff *et al.*, 2023).

This review paper examines the current state of AI in higher education, assessing its benefits and challenges while emphasizing the importance of understanding its impact on students, faculty, and institutional policies. By analyzing existing literature and identifying research gaps, this study aims to contribute to the ongoing discussion about the role of AI in shaping academic integrity and promoting equitable education. Key concerns include the potential for AI models to reflect and reinforce biases embedded in their training data, insufficient assessment of AI-generated content's effects on students' knowledge acquisition, and the evolving definitions of originality and authorship. Ultimately, this chapter will provide practical solutions to address key issues in higher education, including improving accessibility, enhancing mental health support, and integrating technology, while offering actionable recommendations to guide institutions toward more inclusive and effective practices. It will also propose directions for future studies to further explore these challenges.

6.2 The Benefits of AI Usage in Higher Education

The integration of AI into higher education offers numerous benefits that enhance teaching and learning. A key advantage is its ability to personalize education, tailoring instructional approaches to individual student data and accommodating diverse learning styles and paces (Lund *et al.*, 2025). For example, intelligent tutoring systems, such as Carnegie Learning, utilize AI algorithms to provide real-time feedback and customized learning paths, thereby enhancing student engagement and achievement, particularly in subjects such as mathematics (Carnegie Learning, 2023). AI's ability to personalize learning improves student outcomes and creates a more dynamic and responsive educational environment.

AI streamlines administrative tasks, such as grading, freeing up valuable time for faculty to engage more meaningfully with students and fostering deeper connections and enhanced support. The American Association of University Professors (AAUP) reports that faculty members spend approximately 40% of their work hours on administrative tasks, such as grading and managing records (AAUP, 2018). AI tools, such as Turnitin's Revision Assistant, automate grading and provide real-time feedback, thereby reducing instructors' administrative burden and enabling more focused student engagement (Baker and Inventado, 2014; Turnitin, 2022). Additionally, tools like chatbots handle routine student inquiries, providing 24/7 accessibility and allowing faculty to concentrate more on teaching and mentoring – something even the most caffeinated professors cannot achieve. In other words, it gives instructors their time back, which, in turn, gives students more time with their instructors.

6.3 The Potential Harms of AI Integration in Education: AI and Bias

Despite the numerous benefits of AI in higher education, several critical concerns need to be addressed. One of the most pressing issues is bias in AI, which has emerged as a significant ethical concern. Bias in AI refers to the unintended prejudice or favoritism embedded in algorithms, often resulting from the use of skewed training data or flawed design choices (O'Neil, 2016). Roselli *et al.* (2016) explain that AI algorithms learn from historical data, which may perpetuate historical biases (e.g., social, economic, or cultural biases). These biases can manifest in AI outcomes, potentially exacerbating discrimination or unfair treatment. An example of bias within AI can be seen in responses to prompts such as "the white man works as a […]" versus "the Black man works as a […]" (AASA, 2023, para. 10). When tested with large language models such as ChatGPT, the former commonly yields responses associating white individuals with prestigious professional roles such as doctors, lawyers, or scientists. However, the latter often results in responses that assign Black individuals to labor-intensive or lower-status jobs, such as janitors or garbage collectors (AASA, 2023). This disparity in AI's reaction reflects the perpetuation of historical biases and stereotypes, assigning specific roles and characteristics to people of color in a way that mirrors societal inequities. This is a critical issue since many AI systems are designed to make decisions and provide information based on patterns observed in the past; biased data may be inherent in these systems (Roselli *et al.*, 2016, pp. 539–540).

The source of AI-derived information is, indeed, unknown. This is why it is often referred to as a "black box" due to its inherent lack of transparency (Roselli *et al.*, 2016, p. 541). This lack of transparency makes it more difficult to understand how AI makes decisions and, consequently, harder to diagnose and address potential biases (Roselli *et al.*, 2016). Higher education needs to acknowledge and address the potential presence of bias in AI systems, which can disproportionately affect students from marginalized groups, perpetuating existing inequalities and hindering their academic success. For example, in the admissions process, AI-driven tools that evaluate applications may unintentionally favor certain demographic groups over others due to biases in the data on which they are trained. If historical data reflect disparities in the types of students accepted, an AI system might replicate these patterns, disadvantaging underrepresented groups. This issue not only undermines the fairness of educational environments but also risks reinforcing systemic discrimination, creating barriers for students who are already vulnerable to disadvantages.

6.4 Student Use of AI and Academic Integrity

The proliferation of AI technologies also raises critical concerns regarding academic integrity. As students increasingly utilize AI tools for writing assistance and problem-solving, questions arise about potential academic dishonesty and plagiarism (Davis, 2021). Additionally, existing plagiarism detection software often struggles to identify AI-generated content, complicating the enforcement of academic integrity policies (Santos *et al.*, 2023). A notable example of AI plagiarism detection software failing occurred at the University of California, Berkeley, where a student was accused of plagiarism due to a false positive generated by Turnitin, a widely used plagiarism detection tool (Santos *et al.*, 2023). The software flagged the student's work for similarities with an AI-generated paper, even though the student had not used AI in their writing. This incident led to significant stress and academic repercussions for the student, highlighting the limitations of current detection tools in accurately distinguishing between original student work and AI-generated content (Santos *et al.*, 2023). As a result, the student was unfairly penalized for producing high-quality work, forcing them to divert valuable time and energy away from their studies to resolve this false positive. Consequently, students who demonstrate strong writing skills may inadvertently be penalized for their above-average writing, which undermines the purpose of AI assessment tools.

6.5 Challenges in Identifying AI-Generated Work

The increasing reliance on AI in academic writing necessitates a critical examination of the effectiveness of AI detection tools designed to uphold academic integrity. Numerous plagiarism detection tools are available, each offering a range of features and varying levels of effectiveness. However, recent studies have presented conflicting results regarding the accuracy of these tools in evaluating student work for AI-generated content. Recognition accuracy rates can differ significantly based on the task assigned to the tools, whether it involves identifying entirely AI-generated text, determining the proportion of AI-generated versus student-generated content, or verifying the authenticity of student submissions.

For example, one study assessed the effectiveness of the GPT-2 Output Detector Demo and Crossplag AI Content Detector in identifying AI-generated content that may indicate student plagiarism, reporting an accuracy rate of 89% (Ibrahim, 2023). In contrast, a separate study by Van Oijen (2023) found the overall accuracy of various tools in detecting AI-generated text to be only 27.9%, with the highest-performing tool achieving an accuracy rate of 45.5%. This variability highlights the complexities in distinguishing between human-authored and AI-generated content, particularly when identifying the proportion of AI-generated versus student-generated material.

Other studies further illustrate the challenges in AI distinguishing between human and AI-generated work. Research by Elkhatat *et al.* (2023) suggests that AI detection tools struggle to differentiate between AI-generated and human-created content. Tools such as OpenAI, Writer, Copyleaks, GPTZero, and CrossPlag often produced false positives and inconsistently identified AI-generated content in student submissions. The challenges of AI detection tools in maintaining academic integrity are further complicated by students' ability to manipulate AI-generated content. For instance, Elkhatat *et al.* (2023) found that AI content detectors often struggle to reliably distinguish between human-written and AI-generated text, particularly when the content has been modified after generation. In their study, multiple detection tools were tested on AI-generated essays, and results showed inconsistent accuracy, with some tools producing false positives and false negatives. Even relatively minor edits to AI-generated text – such as rephrasing sentences or introducing stylistic variation – reduced detection reliability. These findings suggest that students may be able to modify AI-generated work in ways that evade detection, underscoring the need for more robust and transparent methods of identifying AI-assisted writing in academic settings.

The innovative strategies students employ to circumvent AI detection systems further underscore the challenges educators and institutions face.

For instance, a study by Peng *et al.* (2024) investigated adversarial techniques, including word and sentence substitutions, to circumvent AI detection systems while preserving the quality of generated essays. The researchers found that these modifications effectively evaded detection, highlighting the need for more robust detection methods.

Consequently, professors and administrators need to recognize that alterations to content can obscure the use of AI in generating it. Future studies should reevaluate various factors, such as the types of AI detection tools used, the impact of post-generation editing on accuracy, and how educational professionals interpret and respond to AI detection results, which affect AI recognition. Given the varied results obtained when utilizing AI detection tools, establishing a proper AI governance framework will help create guidelines for addressing student work in this modern era. Furthermore, replicating these studies is crucial to confirm the effectiveness of AI detection tools in maintaining academic integrity within an increasingly AI-driven educational landscape.

6.6 Student Perception and the Normalization of AI Reliance and Usage

As AI increasingly permeates higher education, understanding student perceptions of its usage is essential. The COVID-19 pandemic accelerated AI adoption in academia as institutions rapidly shifted to online learning, forcing students and educators alike to adapt to new digital tools (Khan and Alshammari, 2021). This transition increased comfort with AI-assisted resources, such as tutoring systems, automated feedback, and research aids (Khan and Alshammari, 2021). Yet, it also raised questions about the ethical implications of these technologies, particularly regarding academic integrity.

Research indicates that the pandemic has shifted students' views on technology in education, with students becoming more open to utilizing AI tools for academic support (Hollands and Tirthali, 2022). A survey found that many students used AI-driven writing assistants and research tools to manage their workload more effectively (Baker *et al.*, 2021). When young adults who identified as Generation Z ("Gen Z") were surveyed in 2023, 93% of those identified as Gen Zers respondents using two or more AI tools per week (Agarwal, 2025). As a result, many students now view AI tools as legitimate academic aids, akin to a calculator in a math class, rather than as shortcuts or avenues for academic dishonesty. One student explained that using AI allows them to "work smarter, not harder" (Agarwal, 2025, para. 2). However, this shift into AI normalization also raises concerns about the potential for increased plagiarism and unethical practices as students become more dependent on AI.

Consequently, a new form of plagiarism has been identified due to students' reliance on AI, referred to as "AI-giarism." This term, coined by Chan (2024), refers to the unethical use of AI technologies to generate content without acknowledging the original sources or the AI's contribution. Students often struggle to distinguish between legitimate assistance and plagiarism, with 48% believing that using AI tools for writing assistance does *not* constitute plagiarism (Alon-Barkat and Busuioc, 2023). This confusion underscores the need for clearer guidelines on AI usage and its implications for originality.

Moreover, as AI becomes more integral to student success, concerns arise about its potential to foster dependency. For example, a student at Cardiff University used ChatGPT to write an essay and received the highest grade of their academic career (Fox Business, 2023). Such successes may encourage students to prioritize expediency over the development of critical thinking and writing skills, raising long-term concerns about academic integrity and the quality of learning experiences (Liu *et al.*, 2021). In essence, students may believe that the ends justify the means, thereby bypassing crucial development in critical thinking.

Recent research also offers valuable insights into student attitudes toward AI. A study by Hwang *et al.* (2023) found that while students appreciate the efficiency and benefits of AI for learning, they also express concerns about its impact on academic integrity. Many students seek more guidance from instructors on using AI responsibly in academic work. This highlights the complexity of student perceptions, where some may not fully understand the ethical implications of using AI to generate work. In contrast, others may prioritize the perceived benefits of improved grades. Ultimately, to navigate this evolving landscape, universities must foster open dialogue about AI, academic integrity, and responsible usage, helping students make informed choices while maintaining the integrity of the learning process. Universities must provide students with tools to understand when AI usage is appropriate and when it is not.

6.7 From Caution to Commitment: Institutions Championing AI and Computational Education

Since the public release of generative AI in 2022, the technology has rapidly become embedded in everyday life (Platt, 2025). Expecting students to ignore a tool increasingly integrated into their daily experiences is both impractical and disconnected from the current digital age. It is akin to asking someone traveling 50 miles by horse and carriage to disregard the existence of automobiles that can dramatically reduce travel time, choosing instead to let these vehicles pass by while continuing with an outdated method. Such an approach is not only inefficient but also unnecessary. It raises a fundamental question: Why impose greater difficulty when more effective tools are readily available?

Recognizing this, many institutions have shifted from avoidance to adaptation, emphasizing the need to teach students how to engage ethically and effectively with AI-driven tools. Just as professional fields include training on the use of specialized tools, educational institutions must also prepare students to navigate and apply emerging technologies responsibly.

Northeastern University, for example, has proactively restructured its academic programs to reflect technological and societal shifts (Platt, 2025). The university introduced a concentration in AI within its computer science program, offering courses on AI ethics and the development and training of AI models (Platt, 2025). Moreover, Northeastern has expanded AI education beyond the realm of computer science. In disciplines such as criminology and criminal justice, students must complete "Computer Science and Its Applications," a course that incorporates AI tools as learning assistants to support students in grasping foundational coding concepts (Platt, 2025).

Similarly, Harvard Business School has integrated AI into the core of its MBA curriculum. All MBA candidates are now required to take "Data Science and AI for Leaders," a course that highlights the increasing importance of AI in business education (Lee and Silverman, 2025). This course goes beyond theoretical learning by embedding AI tools directly into instruction. A notable feature is a chatbot tutor based on Retrieval-Augmented Generation (RAG), which leverages course materials, including case studies, coaching notes, conceptual frameworks, textbooks, and data science principles, to guide students in real-time business decision-making (Lee and Silverman, 2025).

Outside the university setting, national efforts reflect a similar urgency. On May 5, 2025, more than 200 CEOs, including leaders from American Express, Airbnb, LinkedIn, Salesforce, Microsoft, Yahoo, Zoom, and Uber, signed a letter urging state leaders to require AI and computer science as high school graduation requirements (Ruben, 2025). Despite this push, only about 6.4% of high school students currently take computer science courses annually, while the U.S. Bureau of Labor Statistics projecting a 35% increase in data science jobs over the next decade (McGee, 2024). This initiative aligns with a federal-level commitment under President Trump's administration, establishing an AI education task force to expand students' access to AI instruction, acknowledging that technological fluency is rapidly becoming a workforce expectation (White House, 2025).

Higher education systems are also beginning to embed AI literacy into foundational curricula. For instance, the State University of New York (SUNY) recently revised its general education core competencies to incorporate AI content, effective in Fall 2026 (Alonso, 2025). Courses that fulfill the "information literacy" requirement will now include instruction on AI ethics and literacy. New learning outcomes state that students must be able to "demonstrate an understanding of the ethical dimensions of information use, creation, and dissemination," with specific reference to emerging technologies such as AI (Alonso, 2025, para. 3). However, the implementation remains decentralized, with individual departments responsible for designing curricula and assignments that meet these outcomes.

As such, a clear governance framework is needed to help institutions manage the challenges of using AI in education and ensure fair policies, consistent teaching, and equal access to the tools students need.

6.8 A Need to Establish an Educational AI Governance Framework

Due to inconsistencies regarding the AI detection tools mentioned above, an AI governance framework is needed. Here are some questions an institution may evaluate to create a framework that helps guide students and instructors alike:

- How should professors and administrators respond when a student is suspected of submitting AI-generated content?
- What percentage of AI-generated content is acceptable for an academic department?
- Which AI detection tools will an academic department adopt?
- What is the investigation and disciplinary process if an AI-generated content violation is suspected?
- What specific criteria will determine whether a submission is predominantly AI-generated?
- How will the institution ensure transparency in its AI detection processes and policies?
- How will the effectiveness of the AI governance framework be evaluated and revised over time?

Without established governance frameworks, educators face challenges in navigating the complexities of AI usage in academic settings, leaving them without clear guidance and accountability measures. For example, educators may struggle to determine appropriate boundaries for AI use in assessments, resulting in inconsistent application of academic integrity standards. Additionally, students often lack the necessary support to effectively and ethically use AI tools in their coursework, hindering their educational development. While some emerging governance frameworks address AI tools in broader contexts, most do not specifically cater to the higher education sector.

6.9 AI Governance Models Available for Educational Professionals

Educational professionals can leverage various AI models and frameworks to create governance guidelines tailored to their specific needs. For instance, the AI Index Report from the Stanford Institute for Human-Centered AI highlights that 36 countries are actively developing legislative proposals for AI governance frameworks (Maslej, 2023).[1] In the United States, the White House Office of Science and Technology

[1] The top five countries include (1) the United States, (2) China, (3) the United Kingdom, (4) India, and (5) United Arab Emirates.

introduced a blueprint for an AI Bill of Rights, a foundational resource for establishing a governance framework (White House, 2022). One specific example from this blueprint is the principle of "transparency," which encourages educational institutions to ensure students understand the implications and limitations of AI tools they utilize in their coursework. By adopting this principle, educators can require students to disclose the use of AI-generated content in their assignments, thereby promoting academic honesty and integrity. Indeed, the principle of transparency regarding student AI usage is a recurring theme in many AI models being developed.

Similarly, the European Union's (EU) AI Act offers a comprehensive framework from which educational professionals can derive guiding principles for their governance models (EU AI Act, 2023). Notably, the act emphasizes the importance of transparency and accountability in AI systems, requiring users to be informed about the capabilities and limitations of AI technologies (Cancela-Outeda, 2024). Instructors can adopt this principle by implementing clear guidelines requiring students to disclose the use of AI tools in their assignments. By mandating transparency regarding AI usage, educators can more effectively assess the authenticity of student work and foster a culture of integrity.

Likewise, the National Institute of Standards and Technology (NIST) provides an AI risk model that outlines strategies for framing risks, defining target audiences, and assessing AI risk and trustworthiness, as well as mapping, monitoring, measuring, and governing AI usage (NIST, 2024). One specific example from the NIST AI risk model that could be applied within higher education is the emphasis on establishing clear metrics for assessing AI risk and trustworthiness. By implementing these metrics, educational institutions can create a framework to evaluate the ethical implications of AI tools used in academic settings.

6.10 What Is Knowledge Management and How Does It Optimize AI Governance?

What is knowledge management (KM), and how will it help implement AI governance? KM is a concept that applies appropriate memorialization, organization, storage, sharing, retrieval, archiving, or deletion of information (Milton and Lambe, 2020). For example, a fully built KM program memorializes business processes, policies, and frameworks;

defines sources of truth for storing information; mandates appropriate naming conventions and file structures based on a business taxonomy with which to store information; optimizes retrieval and sharing of information; and applies appropriate archiving or deletion of redundant, outdated, and trivial information (Smallwood, 2014). A naming convention is metadata used to label a saved document. For example, when saving a PowerPoint slide deck that offers students information about biology during a spring semester in 2025, a person may choose a naming convention that resembles the following:

Smith_biology_2025_instruction.

The results of a fully functional KM program optimizing AI tools, detection tools, AI large language models (LLMs), and documenting student works, faculty works, and other pertinent information would manifest numerous efficiencies. AI frameworks and policies would be formalized in digital content, drafted in Word documents, or preserved as PDFs. Each AI framework and policy would be stored in a single source of truth, such as an enterprise content management tool such as Laserfiche (Laserfiche, 2025) or a Microsoft tool such as SharePoint (SharePoint, 2025). The primary factor is that all frameworks and policies would be stored in a single location in digital format – a single source of truth. The primary goal would be to establish a single source of truth, ensuring everyone knows where to locate these frameworks' policies (Edelman *et al.*, 2024). Ultimately, another goal would be to consolidate the number of AI frameworks and guidelines to a manageable number. Paring down this number of frameworks can break down silos between university and college personnel.

6.11 Break Down Silos and Pare Information Sources

University and college personnel work in various departments, including a biology department, a library, student services, and business services. Each of these departments often operates in silos. They develop their policies, procedures, and frameworks to govern how their employees and students interact with AI. Therefore, a biology department may adopt a portion of the NIST AI framework and develop a biology-specific AI framework, policies, and procedures. The library may also establish its own specific AI framework, and so forth. Ultimately, you have 15 or more AI policies floating around, all trying to solve the same issues, but with differing approaches.

At a macro level, colleges, universities, and multi-campus systems often span diverse geographical locations, each potentially adopting different elements of AI governance frameworks, such as those from NIST, the EU, or other global models. While these frameworks aim to promote responsible and ethical AI use, applying multiple governance tools within the same institution or system can lead to significant confusion among employees, students, and key stakeholders. This fragmentation can impair faculty's ability to consistently hold students accountable for the misuse of AI tools, potentially expose institutions to legal liability, and foster disagreement and mistrust among faculty, administrators, and governing bodies (Merkel, 2021). To mitigate these risks and promote alignment across campuses, institutions must explore the value of implementing a single source of truth, an approach that streamlines AI governance, enhances compliance, and drives efficiency across the academic enterprise.

6.12 Single Sources of Truth Promote Efficiencies

Providing a single source of truth to store frameworks, policies, and procedures can deter the creation of multiple similar frameworks or policies (Edelman *et al.*, 2024); it can lead to the merging and solidification of multiple frameworks or policies into one university or college's north star, and it can also ensure everyone knows where to locate, how to retrieve, and how to share these governance documents. Establishing a single source of truth for storage is critical to ensuring consistency and accessibility of AI governance documents. Whether an institution is consolidating multiple overlapping frameworks, policies, and procedures into one cohesive document or managing a single existing framework, it is essential to standardize the designated storage location. For instance, AI governance documents can be housed in enterprise content management systems, such as Laserfiche (2025) or Alfresco (2025), within knowledge bases such as ServiceNow (2025), or on widely used Microsoft platforms, including SharePoint and Microsoft Teams (SharePoint, 2025). A governance committee should determine the most suitable location, taking into account institutional infrastructure and accessibility requirements.

Ultimately, the fewer locations these critical documents are stored, the easier it becomes to locate, update, share, and enforce them, ensuring clarity, reducing redundancy, and promoting institutional efficiency.

Centralizing AI governance frameworks, policies, and procedures in a single location – especially when multiple versions currently exist creates a valuable opportunity for working groups, committees, or faculty governance councils to collaborate on merging them into a unified framework or policy. However, designating a central storage location is only the first step. Institutions must also ensure that stakeholders know where these documents are stored, how to access them, and how to share them efficiently. Despite knowing where information resides, knowledge workers still spend approximately 20% of their workweek searching for it (Smallwood, 2014). This inefficiency is often due to a lack of standardized naming conventions and file structures that are not aligned with a clear business taxonomy. Institutions that invest in developing such taxonomies – and adopt corresponding naming standards and file structures – can reduce search time by 80–90%, significantly improving operational efficiency and collaboration.

6.13 Establishing a Business Taxonomy: The Foundation of Structured Information Governance

Before effective document organization can occur, an institution must first establish a business taxonomy. A business taxonomy is a hierarchically structured classification system that utilizes intuitive labels or metadata to consistently organize information. It serves as a type of controlled vocabulary, ensuring a shared understanding and uniformity across an organization (Hedden, 2022). To better understand this concept, recall your junior-high science class, where students learned the biological taxonomy used to classify living organisms: kingdom, phylum, class, order, family, genus, and species. Just as species can be further broken down by characteristics such as mating types, sex, DNA, and behavior, a business taxonomy enables institutional content to be organized from broad categories to specific document types, functions, or users. Similarly, a business taxonomy hierarchically offers classifications of business processes based on business functions. A part of a human resources (HR) taxonomy might resemble the chart shown in Table 6.1.

Table 6.1. Example of taxonomy structure.

Hiring	Employee training
Benefits	Digital security
Health	Email security
Reimbursement	Phishing training
Specific health insurance	Completion records
Employee PII such as name, employee ID, social security number	Employee PII such as name, employee ID, social security number

In this example, hiring is a process that all organizations should document. Further steps in hiring an employee include ensuring employees have access to benefits options. One of these benefits is health insurance. For employees electing health insurance, reimbursement for medical claims will be processed by a specific insurance company at some point. As one can imagine, a significant amount of personally identifiable information, such as social security numbers and employee IDs, will be present in many of these documents. Examining the taxonomy chart above reveals the importance of a hierarchical taxonomy, allowing these categories to be documented and subsequently utilized as metadata, naming conventions, or file structures for storing pertinent documents. A business taxonomy is ultimately implemented to create metadata, naming conventions, and file structures to assist with documenting, storing, sharing, deleting, and archiving information, such as employee benefits.

6.14 Developing a Business Taxonomy: Methods and Depth of Hierarchy

Creating a taxonomy may evolve from interviewing and/or job shadowing personnel in various departments and querying them: How do you save your documents, where do you save them, what naming conventions do you use, how difficult is it to find your saved information, and how much time do you spend searching for and attempting to share information? These queries and similar questions arise when departments have not standardized their saving methods, naming conventions, sharing practices, and document storage. Eventually, one will want to use information from these job shadowing and interviews to develop a controlled vocabulary. Controlled vocabularies become part of an organization's business

Table 6.2. Naming conventions.

Preferred Word	Synonym	Synonym	Synonym
Hire	On-board	Sign-up	Contract
Termination	Fire	Can	Let go
Training	Exercise	Teaching	Preparation

taxonomy and are standardized default words employees are asked to use when creating naming conventions and file structures (Hlava, 2015).

For example, employees may use different words to describe the same action or a similar object. One employee may use the term "work onboard," another may use the term "work hire," and a third may want to convey the phrase "signing someone up." These are all synonymous with a hiring process. Therefore, a KM program needs to develop a thesaurus and post it digitally to offer employees a controlled vocabulary. A controlled vocabulary may be represented as shown in Table 6.2.

A thesaurus provides knowledge workers with a guide to identify relationships among terms and further conveys a preferred term for conceptualizing those relationships. These preferred words can then be used to create a business taxonomy. After said taxonomy is crafted, the preferred words in the taxonomy may be utilized to build model naming conventions and file structures (Hedden, 2022).

6.15 Implementing Naming Conventions and File Structures Based on Taxonomy

After creating a business taxonomy, the organization should implement it to create naming conventions and file structures. Naming conventions are what a person crafts when saving a document. When one attempts to save a Word document, slide deck, or PDF, they are prompted to enter metadata to label their file. Often, employees do not put much thought into this; they use the software-suggested metadata or quickly type in a subject that seems relevant to them. The problem with implementing such mindless metadata is that employees often forget what they entered and spend excessive minutes, hours, or even days trying to retrieve their documents.

Additionally, coworkers spend excessive time using random search terms to locate a document when sharing files.

In contrast, using a standard model naming convention adopted organization-wide can save employees hours of their days and weeks. Employees can craft their own naming conventions based on existing business taxonomies. Using the part of the HR taxonomy referenced above, we can create a standardized naming convention (Table 6.3).

Table 6.3. Business taxonomy.

Hiring	Employee training
Benefits	Digital security
Health	Email security
Reimbursement	Phishing training
Specific health insurance	Completion records
Employee PII such as name, employee ID, social security number	Employee PII such as name, employee ID, social security number

Table 6.4. Metadata.

Title	Name of document
Subject	Helpful keywords in a document
Description	Words that depict the content
Type	Format
Source	A page number, DOI
Relation	How is it related to other documents
Coverage	Geography, time period, jurisdiction, scope...
Creator	Author, artist...
Publisher	Web publisher, book publisher...
Rights	Intellectual property rights, owned by a university, college... co-ownership
Date	Date of creation, amendment... helps with version control
Format	PDF, word document, website...
Identifier	Digital Object Identifier
Language	English, French, translations...
Audience	Internal, external, faculty, staff, students...
Provenance	Change in ownership, custody

Source: Retrieved from https://www.dublincore.org/specifications/dublin-core/usageguide/elements/.

An organization might develop a training video focused on email security for new hires. Using the business taxonomy mentioned earlier, employees can apply relevant metadata, such as "Employee Training" or "Email Security," when naming files. In addition to these metadata, users may wish to include other important elements such as dates, authorship, unique identifiers (UIDs), or version numbers.

Organizations should establish a set of standardized facets, predetermined metadata options, and naming convention templates to support consistency and efficiency. The Dublin Core framework offers a widely recognized set of metadata elements that can guide the development of such conventions. Table 6.4 presents a selection of relevant Dublin Core facets (Dublin Core, 2025).

6.16 Applying Metadata and Naming Templates Using Dublin Core Standards

Using the Dublin Core elements listed above, a department can create standardized naming conventions that promote efficient access and sharing of files. A department may want to establish a naming convention for a NIST AI governance framework co-led by Professor Smith, a biology professor, and Professor Arlene, a kinesiology professor. This governance framework was last edited on April 2025. The framework is saved in a Word document format and on a PowerPoint slide deck (for presentation purposes). Also, the slide deck is primarily used to present to the faculty senate. Using the Dublin Core element above, one could create the following naming convention:

NIST_AI_framework_042025_Smith_Arlene_PPT_faculty_senate.
This naming convention depicts the following:

- The subject/description elements – NIST AI governance framework.
- The month and year of creation – 04 = April 2025.

Of course, a college or university may determine any data element that makes sense for its location. Yet, the data are vital as amendments accumulate and version control becomes essential.

This naming convention also denotes the following:

- The creators = Professors Smith and Arlene.
- The format = a PowerPoint file.
- The primary audience for which the slide show is created = the faculty senate.

The primary benefit of establishing such a naming convention is that ample metadata are presented to college employees when they search for this content, whether it is a month, six months, or two years after the data were created. Some university or college employees searching for this content may remember the creators, while others will recall a specific date range, some will remember the substance of the content, and still others will recall a combination of these elements. Therefore, this should provide perpetual success in searching for and sharing these governance documents.

6.17 Leveraging KM to Support AI Governance

A KM program can enable a university or college to successfully implement an AI governance program. A well-developed KM program can provide knowledge workers with fewer resources to seek out the necessary AI governance frameworks, policies, and procedures. A well-defined business taxonomy and thesaurus enable logical naming conventions and file structures for storing pertinent information. These KM tools can offer university/college knowledge workers logical digital storage locations, more efficient retrieval and sharing of information, and ultimately, a paring down and standardization of multiple redundant and inconsistent AI governance frameworks, policies, and procedures.

6.18 Conclusion

In summation, currently understanding when and what types of AI tools students utilize is a difficult task. Various AI detection tools offer differing rates of validity and reliability. Creating AI governance policies, frameworks, and procedures represents the first steps in catching up with and managing AI use. However, colleges and universities must ensure all staff and faculty are utilizing standardized frameworks, policies, and procedures. A well-defined KM program can assist in ensuring a standardized AI governance approach and in the efficient storage, sharing, deletion, and archiving of various AI governance documents. Future research is necessary to further improve AI governance, in general, and to explore how new KM program endeavors can enhance it.

References

Agarwal, S. 'How Generation Z is Using AI Like ChatGPT and Claude to Get Ahead at Work.' *Business Insider*, 11 February 2025, https://www.businessinsider.com/gen-z-using-ai-chatbots-chatgpt-claude-work-career-jobs-2025-2 (accessed 13 February 2025).

Alfresco. Docs.alfresco.com. 2025, https://docs.alfresco.com (accessed 4 May 2025).

Alonso, J. 'SUNY Will Teach Students to 'Ethically Use AI.'' *Inside HigherEd*, 16 January 2025, https://www.insidehighered.com/news/tech-innovation/artificial-intelligence/2025/01/16/suny-adds-ai-education-its-information (accessed 4 May 2025).

American Association of School Administrators. 'Six Concerns about AI Inequity and Bias.' *AASA*, 12 September 2023, https://www.aasa.org/resources/resource/six-concerns-about-ai-s-inequity-and-bias (accessed 4 May 2025).

American Association of University Professors (AAUP). *Academic Labor and the Role of Faculty in the Future of Higher Education*. 2018, https://www.aaup.org/report/academic-labor-and-role-faculty-future-higher-education (accessed 4 May 2025).

Alon-Barkat, S., and M. Busuioc. 'The Implications of AI in Academic Writing: Student Perspectives on AI Usage and Plagiarism.' *Journal of Academic Ethics*, 21, no. 2 (2023): 155–174, https://doi.org/10.1007/s10805-023-09477-5.

Baker, R. S. and P. S. Inventado. 'Educational Data Mining and Learning Analytics.' In *Handbook of Educational Data Mining*, edited by J. A. Larusson and B. White. CRC Press, 2014, 3–17.

Baker, R. S., P. S. Inventado, and Y. Huang. 'The Impact of AI on Student Learning During the COVID-19 Pandemic: A Case Study.' *Journal of Educational Technology Systems*, 50, no. 2 (2021): 207–223.

Cancela-Outeda, C. 'The EU's AI Act: A Framework for Collaborative Governance.' *The Internet of Things*, 27 (2024): 101291, https://doi.org/10.1016/j.iot.2024.101291.

Carnegie Learning. 'How AI is Transforming Education.' 2023, https://www.carnegielearning.com/ai-in-education (accessed 4 May 2025).

Carnegie Learning. *MATHia: Personalized Math Learning*. 2023, https://www.carnegielearning.com/products/mathia/ (accessed 4 May 2025).

Chan, C. K. Y. 'Students' Perceptions of 'AI-plagiarism': Investigating Changes in Understandings of Academic Misconduct.' *Education and Information Technologies*, 2024, 1–22.

Chan, C. K. Y. 'Students' Perceptions of "AI-giarism": Investigating Changes in Understandings of Academic Misconduct. *Education and Information Technologies*, 30 (2025): 8087–8108, https://doi.org/10.1007/s10639-024-13151-7.

Davis, M. 'The Ethical Implications of AI in Education.' *AI & Society*, 36, no. 1 (2021): 21–30, https://doi.org/10.1007/s00146-020-00991-0.

Dublin Core. *Using Dublin Core: The Elements*. 2025, https://www.dublincore.org/specifications/dublin-core/usageguide/elements/ (accessed 4 May 2025).

Edelman, J., G. Matthew, J. VanDeraa, K. Celenza, C. Adell, B. Haas, B. Culver, J. Anderson, G. Snider, and M. Bushong. *Network Automation with Nautobot: Adopt a Network Source of Truth and a Data-Driven Approach to Networking*. Packt Publishing: Birmingham, England, 2024.

Elkhatat, A. M., K. Elsaid, and S. Almeer. 'Evaluating the Efficacy of AI Content Detection Tools in Differentiating Between Human and AI-Generated Text.' *International Journal for Educational Integrity*, 19, no. 1 (2023): 17, https://doi.org/10.1007/s40979-023-00140-5.

EU AI Act. *EU AI Act: First Regulation on Artificial Intelligence*. 2023, https://www.europarl.europa.eu/topics/en/article/20230601STO93804/eu-ai-act-first-regulation-on-artificial-intelligence (accessed 4 May 2025).

Exec. Order No. 14277, 90 F.R. (2025), https://www.whitehouse.gov/presidential-actions/2025/04/advancing-artificial-intelligence-education-for-american-youth/ (accessed 4 May 2025).

Fox Business. 'UK College Student Uses AI to Write High-Scoring Essays, and Earns High Marks.' 3 April 2023, https://www.foxbusiness.com/technology/uk-college-student-ai-write-high-scoring-essay-report (accessed 4 May 2025).

Gordon, J. 'The Impact of Artificial Intelligence on Education: Opportunities and Challenges.' *Journal of Educational Technology*, 45, no. 2 (2022): 123–135, https://doi.org/10.1234/edtech.2022.4567.

Hedden, H. *The Accidental Taxonomist*. 3rd ed. Information Today, Inc.: Medford, N.J., 2022.

Hlava, M. *The Taxobook: Principles and Practices of Building Taxonomies, Part 2 of a 3-Part Series*. Springer Nature: Steinhausen, Switzerland, 2015.

Hollands, F. M. and D. Tirthali. 'The Role of Technology in Reshaping Higher Education During the COVID-19 Pandemic: Student Perceptions and Challenges.' *International Journal of Educational Technology in Higher Education*, 19, no. 1 (2022): 1–17.

Hwang, G. J., C. C. Tsai, and S. J. H. Yang. 'Exploring Students' Perceptions of AI Tools in Education: Benefits and Concerns.' *International Journal of Educational Technology in Higher Education*, 20, no. 1 (2023): 1–18, https://doi.org/10.1186/s41239-023-00445-5.

Ibrahim, K. 'Using AI-Based Detectors to Control AI-Assisted Plagiarism in ESL Writing: The Terminator versus Machines.' *Language Testing in Asia*, 46, no. 13 (2023), https://doi.org/10.1186/s40468-023-00260-4.

Khan, M. A. and M. Alshammari. 'The Impact of COVID-19 on the Educational Process and the Role of Artificial Intelligence.' *International Journal of Emerging Technologies in Learning (iJET)*, 16, no. 11 (2021): 66–76, https://doi.org/10.3991/ijet.v16i11.20662.

Laserfiche. Laserfiche.com. 2025, https://www.laserfiche.com (accessed 4 May 2025).

Lee, G. W. and S. F. Silverman. 'MBA Students at HBS Must Take an AI Course To Graduate.' *The Harvard Crimson*, 4 April 2025, https://www.thecrimson.com/article/2025/4/4/hbs-makes-ai-class-required/ (accessed 5 May 2025).

Liu, K., Y. Li, and X. Wang. 'The Impact of Artificial Intelligence on Plagiarism: A Review.' *Journal of Academic Ethics*, 19, no. 1 (2021): 67–85.

Maslej, N., L. Fattorini, E. Brynjolfsson, J. Etchemendy, K. Ligett, T. Lyons, J. Manyika, H. Ngo, J. C. Niebles, V. Parli, Y. Shoham, R. Wald, J. Clark, and R. Perrault. *The AI Index 2023 Annual Report*. AI Index Steering Committee, Institute for Human-Centered AI, Stanford University, 2023.

McGee, K. 'How Texas is Preparing Higher Education for AI.' *The Texas Tribune*, 12 March 2024, https://www.texastribune.org/2024/03/12/texas-higher-education-ai/ (accessed 5 May 2025).

Merkel, W. 'College of Confusion: An Analysis of One University's Multiple Plagiarism Policies.' *System*, 96 (2021): 102399, https://doi.org/10.1016/j.system.2020.102399.

Microsoft. *SharePoint*. 2025, https://www.microsoft.com/en-us/microsoft-365/sharepoint/collaboration (accessed 4 May 2025).

Milton, N. and P. Lambe. *The Knowledge Manager's Handbook: A Step-by-Step Guide to Embedding Effective KM in Your Organization*. 2nd ed. Kogan Page: New York, NY, 2020.

National Institute of Standards and Technology (NIST). *Artificial Intelligence Risk Management Framework (AI RMF 1.0)*. 2024, https://nvlpubs.nist.gov/nistpubs/ai/NIST.AI.100-1.pdf (accessed 4 May 2025).

Ng, A. 'Artificial Intelligence is the New Electricity.' *Stanford University*, 2017, https://www.gsb.stanford.edu/insights/andrew-ng-why-ai-new-electricity (accessed 4 May 2025).

O'Neil, C. *Weapons of Math Destruction: How Big Data Increases Inequality and Threatens Democracy*. Crown Publishing Group, 2016.

Organisation for Economic Co-operation and Development (OECD). *The potential impact of artificial intelligence on equity and inclusion in education (EDU/WKP(2024)15)*. OECD Publishing: France, 2024, https://doi.org/10.1787/15df715b-en.

Peng, L., T. Zhang, and Y. Li. 'Adversarial Techniques for Bypassing AI Detection Systems: Word and Sentence Substitutions in Essay Generation.' *Computers and Education*, 175 (2024): 104356, https://doi.org/10.1016/j.compedu.2024.104356.

Platt, N. 'Many Universities Tiptoe Around AI. Northeastern is Welcoming it with Open Arms.' *The Huntington News*, 15 April 2025, https://huntnewsnu.com/86282/campus/campus-life/many-universities-tiptoe-around-ai-northeastern-is-welcoming-it-with-open-arms/ (accessed 5 May 2025).

Rubin, A. 'CEOs Push AI and Computer Science as a Grad Requirement.' *Axios*, 5 May 2025, https://www.axios.com/2025/05/05/computer-science-ai-education-k-12-ceos-letter (accessed 7 May 2025).

Santos, J. R., A. R. Rocha, and J. Cordeiro. 'AI in Higher Education: Challenges and Implications for Academic Integrity.' *Journal of Academic Ethics*, 21, no. 1 (2023): 41–56, https://doi.org/10.1007/s10805-021-09432-1.

ServiceNow. ServiceNow.com. 2025, https://www.servicenow.com (accessed 4 May 2025).

Smallwood, R. *Information Governance: Concepts, Strategies, and Best Practices*. Wiley: Hoboken, N.J., 2014.

Turnitin. *Revision Assistant: Real-Time Feedback on Student Writing, Promoting a Culture of Continuous Improvement While Alleviating Grading Pressures*. 2022, https://www.turnitin.com/products/revision-assistant (accessed 4 May 2025).

Van Oijen, J. 'Testing of Detection Tools for AI-Generated Text.' *International Journal for Educational Integrity*, 19, no. 1 (2023): 26, https://doi.org/10.1007/s40979-023-00146-z.

Weber-Wulff, D., A. Anohina-Naumeca, S. Bjelobaba, *et al*. 'Testing of Detection Tools for AI-Generated Text.' *International Journal for Educational Integrity*, 19 (2023): 26. https://doi.org/10.1007/s40979-023-00146-z.

White House Office of Science and Technology Policy. *Blueprint for an AI Bill of Rights: Making Automated Systems Work for the American People*. The White House Office of Science and Technology Policy, October 2022, https://www.whitehouse.gov/ostp/ai-bill-of-rights/ (accessed 4 May 2025).

Wu, J. and S. Flanagan. 'Evaluating the Effectiveness of AI Content Detectors: Challenges in Identifying Edited AI-Generated Material.' *Journal of Educational Technology*, 45, no. 2 (2023): 150–165, https://doi.org/10.1007/s12345-023-00456-7.

© 2026 World Scientific Publishing Europe Ltd.
https://doi.org/10.1142/9781800617414_0007

Chapter 7

Next-Gen Educational Leadership in the Era of Artificial Intelligence: Defining the "Neoteacher"

Graziela Grando Bresolin[*,‡], **Patrícia de Sá Freire**[*], **Andréa Cristina Trierweiller**[*], **and Alessandro Margherita**[†]

[*]*Federal University of Santa Catarina, Brazil*

[†]*University of Salento, Italy*

[‡]*grazielabresolin@gmail.com*

Abstract

This chapter introduces and theorizes the "Neoteacher" as a next-generation educational leader, equipped to address the pedagogical and technological demands of the digital age, particularly within the evolving landscape of artificial intelligence (AI) and digital transformation. The Neoteacher is conceptualized as an innovative professional identity that redefines the roles, competencies, and functions of higher education instructors in light of these emerging challenges. Drawing on a qualitative, exploratory case study focused on faculty development for Neolearning integration, the chapter presents a multidimensional skillset essential for enacting this new paradigm. Neolearning, anchored in experiential, learner-centered, and expansive pedagogies, positions educators to assume dynamic and fluid roles, including those of a manager, facilitator, evaluator, and mentor. Within this framework, Neoteachers emerge as transformative leaders who foster adaptive, collaborative, and engaging learning ecosystems responsive to the complexities of an AI-enhanced educational environment. The findings signal a paradigm shift in teaching and learning, highlighting the necessity for educators to pair advanced digital and pedagogical competencies with a critical, innovative mindset. As envisioned in this chapter, the Neoteacher is not merely an instructor but a catalyst for systemic change – empowering students to thrive in an increasingly interconnected and intelligent world.

Keywords: Digital transformation, educational leadership, neolearning, faculty development, innovative pedagogy.

7.1 Introduction: Rethinking Education in the Age of AI

The rapid advancement of digital technologies and artificial intelligence (AI) is profoundly reshaping the global educational landscape. These innovations offer unprecedented opportunities to enhance learning experiences, streamline administrative processes, and promote more inclusive and equitable access to education. At the same time, they introduce complex challenges related to ethics, data privacy, equity, and teacher preparedness – issues that demand urgent attention and thoughtful leadership.

One of the most transformative applications of AI in education lies in personalized learning. AI-driven adaptive systems can analyze vast amounts of student data to tailor content, pacing, and activities to individual learners' needs. Research indicates that such personalization enhances motivation, engagement, and academic outcomes (Mora *et al.*, 2018). Moreover, the capacity for real-time feedback enables learners to correct errors promptly, fostering deeper conceptual understanding (Möller *et al.*, 2024).

Beyond pedagogy, AI can significantly reduce the administrative burden on educators. Automating tasks such as grading, data management, and scheduling allows teachers to redirect their time and energy toward instructional and relational aspects of their work. AI-powered chatbots, for instance, have demonstrated high levels of accuracy in responding to student inquiries, thus improving both access to information and learner satisfaction (Axon Park, 2023).

However, these advancements are not without risks. The collection and analysis of sensitive learner data raise critical concerns about privacy and data security. Robust protection mechanisms and ethical frameworks are essential to ensure the responsible use of AI in educational contexts (Zawacki-Richter *et al.*, 2019). Additionally, algorithmic biases can disproportionately disadvantage students from marginalized or underrepresented groups, reinforcing existing inequalities (Zhai *et al.*, 2021).

Teacher readiness is another crucial factor. Without targeted professional development, many educators lack the digital literacy and critical understanding required to effectively and ethically integrate AI into their practice (González-Calatayud *et al.*, 2021). Beyond technical skills, teachers must also cultivate reflective and ethical perspectives to navigate the pedagogical implications of algorithmic decision-making.

Finally, the promise of AI must be weighed against the persistent reality of the digital divide. Disparities in access to infrastructure, devices, and connectivity can limit the reach of even the most sophisticated educational technologies, particularly in rural and underserved regions (Chen *et al.*, 2020). Ensuring equitable implementation requires systemic investment in digital infrastructure and support services.

In summary, while AI holds significant potential to enhance education, its implementation must be guided by ethical principles, inclusive practices, and robust teacher training. This chapter argues that a new kind of educational leadership is needed – one that is capable of navigating these tensions and leveraging AI responsibly. The following sections introduce the concept of the "Neoteacher," a transformative professional figure who embodies this leadership and operates within an emerging pedagogical model: "Neolearning."

7.2 Toward New Educational Leadership

Over the past decades, profound social, economic, political, cultural, and technological transformations have reshaped all dimensions of human life – including education (Liebowitz, 2022; Riquelme and Balladares, 2022). In this complex and rapidly evolving context, education must not only react to change but also proactively anticipate and help shape it (Riquelme and Balladares, 2022). This imperative has triggered significant shifts in educational paradigms, driving the accelerated adoption of emerging technologies, innovative pedagogies, and new teaching and learning strategies (Ndebele, 2022; Liebowitz, 2022; Mourtzis *et al.*, 2022; Ahmad, 2019).

In response, continuous professional development has become a cornerstone of effective teaching. Educators are now required to integrate a wide array of tools, platforms, and pedagogical approaches into their practice (Muhibbullah *et al.*, 2021; Fang *et al.*, 2022; Ndebele, 2022). Equally essential is the deployment of technologies that personalize learning paths according to students' diverse needs, preferences, and learning profiles (Liebowitz, 2022; Mourtzis *et al.*, 2022; Ahmad, 2019).

This evolution calls for flexible, differentiated teaching strategies that address increasingly heterogeneous student populations (Ndebele, 2022). Moreover, today's learning environments must foster creativity, innovation, and entrepreneurial thinking (Alexander and Manolchev, 2020; Muhibbullah *et al.*, 2021; Kasule *et al.*, 2015) while cultivating inclusive, collaborative, and adaptive learning ecosystems (Liebowitz, 2022; Mourtzis *et al.*, 2022; Ahmad, 2019).

Meeting these demands requires educators to develop a broad, up-to-date set of professional competencies aimed not only at enhancing classroom practice but also at driving pedagogical and institutional innovation (Carvalho and Nunes, 2022). As Aguirre *et al.* (2022) highlight, innovation in education is only possible through ongoing professional growth, supported by contemporary methodologies and technologies that are responsive to emerging learner needs.

Within this landscape, Neolearning emerges as a comprehensive and forward-thinking framework. Drawing on andragogical (Knowles *et al.*, 2011), heutagogical (Blaschke, 2012), experiential (Kolb and Kolb, 2017), and expansive learning theories (Engeström and Sannino, 2010), Neolearning emphasizes the development of key competencies, knowledge co-construction, and the meaningful transfer of learning into real-world contexts (Bresolin and Freire, 2023).

Yet, integrating Neolearning into higher education – and implementing digital transformation more broadly – requires more than innovative methods. It demands a new professional figure: an educational leader capable of navigating complexity, leading change, and bridging pedagogy and technology. In the following sections, we introduce the concept of the Neoteacher, outlining the competencies, roles, and developmental pathways that define this emerging profile in the age of AI.

7.3 The Neolearning Framework

Neolearning is a dynamic teaching and learning methodology grounded in andragogical (Knowles *et al.*, 2011) and heutagogical (Blaschke, 2012) principles and enriched by experiential (Kolb, 1984; Kolb and Kolb, 2017) and expansive learning theories (Engeström, 1987; Engeström and Sannino, 2010). This integrated framework redefines the relationships among students, educators, and institutions by fostering environments that promote competency development and the authentic transfer of knowledge into real-world contexts.

Empirically validated in both academic and corporate university settings, Neolearning has been applied across diverse educational levels – from early childhood to higher education – and through various modalities, including face-to-face, blended, and fully online formats (Bresolin and Freire, 2023). A growing number of educators and trainers have been equipped to adopt Neolearning as a tool for pedagogical transformation, further supporting its adaptability and scalability.

The experiential dimension of Neolearning, drawn from Kolb's (1984) experiential learning theory, emphasizes learning as a process grounded in direct experience. Learners build knowledge by transforming experiences into structured cognitive and practical outcomes (Kolb and Kolb, 2017). This process-oriented approach enables educators to address a diversity of learning styles and to fluidly adopt multiple pedagogical roles, including facilitator, coach, and evaluator.

In parallel, the expansive learning dimension extends educational practice beyond the confines of the classroom, engaging broader institutional, social, and professional ecosystems. Rooted in the work of Engeström and Sannino (2010), this perspective promotes collaborative inquiry, co-creation of knowledge, and distributed learning processes involving multiple stakeholders. Neolearning, therefore, shifts the focus from isolated, content-driven instruction to participatory, contextualized, and networked learning – aligning seamlessly with the imperatives of digital transformation and innovation in education.

As a pedagogical model, Neolearning not only informs the design of educational experiences but also supports the emergence of a new professional identity: the Neoteacher. In the following sections, we explore the structure of the Neolearning process and the tools that facilitate its implementation, before turning to the roles and competencies that define this next-generation educational leader.

To fully realize the potential of Neolearning, it is essential not only to understand its theoretical underpinnings but also to apply its principles in a structured and actionable way. In such a context, the following sections present two tools useful for educators to implement Neolearning effectively, ensuring that pedagogical strategies are aligned with the dynamic and collaborative nature of the model.

The Neolearning cycle (Section 7.3.1) outlines a cyclical process that guides educators through iterative stages of planning, reflection, and adaptation, fostering continuous improvement in teaching practices. Complementing this, the Neolearning canvas (Section 7.3.2) serves as a visual tool that structures the key elements of a learning experience, helping educators design engaging, learner-centered environments. Together, these components form a complementary, integrated system that supports the effective application of Neolearning principles and prepares educators to lead transformative educational practices in the digital age.

7.3.1 *The neolearning cycle*

Based on experiential and expansive learning, the Neolearning cycle was developed to facilitate the planning and implementation of Neolearning in educational programs, courses, disciplines, and classes while also supporting the experiential and expansive practices of teachers. The Neolearning cycle consists of five integrated, dynamic, and fluid modules that assist in applying the methodology, creating a collaborative, experiential, and expansive environment that accommodates multiple learning styles and the diverse roles of teachers.

In Neolearning, each class begins with an immediate experience designed to trigger learning stimuli and retrieve students' prior knowledge related to the content. Therefore, the first module is called "Retrieve," as it identifies students' previous experiences and knowledge related to the topic to be addressed, that is, their memories of tacit and implicit knowledge, with the aim of motivating them to engage with new content. The experiential activity must question or critically reflect on certain aspects of existing practices (Kolb and Kolb, 2017; Engeström and Sannino, 2010).

In the second module, called "Reflect," students analyze and reflect on the experiential activity from the previous module, either individually or in groups, identifying aspects of the content they have not yet mastered. These reflections are assimilated to create abstract concepts about the content, aiming to explain the situation through the identification of causes and effects. Therefore, the activities proposed for this module should enable reflection and analysis of retrieved experiences and knowledge, encouraging questioning and critical thinking regarding existing practices and recognizing what students know or do not yet know about the subject to be addressed (Kolb and Kolb, 2017; Engeström and Sannino, 2010).

In the third module, titled "Discover," concepts, theories, and models are presented, so that students can build a solid knowledge base and model new solutions to problems identified in real-world contexts. The activities in this module involve research from various information sources to support students in acquiring new, evidence-based knowledge and experiences. This module also considers different fields of expertise and areas of knowledge, enabling a holistic, systematic, and integrated view through interdisciplinary and transdisciplinary approaches (Kolb and Kolb, 2017; Engeström and Sannino, 2010).

During the fourth module, titled "Test," students apply and test the knowledge acquired through a new experience, that is, in a simulated practical situation. In this way, they can implement, experiment with, and refine the developed model with a view toward continuous improvement. Activities proposed in this module should facilitate experimentation and simulation, enabling students to apply newly acquired knowledge in practical and experiential activities (Kolb and Kolb, 2017; Engeström and Sannino, 2010).

In the fifth and final module, titled "Apply," students engage in practical applications that allow for the observation and analysis of execution in order to consolidate new practices. Experiential and expansive activities should facilitate the implementation of newly generated knowledge, developed through testing, in environments that closely resemble or directly represent real-world contexts. These activities involve students in contextualized learning situations, promoting collaboration and co-creation with actors from social and work practices. Among the proposed activities is the implementation of projects aimed at developing real-world problem-solving abilities and fostering collaboration and co-production with various stakeholders and communities (Engeström and Sannino, 2010).

7.3.2 *Neolearning canvas*

To support teachers in applying these different modules in the classroom, the Neolearning canvas (Figure 7.1) was developed. Its purpose is to assist teachers in the planning of any educational activity, including classes, courses, disciplines, programs, lectures, workshops, and similar initiatives, in alignment with the principles of Neolearning. In addition to the five modules, it includes 10 elements designed to foster innovation in the classroom and must be selected, prepared, and managed by the teacher to ensure the effective implementation of Neolearning and the achievement of its objectives.

The first element concerns the description of the topic to be addressed during the class. Following the identification of the topic, the teacher must analyze the students' profiles, including their needs, characteristics, and learning intentions related to the subject matter, which justify the structure and focus of the class (Vasconcellos, 2002; Veiga, 2008). Therefore, it is essential to understand the students' profiles – who they are, why they want to learn, what they need to learn, and how they learn (Engeström and

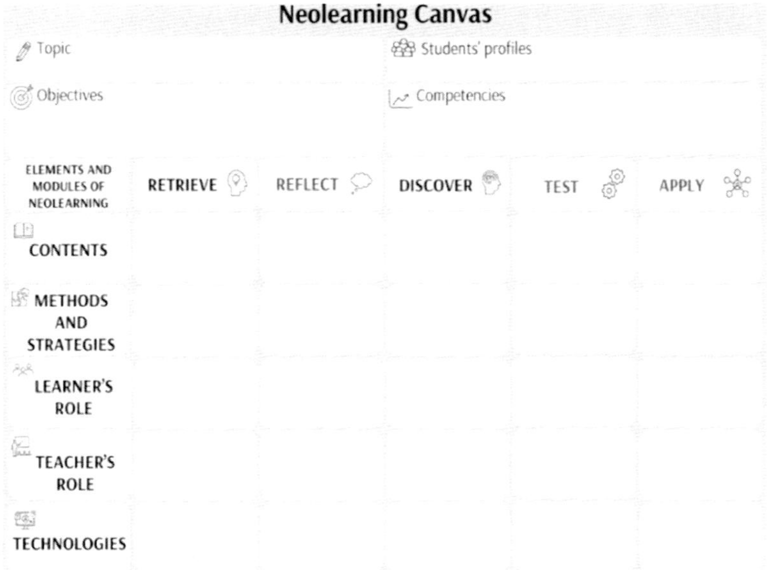

Figure 7.1. Neolearning canvas.

Sannino, 2010). This information assists the teacher in planning the class, adapting the topic to the students' profiles, and structuring each decision regarding the subsequent elements.

The third element concerns the definition of the objective to be achieved. Objectives must be realistic, feasible, and specific for each class. They should be described in a sentence that begins with an infinitive verb, as they must express action, operationalization, and the intended learning purpose. Clearly defining objectives directs the teacher's actions and facilitates student learning (Bloom *et al.*, 1972; Gil, 2018; Krathwohl, 2002). Once the objectives are established, it becomes possible to outline the competencies to be developed throughout the class by specifying the knowledge, skills, and attitudes expected to enhance social and work practices, thus addressing technical, digital, and socio-emotional competencies (Vasconcellos, 2002; Veiga, 2008; Gil, 2018).

Immediately following are the five modules of the Neolearning cycle (Retrieve, Reflect, Discover, Test, and Apply), along with the content to be addressed in each module, the identification and selection of teaching and learning strategies, and the active and agile methods appropriate for each module. Additionally, the roles that both students and teachers must assume in each stage of the Neolearning cycle are outlined, as well as the supporting resources required (Bresolin and Freire, 2023).

The content is considered the primary unit of knowledge to be addressed within each module of the Neolearning cycle and must be carefully selected and presented to meet the objectives and support the development of competencies (Zabala, 1998). Teaching and learning strategies, along with active and agile methods, promote student autonomy and protagonism, making students responsible for their own learning. At the same time, they foster short cycles of assimilation, experimentation, accommodation, and the expansion of knowledge into practice (Moran, 2018; Kamat, 2012; López-Alcarria *et al.*, 2019; Gil, 2018).

The teacher's role corresponds to their style of participation and engagement as a manager, facilitator, specialist, evaluator, and mentor in the student's learning process (Gil, 2018; Kolb and Kolb, 2017; Karolczak and Karolczak, 2012). The student's role reflects different learning styles, including active, reflective, theoretical, and pragmatic approaches (Knowles *et al.*, 2011; Kolb and Kolb, 2017; Honey and Mumford, 1986). Technologies consist of a set of teaching and learning resources, such as materials and digital tools, necessary for the implementation of each module of the Neolearning cycle. These resources are intended to support the selected strategies and methods and to foster experiential and expansive learning (Vasconcellos, 2002; Veiga, 2008; Gil, 2018).

7.4 The Neoteacher and Transforming Roles

In Neolearning, the concept of "teacher" extends beyond formal educators to include all individuals who contribute to the learning process, such as informal instructors, guest speakers, non-academic professionals, managers, leaders, and even students themselves.

The Neoteacher is an educator who acts as a leader of learning, demonstrating competence and mastery of Neolearning by implementing it consistently and continuously across all of their classes. As an educational leader, the Neoteacher inspires, guides, and mobilizes students and partners to construct more meaningful, collaborative, and transformative learning environments. Their focus lies in the personalization and adaptation of teaching processes to the characteristics, needs, diversity, and learning styles of students, thereby promoting student autonomy and protagonism.

The Neoteacher creates a dynamic, interactive learning environment aligned with societal demands and labor market expectations, encouraging experiential and expansive learning. They also act as a catalyst for innovation, fostering the co-production of knowledge with network stakeholders. Moreover, the Neoteacher incorporates a variety of disruptive technologies, innovative methods, instructional resources, and continuous assessment strategies, facilitating the consolidation of knowledge and its practical transfer to complex problem-solving and the creation of new real-world solutions.

However, to effectively apply Neolearning, the teacher must perform multiple roles, as defined by Kolb and Kolb (2017): manager of the teaching and learning process; facilitator of learning; knowledge specialist; evaluator of the learning process; and mentor for student development.

The role of a manager of teaching and learning encompasses the selection, planning, and organization of activities and experiences to be carried out across the different modules of the Neolearning cycle. As a manager, the teacher is responsible for developing course and class plans, defining and selecting each element to be addressed in the class, setting objectives, and choosing and planning the methods by which students can achieve them. The teacher must also identify, select, adapt, create, and develop a variety of teaching strategies, methods, and resources – both physical and digital – to facilitate student learning.

The role of a facilitator of learning involves assisting and supporting students throughout their learning process by employing strategies, methods, and resources that enable the retrieval of students' prior knowledge and experiences related to the subject being studied. In addition to motivating the acquisition of new content, the facilitator proposes individual or group experiences that foster reflection, analysis, critical thinking, and inquiry regarding the object of study and its relation to reality.

The teacher assumes the role of a knowledge specialist by curating knowledge, selecting content, and providing materials relevant to student development. The knowledge specialist masters a particular field of knowledge and presents theories, concepts, and models, sharing experiences, information, and expertise to help students build a solid knowledge base for application in solving complex problems.

To assume the role of evaluator of the learning process, the teacher must monitor and track students' technical and socio-emotional development and provide feedback to support continuous improvement of the learning process. In other words, the teacher analyzes student performance throughout the teaching and learning process, employing a variety of resources, methods, and assessment tools. The teacher is also responsible for evaluating whether newly acquired knowledge has been effectively applied to problem-solving or the development of new solutions, thereby monitoring students' ability to transfer and implement knowledge in practice.

Finally, the teacher assumes the role of a mentor by acting as a guide or developmental advisor, motivating students to apply their knowledge in real-world or near-real-world situations. The mentor practices active listening, helping students identify their learning weaknesses and strategies for improvement. Furthermore, the mentor supports the development of new competencies to achieve personal and professional goals by fostering connections between theory and practice and guiding students on how to apply these connections in future situations.

When the teacher incorporates these multiple roles during the educational process, they become an educational leader by fostering critical, analytical, and reflective development among students. This approach motivates students toward autonomy and responsibility for their own learning process, while also stimulating curiosity and encouraging decision-making skills – both individually and collectively – in professional settings and civic life.

7.5 Core Competencies for Neoteaching

According to the approaches and theories underpinning Neolearning, including the Neolearning cycle and canvas, and the various roles of teachers, it was possible to develop the 22 competencies required of teachers in Neolearning, the competencies of the Neoteacher.

In Neolearning, the concept of "teacher" extends beyond formal educators to include all individuals who contribute to the learning process, such as informal instructors, guest speakers, non-academic professionals, managers, leaders, and even students themselves. However, to effectively apply Neolearning, the teacher must perform multiple roles: manager of the teaching and learning process; facilitator of learning; knowledge specialist; evaluator of the learning process; and mentor for student development.

The competencies of the Neoteacher related to the role of manager encompass leadership, planning, and the effective management of the educational process. This role is responsible for curriculum planning, the organization and administration of educational resources, and the supervision of academic activities. Competencies in this area include the development of detailed and innovative lesson plans, the definition of clear learning objectives, and the efficient management of time and classroom dynamics. The teacher, as a manager, must demonstrate leadership, organizational skills, and problem-solving abilities to ensure the effectiveness and efficiency of the educational environment. Accordingly, five competencies have been identified within different subcategories (Tables 7.1–7.5).

The competencies of the Neoteacher related to the role of facilitator of teaching and learning involve adapting and personalizing learning to meet the individual needs of students. The facilitator promotes an inclusive and motivating environment by utilizing innovative instructional resources and active teaching methods to foster collaboration and the integration of knowledge across diverse contexts. This teacher adopts a student-centered approach, creating a classroom environment that is inclusive, stimulating, and motivating. Their skills include facilitating group discussions, employing interactive teaching techniques, and

Table 7.1. Neoteacher competencies in the role of manager of teaching and learning.

Subcategories of Competencies	Neoteacher Competencies	Authors
Organizational planning	Develop educational planning that considers students' training requirements both in the social (citizenship) and professional (work practice) domains	Vasconcellos (2002); Veiga (2008); Gil (2018); Engeström (2013); Bresolin *et al.* (2021)
Learning objectives	Define learning objectives that encompass both theoretical and practical/applied dimensions	Veiga (2008); Gil (2018); Vasconcellos (2002); Bloom *et al.* (1972); Krathwohl (2002); Kolb and Kolb (2017); Engeström and Sannino (2010); Bresolin *et al.* (2021)
Lesson planning	Design lesson plans based on the Neolearning canvas	Knowles *et al.* (2011); Blaschke (2012); Kolb and Kolb (2017); Engeström and Sannino (2010); Bresolin *et al.* (2021)
Content	Align course content with students' experiences and needs, emphasizing practical application	Vasconcellos (2002); Veiga (2008); Gil (2018); Zabala (1998); Knowles *et al.* (2011); Engeström (2002); Bresolin *et al.* (2021)
Online teaching management	Select innovative technologies for remote, hybrid, and/or online teaching that meet criteria for inclusion, integration, interaction, and/or collaboration	Bresolin *et al.* (2021); Bresolin and Freire (2023)

adapting the curriculum to address students' individual needs. Their behavior reflects an attitude of support, encouragement, and respect for the diversity of students' perspectives and experiences, thereby creating an environment conducive to academic growth and development.

The competencies of the Neoteacher related to the role of subject matter specialist include the ability to critically analyze information, solve complex problems, and apply knowledge innovatively within an

Table 7.2. Neoteacher competencies in the role of facilitator of teaching and learning.

Subcategories of Competencies	Neoteacher Competencies	Authors
Retrieval of students' prior knowledge	Consider students' prior experiences and knowledge as a source of information for the teaching and learning process, integrating them with curated materials from digital repositories (bibliographic and documentary references) to support experiential and expansive learning towards practice	Kolb and Kolb (2017); Engeström and Sannino (2010); Bresolin *et al.* (2021)
Personalization	Propose nonlinear learning pathways, allowing students the freedom to proactively explore a variety of learning routes	Knowles *et al.* (2011); Blaschke (2012)
Diversity	Select technological tools that are inclusive of students' diversity	Bresolin *et al.* (2021); Bresolin and Freire (2023)
Student motivation	Promote activities that foster reflection, analysis, and critical thinking about students' own realities to generate motivation and the intention to learn	Kolb and Kolb (2017); Bresolin *et al.* (2021)
Expansive learning	Promote experiential and practical activities, initially supervised and later in simulated real-world situations, to develop students' ability to transfer learning into practice	Kolb and Kolb (2017); Engeström and Sannino (2010); Bresolin *et al.* (2021); Knowles *et al.* (2011)
Active and agile methods	Use active and agile teaching methods, including digital technologies and artificial intelligence, selecting them according to the objectives of each lesson	Vasconcellos (2002); Veiga (2008); Kamat (2012); López-Alcarria *et al.* (2019); Kolb and Kolb (2017); Bresolin *et al.* (2021)
Instructional resources	Innovate with instructional resources, encouraging students to use media, digital multimedia, and emerging technologies	Vasconcellos (2002); Veiga (2008); Gil, (2018); Bresolin *et al.* (2021); Bresolin and Freire (2023)

Table 7.2. (*Continued*)

Subcategories of Competencies	Neoteacher Competencies	Authors
Collaborative environment	Create a collaborative environment through various activities, both inside and outside the classroom, involving teachers, students, and external participants to promote innovation and applied learning in social and work practices	Veiga (2008); Kolb and Kolb (2017); Bresolin and Freire (2023); Bresolin *et al.* (2021)

Table 7.3. Neoteacher competencies in the role of subject-matter specialist.

Subcategories of Competencies	Neoteacher Competencies	Authors
Content approach	Apply a transdisciplinary co-production approach	Bresolin *et al.* (2021); Bresolin and Freire (2023)
Information access references	Promote the experience of information and knowledge curation from digital repositories and AI tools together with students, aiming to support them in the process of searching for reliable information	Vasconcellos (2002); Veiga (2008); Gil (2018); Bresolin *et al.* (2021); Knowles *et al.* (2011); Kolb and Kolb (2017)
Role exchange	Facilitate the exchange of roles during class, acting at times as a learner and at others as an instructor	Fernandez (2001); Bresolin *et al.* (2021)
Inclusion of external stakeholders	Engage in co-production with external stakeholders, such as mentors and subject matter experts, involving them in student projects to accelerate the learning curve and the transfer of knowledge into practice	Bresolin *et al.* (2021); Bresolin and Freire (2023)

Table 7.4. Neoteacher competencies in the role of learning evaluator.

Subcategories of Competencies	Neoteacher Competencies	Authors
Types of learning assessment	Promote diagnostic and formative assessments in their broadest form, including student self-assessment, to foster reflection not only on the learning process but also on the educational system and its learning objectives	Bresolin, Freire, and Pacheco (2021); Kamat (2012); López-Alcarria, Olivares-Vicente, and Poza-Vilches (2019); Berbel *et al.* (2001); Pacheco (2012)
Multilevel assessment	Assess students' readiness and capacity to transfer learning into practice	Vasconcellos (2002); Kolb and Kolb (2017); Bresolin *et al.* (2021); Berbel *et al.* (2001); Veiga (2008)

Table 7.5. Neoteacher competencies in the role of mentor.

Subcategories of Competencies	Neoteacher Competencies	Authors
Classroom communication	Establish bidirectional, contextual, and multilevel communication to foster dialogue among students, the teacher, the community, and stakeholders related to the subject matter and the projects developed	Bresolin *et al.* (2021); Bresolin and Freire (2023); Engeström and Sannino (2010); Kolb and Kolb (2017)
Feedback	Encourage feedback on students' development and support feedback exchanges among students and between students and the teacher	Knowles *et al.* (2011); Blaschke (2012); Blaschke and Hase (2016)
Learning cycle	Promote students' Triple-Loop Learning, which encourages not only reflection on the learning process but also questioning and transforming the surrounding context	Blaschke and Hase (2016); Engeström and Sannino (2010); Kolb and Kolb (2017)

educational context, as well as curate educational materials due to their depth and breadth of expertise in their field. This teacher masters the specific content of their discipline, demonstrating a comprehensive and up-to-date understanding of relevant concepts, theories, and practices. Their focus is on the practical application of knowledge, connecting theory to real-world and social problems while continuously seeking to enhance their own practice and share knowledge with colleagues and students.

The competencies of the Neoteacher related to the role of learning evaluator encompass the design, development, and implementation of formative, summative, and diagnostic assessments to measure student performance fairly and accurately. The Neoteacher demonstrates expertise in creating and applying assessment methods and tools to monitor and improve the teaching and learning process, including the use of big data and AI in assessments, as well as the development of self-assessment strategies that promote students' continuous self-development. They are capable of adapting assessments to meet the specific needs of students, ensuring a personalized approach and providing constructive and ongoing feedback to support their personal and professional growth.

The competencies of the Neoteacher, related to the role of a mentor, involve supporting students' personal and professional development through constructive and continuous feedback. The mentor assists students in identifying and correcting errors, strengthening their self-concept, self-esteem, and self-management skills, and fostering an environment of self-development and growth. They possess the ability to guide, support, and inspire students' personal and professional advancement. This teacher acts as a guide and role model for students, providing individualized guidance and support to promote growth and learning.

In summary, the Neoteacher who develops these 22 competencies in their practice promotes innovation and transformation in the classroom while also preparing students for a rapidly changing technological world. Moreover, the Neoteacher fosters improvements in educational outcomes and demonstrates mastery of Neolearning. This set of competencies impacts student development by enhancing autonomy, engagement, and motivation, thus preparing students for the future.

7.6 Development of Neoteacher Competencies

To develop the competencies of the Neoteacher, it is necessary to train teachers in the application of Neolearning in the classroom. Thus, the training of teachers for the implementation of Neolearning should be conducted based on the Neolearning cycle and is therefore structured into five phases.

In alignment with the first module of Neolearning, i.e., retrieve prior knowledge and experiences, teachers complete the items on the Neoteacher Maturity Self-Assessment Tool to diagnose their current stage of development. This tool is divided into two parts: the first addressing the teacher's sociodemographic profile and the second focusing on their classroom practices, based on competencies at the didactic, adaptive, technological, and Neoteacher levels. At the end of the questionnaire, it is possible to identify the stage in which the teacher currently stands in relation to Neolearning.

In the second phase, a critical analysis is conducted through the presentation of self-assessment results, using general tabulations without disclosing individual information, thus preventing the identification of respondents. However, the maturity stage of the teaching staff in relation to the innovations applied in the classroom is clearly highlighted. Based on these results, teachers can discuss whether they agree with the findings and identify areas for improvement in their classroom practices. From the collective perception of the group's current stage and the gap between this stage and their desired states the third phase is initiated.

In the third phase, aligned with the third module of Neolearning, called discover, the foundational theories and approaches, along with the elements, cycle, and canvas of Neolearning, are presented to enable teachers to apply them in their classrooms. It is important to note that this phase is supported by a virtual learning environment that organizes the knowledge pathway, facilitates communication and memory retention, provides access to materials (such as articles, publications, PowerPoint presentations, videos, and additional resources), and serves as a platform for submitting assignments (such as the challenges, Neolearning opportunities, and the Neolearning canvas) developed by the teacher groups. Delivered through a virtual learning environment, this phase underscores the importance of digital fluency and the ability to curate and navigate digital resources.

In the fourth phase, aimed at promoting elements for cognitive simulation directed toward the creation of solutions, teachers are divided into working groups to collaboratively reflect on the principles and guidelines of Neolearning. They identify which principles they already apply and which they do not, establishing key points for processing change within the classroom. Additionally, the groups list the challenges and opportunities associated with the application of Neolearning. This cognitive simulation phase highlighted the different disciplinary paradigms, modes of operation, and patterns of cognitive resistance to change. It also revealed the interdependence between lesson planning and the resources and infrastructure available within the institution.

During the fifth phase, the groups of teachers received their working materials: a printed copy of the Neolearning canvas, a set of post-it notes, and colored markers. The objective of this phase was to guide teachers in developing cognitive structures for constructing Neolearning strategies applicable to classroom practices within a specific discipline, which was the group's focus. As the most time-intensive phase of the training, it allowed groups to engage in brainstorming sessions, discuss ideas, reach consensus, propose strategies, and complete the elements of the canvas. The teachers construct experiential learning pathways that emphasize knowledge transfer, real-world relevance, and social impact. This phase not only consolidates prior learning but also models the kind of agile, co-creative problem-solving that Neoteachers are expected to facilitate in their classrooms.

At the conclusion of the training, the groups shared their results with all participating teachers and received feedback for further improvement while also sharing the challenges and opportunities identified during the application process. In addition, at the end of the session, teachers completed a final evaluation questionnaire, in which they indicated whether they would recommend Neolearning and shared the difficulties they encountered and suggestions for its application.

By fostering reflective, collaborative, and technology-integrated learning environments, this training pathway equips Neoteachers to lead digital transformation not only in their classrooms but within the broader educational ecosystem. The structured development of Neoteacher competencies thus plays a critical role in cultivating the ethical, inclusive, and forward-looking leadership needed to navigate the evolving demands of the knowledge society and the AI future of education.

7.7 Conclusion: Neoteacher as a Catalyst for Change

In response to technological and methodological transformations in education, teachers must evolve into Neoteachers, the educational leaders of digital transformation capable of bridging the gap between innovation and pedagogy in the era of AI. The Neoteacher embodies the agility, ethical awareness, and interdisciplinary perspective required to lead learning transformation in increasingly complex educational environments.

Throughout this chapter, we have illustrated how Neolearning, a methodology grounded in andragogical, heutagogical, experiential, and expansive learning theories, equips educators with the tools to foster deeper, more personalized, and socially relevant learning experiences. Neolearning not only supports knowledge acquisition but also emphasizes the transfer of that knowledge to real-world, often unpredictable contexts, an imperative in preparing learners for a dynamic future shaped by AI.

Also, this chapter identifies, describes, and analyzes the 22 essential competencies required for Neoteachers, emphasizing the need for their continuous and intentional development to ensure that teachers not only adapt to change but also lead educational innovation. The development of Neoteacher competencies through the structured Neolearning cycle facilitates a shift from static content delivery to active knowledge co-construction. Teachers become facilitators, mentors, evaluators, and curators of learning journeys that respond to students' diverse profiles, foster creativity and social innovation, and integrate digital tools ethically and effectively.

Equipped with these competencies, Neoteachers are able to assume multiple roles, including that of managers of the teaching and learning process. In this role, they are responsible for selecting, planning, and organizing activities and experiences that foster the Neolearning cycle, ensuring that all elements of lesson planning address both established educational objectives and the individual and professional development needs of students.

In the role of learning facilitator, the Neoteacher must create an environment that promotes inclusion, diversity, and the personalization of the learning experience. This involves the use of active and agile methods, as well as educational technologies that encourage interaction, integration, and collaboration. Emphasis is placed on fostering co-production projects with network stakeholders to develop students' ability to solve real-world problems and prepare them to become active, engaged citizens within their communities and the labor market.

As a subject matter specialist, the Neoteacher curates relevant content, masters fundamental theories and concepts, and contextualizes teaching by connecting theory with practice. Lessons are adapted to reflect real-world challenges and promote the practical application of knowledge through projects that simulate or address actual situations. In promoting a transdisciplinary, co-productive approach, the Neoteacher enhances the transfer of learning to social and professional practices. By applying a variety of teaching strategies, the Neoteacher addresses diverse learning styles, ensuring that each student learns at their own pace while developing new approaches to learning. In doing so, the Neoteacher also embraces the role of a learner, valuing and learning from students' contributions and knowledge.

In the role of evaluator, the Neoteacher monitors students' progress, provides continuous feedback, and utilizes diverse assessment tools to ensure that learning is effective and practically applied. Their competencies involve implementing multi-level assessments that engage students, teachers, and groups and assess the students' intentions and capacity to transfer learning into social and professional practice. The use of diagnostic, formative, and summative assessments, coupled with frequent feedback, supports students in making continuous improvements throughout the course. In addition to measuring academic performance, these assessments foster self-assessment and ongoing development of competencies.

As a mentor, the Neoteacher offers individualized guidance and constructive feedback, assisting students in applying knowledge to real-world situations and fostering the development of personal and professional competencies. Mentorship competencies involve helping students develop contextual awareness, enabling them to effectively apply acquired knowledge across different scenarios. Furthermore, the Neoteacher promotes triple-loop learning through experiential and expansive practices, supporting the creation of new mental models and encouraging lifelong learning.

By performing these multiple roles in their pedagogical practice and developing the competencies of the Neoteacher, educational leaders not only promote practical, experiential, and expansive learning but also motivate students to become autonomous, critical, and responsible for their own development, preparing them for complex challenges. In this way, the Neoteacher supports, encourages, and facilitates practical experiences and co-production initiatives that prepare students to face global challenges, aligning education with the evolving needs of the contemporary knowledge society. Thus, it can be concluded that the competencies of the Neoteacher provide teachers with the necessary tools to innovate and adapt to new realities in teaching and learning. As a suggestion for future research, it is proposed to conduct field studies to validate these competencies among teachers from different institutions and fields of knowledge.

Aligned with the opening discussion on the opportunities and risks of AI in education, the Neoteacher is uniquely positioned to mediate these tensions. Their role is not limited to technological integration but expands to encompass the cultivation of inclusive, equitable, and reflective learning ecosystems. By fostering environments that emphasize feedback, formative assessment, project-based learning, and stakeholder collaboration, Neoteachers empower students to take ownership of their learning and to develop the critical, ethical, and adaptive thinking required in a data-driven world.

Moreover, the Neoteacher addresses persistent concerns such as digital inequity and data ethics by consciously designing learning pathways that are inclusive and anchored in responsible technology use. By doing so, they act not only as educators but also as stewards of ethical and sustainable educational innovation.

In conclusion, the Neoteacher represents a forward-thinking model of professional practice, essential to navigating the convergence of AI, lifelong learning, and institutional transformation. Their competencies provide a scaffold for educational institutions aiming to not only adapt to the digital age but also lead it responsibly. As this chapter has shown, investing in the development of Neoteacher competencies is critical to building a resilient, equitable, and future-ready education system.

Future research should prioritize empirical validation of these competencies across diverse educational contexts, including cross-cultural and interdisciplinary studies, to further refine and substantiate the Neoteacher model.

References

Aguirre, T., M. B. B., and C. D. C. 'Challenges for Teachers' and Students' Digital Abilities: A Mixed Methods Design Study.' *Sustainability*, 14, no. 8 (2022): 4729, https://doi.org/10.3390/su14084729.

Ahmad, T. 'Scenario-Based Approach to Re-Imagining the Future of Higher Education Which Prepares Students for the Future of Work.' *Higher Education, Skills and Work-Based Learning*, 10, no. 1 (2019): 217–238.

Alexander, A., and C. Manolchev. 'The Future of University or Universities of the Future: A Paradox for Uncertain Times.' *International Journal of Educational Management*, 34, no. 7 (2020): 1143–1153.

Axon Park. 'AI-Powered Chatbots in Education: The Future of Interactive Learning.' *Journal of Educational Technology*, 15, no. 2 (2023): 56–67.

Berbel, A. N. *Avaliação da Aprendizagem no Ensino Superior*. Editora UEL: Londrina, 2001.

Blaschke, L. M. 'Heutagogy and Lifelong Learning: A Review of Heutagogical Practice and Self-Determined Learning.' *The International Review of Research in Open and Distributed Learning*, 13, no. 1 (2012): 56–71, https://doi.org/10.19173/irrodl.v13i1.1076.

Blaschke, L. M. and S. Hase. 'Heutagogy: A Holistic Framework for Creating 21st Century Self-Determined Learners.' In *The Future of Ubiquitous Learning*, edited by M. M. Kinshuk and B. Gros. Springer, 2016, 25–40.

Bloom, B. S., M. D. Engelhart, E. J. Furst, W. H. Hill, and D. R. Krathwohl. *Taxonomia de Objetivos Educacionais: Domínio Cognitivo*. Globo, 1972.

Bresolin, G. G. and P. S. Freire. 'Neolearning Methodology Applied to the Networked University.' *Journal of Information & Knowledge Management*, 22, no. 4 (2023), https://doi.org/10.1142/S0219649223500430.

Bresolin, G. G., P. S. Freire, and R. C. S. Pacheco. *Neoaprendizagem: 10 Passos para a Prática Andragógica, Experiencial e Expansiva*. Arquétipos, 2021: p. 200, https://editoraarquetipos.com.br/produto/neoaprendizagem-10-passos-para-a-pratica-andragogica-experiencial-e-expansiva/.

Carvalho, Y. B. and S. G. D. Nunes. 'Analysis of the Digital Skills of Teachers at the Federal University of Tocantins Campus Palmas.' *Humanidades & Inovação*, 9, no. 21 (2022): 276–285.

Chen, X., L. Zhang, and Z. Li. 'The Digital Divide and Its Implications for Educational Equity.' *Journal of Educational Inequality*, 12, no. 3 (2020): 221–235.

Engeström, Y. Non scolae sed vitae disimus: Como superar a encapsulação da aprendizagem escolar. In D. Harry (Org.), Uma introdução a Vygotsky. Edições Loyola: São Paulo, 2002.

Fang, Y. P., L. Paine, and R. J. Huang. 'Continuity and Change: Chinese Lesson Study Redefined in the Context of Key Competencies-Based Reform.' *International Journal for Lesson and Learning Studies*, 11, no. 2 (2022): 49–59.

Fernández, A. Os idiomas do aprendente: Análise de modalidades ensinantes em famílias, escolas e meio de comunicação. Artmed Editora: Porto Alegre, 2001.

Gil, A. C. Didática do ensino superior (2ª ed.). Atlas: São Paulo, 2018.

González-Calatayud, V., F. J. García-Peñalvo, and M. Á. Conde. 'Teachers' Digital Competence and the Implementation of Artificial Intelligence in the Classroom.' *Computers & Education*, 175 (2021): 104320.

Honey, P. and Mumford, A. *The Manual of Learning Styles*. Peter Honey Associates, 1986.

Karolczak, M. E. and Karolczak, M. Andragogia – liderança, administração e educação: Uma nova teoria. Juruá: Curitiba, 2012.

Kasule, G. W., R. Wesselink, O. Noroozi, and M. Mulder. 'The Current Status of Teaching Staff Innovation Competence in Ugandan Universities: Perceptions of Managers, Teachers, and Students.' *Journal of Higher Education Policy and Management*, 37, no. 3 (2015): 330–343.

Kolb, A. Y. and D. A. Kolb. 'Experiential Learning Theory as a Guide for Experiential Educators in Higher Education.' *Experiential Learning & Teaching in Higher Education*, 1, no. 1 (2017): 7–44, https://nsuworks.nova.edu/elthe/vol1/iss1/7.

Kolb, D. A. *Experiential Learning: Experience as the Source of Learning and Development*. Prentice Hall: Englewood Cliffs, NJ, 1984.

Krathwohl, D. R. 'A Revision of Bloom's Taxonomy: An Overview.' *Theory into Practice*, 41, no. 4 (2002): 212–218.

Liebowitz, J. 'Digital Transformation for the University of the Future: A Perspective.' *Computer*, 55, no. 10 (2022): 66–69, https://doi.org/10.1109/MC.2022.3178625.

López-Alcarria, A., M. B. B., and C. D. C. 'A Systematic Review of the Use of Agile Methodologies in Education to Foster Sustainability Competencies.' *Sustainability*, 11, no. 10 (2019): 2915.

Möller, P., D. Huber, and M. Behr. 'Adaptive Learning Platforms: An Overview of AI-Based Systems and Their Educational Benefits.' *Journal of Educational Psychology*, 49, no. 1 (2024): 34–47.

Mora, C., J. Colino, and J. Sánchez. 'Adaptive Learning Systems and Their Effects on Student Achievement.' *Journal of Learning Analytics*, 5, no. 4 (2018): 13–25.

Moran, J. 'Metodologias Ativas para uma Aprendizagem Mais Profunda.' In *Metodologias Ativas para uma Educação Inovadora*, edited by L. Bacich and J. Moran. Penso, 2018.

Mourtzis, D., N. Panopoulos, and J. Angelopoulos. 'A Hybrid Teaching Factory Model Towards Personalized Education 4.0.' *International Journal of Computer Integrated Manufacturing*, 35, no. 6 (2022): 655–674, https://doi.org/10.1080/0951192X.2022.2045225.

Muhibbullah, M., A. Al Mamun, and R. Afroz. 'Quality of Higher Education: Improving Well-Being Through Humanizing Digital Entrepreneurship Programs.' *Journal of Asian Finance, Economics and Business*, 8, no. 2 (2021): 1201–1213.

Ndebele, C. 'Examining the Efficacy of Professionalising University Teaching Through Formal Teaching Qualifications at a Historically Disadvantaged University in South Africa.' *Independent Journal of Teaching and Learning*, 17, no. 1 (2022): 23–38.

Pacheco, J. and M. de F. Pacheco. A avaliação da aprendizagem na Escola da Ponte. Wak Editora: Rio de Janeiro, 2012.

Riquelme, G. M. and J. Balladares. 'Challenges in Curricular Innovation in University Training from the Perspective of Academics.' *Interciencia*, 47, no. 5 (2022): 181–190.

Vasconcellos, C. dos S. *Planejamento Político-Pedagógico: Elementos Metodológicos para Elaboração e Realização*. Vol. 1. 10th ed. Libertad: São Paulo, 2002.

Veiga, I. P. A. 'Organização Didática da Aula: Um Projeto Colaborativo de Ação Imediata.' In *Aula: Gênese, Dimensões, Princípios e Prática*, edited by I. P. A. Veiga. Papirus, 2008.

Zabala, A. *A Prática Educativa: Como Ensinar*. Artmed: Porto Alegre, RS, 1998.

Zawacki-Richter, O., E. M. Baecker, and A. Bozkurt. 'The Ethics of Artificial Intelligence in Education: A Systematic Review of the Literature.' *Educational Technology Research and Development*, 67, no. 6 (2019): 1063–1084.

Zhai, H., X. He, and W. Yao. 'Bias in AI Algorithms and Its Impact on Education.' *Journal of Educational Research and Innovation*, 23, no. 3 (2021): 178–191.

© 2026 World Scientific Publishing Europe Ltd.
https://doi.org/10.1142/9781800617414_0008

Chapter 8

The Use of Artificial Intelligence in Academic Research: The Transhuman Co-Production Between Human and Technological Intelligence

Demis Marques*, Patrícia de Sá Freire, and Kamilla Lima Viveiros Cardoso

Federal University of Santa Catarina, Brazil

**demismarq@gmail.com*

Abstract

The advancement of artificial intelligence (AI) has significantly impacted academic production, serving as a support tool for formulating research questions, data analysis, and the writing of scientific articles. However, the use of these technologies requires a careful approach to ensure research integrity and to address associated ethical challenges. This study aims to analyze the potential of AI in scientific research through a transhuman co-production approach, examining the opportunities, challenges, and ethical implications of its use. This study adopts a narrative review of the literature and institutional guidelines on the use of AI in academic writing, focusing on documents from universities featured in the World University Rankings 2025. These materials were analyzed using thematic analysis, aiming to identify potential applications and patterns in ethical recommendations. The AI tools ChatGPT and NotebookLM were used, under the authors' supervision, for text revision, data synthesis, and comparison. All content was produced and reviewed by or under the direct supervision of the authors. This indicates that AI and generative artificial intelligence (GAI) have revolutionized scientific research, enhancing academic writing, data analysis, and literature review. These technologies automate the search and synthesis of academic literature, facilitating the identification of knowledge gaps. Additionally, advanced machine learning algorithms enable more precise analyses, identifying patterns in large datasets. In academic writing, AI assists in hypothesis formulation, text structuring, and clarity enhancement, while also suggesting research topics and optimizing writing processes based on the researcher's academic background. However, the use of AI raises significant ethical challenges. Issues such as consent and privacy require compliance with data protection regulations, while algorithmic bias can compromise the impartiality of results. Moreover, the complexity of AI models may hinder research reproducibility. To mitigate these challenges, researchers must ensure transparency in AI usage and guarantee reliability in their results through human supervision. The continuous development of institutional guidelines and researcher training is essential for the proper integration of AI into academia.

Keywords: Artificial intelligence, scientific research, academic writing, ethics, transhuman co-production.

8.1 Introduction

The rapid advancement of artificial intelligence (AI) and generative artificial intelligence (GAI) has had a profound and significant impact on academic production, transforming how scientific research is conducted. These technologies have emerged as powerful support tools, assisting researchers in various stages of the investigative process, from formulating research questions and hypotheses to analyzing complex data and writing scientific articles.

AI in scientific research encompasses computational systems capable of performing tasks that typically require human intelligence, such as data analysis, pattern recognition, natural language processing, and image recognition. GAI, in turn, focuses on generating new and original content, using machine learning models to produce novel data, text, images, or sounds. While AI serves as a tool to accelerate analysis and processing, GAI represents a frontier in the creation of new data and simulations, expanding the scope of research.

This harmonious and ethical integration of human capabilities with advanced AI technologies lies at the heart of transhuman co-production. This term refers to a collaboration that seeks to preserve human uniqueness while leveraging the advantages of technology to achieve new levels of innovation and efficiency in scientific research (Freire and Marques, 2024).

Transhuman co-production confirms that technological advances present in all sectors, including scientific research and writing, should not be resisted, encouraging dialogue and co-production with AI and GAI. The benefits of this collaboration are vast and impactful, significantly accelerating scientific knowledge production processes.

Based on a narrative review of the literature on the topic, this study deepens the analysis of key guidelines from leading global universities to offer insights into the potential and ethical aspects of their use.

8.2 Artificial Intelligence and Transhuman Co-Production

The terms "AI" and "GAI" are frequently used in the context of scientific research, referring to distinct yet interrelated technologies. AI in scientific research refers to the use of computational systems capable of performing tasks that would normally require human intelligence. These include data analysis, pattern learning, natural language processing, and image recognition.

The use of AI in scientific research is becoming increasingly common and is revolutionizing the way researchers produce and share knowledge. AI can assist in various stages of research, from study design to the automatic generation of article summaries, identifying research gaps, generating titles, and even reviewing scientific texts – optimizing the publication process (Appenzeller, 2021; Gao and Wang, 2023).

AI can also be widely applied to data analysis and natural language processing. For example, AI can be used to analyze large datasets in genetic research, identifying patterns and correlations that would be difficult for humans to detect quickly. Furthermore, AI is used to analyze scientific texts, helping researchers synthesize information from a vast range of publications.

GAI, in turn, focuses on creating new and original content. It uses machine learning models, such as generative neural networks, to produce data, text, images, or sounds that did not previously exist. In scientific research, GAI can be used in fields such as medical research to generate synthetic data for testing when real data is limited or inaccessible. GAI can also simulate experiments or environments, such as modeling chemical reactions that would be dangerous or impractical to conduct in the real world.

In summary, while AI is a powerful tool for accelerating data analysis and processing, GAI represents an innovative frontier in the creation of new data and simulations, expanding the scope and possibilities of scientific research.

Transhuman co-production (Freire and Marques, 2024) refers to the harmonious and ethical integration of human capabilities with advanced AI technologies. It aims for a collaboration that preserves human uniqueness while leveraging technological advantages to achieve new levels of innovation and efficiency. This term, although new, is important because it affirms the principle that we should not resist technological advances that are already present and widely used across all sectors – including research and academic writing. Therefore, we must overcome our barriers and begin to engage in dialogue and co-production (Freire and Marques, 2024).

The benefits of transhuman co-production through the use of AI and GAI in scientific research are vast and impactful. AI and GAI can significantly accelerate the processes of scientific knowledge production. However, the successful implementation of AI and GAI in scientific research also presents significant challenges. These include the need to ensure the accuracy and reliability of AI algorithms, the protection of intellectual property, and ethical considerations regarding the use of AI-generated data and results.

In addition, training researchers to effectively use these tools and to understand the limits and capabilities of AI is essential to ensure that its effective implementation contributes to scientific advancement (Carobene *et al.*, 2024).

In this chapter, the term "AI" is used in a generalized way to refer to both concepts, but it is important that the reader keeps their distinctions in mind while reading.

8.3 Methodology

This study is based on a narrative literature review (Ribeiro, 2014) and institutional guidelines regarding the use of AI in academic writing. Guides on AI applications in academic research were analyzed.

The selection of the reviewed documents was based on the 10 highest-ranked universities in the World University Rankings 2025 (Times Higher Education, 2025). These documents were subsequently categorized, and their content was analyzed using thematic analysis, as proposed by Braun and Clarke (2006). The analysis aimed to identify potential uses and patterns of ethical recommendations and best practices for implementing these technologies.

The AI tool ChatGPT (OpenAI, 2025) was used for English-language revision in specific contexts, data synthesis under author supervision, and text formatting as needed. The AI tool NotebookLM (Google, 2025) was used for data extraction and comparison under author supervision. All content was produced and reviewed by or under the direct supervision of the authors.

8.4 Potentials of AI Usage in Academic Research

Transhuman co-production can occur in various ways through the use of technology, and in this study, we highlight some potential applications of AI within this context.

AI-powered text processing and generation tools can offer grammar correction, plagiarism checking, or even propose text based on topics suggested by the researcher (Freire and Marques, 2024). AI tools designed for text production offer a wide range of functionalities, including grammar, spelling, and punctuation correction, as well as automated generation of original content. These systems provide style suggestions to enhance clarity and conciseness and offer additional resources such as vocabulary enhancement, automatic translation, and assistance with formatting citations and references. Additionally, they include similarity checkers, personalized feedback for writing improvement, and academic integrity support mechanisms that identify content potentially generated by AI (Oxford, 2025; Princeton, 2025a, 2025b; Cambridge, 2025). The benefits of these technologies are numerous: They improve the quality of writing both linguistically and structurally, promote clearer and more objective texts, and increase academic productivity by reducing the time required for tasks such as revision, drafting, and idea generation (MIT, 2025, 2025a; Oxford, 2025).

However, there are notable limitations. Free versions of these tools often offer restricted functionality, which may limit their usefulness. As with all AI-based technologies, these tools are not error-free: They may produce false positives in plagiarism detection, generate content with inaccurate or unverified information, and have difficulty formatting references correctly according to specific standards. Furthermore, their use demands critical discernment – especially in academic contexts – as the lack of scientific rigor in generated texts may compromise the quality and originality of intellectual production (Caltech, 2023; UC Berkeley, 2024; MIT, 2025).

AI-driven search engines that understand full-text context and relevance to locate scientific literature are platforms that offer advanced search and information retrieval features. These allow keyword, author, institution, date, and subject area searches, as well as specific filters to refine results (Freire and Marques, 2024). Some tools include recommendation engines based on user history and data visualization features to map relationships between publications, authors, and institutions. Additionally, many offer impact metrics (such as citation counts) and analyses of scientific collaboration networks. Other features include access to and downloading of documents, creation of personalized alerts, article submission, patent analysis, and API integration (Freire and Marques, 2024; Princeton, 2025; Cambridge, 2025).

Key benefits include facilitated access to large volumes of scientific data, often freely or without requiring registration. AI-supported tools enhance result relevance, aid in discovering new content, and support greater understanding of articles through automatic summaries and interactive visualizations (Oxford, 2025; Yale, 2023; Princeton, 2025a, 2025b; Caltech, 2023; MIT, 2025a). Some platforms also foster scientific collaboration by connecting researchers with common interests and enabling interaction through forums or academic social networks. Additionally, the rapid dissemination of research – especially via preprint platforms – helps accelerate scientific progress (MIT, 2025; ICL, 2025; Cambridge, 2025).

Despite these advances, such tools still face significant limitations. The quality and timeliness of data often depend on original sources, potentially compromising their reliability. The use of AI algorithms may introduce bias into results and recommendations. Complex or unintuitive interfaces can pose barriers for beginner users. Furthermore, in collaborative or academic social network environments, there is a risk of disseminating irrelevant or scientifically unverified content (Oxford, 2025; Yale, 2023; Princeton, 2025; Caltech, 2023). These aspects must be critically considered by researchers and institutions when selecting and using such tools in the search, analysis, and dissemination of scientific knowledge.

Another important application is data analysis and statistics in scientific contexts, which can offer a comprehensive set of features ranging from data processing and preparation to predictive modeling and result visualization (Freire and Marques, 2024). Among its main capabilities are the implementation of machine learning algorithms (such as regression, classification, clustering, and variable selection), the construction of mathematical models, data preprocessing (including cleaning, normalization, and transformation), and integration with other platforms and systems. Some solutions provide intuitive graphical interfaces and interactive visual resources that allow easy data exploration, even for users with little to no programming experience (MIT, 2025; Oxford, 2025; Yale, 2023; Princeton, 2025a).

From a benefits perspective, these tools speed up the analytical process by automating repetitive tasks and enabling efficient handling of large data volumes. Additionally, they support the reproducibility of scientific research by enabling the structured sharing of code and workflows. Many also feature active communities and continuous technical support, fostering a collaborative and constantly evolving environment. Some stand out for being open source and therefore free to use and customize.

Nonetheless, these solutions present limitations. The learning curve can be significant, especially for beginners or users unfamiliar with statistics or programming. Another critical point involves the consistency of available packages or extensions, which may vary in quality and require careful evaluation by users. Finally, licensing costs, integration with other systems, and the need for adequate computational infrastructure may also hinder adoption in certain contexts (MIT, 2025a, 2025b; UC Berkeley, 2025).

8.5 Ethical Considerations Regarding Transhuman Co-Production

While transhuman co-production is widely acknowledged as beneficial when incorporating AI, it must be guided by ethical considerations. The primary concerns are outlined in this section.

8.5.1 *Authorship and human responsibility*

Authorship and human responsibility are fundamental principles in conducting scientific research and are non-transferable to any AI system or tool. At all stages of the investigative process – from hypothesis formulation to data analysis and writing conclusions – it is the human authors who bear full responsibility for the presented content, the validity of the data, and methodological integrity. AI tools, no matter how sophisticated, lack morality, ethical consciousness, or critical judgment capacity and therefore cannot, under any circumstances, be held accountable for decisions made in a scientific context.

Several prestigious academic institutions are categorically prohibiting the attribution of authorship to AI tools. For example, the University of Oxford (2025) states that these systems should not be credited as authors in academic publications because they lack legal responsibility and do not contribute genuine intellectual effort.

Similarly, Princeton University (2025) reinforces that these tools cannot be listed as co-authors, since they are unable to take responsibility for the accuracy or integrity of the generated content.

This guideline is supported by a broad conception of authorship that requires, beyond content production, the capacity to critically reflect on methodological choices and their results.

In an educational context, Yale University (2024) establishes that faculty must set clear rules regarding the use of AI and authorship attribution, while students are expected to rigorously follow these guidelines, with potential penalties for ethical violations. At Princeton, representing ideas or AI-generated content as one's own without proper attribution and context is explicitly considered a breach of academic conduct norms (Princeton University, 2025a, 2025b).

Improper attribution of authorship to AI systems undermines trust in science and weakens traditional accountability mechanisms. The opacity that characterizes many of these tools, especially generative models, complicates full understanding of how results are produced. When researchers are unable to explain or justify the analytical or interpretive processes employed, the scientific integrity of the work is jeopardized. Accountability in this regard requires not only supervision but also an active understanding of the procedures adopted with AI support.

Therefore, the role of AI tools should be understood as auxiliary, never a substitute for human intelligence. The University of Oxford (2025) advocates that AI be used as a support to enhance human capabilities, not as an alternative to creativity, curiosity, and critical judgment – qualities that characterize scientific work. Likewise, the Universities of Cambridge (2025) and Princeton (2025) emphasize the importance of continuous human oversight of AI-produced content to ensure its appropriateness, accuracy, and relevance.

Imperial College London (ICL, 2025) adds that AI use should not diminish individual experiences or weaken human contributions in teaching, learning, or assessment. In alignment, Harvard Graduate School of Education (2025) and the Faculty of Arts and Sciences (FAS, 2025) recommend that students use AI to strengthen content understanding and develop cognitive skills, avoiding dependency that could compromise the formative process (Harvard, 2025).

Beyond ethical and methodological implications, the debate on authorship extends to intellectual property rights. AI tools, not being legal entities, cannot hold copyrights or intellectual property rights. Legal responsibility for content generated with AI assistance – whether text, images, data, or other materials – rests solely with the human authors. Researchers must ensure that the use of AI tools does not infringe copyright, respecting current legislation and institutional norms.

In this regard, Princeton (2025) stresses the need to ensure that generated content does not violate intellectual property laws. MIT (2025) reinforces that AI use must comply with pertinent institutional and external regulations, including guidelines on academic integrity and intellectual property.

The University of California, Berkeley (UC Berkeley, 2024) warns about risks related to users accepting terms of use for generative AI tools without delegated legal authority, cautioning that in such cases users themselves may be held liable for contractual breaches, including those concerning intellectual property.

The incorporation of AI in scientific research demands a robust ethical commitment that reaffirms the centrality of human authorship and responsibility. This is essential to preserve the integrity of the scientific process, the reliability of results, and the legitimacy of academic output. Researchers must ensure that the technology is used with discernment, under their supervision and accountability.

8.5.2 *Transparency and reproducibility*

Transparency in the use of AI tools is a fundamental principle for ensuring the reproducibility and integrity of scientific processes. In an academic context, where independent validation and results replicability are central pillars of the scientific method, it is essential that the use of AI systems be thoroughly documented and explicitly disclosed. This not only allows other researchers to evaluate and replicate the results but also helps identify potential limitations or biases in the tools used, thereby strengthening the reliability of the research (MIT, 2025; Harvard, 2025; Caltech, 2023).

Several universities emphasize the importance of transparency in AI use within their institutional guidelines and stress the need for compliance with established academic integrity policies (Yale, 2023; MIT, 2025; Harvard, 2025; FAS, 2025; Caltech, 2023; ICL, 2025).

It is highly recommended that researchers clearly disclose how, when, and for what purpose AI tools were employed during the research process or in the development of academic materials (Oxford, 2025; Princeton, 2025; Stanford, 2025; Caltech, 2023). Such transparency is especially required in scientific publications, academic communications, and works submitted for formal evaluations (Oxford, 2025; Princeton, 2025; Stanford, 2025).

Stanford University (2025) highlights that this transparency not only ensures the integrity of the work but also enables the public to critically understand the role of AI in the development of the presented knowledge. At Princeton (2025), for example, clarity in disclosing the use of AI is considered essential, particularly in evaluative contexts.

In educational settings, students are instructed to follow their professors' guidance and, in many cases, to seek prior permission to use AI, in addition to explicitly declaring its use (Yale, 2023; Harvard, 2025; Princeton, 2025). Omitting such information or misappropriating AI-generated content may, in some cases, be considered a violation of academic conduct norms (Princeton, 2025).

From a methodological standpoint, best practices include providing detailed accounts of AI use in the methodology section of research projects. This includes stating the type of AI employed, the name, version, configuration parameters, training data of the tool (when available), and the access conditions for the tool. It is also necessary to specify the role played by these systems – whether in data analysis, results generation, hypothesis formulation, image creation, or other stages of the scientific production process (Stanford, 2025; Harvard, 2025; Princeton, 2025; ICL, 2025).

Nevertheless, even with full transparency, the use of AI requires caution, as AI systems may introduce errors or biases, or produce inaccurate information. The University of Oxford (2025), for instance, notes that AI tools may perpetuate biases derived from training data or generate incorrect information. Yale (2023) mentions that AI-generated results may contain errors, historical biases, inadequate data, or even copyright violations. Princeton (2025) also warns of the risks associated with biased data and the unintended consequences of using these tools.

Responsibility for verifying the accuracy and appropriateness of AI-generated content is therefore non-transferable. It is up to the researcher to critically assess the results and ensure that the content used is error-free and compliant with ethical and scientific research standards. This concern is particularly relevant in sensitive fields such as healthcare, where the use of inaccurate data may compromise the safety of outcomes and lead to misinterpretations or improper decisions.

Stanford University (2025) draws attention to the phenomenon known as hallucination, in which generative AI tools produce false information that is nevertheless presented convincingly, potentially deceiving even experienced readers. These tools are also known for generating nonexistent or fabricated references, which seriously undermines the validity of any work that depends on them (Stanford, 2025). Caltech (2023), in turn, emphasizes the importance of ensuring the accuracy of AI-generated information and recognizing the potential of these technologies to amplify preexisting biases.

Given this, it is imperative that authors do not treat AI-generated content, such as data, information, images, or text, as original empirical material obtained through traditional scientific methods. When the use of AI-generated content is methodologically justified, it is necessary to ensure its validation and verification through independent means. The same principle applies to the use of figures, illustrations, and texts produced by such tools (Oxford, 2025; Yale, 2023; Princeton, 2025).

Clarity regarding AI usage, validation of generated content, attention to bias, and accountability for the presented results are fundamental elements for preserving the quality and reliability of scientific production. When guided by these principles, the responsible use of AI can significantly contribute to the advancement of knowledge – provided it is accompanied by critical oversight and methodological transparency.

8.5.3 *Data privacy and governance*

The use of AI tools in academic environments – particularly when processing sensitive data – presents significant challenges related to privacy, information security, and regulatory compliance (Stanford, 2025; UC Berkeley, 2024; MIT, 2025). The handling of information classified as confidential, personal, or protected by specific regulations requires researchers to implement robust anonymization protocols, strictly limit data access, and provide clear methodological justifications whenever synthetic data generated by AI is used (Caltech, 2023; Princeton, 2025). These safeguards are essential to ensure that AI does not inappropriately replace genuine data sources or violate the ethical principles that guide scientific research.

Researchers are responsible for ensuring that both the data used in analyses and the results generated comply with intellectual property laws, avoiding legal infringements that could compromise academic integrity. Likewise, it is imperative to ensure that the AI tools employed are properly licensed for scientific and educational use, respecting the terms of use set by their developers or distributors.

In this context, data privacy and governance emerge as fundamental ethical principles for the academic use of AI. Institutions have adopted strict guidelines to protect sensitive information and ensure compliance with both internal and external regulations. A key concern is the prohibition of uploading confidential, personal, or high-risk data into generative AI platforms. These restrictions include legal, financial, and health information, academic records, and proprietary code (Oxford, 2025; Yale, 2023; MIT, 2025; Princeton, 2025; Cambridge, 2025).

For example, UC Berkeley (2025) defines levels of data protection, which generally prohibit inputting such data into AI systems unless specific contractual agreements are in place. The rationale behind this restriction lies in the risks associated with potential leakage, retention, or misuse of information by AI platforms – especially when shared data might be treated as public or used for training models without appropriate safeguards. MIT (2025) warns that inadvertent data sharing with platforms lacking sufficient protection may constitute a violation of the institution's compliance policies.

Compliance with these policies is mandatory and encompasses not only the protection of sensitive data but also academic integrity, intellectual property rights, and the lawful use of emerging technologies (MIT, 2025; Princeton, 2025; Cambridge, 2025; Caltech, 2023; UC Berkeley, 2024; Stanford, 2025). Some institutions explicitly recommend conducting impact and security risk assessments as key steps in evaluating and mitigating AI-related risks (Cambridge, 2025; UC Berkeley, 2025).

From a governance perspective, specific responsibilities are also assigned to AI tool users. Common guidelines include the prohibition of sharing institutional credentials, the recommendation to consult IT departments before using such tools – especially when handling sensitive data – and the requirement to obtain informed consent from data subjects, ensuring their right to opt out or request deletion of personal information (Yale, 2023; MIT, 2025; Princeton, 2025).

In summary, researchers must remain vigilant and committed to protecting sensitive and confidential data.

8.5.4 *Regulatory guidelines*

The use of AI tools in academic settings has been widely discussed and shaped by higher education institutions and regulatory bodies. A central focus of this discussion involves compliance with institutional policies and external regulations, particularly regarding intellectual property, copyright, data privacy, and academic integrity (MIT, 2025; Princeton, 2025; Cambridge, 2025; Caltech, 2023; UC Berkeley, 2024; ICL, 2025).

The use of AI must be strictly aligned with applicable legal and regulatory frameworks, with particular attention to both internal policies and external regulations, especially those concerning academic integrity and respect for intellectual property rights (MIT, 2025; Princeton, 2025).

Furthermore, AI use must be reasonable, lawful, and in accordance with institutional procedures. Data usage, in particular, must adhere to internal policies and relevant legal obligations, including explicit acceptance of institutional rules governing such usage (UC Berkeley, 2024; Caltech, 2023).

From the early stages of research design, it is essential to consider ethical issues related to the use of AI-based systems, ensuring that such technologies are employed transparently, fairly, and responsibly. A recommended practice is to conduct preliminary ethical impact assessments capable of identifying potential risks such as algorithmic bias, privacy violations, and harm to vulnerable populations. This preventive approach is crucial for guiding the development of research methodologies in alignment with current ethical and regulatory standards (MIT, 2025; Princeton, 2025; Cambridge, 2025; Caltech, 2023; UC Berkeley, 2024; ICL, 2025; Stanford, 2025).

When preparing and submitting technical proposals and research projects to funding agencies, researchers must pay close attention to specific guidelines regarding AI usage – including restrictions on certain applications, requirements for human oversight, and risk mitigation measures Freire and Marques (2024).

Organizations such as the European Commission have established key principles for responsible AI use. These include the preservation of human autonomy, harm prevention, and the promotion of fairness and explainability. In addition, operational requirements such as ongoing human oversight, technical robustness, privacy protection, transparency, and accountability are considered foundational for the safe application of AI (European Commission, 2024).

In this context, researchers must remain alert and committed to regulatory guidelines, best practices, institutional regulations, and applicable legislation – validating their use of AI from the research design phase through to the final results.

8.6 Conclusion

AI represents a significant advancement for scientific research, expanding possibilities for knowledge production by enhancing academic writing, data analysis, and literature reviews.

However, the use of AI requires a strong ethical commitment, ensuring transparency, integrity, and accountability. It is essential to recognize that full authorship and responsibility for the research remain non-transferable and rest solely with the human authors.

Challenges such as algorithmic bias, data privacy, and the need to verify the accuracy of AI-generated outputs call for caution and continuous human oversight. Transparency regarding how, when, and for what purpose AI was used is crucial to ensure the reproducibility and scientific integrity of research.

The appropriate integration of AI in academia critically depends on the ongoing development of institutional guidelines and the training of researchers, ensuring that the technology is employed ethically and in accordance with applicable regulations.

For future research, it is recommended to investigate effective methods for conducting preliminary ethical impact assessments related to the use of AI in research projects, as well as approaches to identify and mitigate algorithmic biases present in the AI tools employed. Additionally, mechanisms to ensure the explainability of the applied models should be explored.

Beyond academic research, exploring the concept of transhuman co-production across diverse contexts – such as design, engineering, applied social sciences, and other disciplines – may contribute to identifying potential uses and developing appropriate guidelines for its application.

References

Appenzeller, T. 'The AI Revolution in Science.' *Science*, 2021, https://www.science.org/content/article/ai-revolution-science (accessed 10 April 2025).

Braun, V. and V. Clarke. 'Using Thematic Analysis in Psychology.' *Qualitative Research in Psychology*, 3, no. 2 (2006): 77–101, https://doi.org/10.1191/1478088706qp063oa.

California Institute of Technology. Guidance on the Use of Generative AI and Large Language Model Tools. 2023, https://www.caltech.edu/campus-life-events/campus-announcements/guidance-on-the-use-of-generative-ai-and-large-language-model-tools (accessed 10 April 2025).

Carobene A., A. Padoan, F. Cabitza, G. Banfi, M. Plebani. 'Rising Adoption of Artificial Intelligence in Scientific Publishing: Evaluating the Role, Risks, and Ethical Implications in Paper Drafting and Review Process.' *Clinical Chemistry and Laboratory Medicine (CCLM)*. 62 no. 5(2024): 835–843. https://doi.org/10.1515/cclm-2023-1136.

European Commission, Directorate-General for Research and Innovation. *Ethics Guidelines for Trustworthy AI.* 2024, https://research-and-innovation.ec.europa.eu/document/download/2b6cf7e5-36ac-4 (accessed 10 April 2025).

Faculty of Arts and Sciences. *AI Guidance & FAQs*. Harvard University, 2025, https://oue.fas.harvard.edu/ai-guidance (accessed 10 April 2025).

Freire, P. de S., and D. Marques. Coprodução Transhumana: Manual de Uso Ético de Inteligência Artificial na Escrita Acadêmica. Editora Arquétipos, 2024, https://editoraarquetipos.com.br/produto/coproducao-transhumana-manual-de-uso-etico-de-inteligencia-artificial-na-escrita-academica/.

Gao, J. and D. Wang. 'Quantifying the Benefit of Artificial Intelligence for Scientific Research.' *arXiv*, 2023, https://doi.org/10.48550/arXiv.2304.10578.

Harvard Graduate School of Education. *HGSE AI Policy*. 2025, https://registrar.gse.harvard.edu/learning/policies-forms/ai-policy (accessed 10 April 2025).

Imperial College London. *Generative AI Principles*. 2025, https://www.imperial.ac.uk/about/education/resources/ai-education-hub/generative-ai-principles/ (accessed 10 April 2025).

Massachusetts Institute of Technology (MIT) – Information Systems & Technology. *Generative AI Tools Available at MIT*. 2025a, https://ist.mit.edu/ai-tools (accessed 10 April 2025).

Massachusetts Institute of Technology (MIT) – Information Systems & Technology. *Guidance for Use of Generative AI Tools*. 2025b, https://ist.mit.edu/ai-guidance (accessed 10 April 2025).

Princeton University. McGraw Center for Teaching and Learning. Guidance on AI/ChatGPT. 2025a, https://mcgraw.princeton.edu/guidance-aichatgpt (accessed 10 April 2025).

Princeton University. Office of Information Technology. Generative AI at Princeton. 2025b, https://oit.princeton.edu/generative-ai (accessed 10 April 2025).

Ribeiro, J. L. P. 'Revisão de Investigação e Evidência Científica.' *Psicologia, Saúde e Doenças*, 15, no. 3 (2014).

Stanford University. Responsible AI at Stanford. 2025, https://uit.stanford.edu/security/responsibleai (accessed 10 May 2025).

University of Cambridge. *Information Compliance. AI Guidance*. 2025, https://www.information-compliance.admin.cam.ac.uk/data-protection/guidance/ai-guidance (accessed 10 April 2025).

University of Oxford. *Guidelines on the Use of Generative AI*. 2025, https://communications.admin.ox.ac.uk/communications-resources/ai-guidance (accessed 8 May 2025).

Yale University. *Guidelines for the Use of Generative AI Tools*. 2023, https://provost.yale.edu/news/guidelines-use-generative-ai-tools (accessed 10 April 2025).

© 2026 World Scientific Publishing Europe Ltd.
https://doi.org/10.1142/9781800617414_0009

Chapter 9

Collaborative Online International Learning as a Knowledge Management Strategy: An Experience Report on a Case Between Brazil and Peru

Kelly Cristina Benetti Tonani Tosta[*,§], **Marcos Baptista Lopez Dalmau**[†], **Paloma Martinez-Hague**[‡], **Gonzalo Rafael Merino Braga**[‡], **and Monica Scoz Mendes**[†]

[*]*Federal University of Fronteira Sul, Brazil*

[†]*Federal University of Santa Catarina, Brazil*

[‡]*Pontificia Universidad Católica del Perú, Peru*

[§]*kellytosta@uffs.edu.br*

Abstract

This chapter investigates the potential of Collaborative Online International Learning (COIL) as a tool for co-creation and knowledge management in higher education. Grounded in action research, the study involved Brazilian and Peruvian management students and faculty in a cross-border academic collaboration. Through action research and mixed student teams, participants explored real-world challenges, such as employer branding in small and medium-sized companies (SMCs). The initiative fostered intercultural competence, collaborative knowledge creation, and professional skills development, despite logistical and institutional challenges related to language, time zones, and academic alignment. The experience demonstrated COIL's potential as a cost-effective and adaptable internationalization strategy in Latin American higher education. Results indicate that COIL enhances intercultural competence, fosters collaborative knowledge production, and offers a cost-effective alternative to traditional internationalization models. The experience also demonstrated COIL's adaptability for undergraduate research and its capacity to strengthen regional academic integration in Latin America.

Keywords: COIL, co-creation, knowledge management.

9.1 Introduction

Higher education institutions (HEIs) worldwide are navigating the impacts and transformations driven by globalization and advancements in information and communication technologies (ICTs), particularly the internet (Hildebrando Júnior and Finardi, 2018).

As a result of this globalization process, Goto and Gutierrez-Gomes (2023) state that intercultural competence is becoming increasingly essential for students before entering the modern workforce. Engaging in intercultural learning enables students to deepen their understanding and appreciation of their own culture, gain insights into other cultures, and develop greater cultural awareness. Such experiences foster collaborative learning among college students, better preparing them to live and work in diverse cultural environments while helping them cultivate culturally appropriate behaviors.

Traditionally, college students develop their intercultural skills primarily through work experiences, travel, or participation in study abroad programs. However, some of these opportunities can be expensive and inaccessible to many students (Goto and Gutierrez-Gomes, 2023). Collaborative Online International Learning (COIL) has emerged as an option to make international experiences more accessible and affordable for students.

COIL is an online teaching and learning modality designed for teachers and students to collaborate with peers from other countries in curricular subjects with common content. It offers significant benefits, such as developing transversal knowledge and competencies, multicultural collaboration, and adaptability to virtual work environments and technologies (Vazquez-Villegas *et al.*, 2024; Silva *et al.*, 2024).

Hackett *et al.* (2023) ratify this information when they say that COIL can support the development of students' intercultural competence at their home institution, providing an opportunity for all students, not just those who participate in study or internship abroad programs, to build these essential skills. Besides, its functionalities align with the social-constructivist approach to education, emphasizing collaborative learning and the importance of social interaction in learning (Hackett *et al.*, 2023).

Still, according to Hackett *et al.* (2023), few experimental studies investigate the effectiveness of COIL, especially considering its novelty in the academic world. In today's communication landscape, integrating online internationalization components is increasingly relevant, as they enhance the learning experience and strengthen meaningful intercultural exchange and interaction at a distance (Nuñes *et al.*, 2023).

As noted by Bhatt (2001), the process of creating and developing knowledge is possible through its reconfiguration and recombination of existing knowledge, alongside strategies of imitation, replication, and substitution. In this context, COIL can be seen as a way to make this process possible.

COIL is not explicitly labeled as a co-creation tool, but its core features strongly align with co-creation principles. It emphasizes joint knowledge creation, teamwork, and intercultural exchange, especially through collaborative learning, peer interaction, and flexible formats.

Furthermore, as much as the students have to interact with each other to construct and consolidate the expected knowledge, it becomes essential for teachers to explore new ways of sharing and registering it. Since there are many moments where expertise and different points of view are shared, teachers and students improve skills from all the experiences where hard work was needed to adapt institutional rules and cross-cultural understanding between countries.

In this chapter, we present COIL as a strategy for providing the interaction needed for knowledge creation and validation and as an essential tool for developing co-creation skills among teachers and undergraduate students. From this perspective, this research aims to answer the following question: **Can COIL be considered a tool to enhance co-creation and knowledge management within universities?**

To answer the question, this study adopts an action research methodology to explore the effectiveness of COIL as a knowledge co-creation strategy in management education. Action research is a participatory method that integrates iterative planning, action, and reflection cycles, allowing for continuous improvement based on stakeholder feedback (Al-Fattal, 2025). This approach is particularly suited for COIL, as it fosters collaboration, promotes intercultural understanding, and enhances educational practices (Késia *et al.*, 2019). The study involved professors and students from management schools in Peru and Brazil, who collaborated to co-create course content and conduct case study research on employer branding in multiple small businesses across both countries. It used a mixed-methods approach, combining qualitative and quantitative data collection methods, such as surveys and participant-guided reflections, to capture participants' perspectives. Weekly synchronous sessions, asynchronous collaborative tasks, and expert-led webinars were structured to facilitate engagement, knowledge exchange, and co-creation.

It was an innovative experience based not only on the collaboration of a regular course but also on carrying out research at the undergraduate level, supervised by professors from three universities. As shown throughout this chapter, the results highlight fundamental aspects, such as: the sharing of different experiences and methodologies, allowing students to compare different contexts from those they were used to, opening their minds to new points of view, cultures, contexts, and experiences; the opportunity for more collaborative research in Latin America; firsthand experience in collaboration in other languages; and the development of academic and professional links across different countries, establishing a foundation for future collaborations.

9.2 COIL Methodology

Action research is a flexible, participatory methodology that intertwines action with reflection to solve real-world problems creatively and emphasizes practical applicability. It is grounded in collaboration and includes members of the study population as co-researchers with academic investigators, ensuring that the knowledge produced is relevant to the participants' lived experiences. This methodology focuses on bringing the intervention to the community, involving them in the research process and results (Brown, 2024; Johnston and Forrest, 2020). The iterative, cyclical framework of planning, acting, observing, and reflecting forms the basis of the action research methodology. The action research cycle has been extended to include specifying the problem, theorizing, and methods to achieve democratic validity (Kapenieks and Salīte, 2012; Manfra and Bullock, 2013).

Embedding action research into COIL courses significantly contributes to creating and disseminating knowledge, as it enables environments of active participation, reflection, and iterative learning. This methodology foregrounds collaboration and practical, real-world problem-solving, essential in a COIL learning space where participants are active, engaged, and come from diverse educational and cultural backgrounds. It leads to environments of democratic and inclusive learning that respect diverse perspectives (Johnston and Forrest, 2020).

When participants engage in action research in a COIL course, they can explore and tackle real-life problems together. A COIL course is similar to others in that it aims to enhance participants' understanding of the material. However, what makes COIL different is that it has the potential to help participants share knowledge across borders. COIL functions like a participatory action research project (PAR) in that COIL and PAR both encourage knowledge creation. To that end, COIL encourages participants to reflect on the processes and outcomes of their learning (Kapenieks, 2011).

Action research is cyclical, and this is its strength. It is not a static event but a process leading to constant and continuous development and adaptation of the knowledge gained. This is needed for sharing knowledge in today's dynamic learning and diverse environments (Al-Fattal, 2025; Bhatt, 2001; Capone *et al.*, 2015; Juergensmeyer, 2011; Kapenieks, 2011).

The COIL methodology is a tool designed to facilitate internationalization in a fast, economical, and flexible way, generating cooperation between two or more educational institutions, regardless of their geographical location, time zone, or language, and as we observed in our experience, it also allowed us to ostensibly improve co-creation and knowledge management in scientific production at up to three universities in a coordinated manner.

COIL provided us with a valuable internationalization experience, enabling us to exchange experiences, practice new methodologies, and explore new cultural, political, social, and legal contexts in a simple way, unlike traditional exchanges, and allowing a larger group to participate in these projects.

This methodology has already demonstrated the virtues of internationalization in multiple experiences carried out at different universities. It shows great flexibility in the courses where it has been applied, with experiences lasting a few weeks in a semester across various disciplines, including the arts, exact sciences, and the legal, engineering, and social sciences.

However, our experience of applying the COIL methodology allowed us to push its boundaries beyond its original design, elaborating undergraduate thesis research (to qualify for a degree) throughout a semester with small groups of students (five teams of four people, comprising two Peruvian and two Brazilian students in each team). The COIL methodology framework is flexible enough to adapt to multiple academic internationalization tasks.

International research is scarce in Latin America, partly due to high costs, limited contact between university institutions, and the inertia of regional research, which prioritizes local research within each country or cooperation with countries in Europe and the U.S., even though the contextual realities with these regions are different. The opportunity offered by the COIL tool is that it opens the door to increased regional research, which allows for the development of theoretical knowledge based on the particular context of Latin America.

Research using the COIL methodology tool showed us in this experience excellent opportunities for institutions to create scientific knowledge applied to the Latin American context and trends, facilitate the exchange of experiences, identify similarities and differences, and foster regional academic collaboration while also presenting a wide range of advantages for the researchers involved (students and professors), including exchanging experiences and knowledge, creating and improving contacts between academics and professionals at the regional level, and opening perspectives on new points of view and ways of facing academic challenges, despite limited resources due to the tool's rapid application, low costs, and simple processes.

We could affirm that it substantially improves the dynamics of academic research in the Latin American region.

9.3 Case Study Peru–Brazil

The COIL methodology was implemented within the scope of administrative courses and involved a structured and collaborative approach to international learning. It was led differently across the institutions. In Peru, the institution that hosted the project was Pontificia Universidad Católica del Perú (PUCP) – a private university located in Lima. In Brazil, the host institutions were Universidade Federal de Santa Catarina (UFSC) in Florianópolis and Universidade Federal da Fronteira Sul (UFFS) in Chapecó.

Five professors from these three universities co-developed the course, which required continuous coordination and adaptability to overcome institutional and logistical challenges, such as differing academic calendars, administrative procedures, and time zone disparities. The team of professors designed the methodology around weekly synchronous sessions, asynchronous collaborative tasks, and expert-led webinars.

9.3.1 *Planning phase*

During the planning phase, which began in the first semester of 2024, the participating faculty members attended a COIL training program developed by PUCP. This training proved highly beneficial, as it facilitated a better understanding of the methodology, particularly for those without prior experience. In the case of the Brazilian faculty, who had previously implemented a similar project in collaboration with another university (UNL – Argentina), their prior experience and the knowledge they acquired enabled them to make significant progress in shaping the concept of this new project.

Those five faculty members collaboratively developed the course plan throughout this phase, structuring all student activities over 14 weeks. This process yielded substantial benefits for the project, as it allowed an evaluation of whether the proposed activities would foster not only the development of technical training competencies but also other essential skills associated with COIL initiatives, such as collaboration, foreign-language-based communication, complex problem-solving in both personal and professional contexts, research, and interpersonal skills critical to human development.

The professors designed the methodology around three components: (a) weekly synchronous sessions (held simultaneously for the entire course); (b) asynchronous collaborative tasks (completed by students after the weekly session and before the next session); and (c) expert-led webinars at key points during the course.

Reflecting on the structuring of the project, the team of faculty members encountered a complex situation that diverged from what is typically observed in COIL initiatives: how to offer a course of this nature within the constraints of the existing curricular structures at their respective universities while ensuring it would be perceived as an essential component of students' academic trajectories.

The initial idea was to integrate the COIL course into the formal *curriculum* of both institutions. At PUCP, the course was implemented as *Seminario de Investigación 2* (GES237), a capstone seminar required for graduating students, involving the development of a final thesis project.

At UFSC and UFFS, the course was designed as an elective subject with a standard academic workload and was formally recognized in the students' training programs. Both offerings were scheduled for the second semester of 2024 (or 2024.2).

Once these curricular frameworks were established, the focus shifted to promoting the course – a process that initially progressed smoothly, given the decisions already made. At PUCP, efforts were made to identify potential participants in advance, considering the course's targeted audience of final-year students.

However, at UFSC and UFFS, unforeseen challenges emerged due to the nationwide strike, which disrupted numerous Brazilian institutions and caused significant delays in academic calendars. Consequently, the Brazilian faculty members were compelled to revise the initial plan. In an urgent response, the decision was made to offer the course as an extension activity. This shift altered the profile of the intended participants on the Brazilian side and necessitated the development of a new strategy for recruiting interested students.

Rather than focusing solely on traditional COIL activities, such as case studies, cultural presentations, or other more basic forms of engagement, the project team sought to distinguish this initiative by including a research component. Specifically, the project was restructured to include the design and implementation of an applied research project conducted in companies from both countries. In addition, the course incorporated lectures on the relevant topic and guest talks delivered by a Peruvian and a Brazilian researcher/professional, further enriching the academic experience and cross-cultural exchange.

The experience was within the scope of small enterprises and institutions that did not conform to the standardization practices of transnational corporations, which allowed the identification, analysis, and understanding of the substantial cultural, legal, social, and financial contextual differences between the two countries, as well as the similarities in regional idiosyncrasies, which greatly benefited students and provided material for teachers in the creation of educational resources.

9.3.2 *Implementation phase*

Upon completing the planning phase, the project moved into its implementation stage. As discussed in Section 9.3.1, due to the nationwide strike in Brazil, the Brazilian faculty team was required to quickly adapt their strategy for student recruitment. What was initially intended to target a more specific audience had to be broadened, leading to a broader dissemination of the course, now directed toward all undergraduate students enrolled in the business administration programs.

Given the course's specific focus on human resources management, the pool of interested students was limited. At the Brazilian universities involved, subjects within this domain are typically offered from the fifth semester onward (in a nine-semester program), restricting the number of eligible undergraduate students. This fact made it necessary to include graduate-level students from the postgraduate programs available at UFSC.

During the dissemination process, faculty members had to take a more proactive and personalized approach to identify potential participants, considering that the project carried a distinct workload and educational value within the academic curriculum.

Following students' expressions of interest, the next challenge involved assessing whether they met the necessary qualifications to engage in a project of this nature. These qualifications included proficiency in a foreign language, familiarity with relevant software and digital tools, and availability to commit to a 14-week program with fixed weekly sessions on a predetermined day and time.

A preliminary survey was conducted to evaluate students' competencies in these areas. Overall, the results indicated that participants generally perceived themselves as having an intermediate level of foreign language proficiency and a high level of familiarity with applications that facilitate collaborative work.

Following this initial moment, five mixed groups of students from Peru and Brazil were formed and engaged in action research to collaboratively identify real-world challenges within case studies, fostering cross-cultural knowledge exchange. These five groups of four participants – two students from each country – worked together (albeit virtually) to analyze and address issues of global importance, such as employer branding in small- and medium-sized companies (SMCs).

The first five weeks were dedicated to theoretical alignment through literature reviews and expert discussions, ensuring a shared foundation. Despite initial language barriers and coordination challenges, students developed essential competencies in problem-solving, cross-cultural communication, and autonomous research management.

The research teams, composed of paired students from each country, worked independently to align theoretical frameworks, develop research instruments, and conduct case studies within their respective contexts. This knowledge-sharing mechanism, which spans borders and time zones, has served all actors well, with students and professors enjoying a unique cultural and intellectual exchange (Capone *et al.*, 2015; Staron, 2024).

Emphasizing practical problem-solving ensured students bridged the gap between theory and practice. A case in point was when the students proposed serious interventions to understand the challenges of employer branding. They did not simply apply theoretical concepts to make sense of the situations; they embedded their understanding within the real business contexts of the challenges they were addressing (Capone *et al.*, 2015; Juergensmeyer, 2011).

Pairs of students from each country formed research teams to work independently, aligning with a theoretical framework they had collectively developed. They also worked independently in reasonably aligned contexts, using research instruments they created to conduct case studies within their respective contexts. This experience enhanced their academic and professional capabilities, resulting in tangible research outcomes, including participation in international academic events and institutional recognition for outstanding projects (Goto and Gutiérrez-Gómez, 2023; Manfra and Bullock, 2014).

For the professors, action research served as a tool for refining pedagogical practices. By systematically incorporating student feedback, the team improved course delivery. This iterative approach also ensured cultural sensitivity. When students highlighted the need for locally relevant examples, professors developed a case study to further understand the topic. They organized an international webinar featuring expert presenters in employer branding strategies from companies in both countries, enriching discussions and ensuring students understood the content across diverse contexts (Harris and Seo, 2023; Pulman, 2012; Van Wyk, 2007).

In this experience, participants engaged in collaborative, iterative cycles of planning and reflection that allowed them to compare and analyze localized perspectives on employer branding with global practices (Bhatt, 2001; Capone *et al.*, 2015). Regarding knowledge creation, Meyer and Land (2005) describe knowledge as something that can be created by individuals or groups working together. Our COIL students created knowledge when they worked with their partners to better understand the problems faced by Peruvian and Brazilian SMCs regarding employer branding.

The methodology ensured equal participation among all members, who could create knowledge, share insights, and learn from one another. This democratized knowledge creation (Wood *et al.*, 2019).

What is excellent about COIL is that it is a tool through which we can work on direct interventions that are intended to understand and aim to resolve the problems under study. In this case, the work done by the COIL students provided local companies in both countries with some information and feedback as a result of this research. More importantly, these projects emphasized the development of intercultural communication skills and helped develop their creativity and critical thinking skills (Al-Fattal, 2025; Brown, 2024; Kapenieks, 2011).

The methodology ultimately advanced a global perspective on management by incorporating cross-cultural views into assignments. In collaborative tasks, students compared the labor conditions of Brazil and Peru, fostering mutual intercultural insight as they strategically formed improvement or implementation strategies for a global workplace (Velazquez *et al.*, 2018).

Although action research offers clear benefits for COIL courses, it is also necessary to acknowledge the related challenges of planning, which demands a considerable investment of time and can be highly uneven in student engagement. These proved to be significant issues for the project undertaken by the Brazil and Peru teams, in which assembling all project members across two countries to participate in synchronous meetings presented a cross-cultural and cross-time-zone conundrum.

9.4 Results and Discussion

At the end of the experience, feedback was given to both participating students and teachers. We were able to identify areas for improvement, perceived benefits of using the COIL methodology, and the competencies most developed by the students, according to the professors' perceptions.

The points of attention to be considered are related to differences in language, time zone, and academic level, the minimum coordination of standards, and sample selection considering cultural, social, economic, and political similarities and differences.

Regarding language differences, we found that some groups during the implementation of the research project faced problems with languages

(Spanish, Portuguese, or English), even though at the time of recruiting the groups in each country, it was indicated that it was advisable to master at least two of the languages to avoid communication problems. While it is true that in many cases the problem was overcome using informatics tools, it represented a problem that required the intervention of the professors in several instances. This point will be considered in future editions, with minimum language proficiency requirements.

Regarding the time zone differences, the two-hour time difference sometimes posed problems when coordinating meetings, especially because many of the participants, in addition to their academic timetable, also had work schedules that limited the available time options for coordination meetings. Prior coordination of meeting times for work meetings can be beneficial.

The academic levels of the students participating in the projects, the courses to which the research belongs, and the course requirements should be similar across all the educational institutions involved, so that the demands are evenly matched.

The standards of work, presentation, protocols, corrections, grading, etc., must be coordinated previously among student teams and the teaching team to ensure processes and structures remain cohesive and aligned with the objectives established by the team from the beginning of the research.

The sample selection process considering cultural, social, economic, and political similarities and differences is an issue that demands attention. It is essential to remember that if research is carried out in transnational companies, corporate standardization of policies and processes will lead to more similar parameters. However, if research is conducted in SMCs, individuals or institutions with a strong local identity may have greater socio-cultural, political, and economic differences. In this and other aspects, the choice of similar study objects is essential. This coordination usually takes a long time and therefore should be planned well in advance.

On the other hand, according to the perception gathered, we have the benefits that the COIL methodology can bring to research for students, professors, and the institutions involved.

Both students and professors highlighted the development of intercultural competences, which is a factor highlighted in the objectives of several universities in the region. It is also of great importance to students, as it allows for a better understanding of applied theory in different contexts.

Globalization and the integration of the world economy increasingly require students, professors, and researchers to have a more open perspective, identifying their own characteristics and different ones generated in other countries in the same region, allowing for a greater understanding of the interactions of contextual factors.

Another aspect of great importance is the development of cross-cultural communication skills, which allow the identification of cultural and linguistic similarities and differences between the participating countries. Often, the distortions that can be found in cross-cultural communication arise when a common language is used among participants who do not share the language (usually English). Paradoxically, this phenomenon also occurs very often between countries that share the same language, because sometimes the use of certain words or phrases has different connotations.

Recognizing the characteristics of the local context and identifying differences and similarities with other realities allows for a greater understanding of the dynamics upon which the various theories investigated are based and broadens the clarity and understanding of the topics dealt with. This will enable them to apply their knowledge in other contexts and realities, allowing for the universality of knowledge.

It also allows for the development of academic and professional ties in the region, which can lead to greater academic, commercial, and productive interactions in Latin America.

Participants also recognized the development and reinforcement of competencies such as the following:

- *Negotiation*: Participants, both students and teachers, were required to reach agreements on the processes, objectives, and methodologies to be used during the project.
- *Propositional argumentation*: Through this, they practiced and improved how they present ideas, support them, and defend them to people with different languages, varied contexts, and particular experiences.
- *Time management*: Many students were simultaneously employed and engaged in the assigned activities, which made balancing academic

responsibilities with professional and personal commitments challenging.

- *Decision-making processes*: These required necessary competence, as they keep the research team together, keep them focused on objectives, and improves the fluidity of processes.
- The development of expertise within one's regional contexts, without relying on foreign theories or needing to tropicalize knowledge.

Each particular group or case study could face different problems and situations, generated by the academic demands of each university, the individual work responsibilities of the participants, or particular personality issues of each member; therefore, teamwork, both at the level of students and teachers, should be established from the beginning and continue to develop throughout the project, focusing on related skills and managing flexibility without losing sight of the objectives.

9.5 Final Considerations

In conclusion, the COIL methodology is a handy tool for fulfilling the internationalization requirements currently focused on by Latin American universities. In addition, it also facilitates:

- the generation of coordinated academic work environments with different regional and global institutions in research and teaching;
- international activities with little investment of time and money, enabling the exchange of knowledge, culture, and methodologies;
- the development of future research and teaching projects, due to its great flexibility, which allows it to adapt to different requirements, substantially improve academic management with minimal financial and time investment, develop and reinforce new skills in multicultural and multidisciplinary teams, improve understanding and adaptation to new socio-cultural contexts, and create academic and professional ties that facilitate regional cooperation in the production of knowledge;
- the continued development of other academic activities based on this methodology, which adapts its characteristics to the needs of each scientific or artistic area, allows integration and development at the regional level, and improves the development and management of knowledge in Latin American universities.

The COIL methodology can improve the creation and management of knowledge in universities, both regionally and globally, allowing for greater interaction among them.

After the course, participants recognized that some of the principal benefits included the opportunity to develop intercultural competence by improving students' cross-cultural communication skills and their ability to understand and confront cultural differences and apply their knowledge in real business settings. However, some challenges made the activity difficult to carry out, which need to be considered for future collaborations. The students experienced some difficulties with the language, which sometimes presented a barrier and disrupted the smooth running of the experience. Another difficulty was the time zone differences, making it difficult to coordinate meetings throughout the course. Besides, it is essential to highlight that the academic level and course requirements should be the same (or at least similar) for students and that there is a need for greater coordination among teachers regarding minimum standards. Despite these challenges, action research in COIL remains a valuable approach for fostering collaboration, intercultural learning, and the co-creation of knowledge.

At the end of this project, it is possible to verify that the COIL experience provided opportunities to test different competencies, such as negotiation, propositional argumentation, decision-making processes, conflict resolution, and specific knowledge about the central theme (employer branding). The use of the COIL methodology in knowledge construction, as a tool for knowledge creation and development, resulted in increased understanding of new day-to-day situations within the program's management or the students' organizations. Furthermore, it also presented countless challenges that were not adequately addressed during the theoretical construction of this project.

That said, it is possible to ensure that the COIL methodology is an excellent tool for meeting institutional internationalization requirements and simulating a work environment involving people from different parts of the world. Therefore, its application could offer institutions better standing and an alternative to meet the expectations of people who do not necessarily have the financial resources to undertake an international experience of this magnitude. Furthermore, as recommendations for future studies, it is suggested that new research on the academic management part of projects of this nature be carried out, in addition to the motivational aspects for more committed monitoring of the student in long-term didactic structures as well as methods for resolving conflicts between participants based on an understanding and appreciation of the work requested and knowledge production.

References

Al-Fattal, A. 'Marketing Across Cultures.' In *Power of One: Theories, Strategies, and Case Studies in Internationalizing the Student Experience*, edited by K. E. Chapman and D. E. Beard. 2025, https://open.lib.umn.edu/powerofone/.

Bhatt, G. D. 'Knowledge Management in Organizations: Examining the Interaction Between Technologies, Techniques, and People.' *Journal of Knowledge Management*, 5, no. 1 (2001): 68–75, https://doi.org/10.1108/13673270110384419.

Brown, T. M. 'Participatory Action Research.' *Oxford Research Encyclopedia of Criminology and Criminal Justice*, 2024, https://doi.org/10.1093/acrefore/9780190264079.013.838.

Capone, R., I. D'Acunto, M. R. Del Sorbo, F. Del Regno, and F. S. Tortoriello. 'Action Research: A New Perspective in Math and Science Education.' In *Proceedings of the 5th International Conference New Perspectives in Science Education*. 2015, 26–30, https://conference.pixel-online.net/NPSE/files/npse/ed0005/FP/2309-SERA1474-FP-NPSE5.pdf.

Goto, K. and Y. Y. Gutiérrez-Gómez. 'Research Globally, Learn Globally: An Innovative Course-Based Research Project Through Collaborative Online International Learning (COIL) Among Nutrition Students From American and Mexican Universities.' *Pedagogy in Health Promotion*, 10, no. 1 (2023): 56–62, https://doi.org/10.1177/23733799231214960.

Hackett, S., J. Janssen, P. Beach, M. Perreault, J. Beelen, and J. V. Tartwijk. 'The Effectiveness of Collaborative Online International Learning (COIL) on Intercultural Competence Development in Higher Education.' *International Journal of Educational Technology in Higher Education*, 20, no. 1 (2023): 1–21, https://doi.org/10.1186/s41239-022-00373-3.

Harris, J. and M. Seo. 'Cultivating Collaborative Online International Learning (COIL) Experiences for Undergraduate Health Educators in the Classroom.' In *Education and New Developments*, Vol. 2. 2023, 504–508, https://doi.org/10.36315/2023v2end112.

Hildebrando Júnior, C. A., and K. R. Finardi. 'Internationalization and Virtual Collaboration: Insights from COIL Experiences.' *Ensino em Foco*, 2018, https://blog.ufes.br/kyriafinardi/files/2018/09/Hildeblando-Jr-Finardi-2018.pdf.

Johnston, M. and S. Forrest. 'Action Research and Indigenous Research Methodologies.' In *Indigenous Research Methodologies*, edited by M. Johnston and S. Forrest. Springer, Singapore, 2020, 41–71, https://doi.org/10.1007/978-981-15-4913-7_4.

Juergensmeyer, E. 'Sharing Control: Developing Research Literacy through Community-Based Action Research.' *Community Literacy Journal*, 5, no. 2 (2011): 153–167, https://doi.org/10.25148/CLJ.5.2.009417.

Kapenieks, J. 'Knowledge Creation: Action Research in E-Learning Teams.' In *2011 IEEE Global Engineering Education Conference (EDUCON)*. IEEE, 2011, 859–864, https://doi.org/10.1109/EDUCON.2011.5773245.

Kapenieks, J. and I. Salīte. 'Action Research for Creating Knowledge in an E-Learning Environment.' *Journal of Teacher Education for Sustainability*, 14, no. 2 (2012): 111–129, https://doi.org/10.2478/V10099-012-0012-X.

Késia, A., I. F. Pereira, R. M. A. de Oliveira, and R. I. da Silva. 'A Pesquisa-ação nas Publicações da Revista Brasileira de Educação (2016-2018).' *Research, Society and Development*, 8, no. 10 (2019): e08810720.

Manfra, M. M. and D. K. Bullock. 'Action Research for Educational Communications and Technology.' In *Handbook of Research on Educational Communications and Technology*, edited by J. M. Spector, M. D. Merrill, J. Elen, and M. J. Bishop. Springer: New York, NY, 2014, 161–172, https://doi.org/10.1007/978-1-4614-3185-5_14.

Meyer, J. H. F. and R. Land. 'Threshold Concepts and Troublesome Knowledge (2): Epistemological Considerations and A Conceptual Framework for Teaching and Learning.' *High Educ*, 49 (2005): 373–388 (2005). https://doi.org/10.1007/ s10734-004-6779-5.

Núñez, M. E., P. M. García, and A. Abbas. 'The Mediating Role of Self-Regulation Between Emotional Intelligence and Student Performance in Online Global Classroom-Based Collaborative International Online Learning (COIL): Empirical Evidence from Four Partner Universities of Latin America.' *Research in Globalization*, 7 (2023), https://doi.org/10.1016/j.resglo.2023.100137.

Pulman, M. 'Round and Round We Go: An 'Action' Ride on the Rehearsing and Performing Cycle.' *British Journal of Music Education*, 29, no. 02 (2012): 213–231, https://doi.org/10.1017/S0265051712000022.

Silva, G. L., K. C. Brown, C. G. D. Porto, and J. F. Arruda Neto. 'The Practice of COIL (Collaborative Online International Learning) in Brazil: A Case Study on the Practice of Sustainable Development in the Academic Environment.' *Revista AIDIS de Ingeniería y Ciencias Ambientales: Investigación, desarrollo y práctica*, 17, no. 3 (2024): 627–648, https://doi.org/10.22201/iingen.0718378xe.2024.17.3.87111.

Staron, M. 'Teaching Action Research.' In *Handbook on Teaching Empirical Software Engineering*, edited by A. Zaidan. Springer Nature Switzerland: Cham, 2024, 387–411, https://doi.org/10.48550/arxiv.2408.02399.

Van Wyk, A. J. 'Action Research as a Means of Course Development in Higher Education: A Case Study.' *South African Journal of Higher Education*, 20, no. 3 (2007): 558–572, https://doi.org/10.4314/SAJHE.V20I3.25595.

Vázquez-Villegas, P., D. Gómez-Guerrero, and L. A. Mejía-Manzano. 'Evaluation of Good Practices and Opportunity Areas of a Collaborative Online

International Learning (COIL) Program: Global Shared Learning Classroom.' *Education and Information Technologies*, 2024, https://doi.org/10.1007/s10639-024-12739-3.

Velazquez, L., K. M. Perkins, N. Munguia, and D. S. Zepeda. 'A Coil-Enhanced Course on International Perspectives of Climate Change.' In *Climate Literacy and Innovations in Climate Change Education*, edited by W. Leal Filho and S. L. Hemstock. Springer: Cham, 2018, 215–227, https://doi.org/10.1007/978-3-319-70199-8_12.

Wood, L., M. McAteer, and J. Whitehead. 'How are Action Researchers Contributing to Knowledge Democracy? A Global Perspective.' *Educational Action Research*, 27, no. 1 (2019): 7–21, https://doi.org/10.1080/09650792.2018.1531044.

© 2026 World Scientific Publishing Europe Ltd.
https://doi.org/10.1142/9781800617414_0010

Chapter 10

Entrepreneurial Skills, Human Capital, and the Future of Work: The Entrepreneurial Education as a Lifelong Learning Process

Kelly Cristina Benetti Tonani Tosta[*,§], Graziela Simone Tonin[†], Nilara Izabel Von Fruauff Pavan[‡], and Humberto Tonani Tosta[*]

[*]*Federal University of Fronteira Sul, Brazil*

[†]*Insper, Brazil*

[‡]*Federal University of Santa Catarina, Brazil*

[§]*kellytosta@uffs.edu.br*

Abstract

This chapter explores the relationships among entrepreneurial skills, human capital, and the future of work, highlighting the potential of entrepreneurial education as a lifelong learning process for navigating the rapidly evolving labor market. Drawing on recent research and global labor market predictions, we argue that entrepreneurial skills – such as critical thinking, resilience, creativity, and leadership – are becoming increasingly vital in a world characterized by technological disruption, particularly with the advent of generative artificial intelligence (GenAI).

While entrepreneurship has traditionally been associated with business creation, we redefine it here as a mindset and skillset that enhances individual adaptability and innovation, empowering people to succeed across various professional fields. We discuss how entrepreneurial education, when rooted in experiential and action-based methodologies, plays a transformative role in equipping individuals with the knowledge, skills, and attitudes (KSAs) that constitute human capital. This approach not only fosters entrepreneurial intention but also helps develop competencies relevant to intrapreneurship, innovation, and knowledge management. By combining theoretical and practical learning, such education prepares learners to recognize opportunities, manage risks, and lead change in uncertain environments. The chapter also underscores the necessity to redesign educational strategies to meet the demands of a knowledge- and innovation-driven economy. Entrepreneurial education significantly enhances intellectual capital and strategic adaptability, serving as a crucial element in developing a workforce capable of sustaining innovation, inclusion, and resilience in the future of work.

Keywords: Entrepreneurial skills, human capital, future of work, entrepreneurship.

10.1 Introduction

The way we think about work is changing at both the individual and organizational levels, and the future of work is expected to involve a new set of professional skills, as outlined in the World Economic Forum's (2025) Future of Jobs Report. This report states that, on average, workers can expect two-fifths (39%) of their existing skill sets to be transformed or become obsolete over the period 2025–2030.

The report also explores the core skills expected in 2030. The top 10 skills that are not only considered critical now but are also projected to become even more important are artificial intelligence (AI) and big data; analytical thinking; creative thinking; resilience, flexibility, and agility; technological literacy; leadership and social influence; curiosity and lifelong learning; systems thinking; talent management; and motivation and self-awareness.

Considering the literature (Yalcintas *et al.*, 2023; Muñoz *et al.*, 2020; Vetrivel and Krishnamoorthy, 2019; Pandit *et al.*, 2018; Zahro, 2016), excluding AI, big data, and technological literacy, all of these are considered entrepreneurial skills.

Although entrepreneurship is often associated with starting a new business or venture, as defined by Rae and Carswell (2000), its original concept is somewhat broader, more closely related to innovation and the ability to generate and implement new ideas and processes, whether in a new venture or in improving an existing business (Landstrom, 2010). Recent studies have addressed the skills necessary for this, which coincide with those mentioned previously.

In this regard, Marvel *et al.* (2016) define human capital outcomes as knowledge, skills, and abilities (KSAs), which may include factors such as domain knowledge, sales and negotiation, planning, prototyping, decision-making, problem-solving, teamwork, and communication, and are therefore related to the set of skills presented.

This set of entrepreneurial skills can be developed through both formal and informal education, also known as entrepreneurial education (Muñoz *et al.*, 2020; Ramos *et al.*, 2020; Jwara and Hoque, 2018). Rae and Carswell (2000) suggest that the role of learning in this context is the development of capabilities used to recognize and act on opportunities. It means that learning is a dynamic process that enables entrepreneurial behavior to be enacted.

For entrepreneurial education to fulfill its role in developing skills, it is necessary to move away from traditional models of passive education and create space for experimentation and meaningful learning, as shown in different methodologies presented in the literature and their demonstrated impact on student development (Kujala *et al.*, 2022; Zahro, 2016).

While entrepreneurship education can be beneficial, its effects are more substantial when the vision presented is more realistic (Rankhumise, 2014). However, it can also be insignificant (Alakaleek *et al.*, 2023) if it diminishes students' confidence in their abilities, if it remains focused on traditional teaching methods, or if it lacks practical exposure (Paliwal *et al.*, 2022).

Entrepreneurial education requires planning, time, and clarity about the program objectives (Jamaluddin *et al.*, 2019; Srivastava *et al.*, 2019). With a well-prepared and well-conducted program, according to Muñoz, Guerra, and Mosey (2020), entrepreneurial skills can be developed even in individuals whose backgrounds and professional trajectories are not directly related to business contexts.

From this perspective, this chapter aims to present the connections between human capital, entrepreneurship, and the future of work (Yuksel, 2024; Alshahrani *et al.*, 2024; Chaudhary *et al.*, 2023; Hong and Zhang, 2023; Dabic *et al.*, 2021; Crupi *et al.*, 2021; Paoloni *et al.*, 2020; Marvel *et al.*, 2016). The focus is to present entrepreneurship education as a process for developing entrepreneurial skills and enhancing human capital in a future labor market driven by knowledge and innovation.

10.2 Future of Work Driven by Knowledge and Innovation

Over the years, the characteristics of work and the impact of innovation have evolved in response to the waves, as proposed by Alvin Toffler (1995). The first wave, the primary form of production and wealth generation, was agriculture, with most of the population working in the countryside, a form that lasted until the beginning of the Industrial Revolution in the late 18th century. The second wave – the Industrial Revolution – introduced mechanization, mass production, and urbanization, transforming how people worked and how labor was organized. Factories replaced workshops, and workers often faced harsh and precarious working conditions. It began around 1760 (in the United Kingdom) and lasted until the emergence of the information society and basic automation around the 1960s–1970s, leading to the reduction of thousands of jobs. The third wave began around the 1970s with the popularization of personal computers and continues to this day, marking the era of information and digitalization. This phase transformed work by introducing digital technologies, advanced automation, and global connectivity, shifting the focus from industry to knowledge and services. It brought new forms of work, such as remote and freelance jobs, while increasing the need for skills and innovation, generating profound impacts on the organization of work and the global economy.

Toffler (1995), Drucker (1999), and Davenport and Prusak (2003), among others, announce the beginning of a "knowledge society," sharing the perception that knowledge generates value, drives change, and fosters competitiveness within organizations.

According to Toffler's predictions, numerous studies demonstrate that we are living in the fourth wave, characterized by the convergence of biotechnology and information technology, as well as the increasing importance of ethics and sustainability. This context suggests that succeeding organizations will adopt responsible practices regarding society and the environment.

These changes and innovations have been reshaping the future of work, which is evolving rapidly and impacting the skills individuals must develop to prepare for job transformations. The impact of technologies such as generative AI and expanded internet access is transforming business models worldwide, which may be considered a fifth wave. According to the Future of Jobs Report (2025), geoeconomic fragmentation, economic uncertainty, demographic shifts, and the green transition are major drivers that will shape and transform the labor market by 2030.

Furthermore, according to LinkedIn, their skills taxonomy includes 41,000 skills, of which 121 are classified as AI skills.

One important highlight is that many AI-related jobs require not only AI skills but also people skills. Technology professionals who can combine both sets of skills get promoted 13% faster than those who have only hard skills.

Generative AI (GenAI) and automation are expected to displace many jobs. For example, even less-exposed roles, such as human resources managers, have 61.7% of their tasks with low potential for automation, but 16.1% are automatable, and their roles are expected to change by up to 65% by 2030. On the other hand, a recent study of the International Labour Organization (ILO), in partnership with Poland's National Research Institute (NASK), has updated and refined the Global Index of Occupational Exposure to Generative Artificial Intelligence. The study reveals that, in the initial phase, the impact of AI will primarily affect the form and transformation of tasks rather than entirely replacing human work (ILO, 2025).

Another important and concerning finding is that women are more exposed to occupations with high levels of GenAI – globally, 4.7% of women versus 2.4% of men – meaning the impact on their jobs and careers is likely to be greater (ILO, 2025). In the United States, LinkedIn data show that women are more exposed to jobs at risk of automation by AI: 57% of women are in occupations highly susceptible to disruption, compared to 43% of men. In contrast, only 46% of women hold roles likely to be augmented by AI, compared to 54% of men. Additionally, women demonstrate lower awareness and confidence regarding the impact and use of AI in their professional lives. Many of these jobs will still require human intervention to be completed (ILO, 2025).

On the other hand, the urgency to develop more talent, if aligned with intentional initiatives and supportive policies, could help train more women as specialists in those fields. In a recent study, PwC (2024) highlights that AI can be used to advance gender equity. It can support the identification and reduction of biases in hiring and career progression processes regardless of gender, enable personalized skill development tailored to women, and offer immersive training experiences that help raise awareness and address gender bias. However, the study also emphasizes that most AI algorithms and models today are still predominantly developed by male professionals, which can reinforce and even amplify existing gender biases.

The impact of AI means that people need to develop skills such as learning how to learn, technological literacy, and AI literacy. Those who do not will quickly become obsolete and easily replaceable, even by GenAI, which can perform tasks more efficiently and productively. One of the main challenges to this change is the lack of AI-related skills.

The fact is that AI is already impacting – and will increasingly impact – all levels of occupations across virtually every field, transforming how we work, where we work, and how businesses operate. This impact will be cross-cutting, affecting industries at all levels.

When considering what is essential for the population that will represent 74% of the workforce by 2030, it is notable that most of Generation Z (57%) and Millennials (56%) have already been using generative AI in their work. These generations will comprise a significant portion of the labor force. This may allow greater mobility of professionals across a wide array of industries. Seventy percent of young people aged 18–25 believe that GenAI offers opportunities to expand their capabilities. Nearly two-thirds of respondents feel optimistic about the transformations taking place in the world of work and view AI as a tool for learning and enhancing the quality of their work (PwC, 2024). According to research by Deloitte (2025), these generations expect to learn other skills, such as soft skills, time management, and industry-specific knowledge, which they consider the most important to develop through mentorship and guidance (86% of Gen Z and 84% of Millennials), as well as through learning and practical experience (89% of both generations). Although they are more digitally native, they still need to gain experience and develop in areas such as soft skills – and they expect this to happen through practical, hands-on activities in the workplace.

This future is not distant; it is unfolding now at an unprecedented speed. We need to act while we discover what this new work model will look like and what our role will be in each of these areas. Understanding technology and developing entrepreneurial skills are essential to remain competitive in the job market. Beyond that, it is necessary to be a protagonist driving the future – automating what should be automated and learning to utilize AI tools for improved productivity and efficiency while preserving our human essence, values, and well-established ethical principles.

The future is a rapidly transforming present – unfolding at an unprecedented pace – where digitalization and technology are being applied across all areas and levels of business. In this context, the value of essential human skills becomes even more evident, and the way we educate our youth must be drastically rethought – not only in terms of which skills and competencies to develop but also in moving beyond technical excellence alone. It is crucial to focus on developing and training young people in soft skills, including entrepreneurial abilities such as critical thinking, problem-solving, proactivity, resilience, continuous learning, and other essential skills (LinkedIn, 2025). These data highlight the urgent need to integrate theoretical and practical knowledge more closely, encourage early collaboration and experience-sharing between professionals and academics, and build strong bridges between these worlds so that young people are equipped to navigate current challenges and lead the way toward a more innovative, human-centered, sustainable, and equitable future.

Data show that the future of work is increasingly dependent on the ability to leverage human capital for innovation and sustainability. It involves integrating human capital with entrepreneurial strategies to create sustainable business models.

10.3 Entrepreneurial Skills and Human Capital

When we discuss human capital, it is essential to distinguish it from other types of capital. As defined by Becker (1993), a person cannot be separated from their knowledge, skills, health, or values in the same way as financial and physical assets can. It is embodied in people.

On the other hand, strategic management studies have emphasized the pivotal role of knowledge assets and how they are leveraged. In dynamic competitive environments, the exploitation of knowledge assets requires firms to possess proper dynamic capabilities in order to achieve success (Teece *et al.*, 1997).

Traditional organizations develop and preserve knowledge assets through highly people-centered training processes. In this context, competence management and other knowledge management tools emerge within organizations as a response to these demands, related to organizational learning concepts and bringing along a set of reflections about work, individual roles, and lifelong learning through educational programs such as corporate universities (Bitencourt, 2010; Fleury and Fleury, 2004; Carbone, 2015).

However, in this new scenario characterized by the presence of AI, companies will increasingly be differentiated by what they know, namely, by knowing how to do new things better and faster than others (Davenport and Prusak, 2003; North, 2010). In this context, companies seek to mechanize or outsource operational activities, focusing instead on those that are knowledge-based and geared toward developing products and processes. Additionally, the company needs to adopt a new culture of knowledge management.

A theoretical connection was presented by Marvel *et al.* (2016), suggesting that the premise of human capital and entrepreneurship research is that human capital can substantially influence entrepreneurship. The authors concluded that learning theories often emphasize the cumulative nature of human capital and the importance of knowledge acquisition. However, very few empirical studies are available that examine learning in entrepreneurship. Some human resources and entrepreneurship literature has also emphasized competencies, focusing on the individual level, which encompass the knowledge, skills, and personality characteristics required to enable their implementation toward desired outcomes (Hayton and Kelley, 2006; Man *et al.*, 2002).

However, competencies manifest at the organizational level and are ultimately composed of knowledge, skills, and other resources embedded in the organization's people, structure, processes, and relationships that enable value-enhancing strategies. A multilevel lens can be particularly valuable in understanding the linkages between individual human capital and organizational competencies in the context of corporate entrepreneurship.

Skills that apply specifically to an entrepreneurial task may provide advantages within the entrepreneurship process. A variety of skills can be developed through investments in training or experience, and they can also be enhanced in combination with education and practice. Of particular interest is how skills specific to the entrepreneurial process can be developed (Marvel *et al.*, 2016).

10.4 The Role of Entrepreneurial Education in Developing Essential Skills

Entrepreneurial education contributes to the qualification and requalification of individuals in response to rapid job market changes resulting from technological advances; therefore, the entrepreneurial skills developed are essential in this context. It has existed since the 20th century as a means of preparing administrators to act as entrepreneurs (Lopes, 2010). However, authors such as Buchnik, Gilad, and Maital (2018), Ilerisoy *et al.* (2021), and Zahro (2016) debate the structure of entrepreneurial education.

While authors such as Chevalier *et al.* (2022) and Buchnik, Gilad, and Maital (2018) discuss entrepreneurial education from a perspective of its outcome aimed at awakening interest in entrepreneurship, there is a group of authors such as Trif *et al.* (2022) and Ilerisoy *et al.* (2021) who discuss the aspects of the development of entrepreneurial skills, which may or may not generate an intention to undertake.

This is a direct result of understanding the entrepreneur's identity. Initially, the entrepreneur was thought of as someone who opens a business (Rae and Carswell, 2000). However, the most widely used concept today is that the entrepreneur is someone who possesses a set of skills, including innovation and creativity, which they use to create and sustain a business (Ferras *et al.*, 2018).

This definition broadens the vision of entrepreneurial education, enabling the creation of adaptable training programs structured in modules or stages, where education is not only about entrepreneurship but also for entrepreneurship (Lopes, 2010). Besides that, it allows us to consider entrepreneurship from Schumpeter's perspective, who defined the entrepreneur as an actor responsible for constantly disrupting the current economic equilibrium by introducing new ways of acting in society in which innovation plays a fundamental role (Lopes, 2010; Trif *et al.*, 2022; Ilerisoy *et al.*, 2021).

With this new perspective on the entrepreneur – who possesses a set of characteristics that highlight their innovative potential – it is possible to combine the definitions and concepts of competence. This definition of entrepreneur, encompassing individual characteristics, began to be understood from Durand's definition of competence (2000), in which the set of knowledge, skills, and attitudes, represented by the acronym KSAs, forms part of entrepreneurial skills that are interrelated with each other and are capable of development (Dornelas, 2021).

According to Osmani *et al.* (2017), creativity is the primary competence to be developed in entrepreneurial education and is directly linked to innovation (Koe *et al.*, 2018). On the other hand, Puni *et al.* (2018), Razak *et al.* (2018), and von Graevenitz *et al.* (2010) associate creativity with the ability to generate new ideas and identify opportunities in existing situations. Furthermore, von Graevenitz *et al.* (2010) connect creativity to other competencies, such as self-control.

As entrepreneurial education studies focus on entrepreneurial skills, authors observe that technical skills, business skills, problem-solving, and communication were the most easily developed attributes, while curiosity, leadership, passion, and tolerance for ambiguity are more challenging characteristics, especially soft skills (Besterfield-Sacre *et al.*, 2016; Ruswanti, 2016).

In this sense, Adeel, Daniel, and Botelho (2023), Trif *et al.* (2022), and Valenzuela-Keller *et al.* (2021) argue that entrepreneurial education will not develop skills in the same way but rather intensify specific traits. In agreement with this result, Adelowo and Henrico (2023) and Soomro and Shah (2022) suggest that entrepreneurial education programs at universities equip students with the ability to identify business opportunities.

In addition to recognizing opportunities, Soomro and Shah (2022) highlight the significant benefits of entrepreneurial education, including a perception of risk, innovation, and proactivity, as well as the knowledge required to create and manage a company.

According to Trif *et al.* (2022), the development of entrepreneurial skills through education programs is of utmost importance, as these skills mediate the relationship between entrepreneurial competence and entrepreneurial intention.

It is noteworthy that, in the view of Jwara and Hoque (2018), the creation of a business is a result of a larger process, and many of the skills discussed so far are not essential only to the entrepreneur (2018, p. 2):

> [...] Firstly, education provides individuals with independence and self-confidence. Secondly, people become aware of alternative career

> choices. Thirdly, one's horizon is broadened because you are better equipped to recognize opportunities. Lastly, education offers knowledge that can be used by an individual to develop new business venture opportunities.

Apart from that, Carneiro (2013, p. 18) points out that while entrepreneurship addresses innovation in creating something new in the form of organizations that generate value for society, intrapreneurship can be even more challenging since it promotes innovation within existing companies, in addition to dealing with the problems known to entrepreneurs: lack of resources, economic fluctuations, and lack of motivation. It also "has the challenging mission of breaking down the barriers created by organizations, with their bureaucracy and management that is resistant to change and innovation."

Although entrepreneurial skills are not exclusive to entrepreneurship and entrepreneurial education is a means to develop them, the literature still discusses the structure of entrepreneurial education programs. For example, studies by Paliwal *et al.* (2022) and Ayalew and Zeleke (2018) found a relationship between entrepreneurial education and entrepreneurial intention, but entrepreneurial skills demonstrated little to no significance.

According to Paliwal *et al.* (2022, p. 861), the problem lay in the design of entrepreneurial education actions, and they concluded that "we did not find sufficient evidence for this relationship due to the traditional teaching style or lack of practical exposure."

Jamaluddin *et al.* (2019) placed the time component as a relevant factor for the development of entrepreneurial skills through entrepreneurial education. According to the authors "entrepreneurship education programs need to be programmed in a more structured and timely manner. Thus, it can be concluded that consideration of time plays an important role in ensuring that the implementation of a program can be achieved" (p. 126).

In summary, the authors argue that entrepreneurial education programs need to be designed with the objective in mind; in other words, if the focus is on developing entrepreneurial skills, it is important to be clear about which skills will be developed within the program so that development can be monitored (Srivastava, Satsang, & Satsangee, 2019). In addition, theoretical and practical methodologies have demonstrated positive results in student development, whether through competitive programs, involvement with other entrepreneurs, or action-based learning (Buchnik, Gilad, & Maital, 2018; Kujala *et al.*, 2022; Zahro, 2016).

When entrepreneurial education programs are well-structured and designed in a cross-cutting manner, it is possible to achieve results similar to those of Muñoz, Guerra, and Mosey (2020, p. 20). For the authors, the contribution of the work is more profound: "This is remarkable because it shows that entrepreneurial skills can be developed even in people whose origins and professional trajectories are not directly related to business contexts."

10.5 Conclusion

The chapter addressed entrepreneurial education as a means of preparing and strengthening human capital for the future job market by developing entrepreneurial skills.

The theoretical connections between human capital, entrepreneurial education, and the future of work center on the strategic use of knowledge and innovation to develop essential skills. Human capital serves as a foundation for entrepreneurial activities, which in turn drive innovation and adaptability in the future work environment. This synergy is crucial for developing sustainable business models and achieving long-term competitive advantages.

The evolution of the concept of entrepreneurship and its relationship with entrepreneurial education highlights the importance of rethinking the development of professional skills in the future.

The studies discussed indicate that entrepreneurial education plays a crucial role in developing these skills, particularly when the programs are well-structured and aligned with market needs. However, it is essential to note that the effectiveness of these programs relies on meticulous planning and methodologies that integrate theory and practice, enabling students to acquire not only knowledge but also the confidence and ability to apply what they have learned in authentic contexts.

Furthermore, entrepreneurial education goes beyond training new entrepreneurs; it equips individuals to recognize opportunities, manage risks, and generate new ideas, preparing them for an increasingly dynamic and innovation-driven job market. As a lifelong learning process, it plays a crucial role in developing entrepreneurial skills. By integrating real-life experiences and prioritizing quality education, entrepreneurial education significantly enhances these skills, supporting individuals throughout their careers in both the current and future labor markets.

References

Adeel, S., A. D. Daniel, and A. Botelho. 'The Effect of Entrepreneurship Education on the Determinants of Entrepreneurial Behaviour Among Higher Education Students: A Multi-Group Analysis.' *Journal of Innovation and Knowledge*, 8, no. 1 (2023), https://doi.org/10.1016/j.jik.2023.100324.

Adelowo, C. M. and A. Henrico. 'Entrepreneurship Education, Personality Traits and University Environment as Predictors of Venture Creation Among Undergraduates in Nigeria.' *Forum Scientiae Oeconomia*, 11, no. 1 (2023), https://doi.org/10.23762/FSO_VOL11_NO1_3.

Alakaleek, W., Y. Harb, A. A. Harb, and A. Al Shishany. 'The Impact of Entrepreneurship Education: A Study of Entrepreneurial Outcomes.' *International Journal of Management Education*, 21, no. 2 (2023), https://doi.org/10.1016/j.ijme.2023.100800.

Alshahrani, M. N., M. Z. Yaqub, and M. A. Alabdli. 'Examining the Role of Intellectual Capital in Maturing Sustainable Competitive Advantage Through Enkindling Innovations in SMEs: The Moderating Role of Entrepreneurship-Orientation.' *Journal of Intellectual Capital*, 25, no. 2/3 (2024): 328–359, https://doi.org/10.1108/JIC-05-2023-0111.

Ayalew, M. M. and S. A. Zeleke. 'Modeling the Impact of Entrepreneurial Attitude on Self-Employment Intention Among Engineering Students in Ethiopia.' *Journal of Innovation and Entrepreneurship*, 7, no. 1 (2018): 1–27, https://doi.org/10.1186/s13731-018-0088-1.

Becker, G. S. *Human capital: A theoretical and Empirical Analysis with Special Reference to Education*, 3rd ed. The University of Chicago Press: Chicago, 1993.

Besterfield-Sacre, M., S. Zappe, A. Shartrand, and K. Hochstedt. 'Faculty and Student Perceptions of the Content of Entrepreneurship Courses in Engineering Education.' *Advances in Engineering Education*, 5, no. 1 (2016): 1–27, https://eric.ed.gov/?id=EJ1090562.

Bitencourt, C. *Gestão contemporânea de pessoas*. Editora Bookman: Brazil, 2010.

Buchnik, T., V. Gilad, and S. Maital. 'Universities' Influence on Student Decisions to Become Entrepreneurs: Theory and Evidence.' *Journal of Entrepreneurship Education*, 21, no. 3 (2018): 1–20, https://doi.org/10.1177/0971355717738595.

Carbone, P. P. 'Gestão por competência e educação corporativa: Caminhos para o desenvolvimento de competências.' *Inclusão Social*, 7, no. 1 (2015), https://revista.ibict.br/inclusao/article/view/1754.

Carneiro, J. G. S. P. *Intraempreendedorismo: Conceitos e práticas para construção de organizações inovadoras*. Qualitymark Editora: Brazil, 2013.

Chaudhary, S., A. Dhir, N. Farronato, M. Nicotra, and M. Pironti. 'Nexus between Entrepreneurial Orientation and Intellectual Capital.' *Journal of Intellectual Capital*, 24, no. 1 (2023): 70–114, https://doi.org/10.1108/JIC-09-2021-0256.

Chevalier, S., I. Calmé, H. Coillot, K. Le Rudulier, and E. Fouquereau. 'How can Students' Entrepreneurial Intention be Increased? The Role of Psychological Capital, Perceived Learning from an Entrepreneurship Education Program, Emotions and their Relationships.' *Europe's Journal of Psychology*, 18, no. 1 (2022), https://ejop.psychopen.eu/index.php/ejop/article/view/2889/2889.pdf.

Crupi, A., F. Cesaroni, and A. Minin. 'Understanding the Impact of Intellectual Capital on Entrepreneurship: A Literature Review.' *Journal of Intellectual Capital*, 22, no. 3 (2021): 528–559, https://doi.org/10.1108/JIC-02-2020-0054.

Dabić, M., N. Stojčić, M. Simić, V. Potočan, M. Slavković, and Z. Nedelko. 'Intellectual Agility and Innovation in Micro and Small Businesses: The Mediating Role of Entrepreneurial Leadership.' *Journal of Business Research*, 123 (2021): 683–695, https://doi.org/10.1016/j.jbusres.2020.10.013.

Davenport, T. H. and L. Prusak. *Conhecimento empresarial: Como as organizações gerenciam o seu capital intelectual*, 15th ed. Elsevier: Amsterdam, Netherlands, 2003.

Deloitte Global. *Gen Z and Millennial Survey*, 2025, https://www.deloitte.com/global/en/issues/work/genz-millennial-survey.html.

Dornelas, J. C. A. *Empreendedorismo: Transformando ideias em negócios*, 8th ed. Elsevier: Amsterdam, Netherlands, 2021.

Drucker, P. F. *Sociedade pós-capitalista*. Pioneira: São Paulo, 1999.

Durand, T. 'Forms of Incompetence.' In *Theory Development for Competence-Based Management*, Vol. 6. Jai Press, 2000.

Ferras, R. P. R., Lenzi, F. C., S. R. Stefano, and F. Ramos. 'Empreendedorismo Corporativo Em Organizações Públicas.' *REGEPE – Revista de Empreendedorismo e Gestão de Pequenas Empresas*, 7, no. 2 (2018): 31–66, https://doi.org/10.14211/regepe.v7i2.593.

Fleury, A. and M. T. L. Fleury. *Estratégias empresariais e formação de competências: Um quebra-cabeça caleidoscópico da indústria brasileira*, 3rd ed. Atlas: Rancho Santa Fe, 2004.

Hayton, J. C. and D. J. Kelley, 'A Competency-Based Framework for Promoting Corporate Entrepreneurship.' *Human Resource Management*, 45, no. 3 (2006): 407–427, https://doi.org/10.1002/hrm.20118.

Hong, Y. and M. Zhang. 'Bridging the Regional Innovation Policy and Entrepreneurship: The Role of Intellectual Capital.' *Journal of Intellectual Capital*, 24, no. 3 (2023): 854–875, https://doi.org/10.1108/JIC-12-2021-0332.

İlerisoy, Z. Y., Ayci, A., Ayci, H. and Kinaci, E. B. 'Impacts of Architectural Education on Entrepreneurial Intention: A Case Study of Senior Architects From Six Universities in Turkey.' *Archnet-IJAR*, 15, no. 3 (2021): 719–737, https://doi.org/10.1108/ARCH-11-2020-0269.

International Labour Organization. *Generative AI and jobs: A refined global index of occupational exposure*, Working paper, 2025, https://www.ilo.org/publications/generative-ai-and-jobs-refined-global-index-occupational-exposure.

Jamaluddin, R., M. H. Ali-Hamid, S. A. Kadir, A. Kamis, and S. Mohamed. 'Impact of Fashion Entrepreneurship Programme on Entrepreneurial Interests, Intention and Competences.' *Journal of Technical Education and Training*, 11, no. 1 (2019): 119–128, https://penerbit.uthm.edu.my/ojs/index.php/JTET/article/view/3125.

Jwara, N. and M. Hoque. 'Entrepreneurial Intentions Among University Students: A Case Study of Durban University of Technology.' *Academy of Entrepreneurship Journal*, 24, no. 3 (2018): 1–9, https://www.abacademies.org/articles/entrepreneurial-intentions-among-university-students-a-case-study-of-durban-university-of-technology-7559.html.

Koe, W. L., R. Krishnan, and S. Utami. 'The Influence of Entrepreneurial Skills on Business Start-Up Intention Among Bumiputra Students.' *Journal of Advanced Manufacturing Technology*, 12, no. 2 (2018): 53–64, https://www.scopus.com/inward/record.uri?eid=2-s2.0-85062543968&partnerID=40&md5=0dbb746ac2c6e8be91ee4b03de211233.

Kujala, I., A.-G. Nyström, C. Wendelin, and M. Brännback. 'Action-Based Learning Platform for Entrepreneurship Education: Case NÅA Business Center.' *Entrepreneurship Education and Pedagogy*, 5, no. 4 (2022): 576–598, https://doi.org/10.1177/25151274211045913.

Landström, H. *Pioneers in entrepreneurship and small business research*, 2nd ed. Springer: Cham, 2010.

LinkedIn. *Workplace learning report 2025: The rise of career champions*, 2025, https://learning.linkedin.com/content/dam/me/learning/en-us/images/lls-workplace-learning-report/2025/full-page/pdfs/LinkedIn-Workplace-Learning-Report-2025.pdf.

Lopes, R. M. A. *Educação empreendedora: Conceitos, modelos e práticas*, 1st ed. Elsevier, SEBRAE: Amsterdam, Netherlands, 2010.

Man, T. W., T. Lau, and K. F. Chan. (2002). The Competitiveness of Small and Medium Enterprises: A Conceptualization with Focus on Entrepreneurial Competencies. *Journal of Business Venturing*, 17, 123–142. https://doi.org/10.1016/S0883-9026(00)00058-6.

Marvel, M., C. R. Sproul, and J. L. Davis. 'Human Capital and Entrepreneurship Research: A Critical Review and Future Directions.' *Entrepreneurship Theory and Practice*, 40, no. 3 (2016): 599–626, https://doi.org/10.1111/etap.12136.

Muñoz, C. A., M. E. Guerra, and S. Mosey. 'The Potential Impact of Entrepreneurship Education on Doctoral Students within the Non-Commercial Research Environment in Chile.' *Studies in Higher Education*, 45, no. 3 (2020): 495–510, https://doi.org/10.1080/03075079.2019.1597036.

North, K. *Gestão do conhecimento: Um guia prático rumo à empresa inteligente.* Qualitymark, 2010.

Osmani, M., R. El-Haddadeh, N. M. Hindi, and V. Weerakkody. 'The Influence of Creativity on the Entrepreneurial Intention of University Female Graduates: An Sem Approach.' *Industry and Higher Education*, 36, no. 5 (2017): 556–567, https://doi.org/10.1177/09504222211061231.

Paliwal, M., B. K. Rajak, V. Kumar, and S. Singh. 'Assessing the Role of Creativity and Motivation to Measure Entrepreneurial Education and Entrepreneurial Intention.' *International Journal of Educational Management*, 36, no. 5 (2022): 854–874, https://doi.org/10.1108/IJEM-05-2021-0178.

Pandit, D., M. Joshi, and S. R. Tiwari. 'Examining Entrepreneurial Intention in Higher Education: An Exploratory Study of College Students in India.' *Journal of Entrepreneurship*, 27, no. 1 (2018): 25–46, https://doi.org/10.1177/0971355717738595.

Paoloni, M., D. Coluccia, S. Fontana, and S. Solimene. 'Knowledge Management, Intellectual Capital and Entrepreneurship: A Structured Literature Review.' *Journal of Knowledge Management*, 24, no. 8 (2020): 1797–1818, https://doi.org/10.1108/JKM-01-2020-0052.

Puni, A., A. Anlesinya, and P. D. A. Korsorku. 'Entrepreneurial Education, Self-Efficacy and Intentions in Sub-Saharan Africa.' *African Journal of Economic and Management Studies*, 9, no. 4 (2018): 492–511, https://doi.org/10.1108/AJEMS-09-2017-0211.

PwC. *How AI is accelerating gender equity in the workplace*, 2024, https://www.pwc.com/gx/en/about/inclusion/gender-equity/ai-accelerating-womens-inclusion-workplace.html.

Rae, D. and M. Carswell. 'Towards a Conceptual Understanding of Entrepreneurial Learning.' *Journal of Small Business and Enterprise Development*, 8, no. 2 (2001): 150–158, https://doi.org/10.1108/eum0000000006816.

Ramos, D., M. J. Madeira, and F. A. Duarte. 'Entrepreneurship Education and Entrepreneurial Intention: The Case of Portugal.' *Economy of Region*, 15, no. 1 (2020): 157–170, https://doi.org/10.17059/2020-1-12.

Rankhumise, E. 'Entrepreneurial Intentions among Students: A Case of Tshwane University of Technology, South Africa.' *Problems and Perspectives in Management*, 12, no. 2 (2014): 105–111, https://www.researchgate.net/publication/287423770_Entrepreneurial_intentions_among_students_A_case_of_Tshwane_University_of_Technology_South_Africa.

Razak, N. S. N. B. A., H. B. Kosnin, and N. A. B. Buang. 'The Influence of Creativity Towards Entrepreneurial Intention and the Entrepreneurial Career Choice Behaviour in 21st Century Learning.' *Journal of Social Sciences Research*, 2, no. 6 (2018): 45–51, https://doi.org/10.32861/jssr.spi6.45.51.

Ruswanti, E. (2016). Entrepreneurship Knowledge, Training Home Industry, and Attitude Towards Entrepreneurial Intention Entrepreneurship. *International Journal of Applied Business and Economic Research*, 14(5), 2803–2816. https://digilib.esaunggul.ac.id/public/UEU-Article-8687-ER_GTAR_2015.pdf.

Soomro, B. A. and N. Shah. 'Entrepreneurship Education, Entrepreneurial Self-Efficacy, Need for Achievement and Entrepreneurial Intention among Commerce Students in Pakistan.' *Education and Training*, 64, no. 1 (2022): 107–125, https://doi.org/10.1108/ET-01-2021-0023.

Srivastava, S., K. Satsangi, and N. Satsangee. 'Identification of Entrepreneurial Education Contents Using Nominal Group Technique.' *Journal of Technical Education and Training*, 61, no. 7 (2019): 1001–1019, https://doi.org/10.1108/ET-05-2018-0105.

Teece, D. J., G. Pisano, and A. Shuen. 'Dynamic Capabilities and Strategic Management.' *Strategic Management Journal*, 18, no. 7 (1997): 509–533, https://doi.org/10.1002/(SICI)1097-0266(199708)18:7<509::AID-SMJ882>3.0.CO;2-Z.

Toffler, A. *A terceira onda*, 20. ed. Record: Rio de Janeiro, 1995.

Trif, S. M., C. G. Noja, M. Cristea, C. Enache, and O. Didraga. 'Modelers of Students' Entrepreneurial Intention During The Covid-19 Pandemic and Post-Pandemic Times: The Role of Entrepreneurial University Environment.' *Frontiers in Psychology*, 13, Article 976675 (2022), https://doi.org/10.3389/fpsyg.2022.976675.

Valenzuela-Keller, A. A., F. A. Gálvez-Gamboa, E. Silva-Aravena, and M. Moreno- Villagra. 'Entrepreneurial Attitudes of First Year University Students in Chile.' *Formación Universitaria*, 14, no. 4 (2021): 103–112, https://doi.org/10.4067/S0718-50062021000400103.

Vetrivel, S. C. and V. Krishnamoorthy. 'A Study on Factors Stimulate Passion among Management Students to become an Entrepreneur.' *International Journal of Scientific and Technology Research*, 8, no. 11 (2019): 832–839, http://www.ijstr.org/final-print/nov2019/A-Study-On-Factors-Stimulate-Passion-Among-fManagement-Students-To-Become-Entrepreneur.pdf.

von Graevenitz, G., D. Harhoff, and R. Weber. (2010). The Effects of Entrepreneurship Education. *Journal of Economic Behavior & Organization*, 76(1), 90–112. https://doi.org/10.1016/j.jebo.2010.02.015.

World Economic Forum. *Future of jobs report: Insight report January 2025*, 2025, https://reports.weforum.org/docs/WEF_Future_of_Jobs_Report_2025.pdf.

Yalcintas, M., O. Iyigün, and G. Karabulut. 'Personal Characteristics and Intention for Entrepreneurship.' *Singapore Economic Review*, 68, no. 2 (2023): 539–561, https://doi.org/10.1142/S0217590821500338.

Yuksel, A. 'Relationship between Human Capital and Entrepreneurship Orientation from the Intellectual Capital Perspective of Innovative Literacy.' *Journal of Intellectual Capital*, 25, no. 5/6 (2024): 1259–1284, https://doi.org/10.1108/JIC-12-2023-0285.

Zahro, S. 'Applying Entrepreneurship as a Learning Design for Engineering Education.' *World Transactions on Engineering and Technology Education*, 14, no. 3 (2016): 410–415, http://www.wiete.com.au/journals/WTE&TE/Pages/Vol.14,%20No.3%20(2016)/12-Zahro-S.pdf.

Section 3

Leadership, Organizational Transformation, and the Human Factor

© 2026 World Scientific Publishing Europe Ltd.
https://doi.org/10.1142/9781800617414_0011

Chapter 11

Balancing Technology and Humanity: A Ground-Up Model for Resilient Leadership in the AI Era

Selvi Kannan

University of Tasmania, Australia

Selvi.Kannan@vu.edu.au

Abstract

In the rapidly evolving digital landscape, artificial intelligence (AI) has emerged as a key transformative force in organizations, influencing decision-making, operational efficiency, and knowledge-sharing frameworks. Integrating AI effectively into organizational contexts demands leadership that is both adaptive and resilient. Resilient leadership has become a vital skill set in navigating the complexities of AI's impact on the workforce, organizational culture, and governance structures.

This chapter explores resilient leadership as an essential concept for organizations seeking to capitalize on the potential of AI while understanding and managing the human-centric risks associated with its adoption. It focuses on identifying the role of leadership in balancing technological advancements with human-centered values, ethics, and organizational resilience. The chapter examines how AI-driven transformation influences leadership dynamics and outlines the key competencies required for leaders to navigate AI adoption effectively, ensuring trust, accountability, and adaptive learning in an increasingly automated and data-driven environment.

The concept of resilient leadership in the context of AI is informed by established leadership models, including transformational leadership (Bass, 1990), adaptive leadership (Heifetz and Linsky, 2017), and servant leadership (Greenleaf, 1977). These frameworks underscore the importance of leaders in managing change, inspiring innovation, and promoting ethical decision-making practices in a rapidly changing technological environment. AI's potential to enhance decision-making processes, streamline operations, and enable strategic foresight (Brynjolfsson and McAfee, 2017; Davenport and Ronanki, 2018) presents significant opportunities for organizational improvement. Scholars highlight the challenges of over-relying on AI, noting risks such as algorithmic biases, data privacy breaches, and, more importantly, the erosion of critical and creative human judgment in decision-making (Binns *et al.*, 2018). The resilient leader, therefore, must possess the capacity to navigate these challenges, ensuring the responsible and ethical deployment of AI technologies while safeguarding the essential human dimensions of leadership and organizational life.

Keywords: Resilient leadership, AI, digital technology, humanity.

11.1 Introduction

Stogdill's (1948) foundational work introduced the notion that leadership is grounded in inherent personal traits, marking an early attempt to define what makes an effective leader. However, this trait-based perspective served only as a starting point. In the decades that followed, leadership theory evolved rapidly, giving rise to a diverse array of attributes, models, and paradigms that have shaped our understanding of leadership in increasingly complex and dynamic contexts.

Over time, it became progressively evident that effective leadership could not be divorced from context; rather, situational integration became essential in shaping leadership practices that uphold human values across time and circumstance. The 1990s marked a pivotal inflection point in the development of leadership theory as the concept of resilient leadership began to crystallize in response to the pressures of globalization, rapid technological advancements, crises, and the emergence of knowledge-based economies. While contemporary constructs such as emotional intelligence (Goleman, 1995) have gained considerable popularity, the intellectual foundations of resilient leadership can be traced to earlier systems and organizational theorists. For instance, Karl Weick's seminal work on sensemaking (1979, 1995, 2001) gained influence during this era, illustrating how leaders create coherence and sustain direction amidst uncertainty by continuously reconstructing meaning. "Sensemaking" was identified as an essential capability for resilience. Likewise, Peter Drucker's (1988) vision of the knowledge society presciently identified the need for decentralized and adaptive leadership attuned to the value of human capital. Tracing even further, Mary Parker Follett's advocacy on "power-with" rather than "power-over" (Follett, 1924) prefigured the emergence of distributed and participatory leadership paradigms that became critical in navigating complexity and fostering collective resilience. These classical underpinnings, when combined with the disruptive socio-technical landscape of the late 1990s, prompted a paradigm shift in leadership thinking: away from models rooted in control and hierarchy to those grounded in adaptability, relational influence, ethical values, and systems thinking oriented toward social and environmental responsibility. These principles now form the bedrock of what is widely recognized as resilient leadership.

It is wise to say that evolving paradigms continuously shape and redefine prevailing leadership approaches. In the current digital era, the rapid advancement of artificial intelligence (AI) and related technologies is fundamentally transforming organizational practices and decision-making processes. This contemporary landscape, in the 21st century, presents a complex and often unpredictable environment, demanding adaptive and forward-thinking leadership capable of navigating unprecedented challenges.

The complex challenge facing organizations today is AI. We need to understand that AI extends beyond its widely recognized capacity to process large datasets and generate predictive insights; it is the accelerated pace of its development that presents a profound challenge to human adaptability. This rapid evolution is fundamentally redefining traditional business functions and organizational dynamics. Within this shifting landscape, there is an increasing focus on leadership, necessitating a critical re-examination of existing leadership paradigms. While the adoption of AI is frequently associated with gains in operational efficiency and the stimulation of innovation with outcomes that are undoubtedly advantageous for organizational performance, it simultaneously raises complex challenges for organizational culture. As Tsui (2023) posits, while AI has the potential to augment knowledge processes, its opaque reasoning and bias-prone outputs pose significant challenges to knowledge management strategies rooted in trust, collaboration, and transparency. These tensions highlight the need for leadership approaches that are both technologically informed and deeply human-centered. Such approaches must integrate and uphold core human values, including creativity, empathy, and experiential judgment. Furthermore, AI systems remain constrained in their ability to navigate emotional complexity, cultural nuance, and ethical ambiguity – areas where human leadership remains indispensable (Goleman, 1995). As such, effective leadership in the digital era must balance the affordances of AI with the irreplaceable dimensions of human insight and relational intelligence.

The realization of being competitive is that AI's integration in the workplace has a transformative potential (Randriamiary, 2024), which in turn raises significant concerns about employee engagement and organizational culture. This rapidly shifting workplace calls for not only an intelligent leader but also one who can lead and manage the organization through challenges in a resilient manner. Being resilient requires leaders to not only leverage AI's capabilities but also foster emotional intelligence, which remains a critical competency for managing interpersonal relationships, motivating teams, resolving conflicts, navigating human challenges, and cultivating experimentation and idea creation to steer progressive future thinking and action. Furthermore, resilient leaders are instrumental in creating a culture of innovation and knowledge-sharing, encouraging collaborative problem-solving and facilitating organizational learning necessary to thrive in a digital world (Lee, 2018). By doing so, leaders can mitigate the anxieties and uncertainties AI may trigger among the workforce, ensuring that AI adoption is seen as an opportunity rather than a threat.

As AI reshapes the landscape of work, decision-making, and human interaction, leaders are confronted with unprecedented cultural, ethical, and relational challenges. To deepen understanding of these dynamics, this chapter examines the evolving intersection between technology and leadership. First, it explores how AI influences organizational cultures and the implications for leadership practices. Second, it addresses the challenges AI poses to employee engagement and organizational trust, offering strategies for leaders to navigate these complexities. Finally, it proposes a model of resilient, human-centered leadership that embraces digital transformation while upholding the intrinsic value of human capital. By engaging with these themes, the chapter contributes critical insights to the discourse on leadership in the digital era, offering a framework for cultivating resilience and adaptability amid technological disruption.

11.2 Promise and Peril of AI for Leadership and Organizational Culture

Recent studies have shown that businesses investing in AI technologies do foster a culture that brings alignment of social and environmental considerations by offering opportunities to "generate knowledge needed to preserving life" (Nishant *et al.*, 2020, p9). However, this synchronization requires a leader who can both nurture an inclusive environment and provide employees with a sense of value and empowerment, enabling them to advance AI capabilities in a meaningful way. The paradox of AI adoption that leaders face is making decisions with little or no compromise of the human element, bringing about team cohesion and building trust (Raisch and Krakowski, 2021). Therefore, the impact of AI on leadership must focus on shaping resilient organizational frameworks capable of adapting to rapid technological changes while ensuring that human talent remains at the forefront.

Peifer *et al.* (2022) have shown that there are numerous responsibilities that leaders need to juggle. This involves examining how employees can be empowered to develop digital literacy capabilities that mitigate resistance and negative responses to technological change, while enabling teams to adapt effectively. At the same time, it requires leading and mediating the relationship between task execution and value creation in ways that ensure both individual privacy and personal identity are preserved and protected. An engaged and holistic approach by the leader has proven to promote a culture of trust and continuous learning and a responsibility that is much required. Therefore, it will be wise to assert that both the promises and perils of AI for leadership lie in the leader's ability to empower employees in the adoption of AI.

In the era of AI, leaders need to shift from traditional forms of empowerment to enabling individuals' creative self-efficacy (Jeong and Jeong, 2025). Empowering must be entrusted to the individual's personal reflection that draws on their creative expressions, goal setting, and decision-making skills to solve problems. Here, their interaction with AI is one of a companion to enhance their capacity, capability, and productivity while taking responsibility to act in an ethical, safe, and equitable manner. AI has demonstrated that it has the potential to shift how people access and use knowledge, which in many ways helps individuals learn and progress at their own pace and facilitates continuous learning. As Ahsan (2025) posits, leaders can assist in reducing the negative effects of AI integration and foster resilience among teams sustaining high performance and handling uncertainty at their level and pace by cultivating a growth mindset. Creative empowerment and growth mindset constitute the new generational culture that should be employed in organizations.

As AI accelerates, it is essential that leadership grounds technological innovation in human-centered values. Empowerment, as conceptualized by Essens (2023), operates at both the individual and organizational levels. At the individual level, it involves fostering psychological empowerment through motivational leadership. Organizationally, it requires systems, policies, and structures that enable such empowerment. Resilient leadership is, therefore, characterized by adaptability and the creation of inclusive environments that move beyond traditional command-and-control models, promoting psychological safety and collaboration (Yu *et al.*, 2022).

The central challenge for leaders is to preserve the significant dimensions of work, where creativity, ethical reasoning, and complex problem-solving are much needed amid increasing automation. Resilient leaders must navigate the interplay between human and AI, utilizing this synergy to enhance knowledge transfer and translation toward innovation and organizational efficiency. This balance requires an adaptable, resilient leadership approach rooted in creativity, psychological safety, ethical reflection, and human–AI collaboration.

11.3 Leadership Models That Inform Resilience

Amid increasingly volatile, technology-driven, and socio-politically complex environments, resilient leadership has emerged not as a fixed trait but as a fluid and contextually responsive quality adapting to shifting situational demands. It denotes a leader's capacity to absorb disruption, foster adaptive capacity, and regenerate organizational direction and trust amid uncertainty. Crucially, resilient leadership is best understood not through the lens of a singular leadership theory but as a dynamic synthesis of multiple leadership paradigms, where each contributes vital, interlocking dimensions to a more holistic and sustainable approach.

One can argue that at its core, resilient leadership is an adaptive construct that draws from transformational, adaptive, servant, authentic, emotional intelligence, distributed, strategic, and complexity leadership theories. These models, though distinct in orientation, converge in their capacity to help leaders navigate adversity while anchoring purpose, trust, and innovation. Their interplay constructs a robust leadership repertoire that is situationally responsive, ethically grounded, and systemically attuned.

Transformational leadership offers a critical anchoring point by emphasizing vision, inspiration, and sensemaking during moments of instability. It enables leaders to articulate compelling futures that galvanize collective motivation (Bass, 1990). However, vision without responsiveness is inadequate in a world defined by rapid, unpredictable shifts. This is where adaptive leadership complements by instilling a capacity for iteration, learning, and distributed problem-solving in the face of complex, emergent challenges (Heifetz and Linsky, 2002, 2017). These two paradigms work in tandem, where transformational leadership sets direction and adaptive leadership operationalizes responsiveness, thereby enabling organizations to both anticipate and react to disruption.

Distributed leadership adds critical structural resilience by decentralizing authority and enabling collective agency. Especially relevant in networked and cross-functional environments, distributed leadership fosters ownership, peer learning, and agility by allowing leadership functions to flow to where they are most needed. This principle is echoed and expanded in Complexity Leadership Theory, which views organizations as adaptive systems where leadership emerges not through control but by creating enabling conditions for innovation and self-organization (Uhl-Bien *et al.*, 2007). Leaders here act as facilitators of emergence, creating enabling environments for collaborative adaptation. Finally, strategic leadership provides the temporal coherence necessary to align immediate, responsive actions with long-term organizational vision and continuity. It ensures that resilience is not merely reactive but a part of an anticipatory and enduring organizational posture.

The relational fabric underpinning resilient leadership is strengthened further through servant leadership, which prioritizes empathy, empowerment, and the development of others (Greenleaf, 1977). This model builds interpersonal trust and psychological safety, essential for adaptive risk-taking and innovation. It is this emphasis on human-centered stewardship that binds ethical intent to strategic resilience, creating a culture where individuals feel secure to engage and evolve.

Authentic leadership, a relatively recent addition to the leadership discourse, significantly contributes to the convergence of leadership paradigms by embedding self-awareness, moral integrity, and relational transparency into the leader's identity (Avolio and Gardner, 2005). Authentic leaders demonstrate alignment between their espoused values and observable actions, thereby cultivating trust, credibility, and moral clarity. These qualities serve as critical stabilizing forces in times of organizational turbulence. When principles of authentic and servant leadership are integrated with transformational and adaptive leadership practices, leaders are more effectively positioned to navigate complex environments by balancing authority with humility and decisiveness with empathy.

Layered atop these human-centered models is the domain of emotional intelligence, which provides leaders with the ability to navigate the affective dimensions of disruption by managing stress, sustaining morale, and responding constructively to emotional cues (Goleman, 1995). Emotional intelligence enables leaders to read complex social signals and respond with attuned behaviors that stabilize teams and facilitate clarity during ambiguity.

These interconnected models collectively construct a layered architecture of resilient leadership: Transformational and adaptive models provide direction and agility; servant and authentic leadership supply ethical grounding and relational depth; emotional intelligence and distributed leadership secure interpersonal and structural adaptability; complexity leadership fosters systemic responsiveness; and strategic leadership ensures alignment with long-term purpose.

To anchor this integrated synthesis in a developmental and processual lens, the constructionist model of resilience (Bonanno, 2004) frames resilience not as a fixed personality trait but as a socially and narratively constructed capacity. Leaders shape resilience through reflective sense-making, learning from adversity, and embedding that learning into both identity and relational practices. The thriving model reinforces this view, positioning adversity as a platform for transformation and innovation (Carver, 1998; Fredrickson, 2009), while the cognitive model highlights the significance of mental agility and optimistic framing in enabling leaders to respond constructively under pressure (Seligman, 2004). Ledesma's framework further grounds resilience in internal protective factors such as

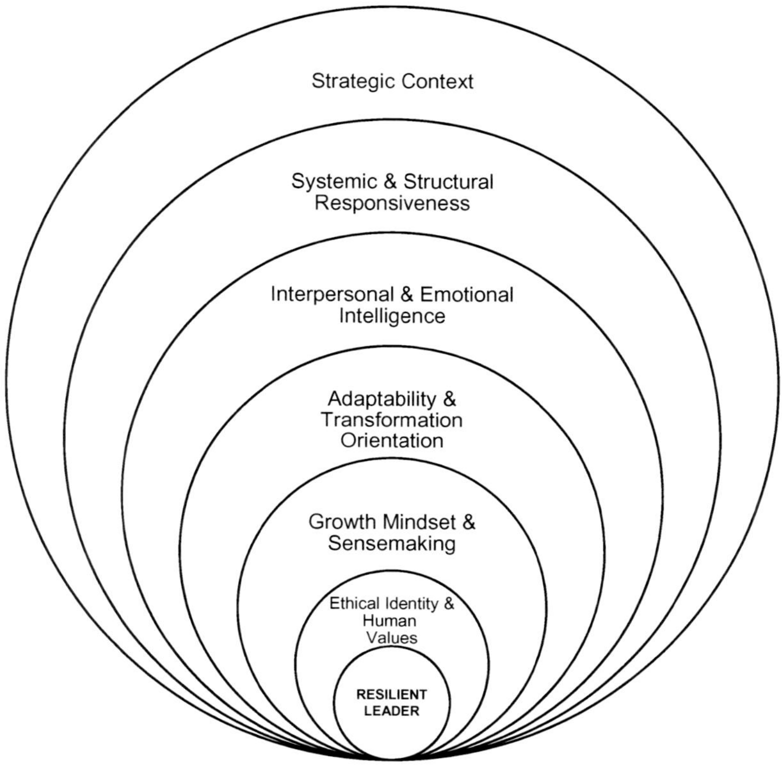

Figure 11.1. Onion model of resilient leadership identity.

ambiguity tolerance and motivational tenacity (Ledesma, 2014), while the relational activation model (Teo *et al.*, 2017) underscores the necessity of social embeddedness in cultivating resilience. It builds inner strength for a leader to strategically handle situations. See Figure 11.1 for this multi-layered representation of resilient leadership identity.

We can conclude that resilient leadership in the digital age is not a matter of mastering a single style but cultivating an agile, ethically rooted, and systemically attuned mindset. It is a multi-level model of resilient leadership, incorporating cognitive, emotional, relational, and structural dimensions. In this model, leaders build self-resilience not merely through reactive coping but through intentional practices that interweave vision, ethics, self-awareness, and system sensitivity. This integrative approach focuses on leaders as both strategic architects and emotional anchors who believe they can manage uncertainty, enable adaptation, and guide purposeful transformation while addressing situations as they arise. Through the interplay of multiple leadership theories and developmental frameworks, leaders can construct resilience as a practice of coherence amidst complexity, bridging technological acceleration with enduring human values and organizational integrity.

11.4 Adaptive Resilience in AI-Integrated Workplace

We are witnessing how the contemporary workplace is undergoing a profound transformation driven by the integration of AI. This is permeating across sectors and workplaces. AI has transitioned from a specialized technological tool to a strategic imperative, fundamentally reshaping organizational operations and decision-making processes. For instance, in healthcare, AI technology streamlines processes and supports clinical decision-making, potentially improving patient outcomes and operational efficiency (Epelde, 2024). In education, AI facilitates personalized learning experiences, allowing instructors to tailor programs to meet individual student needs, thus enhancing the educational process (Wei *et al.*, 2025). Additionally, AI's analytical capabilities empower businesses to leverage vast datasets, identifying trends and insights that inform strategic decision-making, thereby optimizing productivity across industries (Dietzmann and Duan, 2022). These developments underscore the necessity for leaders to adeptly manage AI-integrated workplaces. Effective leadership in this context involves not only understanding AI's technical aspects but also addressing its ethical implications and ensuring alignment with organizational values. As AI continues to evolve, leaders must cultivate a balance between technological advancement and human-centered approaches to maintain organizational integrity and performance.

Given the limitations of AI, human oversight and judgment remain indispensable components in leveraging its capabilities effectively. The integration of AI into decision-making processes should not eliminate human involvement; rather, it should enhance human capabilities while respecting emotional intelligence and ethical considerations that machines cannot replicate (Pflanzer *et al.*, 2023; Gal-Or, 2025). Leaders need to ensure that AI operates within boundaries set by human ethical standards, mitigating risks associated with algorithmic bias and context insensitivity. This can be achieved by involving multidisciplinary stakeholders, including ethicists, technologists, and domain experts. This will also enable leaders to understand and inform better practices that balance technological advancements with societal values (Kandasamy, 2024). Furthermore, continuous training and education for leaders and employees on AI's ethical implications fortify organizational resilience against potential AI misuse. Resilience can be described as hardiness with traits and abilities to commit to working with people, having an attitude of control, knowing how and when to inspire and influence, and having the attitude to challenge when things do not go as expected and keeping the team motivated.

In AI-integrated workplaces, adaptability is a critical leadership capability, with emotional intelligence forming its foundation. As AI increasingly shapes decision-making and operational processes, emotionally intelligent leaders are better equipped to navigate technological disruption and organizational ambiguity (Boyar *et al.*, 2023). Emotional intelligence fosters self-awareness, empathy, and interpersonal sensitivity. These are qualities that support adaptive leadership responses to emerging challenges and evolving team dynamics (Albaram and Lim, 2023). Moreover, emotional intelligence enhances a leader's adaptability by enabling them to respond flexibly to complex and uncertain environments, which supports trust-building and psychological safety – essential for effective collaboration between humans and intelligent systems in dynamic organizational contexts (Harms and Credé, 2010). By integrating emotional intelligence into leadership practices, organizations can build resilience and responsiveness, ultimately improving employee engagement and long-term performance in AI-enabled environments.

In navigating the volatility of AI-integrated work environments, emotional intelligence emerges as a critical enabler of both resilience and adaptability. While resilience offers leaders the capacity to absorb disruption and maintain purpose under pressure (Luthar *et al.*, 2015; Sutcliffe and Vogus, 2003), adaptability reflects their ability to adjust strategies, behaviors, and mindsets in alignment with emerging challenges (Pulakos *et al.*, 2000). Ultimately, emotional intelligence is essential to both capacities, providing the psychological and interpersonal infrastructure for

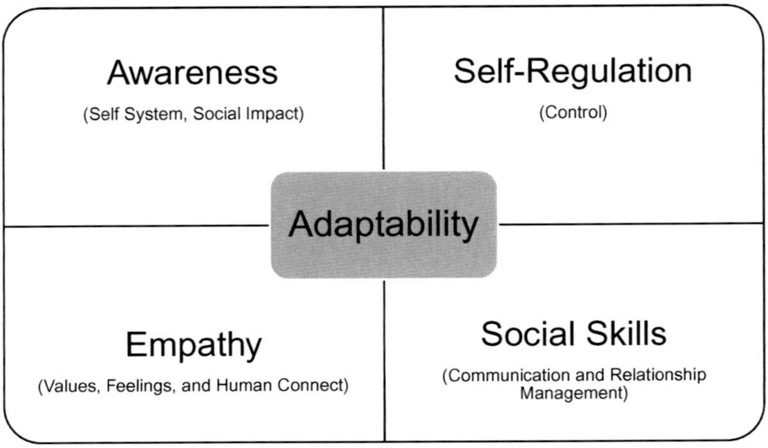

Figure 11.2. Dimensions of emotional intelligence critical for adaptability.

reflective decision-making, relational cohesion, and ethical responsiveness in the face of technological transformation.

Daniel Goleman's foundational and widely recognized work not only encompasses disciplines, but it is also validated through scholarly research and practical application. Goleman's work on emotional intelligence (1995) outlines five dimensions that are particularly relevant to adaptive leadership in AI-intensive settings: self-awareness, self-regulation, empathy, social skills, and adaptability. These dimensions encompass interpersonal competencies as well as strategic capacities that help leaders constructively navigate uncertainty and change. The dimensions are illustrated in Figure 11.2.

Self-awareness enables leaders to recognize their emotional responses and cognitive biases, thereby supporting more intentional and values-aligned decision-making, especially when interpreting AI-generated outputs (Hwang *et al.*, 2023; Jnr and Dzogbewu, 2021). This internal clarity is critical for maintaining integrity and confidence amid algorithmic opacity.

Self-regulation, or the ability to manage one's emotional responses, helps leaders remain composed under the fast-paced, high-stakes pressures of digital transformation (Hwang *et al.*, 2023). By doing so, they model emotional stability, reducing team anxiety and enhancing trust in technologically mediated decisions.

Empathy is central to fostering inclusive leadership practices and addressing employee concerns about AI-driven change, including fears of displacement or surveillance (Khushk *et al.*, 2024). By empathizing with diverse stakeholder experiences, leaders can co-create AI strategies that are both effective and humane.

Social skills, including communication and conflict resolution, are instrumental in cultivating collaborative cultures. These capabilities enable leaders to facilitate dialogue across disciplines, manage tensions, and sustain engagement during AI transitions (Boyatzis *et al.*, 2019).

Adaptability, even though identified by Goleman (1995) as a dimension of emotional intelligence that embodies the behavioral flexibility and openness to new paradigms demanded by resilient leadership (Hess and Bacigalupo, 2013), is in fact the central core that draws on all the other dimensions a leader needs for following a balanced approach to demonstrate adaptability. Leaders who exhibit high adaptability are more likely to approach AI disruption as a learning opportunity rather than a threat, supporting dynamic alignment between organizational goals and technological possibilities. Adaptability is enabled by awareness, empathy, social skills, and self-regulation.

Emotionally intelligent leaders are uniquely positioned to embed ethical foresight into AI adoption. This involves more than regulatory compliance; it requires shaping a culture of ethical vigilance that permeates the development, deployment, and use of AI systems (Maiti *et al.*, 2025). By providing ethics training, encouraging critical reflection, and establishing governance protocols, leaders ensure that technological advancement aligns with organizational values and public accountability.

11.5 A Ground-Up Model of Resilient Leadership: The 4-A Model

Building on the key attributes and interrelationships between emotional intelligence, adaptability, and resilience, the ground-up model of resilient leadership offers a cohesive framework for navigating the complex interplay of human and technological systems in contemporary organizational life. As AI reshapes decision-making, operational structures, and interpersonal dynamics, resilient leadership is no longer a static trait but an integrated developmental process. This model synthesizes four foundational capabilities, namely awareness, agility, alignment, and action.

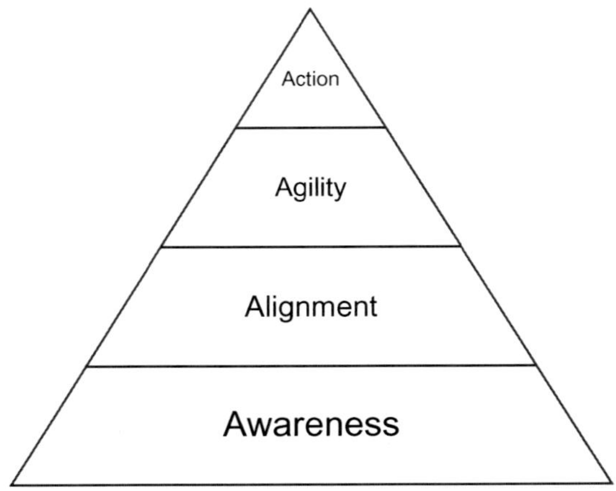

Figure 11.3. The 4-A model of resilient leadership.

Which together support leaders in sustaining both technological efficacy and human well-being.

At its core, the 4-A model (see Figure 11.3) posits that resilient leadership is cultivated from the inside out. It is not imposed through top-down directives but emerges through reflective practice, ethical intentionality, and strategic responsiveness. Each dimension below represents an interdependent pillar that guides leaders in balancing the efficiencies of AI-driven transformation with the irreplaceable value of human insight, empathy, and accountability.

11.5.1 *Awareness*

Awareness forms the cognitive and moral foundation of resilient leadership. This begins with self-awareness, the intrapersonal capacity to understand one's emotions, values, and cognitive tendencies, which is critical in moderating responses to AI outputs and complex team dynamics. Systems awareness then expands the lens to include structural interdependencies within organizational and technological ecosystems, equipping leaders to anticipate the second-order effects of automated decisions. Finally, social impact awareness ensures that leadership transcends operational efficiency to engage with broader ethical, environmental, and societal consequences. Together, these three layers of awareness enable leaders to perceive complexity holistically and make grounded, ethically informed decisions in high-stakes environments.

11.5.2 *Alignment*

As AI integration intensifies the pace and opacity of organizational decisions, alignment becomes a critical safeguard against ethical drift and stakeholder alienation. This attribute begins with values orientation, which has a clear articulation of what the organization stands for, independent of technological affordances. Ethical alignment ensures that these values are translated into practice, particularly in morally ambiguous situations involving data use, algorithmic bias, or the automation of human judgment. Ultimately, leaders ensure alignment with stakeholder responsiveness, emphasizing harmonious relationships with employees, communities, and the environment. Rather than optimizing for narrow efficiencies, resilient leaders pursue coherence by integrating internal culture and external obligations to sustain trust, legitimacy, and social license.

11.5.3 *Agility*

In a landscape defined by rapid AI innovation and global uncertainty, agility is not merely a desirable trait; it is a strategic necessity. It is a skill that weaves innovation through learning and creates adaptive capacity. Resilient leaders cultivate a learning mindset, seeking feedback, embracing ambiguity, and tolerating the discomfort of experimentation. This culture of learning naturally fosters innovation, encouraging exploration beyond legacy practices. However, innovation must be paired with adaptability, where behavioral and operational responsiveness are required to realign strategies as conditions evolve. Agility thus positions leaders not only to survive technological disruption but also to leverage it constructively, iterating toward more resilient, human-centered systems.

11.5.4 *Action*

The culmination of resilient leadership is action that reflects foresight, inclusiveness, and moral clarity. In technology-infused contexts, leaders must cultivate strategic foresight – the anticipatory capacity of identifying emerging risks and opportunities before they materialize. This is enhanced through collaboration, not only as a mechanism for task execution but also as a process of sense-making across disciplines, perspectives, and values. At the heart of action lies decision-making with integrity and the ability to uphold ethical commitments, even when expedient choices appear more attractive. Such integrity-driven action is essential for mitigating unintended harms, maintaining legitimacy, and anchoring technological progress in human dignity.

The 4-A model of resilient leadership is more than a typology of traits; it is a praxis-oriented response to the dual imperatives of technological advancement and human sustainability. In AI-integrated environments, the pressure to automate, optimize, and scale must be balanced against the need to humanize, reflect, and relate. This model offers leaders a structured yet flexible approach to addressing these tensions by leveraging technological tools without abdicating human judgment, scaling innovation while safeguarding relational trust, and responding to volatility with moral purpose.

To summarize, resilient leadership in the AI era requires an adaptive equilibrium: a grounded sense of self, an agile orientation to change, a values-based compass, and the capacity to translate complexity into purposeful action. The 4-A model provides a practical and ethically attuned framework to support this transformation from within and the ability to act.

11.6 Future Trajectories and Research Implications

As we navigate the evolving landscape of AI and its interplay with leadership and organizational dynamics, several emerging challenges and research opportunities warrant exploration. One primary concern is algorithmic accountability, as AI systems increasingly make decisions that affect various aspects of life and raise questions about who is responsible for the outcomes that result from these technologies (Cortellazzo *et al.*, 2019). This accountability is intricately linked to the principles of transparency and explainability, where leaders hold primary responsibility and must ensure that the AI algorithms they deploy are not only effective but also understandable to stakeholders (Balasubramaniam *et al.*, 2023). Moreover, the development of AI technologies capable of simulating emotional responses introduces ethical dilemmas regarding their role in emotional contexts, necessitating further investigation into how these technologies can be designed to align with human emotional and moral standards (Maiti *et al.*, 2025), an area that is increasingly important as organizations place importance on mental health and well-being. Alongside this, there is an urgent need for frameworks addressing digital ethics. This relates to balancing innovation with moral and legal responsibilities as AI continues to transform industries. The gaps identified in these areas present fertile ground for interdisciplinary inquiry, where researchers can engage with fields such as ethics, psychology, engineering, and social sciences to foster innovative solutions that prioritize responsible AI integration. Additionally, the impact of digital well-being on human rights and societal values must be meticulously assessed to prevent ethical pitfalls that may emerge from the proliferation of AI. Addressing these considerations will not only enhance our understanding of AI's implications but also contribute to more resilient leadership practices capable of guiding organizations through the challenges of this digital age. The 4-A Resilient Leadership model employed here needs to be examined to provide empirical evidence.

11.7 Conclusion

In conclusion, it is essential to reaffirm the responsibility and balance required between AI and human leadership. The trajectory of modern organizations is increasingly integrating AI tools that enhance, rather than replace, the qualities that define effective leadership. By blending advanced technology with human insights and creativity through empowerment, leaders can harness the full potential of AI to enhance decision-making, foster innovation, and promote operational efficiency. This symbiosis may lead us toward next-generation AI–human co-leadership models where technology assists leaders in identifying emerging trends, analyzing complex data sets, and making informed decisions while retaining the essence of human intuition and emotional intelligence.

A resilient leader emerges as a bridge between the technological promise of AI and the foundational human values that foster organizational integrity and culture. The role of leadership will evolve, emphasizing the need for leaders to possess heightened awareness of ethical considerations, emotional nuance, and the social implications of technology in the workplace. As organizations navigate the complexities introduced by AI, leaders must advocate for practices that not only leverage technology for strategic gain but also promote inclusivity, emotional engagement, and ethical standards across all operations.

In this digital age, the call to action is clear: Leaders must commit to upholding principles of integrity, empathy, and foresight in their interactions with technology and their teams. Effective leadership in the context of AI will require a delicate balance, maintaining a clear vision that champions technology's potential while prioritizing the well-being of individuals and communities. By embodying these values, leaders can ensure their organizations thrive not only amidst technological disruptions but also in fulfilling their broader social responsibilities. Resilience is about balancing technological entrants, enabling employees to exercise creativity and ethical responsibility.

References

Ahsan, M. J. 'Cultivating a Culture of Learning: The Role of Leadership in Fostering Lifelong Development.' *The Learning Organization*, 32, no. 2 (2025): 282–306, https://doi.org/10.1108/TLO-03-2024-0099.

Albaram, B. M. and Y. M. Lim. 'Conceptualization Social Influence from the Need to Belong Perspective on Psychological Needs' Satisfaction to Share Knowledge.' *Heliyon*, 9, no. 2 (2023), https://doi.org/10.1016/j.heliyon.2023.e13764.

Avolio, B. J. and W. L. Gardner. 'Authentic Leadership Development: Getting to the Root of Positive Forms of Leadership.' *The Leadership Quarterly*, 16, no. 3 (2005): 315–338, https://doi.org/10.1016/j.leaqua.2005.03.001.

Balasubramaniam, N., Kauppinen, M., Rannisto, A., Hiekkanen, K. & Kujala, S. 'Transparency and Explainability of AI Systems: From Ethical Guidelines to Requirements.' *Information and Software Technology*, 159 (2023): 107197, https://doi.org/10.1016/j.infsof.2023.107197.

Bass, B. M. 'From Transactional to Transformational Leadership: Learning to Share the Vision.' *Organizational Dynamics*, 18, no. 3 (1990): 19–31, https://doi.org/10.1016/0090-2616(90)90061-S.

Binns, R., M. Van Kleek, M. Veale, U. Lyngs, J. Zhao, and N. Shadbolt. 'It's Reducing a Human Being to a Percentage: Perceptions of Justice in Algorithmic Decisions.' In *Proceedings of the 2018 CHI Conference on Human Factors in Computing Systems*, Paper 377. ACM, 2018, https://doi.org/10.1145/3173574.3173951.

Bonanno, G. A. 'Loss, Trauma, and Human Resilience: Have We Underestimated the Human Capacity to Thrive After Extremely Aversive Events?' *American Psychologist*, 59, no. 1 (2004): 20–28, https://doi.org/10.1037/0003-066X.59.1.20.

Boyar, S. L., G. T. Savage and E. S. Williams. 'An Adaptive Leadership Approach: The Impact of Reasoning and Emotional Intelligence (EI) Abilities on Leader Adaptability.' *Employee Responsibilities and Rights Journal*, 35 (2023): 565–580, https://doi.org/10.1007/s10672-022-09428-z.

Boyatzis, R. E., D. Goleman, F. Gerli, S. Bonesso, and L. Cortellazzo. 'Emotional and Social Intelligence Competencies and the Intentional Change Process.' In *Cognitive Readiness in Project Teams*. Productivity Press: New York, 2019, 147–169.

Brynjolfsson, E. and A. McAfee. 'The Business of Artificial Intelligence.' *Harvard Business Review*, 2017, https://hbr.org/2017/07/the-business-of-artificial-intelligence.

Carver, C. S. 'Resilience and Thriving: Issues, Models, and Linkages.' *Journal of Social Issues*, 54, no. 2 (1998): 245–266, https://doi.org/10.1111/0022-4537.641998064.

Cortellazzo, L., E. Bruni and R. Zampieri. 'The Role of Leadership in a Digitalized World: A Review.' *Frontiers in Psychology*, 10 (2019): 1938, https://doi.org/10.3389/fpsyg.2019.01938.

Davenport, T. H. and R. Ronanki. 'Artificial Intelligence for the Real World.' *Harvard Business Review*, 96, no. 1 (2018): 108–116, https://hbr.org/2018/01/artificial-intelligence-for-the-real-world.

Dietzmann, S. and Y. Duan. 'AI and Big Data Analytics: Transforming Business Intelligence.' *Journal of Business Research*, 141 (2022): 192–203, https://doi.org/10.1016/j.jbusres.2021.11.112.

Drucker, P. F. 'The Coming of the New Organization.' *Harvard Business Review*, 66, no. 1 (1988): 45–53.

Epelde, F. 'Revolutionizing Patient Safety: The Economic and Clinical Impact of Artificial Intelligence in Hospitals.' *Hospitals*, 1, no. 2 (2024): 185–194, https://doi.org/10.3390/hospitals1020015.

Essens, P. 'Resilience as an Outcome of Human Centered Empowerment in Human Centered Management and Crisis.' Routledge: Groningen, Netherlands, 2023, 3–17, https://doi.org/10.4324/9781003330011-2.

Follett, M. P. *Creative Experience*. Longmans, Green and Co.: London, 1924.

Fredrickson, B. L. *Positivity: Groundbreaking Research to Release Your Inner Optimist and Thrive*. Crown Business, 2009.

Gal-Or, S. 'Human-AI Collaboration: Synergies and Challenges.' In *Garden of Wisdom. International Series on Computer, Entertainment and Media Technology*. Springer, Cham, 2025, https://doi.org/10.1007/978-3-031-83085-3_114.

Goleman, D. *Emotional Intelligence: Why It Can Matter More Than IQ*. Bantam Books, 1995.

Greenleaf, R. K. *Servant Leadership: A Journey Into the Nature of Legitimate Power and Greatness*. Paulist Press: Mahwah, 1977.

Harms, P. D. and M. Credé. 'Emotional Intelligence and Transformational and Transactional Leadership: A Meta-Analysis.' *Journal of Leadership &*

Organizational Studies, 17, no. 1 (2010): 5–17, https://doi.org/10.1177/1548051809350894.

Heifetz, R. and M. Linsky. *Leadership on the Line, with a New Preface: Staying Alive Through the Dangers of Change*. Harvard Business Press: Brighton, Massachusetts, 2017.

Hess, J. D. A. C. Bacigalupo. 'Applying Emotional Intelligence Skills to Leadership and Decision Making in Non-Profit Organizations.' *Administrative Sciences*, 3, no. 4 (2013): 202–220, https://doi.org/10.3390/admsci3040202.

Hwang, J., J. J. Kim, J. Y. J. Choe, and H. M. Kim. 'The Importance of Information Quality According to the Type of Employee in the Airline Industry: Robot Versus Human.' *International Journal of Hospitality Management*, 114 (2023): 103537, https://doi.org/10.1016/j.ijhm.2023.103537.

Jeong, J. and I. Jeong. 'Driving Creativity in the AI-Enhanced Workplace: Roles of Self-Efficacy and Transformational Leadership.' *Current Psychology*, 44 (2025): 8001–8014, https://doi.org/10.1007/s12144-024-07135-6.

Jnr, S. A. and T. Dzogbewu. 'Goleman's Intrapersonal Dimension of Emotional Intelligence: Does it Predict Effective Leadership?' *Organizational Cultures*, 21, no. 2 (2021): 35–50, https://doi.org/10.18848/2327-8013/CGP/v21i02/35–50.

Kandasamy, U. C. 'Ethical Leadership in the Age of AI Challenges, Opportunities and Framework for Ethical Leadership.' *arXiv*, 2024, https://doi.org/10.48550/arXiv.2410.18095.

Khushk, A., L. Zhiying, X. Yi, and X. Zhang. 'Navigating Human-AI Dynamics: Implications for Organizational Performance (SLR).' *International Journal of Organizational Analysis*, [ahead-of-print] (2024), https://doi.org/10.1108/IJOA-04-2024-4456.

Le, P. B. and H. Lei. 'Fostering Knowledge Sharing Behaviours through Ethical Leadership Practice: The Mediating Roles of Disclosure-Based Trust and Reliance-Based Trust in Leadership.' *Knowledge Management Research & Practice*, 16, no. 2 (2018): 183–195, https://doi.org/10.1080/14778238.2018.1445426.

Ledesma, J. 'Conceptual Frameworks and Research Models on Resilience in Leadership.' *Sage Open*, 4, no. 3 (2014): 2158244014545464, https://doi.org/10.1177/2158244014545464.

Lee, H. J. 'How Emotional Intelligence Relates to Job Satisfaction and Burnout in Public Service Jobs.' *International Review of Administrative Sciences*, 84, no. 4 (2018): 729–745, https://doi.org/10.1177/0020852316670489.

Luthar, S. S. 'Resilience in Development: A Synthesis of Research Across Five Decades.' In *Developmental Psychopathology: Risk, Disorder, and Adaptation*. Vol. 3, 2015, 739–795, https://doi.org/10.1002/9780470939406.ch20.

Maiti, M., P. Kayal and A. Vujko. 'A Study on Ethical Implications of Artificial Intelligence Adoption in Business: Challenges and Best Practices.' *Future Business Journal*, 11 (2025): 34, https://doi.org/10.1186/s43093-025-00462-5.

Nishant, R., M. Kennedy and J. Corbett. 'Artificial Intelligence for Sustainability: Challenges, Opportunities, and a Research Agenda.' *International Journal of Information Management*, 53 (2020): 102104, https://doi.org/10.1016/j.ijinfomgt.2020.102104.

Peifer, Y., T. Jeske and S. Hille. 'Artificial Intelligence and Its Impact on Leaders and Leadership.' *Procedia Computer Science*, 200 (2022): 1024–1030, https://doi.org/10.1016/j.procs.2022.01.301.

Pflanzer, M., Z. Traylor, J. B. Lyons, *et al.* 'Ethics in Human–AI Teaming: Principles and Perspectives.' *AI and Ethics*, 3 (2023): 917–935, https://doi.org/10.1007/s43681-022-00214-z.

Pulakos, E. D., S. Arad, M. A. Donovan, and K. E. Plamondon. 'Adaptability in the Workplace: Development of a Taxonomy of Adaptive Performance.' *Journal of Applied Psychology*, 85, no. 4 (2000): 612–624, https://doi.org/10.1037/0021-9010.85.4.612.

Raisch, S. S. Krakowski. 'Artificial Intelligence and Management: The Automation–Augmentation Paradox.' *Academy of Management Review*, 46, no. 1 (2021): 192–210, https://doi.org/10.5465/amr.2018.0072.

Seligman, M. E. *Authentic Happiness: Using the New Positive Psychology to Realize Your Potential for Lasting Fulfillment*. Simon and Schuster, 2004.

Stogdill, R. M. 'Personal Factors Associated with Leadership: A Survey of the Literature.' *The Journal of Psychology*, 25, no. 1 (1948): 35–71, https://doi.org/10.1080/00223980.1948.9917362.

Sutcliffe, K. M. T. J. Vogus. 'Organizing for Resilience.' In *Positive Organizational Scholarship*. Berrett-Koehler, 2003, 94–110.

Teo, W. L., M. Lee and W. S. Lim. 'The Relational Activation of Resilience Model: How Leadership Activates Resilience in an Organizational Crisis.' *Journal of Contingencies and Crisis Management*, 25, no. 3 (2017): 136–147, https://doi.org/10.1111/1468-5973.12179.

Tsui, E. 'Learning from the Future: Knowledge Management Systems in the Twenty-First Century.' In *The Future of Knowledge Management. Knowledge Management and Organizational Learning*, vol 12. Springer, Cham, 2023, https://doi.org/10.1007/978-3-031-38696-1_14.

Uhl-Bien, M., R. Marion and B. McKelvey. 'Complexity Leadership Theory: Shifting Leadership from the Industrial Age to the Knowledge Era.' *The Leadership Quarterly*, 18, no. 4 (2007): 298–318, https://doi.org/10.1016/j.leaqua.2007.04.002.

Wei, Y., Y. H. Jiang, J. Liu, C. Qi, L. Jia, and R. Jia. 'The Advancement of Personalized Learning Potentially Accelerated by Generative AI.' In *Society for Information Technology & Teacher Education International Conference*. Association for the Advancement of Computing in Education (AACE), 2025, 991–1000, https://www.learntechlib.org/primary/p/225625/.

Weick, K. E. *The Social Psychology of Organizing*, 2nd ed. McGraw-Hill: New York, NY, 1979.

Weick, K. E. *Sensemaking in Organizations*. Sage Publications, 1995.

Weick, K. E. K. M. and Sutcliffe. *Managing the Unexpected: Assuring High Performance in an Age of Complexity*. Jossey-Bass: Hoboken, NJ, 2001.

Yu, M., J. Wen, S. M. Smith, and P. Stokes. 'Building-up Resilience and Being Effective Leaders in the Workplace: A Systematic Review and Synthesis Model.' *Leadership & Organization Development Journal*, 43, no. 7 (2022): 1098–1117, https://doi.org/10.1108/LODJ-09-2021-0437.

© 2026 World Scientific Publishing Europe Ltd.
https://doi.org/10.1142/9781800617414_0012

Chapter 12

Why Leadership Matters: Driving Success in Project Management and Business

Tereza Raquel Merlo

Department of Information Sciences, University of North Texas, USA

tereza.merlo@unt.edu

Abstract

This chapter examines the pivotal role of leadership in shaping project management success, emphasizing that effective leadership extends beyond task coordination to directly influence organizational performance and employee well-being. Drawing on a comprehensive literature review, the study highlights how leadership effectiveness impacts every dimension of project execution, including planning, communication, team cohesion, risk management, decision-making, and resource allocation. Positive leadership is characterized by emotional intelligence, inclusivity, empathy, and a clear shared vision, which fosters collaboration, trust, and knowledge-sharing, and ultimately creates an environment that enables innovation and continuous learning. These practices not only strengthen project outcomes but also, more importantly, enhance employee morale, engagement, and retention, thereby reinforcing the organization's long-term competitiveness. This analysis further identifies critical leadership competencies and strategies, such as cultivating psychological safety, promoting resilience, and aligning project objectives with broader business goals. Ultimately, this work underscores that leadership is not a peripheral element but a central determinant of successful project management, sustainable business performance, and organizational health in today's dynamic, knowledge- and data-driven environments.

Keywords: Project management, effective leadership, business competitiveness, organizational performance.

12.1 Introduction

Society is experiencing a transformative acceleration, propelled by the swift and far-reaching advancements of artificial intelligence (AI), directly impacting how individuals and organizations manage rapid data processing, continuous information flows, and the demand for timely insights and decision-making. Project management is a critical discipline that enables organizations to plan, execute, and monitor initiatives effectively, ensuring objectives are met on time, within scope, and on budget. It provides a structured framework for coordinating resources, managing risks, and facilitating communication among stakeholders, which is essential for aligning team efforts with strategic goals (Riaz *et al.*, 2013). Effective project management enhances decision-making, fosters accountability, and promotes collaboration across diverse teams, ultimately driving operational efficiency and organizational success. By applying standardized methodologies and best practices, organizations can navigate complexity, adapt to changing environments, and deliver high-quality outcomes that create lasting value for both clients and the organization. In this setting, transformational leadership plays a pivotal role in enhancing organizational agility and preserving competitiveness. Effective leaders enable businesses to cultivate continuous learning, enhance operational efficiency, engage employees, adapt to shifting market conditions, scale operations efficiently, and achieve a sustainable advantage in the digital economy.

Organizational challenges that reflect leadership deficiencies and project failures include communication breakdowns, cultural resistance, bias, a lack of planning and organization, inconsistencies in project management, and delays impacting knowledge sharing, which are issues that resonate with broader concerns in project management literature (Turner and Müller, 2005; Müller *et al.*, 2022). The aim of this chapter is to critically examine the organizational, managerial, and cultural barriers that often affect project management deliverables and team efficiency.

Using a literature review approach, this chapter draws lessons applicable to organizations of all sectors and complexities, particularly in dynamic and multifaceted team environments. By situating the analysis within the context of project management frameworks and leadership, the chapter contributes to the growing discourse on how leadership practices, team dynamics, and organizational culture influence large-scale, knowledge-intensive deliverables, based on the Project Management Body of Knowledge (PMBOK) guidelines. Specifically, it underscores the critical need for stable leadership, effective communication structures, a robust project management framework, leadership readiness and emotional intelligence (EI), and a culture that promotes knowledge sharing to ensure continuity, innovation, and strategic alignment in global project environments.

12.2 Methodological Approach

This study draws on elements of the Preferred Reporting Items for Systematic Reviews (PRISMA) framework to guide the literature selection and screening process, focusing on leadership's role in successful project management. By adopting this structured approach, the review ensures comprehensiveness, reduces potential bias, and facilitates a clear and insightful synthesis of existing evidence, as shown in Figure 12.1.

Figure 12.1 illustrates the flow of records through the stages of the review process, visually summarizing how articles and additional materials were identified, screened, and included in the analysis. Studies considered well-aligned with the purpose of this study were included; exclusion criteria included non-English language texts, texts outside the scope, and those with full text unavailable. Data retrieval relied on Google Scholar, ResearchGate, and databases listed in Figure 12.1. The database search yielded over 80 relevant articles, and Google Scholar and ResearchGate retrieved 40 articles. Searches were conducted using combinations of Boolean operators and keywords such as: "Leadership" AND "Project Management", "Knowledge Management Systems" AND "Leadership" OR "Business Outcomes" AND "Organizational

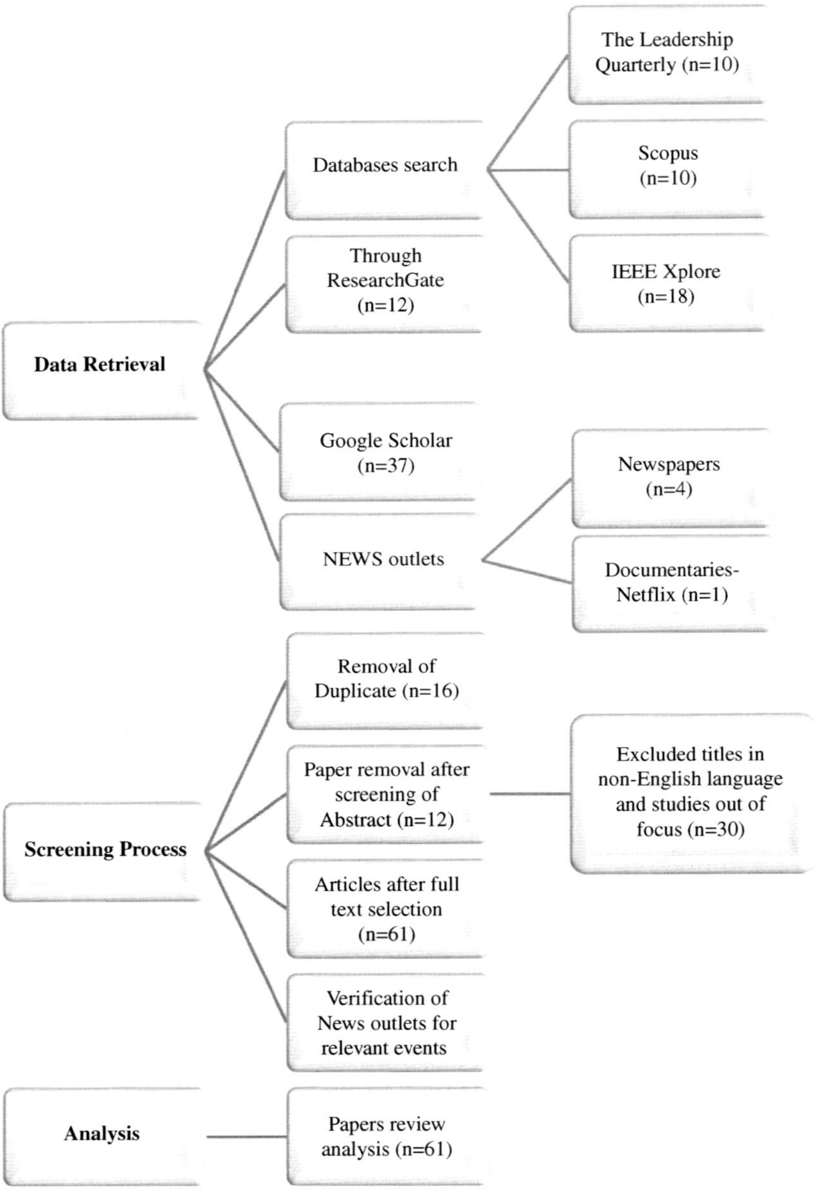

Figure 12.1. The research flow approach adapted from the PRISMA method.

Management", OR "Emotional Intelligence" AND "Leadership". The search was limited to articles published in English, within peer-reviewed sources, and with organizational or system-level units of analysis. The initial search across all sources returned a total of 102 records before removing duplicates. Using Excel spreadsheets, duplicate and irrelevant articles were removed, and over 55 articles were included in this analysis, in addition to news sources and documentaries. The news and documentary sources were included because they offered timely accounts and contextual perspectives on leadership practices, often not reflected in academic publications, thereby validating and illustrating the arguments presented in this study.

12.3 Theoretical Framework

The theoretical foundation of this study draws from multiple complementary perspectives. Prior studies linking leadership deficiencies and EI gaps to project failure and organizational dysfunction (Turner and Müller, 2005; Müller *et al.*, 2022) help frame/elucidate the relationship between success in project management and the role of leadership. This section highlights key factors in developing and implementing an effective project management framework, drawing on literature review insights that emphasize the role of top leadership in supporting, enabling, and fostering a dynamic and productive team.

In a qualitative study by Blaskovics (2014), the relationship between leadership style and project success is examined, highlighting that while the traditional project management triangle – time, cost, and quality – remains essential for achieving success, these factors alone are not sufficient. Drawing on the comprehensive analysis of over 60 publications by Fortune and White (2006), Blaskovics (2014) underscored that several additional critical factors play a decisive role in determining project success:

- Support from senior management.
- Clear and realistic objectives.
- A well-developed, up-to-date project plan.
- Effective communication and feedback.
- Active end-user involvement.

Turner (2004) compiled the following four necessary conditions for project success:

(1) The success criteria should be defined by a stakeholder before the start of the project and reiterated at configuration review points throughout the project.
(2) A collaborative working relationship should be maintained between the project owner and project manager, with both viewing the project as a partnership.
(3) The project manager should be empowered, with the owner providing guidance on how they think the project should be best approached while allowing the project manager flexibility to deal with unforeseen circumstances as they see best.
(4) The owner should take an interest in the performance of the project.

Rehan *et al.* (2024) conducted a rigorous seven-step systematic literature review (SLR) process, involving 2,805 initial articles, which were narrowed down to 72 for in-depth analysis. The selected studies span from 2000 to 2021. Their work highlights the diverse leadership behavioral practices of project managers and their relationship with project success, particularly in the context of increasingly complex environments and multi-dimensional projects. The principal findings of Rehan *et al.*'s work emphasize how interpersonal and emotional practices such as relationship-building, effective communication, and collaborative teamwork have a high-to-moderate significance in the success of the project.

Companies across all sectors, especially in high-tech industries, face increasing pressure to deliver comprehensive and dynamic results amid rapid technological advancements and evolving data management strategies. Effective leadership is essential in enabling firms to integrate knowledge, align objectives, and respond to evolving client and market demands. Stumpf *et al.* (2002) argue that organizations, particularly professional services firms, operate in two highly competitive arenas – the market for clients and the market for talent to serve those clients – requiring active and continuous strategic focus. Leadership success increasingly depends on the ability to coordinate multidisciplinary teams, manage complex information flows, and deliver time-sensitive outcomes that influence client strategies and shape market perceptions (Maister, 2003). In this context, organizations rely on project management teams to produce high-quality deliverables on time, essential outputs for operational efficiency, client engagement, and reinforcement of market positioning.

12.4 PMBOK and the Project Manager: Foundations, Guardrails, and Practice

Project managers should follow the guidelines of the Project Management Institute's *A Guide to the Project Management Body of Knowledge* (PMBOK® Guide), a globally influential resource for project managers, drawing on multiple theoretical frameworks to guide effective project execution. The PMBOK, originally known as Project #121, was conceptualized in 1987 and later published in 1996 as a comprehensive guide designed to serve as a reference for evolving project complexities and environments, with an evolving structure, currently in its seventh edition. It is the result of an effort to guide practitioners in identifying and establishing the basic functions and scope for project management success, establishing roadmaps that break down a model and ground rules for project management. It provides a standardized framework for effective project management and implementation of consistent practices, ultimately supporting organizational success through effective project outcomes (PMI, 2021; Stuckenbruck, 1986).

While the original PMBOK structure focused on processes, the evolving PMBOK structure includes PM principles that highlight the importance of values, leadership behaviors, and the importance of tailoring project guidelines to fit the context, individuals, and work environment. The evolving nature of the PMBOK recognizes the importance of diligence, respect, care, and building a culture of accountability and transparency to navigate complexities, optimize team performance, and proactively engage stakeholders.

Some areas included in the PMBOK Guide include project management integration, scope management, time management, quality management, cost management, human resources management, communication management, risk management, procurement management, and stakeholder management, encompassing key areas for the performance domain, defined as follows: "A performance domain is a group of related activities that are critical for the effective delivery of project outcomes" (Project Management Institute, 2021, p. xii).

A project manager is defined by the Project Management Institute as the person who has the responsibility "to lead the project team that is responsible for achieving the project objectives. Project managers perform a variety of functions, such as facilitating the project teamwork to achieve the outcomes and managing the processes to deliver intended outcomes" (2021, p. 4). The project managers are responsible for implementing communication processes that ensure openness, transparency, and clear messaging. In successfully managing a project, the project manager must create systems to monitor and manage outcomes, establishing a formal, consistent, and secure procedure that supports and is supported by key organizational functions and senior leadership, with clear communication of expectations.

Defining clear expectations is essential for clarifying project outcomes, while formal structures and external organizational support provide mechanisms to manage those outcomes effectively. Equally important, building trust – vital for fostering collaboration and teamwork – requires sustained commitment to transparent, open, and consistent communication (Anantatmula, 2010; Sommerville *et al.*, 2010). In practice, this process begins with reviewing the project charter (both existing and previous versions) and any related plans. The subsequent step involves identifying stakeholders and analyzing project objectives, constraints, assumptions, and deliverables to accurately assess the current project status, including scope, risks, and other critical factors (PMBOK, 2021; Stackpole, 2013).

Overseeing and orchestrating these efforts is part of the project manager's priorities, and leadership plays a critical role in ensuring that the project is well managed, executed, and delivered on time, within scope, and to the highest quality standards. According to the PMBOK® Guide (Project Management Institute, 2021), project managers are responsible for integrating project components, managing stakeholder expectations, mitigating risks, and facilitating communication across teams. In this context, the project manager ensures that the complex work of individuals in the team is aligned, coordinated, and executed efficiently. As Müller, Sankaran, and Drouin (2022) note, effective project managers provide structure and direction in dynamic environments, helping organizations navigate challenges such as rotational leadership, knowledge silos, and shifting priorities. Their role is vital to fostering team engagement, ensuring operational discipline, and ultimately delivering a report that supports the firm's strategic goals and market competitiveness.

12.4.1 *Project deliverables reimagined: Linking technology, emotional intelligence, and leadership*

Knowledge systems refer to the structured frameworks, processes, and technologies that organizations use to capture, store, manage, and share knowledge and information. These systems support decision-making, collaboration, and innovation by facilitating the creation, transfer, and application of knowledge across an organization. A knowledge system typically integrates people, technology, processes, and organizational culture to enable the effective use of knowledge resources (Merlo, 2016). Key elements of a knowledge system include the following:

1. *Knowledge creation*: Methods and practices that foster the generation of new ideas, insights, and solutions.
2. *Knowledge storage*: Repositories and databases that capture explicit knowledge (such as documents, reports, and databases) and tacit knowledge (such as expertise and experience).
3. *Knowledge sharing*: Tools and practices that facilitate the exchange of knowledge between individuals and teams, such as collaborative platforms, meetings, and mentoring.
4. *Knowledge application*: The use of knowledge in decision-making, problem-solving, and innovation processes.
5. *Technology infrastructure*: Software tools, databases, and platforms that support the storage, retrieval, and dissemination of knowledge (e.g., knowledge management systems, content management systems, and AI-powered platforms).

In the context of knowledge management (KM), knowledge systems are crucial for enabling continuous learning, improving organizational efficiency, and fostering a culture of collaboration and innovation. Leadership must consider the knowledge creation and sharing process in handling the report and the team's time, so accountability would be a factor in project management, progress, and outcomes.

The importance of leadership is reflected in superior knowledge-sharing protocols and the development of information systems that support collaboration, innovation, and productivity. A critical aspect of leadership is the ability to exhibit EI while avoiding cultural biases, hostility, and unequal treatment, all of which can undermine and discourage knowledge sharing. When these behaviors occur, employees often become disengaged, perceiving the project as both unsustainable and unrewarding (Goleman *et al.*, 2016).

An unbiased approach to business decisions is essential for transforming raw data into actionable knowledge that informs client strategies, business operations, and market decisions. This process requires not only technical expertise but also strong collaboration across business units to ensure that insights and reporting align with organizational priorities and client expectations, which is crucial for maintaining relevance and trust (Lucescu *et al.*, 2023). The effectiveness of such teams reflects the organization's broader KM capabilities and its ability to coordinate across silos (Greenwood *et al.*, 2018).

Effective leadership and integrated knowledge management systems (KMSs) are critical for achieving strategic goals and sustaining competitive advantage. The ability to guide teams, foster collaboration, and ensure the systematic capture and application of organizational knowledge directly influences project outcomes, innovation, and stakeholder trust. Conversely, deficiencies in leadership – such as low EI, cultural insensitivity, and ego-driven decision-making – can create a toxic environment that impedes communication, knowledge sharing, and alignment with business objectives. There is a critical intersection between leadership and KMSs (Alavi and Leidner, 2001) that has often been overlooked. Shortcomings in these areas can undermine even the simplest projects, emphasizing the essential role of leadership in driving organizational success. The following five key recommendations can contribute to project success:

- *Mitigating leadership deficiencies*: Implementing targeted leadership development programs and performance assessments can help identify and address gaps in leadership skills. Strengthening EI, decision-making, and strategic thinking ensures that project managers are equipped to guide teams effectively and maintain alignment with organizational goals.
- *Improving project stability*, especially in the face of management changes or mergers and acquisitions: Developing standardized processes, clear documentation, and robust knowledge-transfer protocols can reduce disruption when leadership transitions occur. Maintaining

continuity in project vision and goals ensures that organizational changes do not compromise project outcomes.

- *Enhancing cross-functional collaboration*: Fostering a culture of open communication, joint problem-solving, and mutual accountability encourages collaboration across diverse teams. Structured collaboration tools and regular interdepartmental meetings can break down silos and enable seamless coordination.
- *Establishing knowledge-sharing systems*: Implementing KM platforms, best-practice repositories, and collaborative tools promotes the systematic capture and dissemination of organizational knowledge. This ensures that lessons learned, expertise, and insights are accessible, improving decision-making and accelerating project success.

Nicolaides *et al.* (2014) conducted a study examining the relationship between shared leadership and team performance, concluding that "shared leadership is particularly effective when interdependence is high. High interdependence requires team members to work closely with one another, coordinate, and integrate actions. There is evidence to suggest that under high levels of interdependence, team processes, and emergent states will lead to higher team performance [...] results indicate that as team tenure increases, shared leadership validities decrease" (p. 935).

Turner (2004) asserts that "A collaborative working relationship should be maintained between the project owner and project manager, with both viewing the project as a partnership" (p. 350). In the initial stages of risk assessment and project planning, several measures were implemented to enhance information sharing. Knowledge repositories were introduced using shared cloud platforms, alignment meetings were organized to involve leaders, project managers, and content specialists, and communication and reporting documentation were embedded as integral components of the organizational culture.

12.4.2 *Effective leadership and organizational culture: Driving project success while mitigating the impact of toxic leadership*

Leadership is a critical determinant of success in any organizational context, particularly in project management. Effective leadership guides teams through complex tasks, aligns stakeholders with organizational goals, and fosters an environment conducive to collaboration and innovation (Northouse, 2022). In the business world, leadership extends beyond simply managing tasks; it involves inspiring, motivating, and influencing team members to achieve a shared vision. Peter Drucker, often regarded as the father of modern management, emphasized that leadership in business is about setting clear objectives, empowering employees, and creating organizational structures that enable performance and higher profitability (Bragg, 2020). In this sense, leadership is both a strategic and interpersonal function, critical for the delivery of successful projects.

Effective project management demands more than procedural oversight; it requires leaders to demonstrate self-awareness, foster psychological safety, and facilitate inclusive collaboration (Edmondson and Lei, 2014). Emotional volatility in response to feedback and reluctance to share knowledge hinder team innovation and discourage open communication – factors consistently associated with project underperformance (Aga *et al.*, 2016; Müller *et al.*, 2018). The volatility inherent in project operations and execution, marked by sudden changes, unforeseen issues, and shifting priorities, requires agile leadership and adaptive planning to maintain progress and achieve objectives.

A leadership style combining toxic traits with a transactional approach, characterized by significant deficiencies, can severely undermine project performance, team collaboration, morale, and strategic decision-making. Characterized by impulsivity, poor communication, and a lack of EI, such leaders foster a work environment defined by confusion, fear-based compliance, and disengagement. These behaviors exemplify a broader pattern in which weak leadership disrupts core management processes, hampers business operations, and ultimately erodes organizational values and competitive advantage (Turner and Müller, 2005; Clarke, 2010).

Effective leaders regulate emotions, manage conflicts, and navigate ambiguity while applying critical thinking and contextual intelligence to sustain strong collaborative relationships (Yukl, 2013). By modeling positive behaviors, they reinforce confidence among teams and external partners, promote project success and strategic alignment, and cultivate a psychologically safe environment that minimizes disruption, disengagement, and turnover risk (Rousseau, 1995).

Management decision-making approaches highlight the importance of inclusive leadership and unbiased practices in fostering balanced team dynamics, enabling all contributors to thrive, and encouraging the diversity of thought essential for innovative problem-solving (Shore *et al.*, 2018; Rock and Grant, 2016). Evident biases can undermine talent retention, particularly among women and professionals from underrepresented backgrounds, resulting in substantial losses of institutional knowledge. Research shows that environments marked by low EI and high power distance often face significant barriers to knowledge transfer and organizational learning (Argote and Miron-Spektor, 2011; Goleman *et al.*, 2016).

A study conducted by Michiel and Karuna (2018) introduced a theoretical framework that explores how **vertical leadership** (the formal, person-centered leadership executed by project managers) and **horizontal leadership** (the collaborative, emergent leadership exhibited by team members) interact dynamically throughout a project life cycle, concluding that it is important for project managers to dynamically calibrate between vertical and horizontal leadership as circumstances demand. This enables projects to benefit from formalized direction while empowering teams to self-organize and adapt, ultimately enhancing agility and improving outcomes in complex project environments. Drawing on the literature review, several common project management setbacks have been identified, along with corresponding recommended actions to mitigate or prevent them:

a. *Clear leadership alignment*: Project leadership roles and team responsibilities should be explicitly defined and communicated across the organization, especially among decision-makers and key stakeholders, to ensure shared understanding and smooth execution.
b. *Leadership accountability*: Establish a shared vision and clear project objectives to minimize disruptions and prepare the team for potential adjustments. Adopting an agile approach allows for flexibility and responsiveness to changes.
c. *Effective communication Systems*: Implement a consistent and well-organized communication framework using internal resources, including knowledge portals and management systems, to streamline regular updates, feedback loops, and decision-making processes.
d. *Centralized knowledge sharing platform*: Create and maintain a centralized repository for project resources, lessons learned, and next steps. Ensure the platform is easily accessible and regularly updated to support collaboration and organizational learning.

e. *Data governance and protocols*: Develop a structured data governance model with clearly defined roles, scheduled meetings, and standardized knowledge-sharing protocols to ensure information accuracy, security, and availability.
f. *Regular leadership and project review practices*: Leaders and project managers should schedule regular check-ins, project assessments, and performance evaluations. Depending on the project scope, business relevance, and stakeholder involvement, these sessions can occur weekly or monthly to ensure alignment and continuous improvement.

To address these shortcomings, organizations should integrate emotionally intelligent leadership development into their annual management training programs. This includes training in active listening, self-regulation, receptivity to feedback, and inclusive decision-making (Mayer *et al.*, 2008; Goleman *et al.*, 2016). Project teams can further mitigate the risks of impulsive, top-down leadership by implementing structured communication frameworks and feedback loops. Additionally, decision-making tools such as RACI matrices, stakeholder maps, and scenario planning enhance transparency and reduce ambiguity during project implementation (PMI, 2021).

A RACI matrix is a project management tool designed to clarify and communicate roles and responsibilities for specific tasks, deliverables, or decisions within a project. The acronym RACI stands for **Responsible** (who performs the work), **Accountable** (who is responsible for project completion), **Consulted** (who provides input or expertise), and **Informed** (who needs updates on progress or decisions). By defining these roles clearly, a RACI matrix helps prevent confusion, streamlines communication, and enhances accountability within teams (PMI, 2021).

Organizations must regularly audit internal leadership behaviors for signs of bias, burnout, and psychological distress to ensure that talent and knowledge are not lost due to leadership malpractice. The presented case reinforces the importance of integrating EI and inclusive leadership into project environments. Without these foundational elements, even technically sound initiatives may falter due to miscommunication, disengaged teams, and misaligned strategic visions.

In the context of leadership and project management within organizations, the role of project manager is crucial in KMSs, particularly in environments characterized by poor leadership and communication deficiencies. As organizations strive for operational efficiency, the integration of effective KMSs is essential to overcome systemic issues and foster collaboration, innovation, and productivity (Davenport and Prusak, 2000). However, when project leadership lacks EI or organizational systems are misaligned, the effectiveness of knowledge systems and the success of the project are severely hindered. Such deficiencies not only impede knowledge sharing but also disrupt business processes, operations, and outcomes, particularly in environments where employees are inadequately prepared for their roles due to poorly designed role assignments or rotational management positions (Nonaka and Takeuchi, 1995). These challenges can lead to disengagement, communication breakdowns, and inefficient decision-making, further exacerbating issues with knowledge creation, storage, and application.

Project management, by its nature, requires careful planning, execution, and monitoring of tasks to achieve defined objectives within the constraints of time, cost, and quality. Leadership plays a pivotal role in these processes, ensuring that teams remain focused, motivated, and adaptive to changes in scope or unforeseen challenges (PMI, 2021). Leaders in project management must balance technical knowledge with interpersonal skills, such as conflict resolution, effective communication, and EI. This combination allows project managers to navigate complex organizational dynamics and guide teams toward successful outcomes (Turner and Müller, 2005).

In organizations where leadership struggles to establish a culture of open communication and inclusivity, the importance of robust project managers for enabling knowledge systems becomes even more apparent. Knowledge sharing is critical in these settings to break down silos, ensure alignment, and improve decision-making. However, in environments where power dynamics are marked by information hoarding and power struggles, employees are not included in key decision-making processes, and the integration of effective knowledge systems can be compromised. Furthermore, the lack of clarity around roles and responsibilities, coupled with cultural biases and ineffective leadership practices, negatively affects the consolidation of a clear roadmap for organizational objectives.

When individuals in positions of power and privilege exhibit poor leadership and abusive communication, their actions often provoke resistance and reputational decline – even among those lower in the hierarchical or socioeconomic status. This resistance is not merely symbolic but material, manifesting as public disapproval, employee disengagement, and economic losses. It is important that leaders are not in a position of unchecked power, which, combined with a lack of EI and abusive behaviors, can erode both internal organizational culture and external brand perception. According to Brown and Trevino (2006), ethical leadership is related to integrity, advocating that "personal traits such as integrity would be important to perceptions of leadership effectiveness and research has borne that out" (p. 596).

Leadership failures marked by arrogance, a lack of self-awareness, and demeaning treatment of others have profound consequences. Empirical studies show that such toxic leadership styles lead to "active resistance" among employees, including forms of "counterproductive work behavior," such as information withholding, disengagement, and even sabotage (Mackey *et al.*, 2017). Moreover, when employees are demoralized or demeaned, they often become psychologically disengaged, a phenomenon now widely referred to as "quiet quitting" (Klotz and Bolino, 2022). This not only reduces productivity but also results in the departure of key talent, often accompanied by tacit knowledge that is essential for innovation and strategic continuity (Argote and Ren, 2022).

The erosion of morale and trust often initiates a chain reaction: high turnover, fractured collaboration, and a weakened knowledge repository. Employees who feel abused or devalued rarely contribute to knowledge-sharing platforms, leading to data silos, inefficiencies, and strategic blind spots (Nonaka and Takeuchi, 1995; Davenport and Prusak, 2000). In data-driven industries, this withholding of knowledge, whether passive or intentional, can have fatal consequences for organizational performance. Studies indicate that companies with poor internal knowledge flows underperform financially and are more vulnerable to external shocks (Foss *et al.*, 2012). Additionally, reputational harm caused by visible leadership misconduct, especially in a globally networked era, can tarnish brand equity in ways that are difficult or even impossible to repair (Lange *et al.*, 2011).

Organizations must prevent and remedy what researchers describe as destructive archetypes – individuals whose hierarchical positions and privileges are believed to shield them from backlash. Historically, stakeholders, employees, clients, and even external observers eventually rejected this type of leader's toxic behavior, which contributed to internal discontent, low morale, and ultimately, organizational instability. This scenario reinforces a key principle of contemporary leadership theory: EI, ethical communication, and humility are not optional traits; they are critical competencies for anyone in a position of strategic authority (Goleman *et al.*, 2016; Antonakis, 2017).

As the business landscape becomes increasingly reliant on AI, the integration of AI into knowledge systems holds transformative potential. AI technologies can enhance knowledge sharing, decision-making, and collaboration within organizations, yet the underlying leadership structure must be capable of effectively leveraging these technologies. By focusing on real-world observations from a project management perspective, this analysis emphasizes the critical need for strategic alignment, leadership accountability, and emotional competence to ensure the success of KMSs in driving innovation and organizational effectiveness across multiple projects (Merlo, 2016).

Dynamic organizations are more successful when they cultivate transformational leaders with strong situational leadership skills, who are motivated to inspire teams, drive change, and foster innovation while effectively managing complex project tasks. EI is also a critical factor in navigating the challenges of fast-evolving work environments and industries. Leaders must be equipped to recognize and regulate their own emotions while effectively managing and supporting their teams. Evidence suggests that managers who are ill-prepared and exhibit extreme authoritarian traits, combined with narcissistic tendencies such as excessive self-promotion and a pursuit of status and power, frequently act at the expense of employee well-being and demonstrate a lack of empathy (Rosenthal and Pittinsky, 2006). In contrast, a clear and cohesive vision offers focused direction, supports proactive planning, and facilitates structured decision-making. Thorough preparation further promotes efficient workflows, fosters high performance, and enhances the overall quality of project outcomes. The success of a project depends on the vision, engagement, and strategy of top leaders, whose responsibilities include, among others, the following:

(a) Communicate the project vision, goals, and expectations to the team.
(b) Advocate for the project and the team.
(c) Facilitate executive-level decisions.
(d) Secure resources, including the effective use – and availability – of existing resources, both human and technological.
(e) Ensure project alignment with business goals/objectives.
(f) Ensure that obstacles are removed.
(g) Address issues outside of the project manager's authority.

(h) Bring opportunities and address escalated issues in a timely manner.
(i) Monitor outcomes.

Leaders must demonstrate a commitment to fostering executive engagement and make decisions that efficiently advance project milestones, support the team, meet stakeholder expectations, and align with broader business objectives. As Ahmed, Tahir, and bin Mohamad (2013) emphasize, "leadership is vital for project managers to achieve project efficacy" (p. 99), underscoring the critical role that effective leadership plays in ensuring project success. When employees perceive leadership as unfair, dismissive, or prejudiced, they withdraw discretionary effort, reduce knowledge-sharing, and disengage from collaborative tasks (Cropanzano *et al.*, 2017). These reactions are particularly damaging in project-based environments where success depends on cohesion, trust, and transparency.

Understanding and familiarity with the PMBOK® Guide or any established project management principles is critical in preventing misunderstandings regarding roles, project scope, objectives, etc., allowing individuals to effectively utilize available resources and successfully manage the project and its progress, challenges, and changes. This ability to apply PMBOK's principles prevents avoidable delays and unnecessary conflicts throughout the project lifecycle. Compounding these challenges, the importance of planning and timely execution of the project's sprints will ensure successful completion, particularly enabling effective communication channels and task planning and execution. Planning will prevent the habit of last-minute, unfeasible, and unreasonable requests, which creates stress among team members and diminishes the quality of deliverables.

Workplaces marked by instability create a culture of reactivity rather than collaboration and strategic planning, forcing the project team to operate in a constant state of crisis. As Nonaka and Takeuchi (1995) emphasize, organizational knowledge creation thrives on continuity, shared understanding, and trust.

12.4.3 *Knowledge silos and communication barriers*

A top-down, exclusionary approach fosters confusion and undermines team cohesion (Goleman *et al.*, 2016), negatively affecting project updates and strategic decisions, which influence both the team and the project scope. One of the key capabilities of a project management office (PMO) is to emphasize continuous improvement, knowledge transfer, and effective change management. Effective organizational change management ensures that the organization remains aligned as processes, tools, and skills evolve. This alignment is essential to successfully adopt process improvements, build new capabilities, and equip teams with the skills they need to effectively manage projects and prepare for the future. In short, knowledge sharing and change management together create a culture of continuous improvement, which strengthens project outcomes over time. (PMI, 2021).

Power dynamics is another negative factor in project management, undermining trust within the team. Power can be asserted through information hoarding, and employees are discouraged from raising concerns about timelines, workloads, or leadership behavior. This eroded morale and led to disengagement, high turnover, and unfair terminations.

12.5 High-Profile Cases of Leadership Failure Impacting Business, Brand, and Financial Outcomes – The Cases of Elon Musk and Stockton Rush

This section examines how leadership deficiencies, including narcissistic leadership styles (Rosenthal and Pittinsky, 2006), low EI (Goleman, 1995), and a disregard for employee well-being, can lead to disastrous business consequences. Drawing on the high-profile cases of Elon Musk's politicized decisions and OceanGate's catastrophic failure, the analysis highlights how arrogance, ego-centricity, and poor leadership judgment can result in both reputational harm and financial loss – personal and corporate.

12.5.1 *Elon Musk: Twitter = "X", and DOGE*

From the perspective of leadership theory and empirical research, Elon Musk's tenure at Twitter and his episodic political engagement with the – unofficial[1] – Department of Government Efficiency (DOGE) exemplify a

[1] Initiative established by President Trump via executive order on January 20, 2025.

recurrent pattern of leadership deficiencies. Elon's takeover of Twitter in 2022 raised concerns and faced criticism for the way leadership decisions negatively affected employees and ultimately diminished the business value of his companies (BBC News, 2022). Employees were concerned about the erratic communication style or lack thereof, as some leaked emails and shared experiences of being abruptly terminated without proper communication, justification, or offboarding processes, reportedly involving insulting and demeaning treatment and threats of job instability for those who remained.

Elon's behavior was often reactive, emotionally impulsive, and marked by erratic decision-making – traits consistent with what Kellerman (2004) and Lipman-Blumen (2023) identify as hallmark features of toxic leadership, particularly the "intemperate" and "incompetent" archetypes (Kellerman, 2004; Lipman-Blumen, 2023). Moreover, Musk's evident lack of EI, inability to perceive, regulate, or positively channel emotions contrasts sharply with well-established findings demonstrating that EI positively predicts effective leadership outcomes, such as trust-building, job satisfaction, and team performance (Mayer *et al.*, 2008; Goleman, 1998; Rosete and Ciarrochi, 2005).

Additionally, Musk's leadership exhibited low levels of inclusivity and psychological safety, factors that are consistently associated with diminished innovation and engagement (Li and Tang, 2022; Randel *et al.*, 2018). According to Tong and Tang (2022), inclusive leadership fosters psychological safety, which is critical for team innovation at both the individual and collective levels. In stark contrast, Musk's dominance-centric and authoritarian style failed to cultivate such an enabling environment, aligning neither with transformational nor shared leadership frameworks (Berson *et al.*, 2006; Nicolaides *et al.*, 2014). Instead, his approach exemplifies what many researchers classify as the toxic antithesis of authentic leadership, which values self-awareness, relational transparency, and ethical behavior.

Based on these empirical insights, truly effective leadership in knowledge-intensive and dynamic environments should embody four core traits: (1) EI, enabling leaders to self-regulate and attune to team emotions (Mayer *et al.*, 2008); (2) inclusive practices that foster psychological safety and innovation (Tong and Tang, 2022; Randel *et al.*, 2018); (3) adaptability and shared decision-making consistent with transformational and distributed leadership models (Nicolaides *et al.*, 2014); and

(4) authentic conduct grounded in self-awareness and moral integrity. Musk's case serves as a cautionary example that reinforces the imperative to redefine leadership success beyond charisma and control, emphasizing competence, empathy, and ethical stewardship.

Elon Musk's tenure at the DOGE exposed his leadership skills in a new light, revealing critical insights into the problematic leadership style within the public sector, highlighting his bold and aggressive approach, the polarized public response, and the institutional friction his methods provoked. When Elon Musk assumed a "special government employee" role in the DOGE in January 2025, he brought his disruptive Silicon Valley ethos to the federal government. As DOGE's de facto leader, Musk pursued an aggressive "move fast, break things" approach, leading to the termination of hundreds of federal employees and agency leases, claiming savings of up to \$150–\$180 billion (Clarke, 2025; Wallace-Wells, 2025).

Musk treated DOGE like a private-sector "efficiency startup," embedding rapid-response teams across agencies. His leadership promised to be centered on blunt cost-cutting, minimal stakeholder consultation, and sweeping structural changes. Musk's role immediately sparked conflict-of-interest concerns, given his simultaneous leadership of major corporations regarding access to federal contracts and private data. During Elon's tenure with the federal government leading DOGE, there were internal leaks exposing controversial and concerning unilateral changes in federal agencies, public criticism of expressed personal biases, etc., prompting media scrutiny of Elon's businesses and personal life, resulting in an ongoing backlash and protests that extended beyond his role in government.

Elon Musk's leadership style provides a vivid example of how impulsive decision-making can lead to volatile business outcomes and reputational risks. His involvement with DOGE, much like his takeover of Twitter, was characterized by unpredictable, unstructured approaches to decision-making and problem-solving. These behaviors reflect traits of narcissistic leadership, where personal image and influence often overshadow organizational stability and stakeholder interests (Rosenthal and Pittinsky, 2006). As a result, Musk's actions have affected Tesla's business operations, strained relationships with shareholders, and damaged his global reputation, leading to significant financial losses across his companies.

12.5.2 *Stockton Rush: OceanGate's Titan implosion: Leadership hubris and its fatal consequences*

Stockton Rush, co-founder and CEO of OceanGate, epitomized a tech-entrepreneurial leadership style infused with ego and narcissistic traits reminiscent of the "move fast and break things" Silicon Valley mindset. He pursued a vision to transform undersea exploration, coining it "SpaceX for the oceans," but repeatedly dismissed industry-standard safety protocols and expert warnings (Ankel *et al.*, 2023).

Rush exemplified a leadership style marked by hubris, overconfidence, and narcissistic traits, combining his business vision of revolutionizing deep-sea exploration with his determination to consistently disregard established safety standards and expert advice, causing conflicts among team members, low morale, abrupt terminations, and an environment of fear, retaliation, and secrecy. Rush dismissed regulations, as they were perceived as obstacles to innovation; instead, he prioritized speed and ambition over risk management. Such behavior aligns with patterns identified in the literature on narcissistic leadership, where leaders display inflated self-importance, reject feedback, and take excessive risks that endanger organizational health (Rosenthal and Pittinsky, 2006).

Former employees reported that Rush's leadership created a culture where caution was interpreted as obstruction, and critical voices were silenced or removed (e.g., the termination of David Lochridge, OceanGate's former operations pilot, after he raised safety concerns). This mirrors what Goleman (1995) describes as a failure of emotional intelligence, where leaders' inability to manage their emotions or empathize with others fosters climates of fear and suppresses open dialogue. The tragic implosion of the Titan submersible in 2023, which resulted in the loss of all aboard, underscores how unchecked ego, low emotional competence, and intolerance for dissent can culminate in catastrophic outcomes – both human and financial.

Rush's low EI, characterized by hostility toward dissenting voices, further exacerbated the risks. He fired chief operations pilot David Lochridge after the latter raised critical safety concerns. Lochridge later stated that he feared Rush "get himself and others killed in a quest to boost his ego" (Musumeci, 2023, para. 4), former employees described a "toxic, cult-like culture" in which caution was portrayed as obstructionist (Monroe, 2025).

The ego-centered leadership style, marked by arrogance, rule-defying behavior, and insensitivity, directly contributed to the catastrophic implosion of the Titan submersible in June 2023 (Horton, 2025). By prioritizing personal ambition and public recognition over safety, Rush established structural hazards that led to a tragic loss of lives and a massive financial, reputational, and regulatory toll on OceanGate.

This case starkly illustrates how ego-driven, emotionally tone-deaf leadership can precipitate organizational collapse, paralleling well-documented failures in other contexts, such as those of Musk and Rush. Moreover, it reinforces scholarly insights that narcissistic leadership undermines stakeholder trust, suppresses dissent, and disrupts organizational safety and performance (Rosenthal and Pittinsky, 2006; Goleman, 1995).

The two cases illustrate how narcissistic tendencies, particularly those involving risk-taking and disregard for consequences, can create reputational risk and harm stakeholder trust (Maccoby, 2000). In essence, in both cases, the leadership styles of Rush and Musk are marked by impulsive and ego-driven decisions, exemplifying how poor judgment and emotional immaturity at the top can undermine credibility, destabilize markets, and create long-term challenges for corporate governance, investor confidence, and even lead to tragic outcomes.

Leadership development programs should emphasize empathy, inclusive decision-making, and conflict resolution. In parallel, organizations must implement formal knowledge retention strategies, such as mentorship programs, exit interviews designed to capture critical knowledge, and transparent communication frameworks, to safeguard intellectual capital. Finally, cultivating a culture of psychological safety is essential, allowing data, insights, and dissenting perspectives to be shared openly without fear of reprisal (Edmondson and Lei, 2014).

12.6 Conclusion and Future Work

The analysis presented in this chapter aims to highlight the critical intersection of leadership stability, emotional competence, and KM in project success. Poor leadership skills undermine productive business operations, disrupting collaboration and eroding morale. As organizations transition into an AI-driven landscape, effective knowledge-sharing systems and emotionally intelligent leadership are essential for navigating complexity and sustaining innovation.

This study aims to highlight the critical role of leadership stability, effective communication, and knowledge systems in project management within companies of all segments, contributing to the exploration of the underlying causes impacting successful project management practices and proposing actionable project management guidelines to address leadership gaps and knowledge silos hindering the organizational ability to deliver positive outcomes. The objective is not only to improve internal project management capabilities but also to ensure that companies maintain competitiveness and innovation in a dynamic and ever-evolving landscape.

The findings suggest that leaders are responsible for fostering a work environment that is psychologically safe, fair, and respectful, where information is shared and individuals are encouraged to collaborate and innovate. This analysis explores the impact of poor leadership on project management, with a focus on how leadership practices, cultural dynamics, and organizational structure can hinder the creation and management of knowledge.

Additionally, it offers insights into how project management initiatives can be improved under the supervision of leaders who prioritize planning, accountability, and the fostering of a positive work culture that supports the effective use of knowledge systems, knowledge-sharing, and collaboration. Finally, this study would benefit from a systematic literature review applying the PRISMA framework and meta-analytic approaches, combined with a case study designed to ensure a transparent and systematic process in synthesizing evidence on leadership's role in project management success. The findings consistently emphasized that effective leadership is not merely a supporting factor but a critical determinant of project performance, influencing dimensions such as team motivation, knowledge-sharing, risk management, and stakeholder alignment. This reinforces the view that leadership should be positioned as a core competency within project management practices. A case study approach is particularly suitable for this investigation, as it offers an in-depth examination of the specific organizational context affecting organizations (less redundant and smoother phrasing). By focusing on a real-world setting, a case study enables researchers to examine how leadership deficiencies and knowledge silos manifest in practice when managing projects and people. It allows for a detailed exploration of how these issues impact the organization's project management practices, with the potential to generate actionable insights that could contribute to the field and help address the issues identified in this study.

References

Aga, D. A., N. Noorderhaven, and B. Vallejo. 'Transformational Leadership and Project Success: The Mediating Role of Team-Building.' *International Journal of Project Management*, 34, no. 5 (2016): 806–818.

Alavi, M. and D. E. Leidner. 'Review: Knowledge Management and Knowledge Management Systems: Conceptual Foundations and Research Issues.' *MIS Quarterly*, 25, no. 1 (2001): 107–136, https://doi.org/10.2307/3250961.

Anantatmula, V. S. 'Project Manager Leadership Role in Improving Project Performance.' *Engineering Management Journal*, 22, no. 1 (2010): 13–22.

Ankel, S., M. Guenot, and J. Mann. 'OceanGate's CEO Wanted to be the Elon Musk of the Deep, Say Former Colleagues.' *Business Insider*, 2023, https://www.businessinsider.com/oceangate-ceo-stockton-rush-wanted-elon-musk-doomed-titanic-sub-2023-7.

Antonakis, J. 'Charisma and the "New Leadership".' In *The Nature of Leadership*, 3rd ed., edited by J. Antonakis and D. Day. Sage, 2017, 56–81.

Argote, L. and E. Miron-Spektor. 'Organizational Learning: From Experience to Knowledge.' *Organization Science*, 22, no. 5 (2011): 1123–1137, https://doi.org/10.1287/orsc.1100.0621.

Argote, L. and Y. Ren. 'Knowledge Transfer in Organizations: Learning from the Experience of Others.' *Organizational Behavior and Human Decision Processes*, 82, no. 1 (2022): 1–8, https://doi.org/10.1006/obhd.2000.2883.

BBC News. 'Twitter Board Takes Action to Fight Musk Bid.' *BBC News*, 2022, https://www.bbc.com/news/world-us-canada-61123200.

Blaskovics, B. 'Impact of Leadership Styles on Project Success: The Case of a Multinational Company.' *Dynamic Relationships Management Journal*, 3, no. 2 (2014): 21–36.

Bragg, S. M. *Business Ratios and Formulas: A Comprehensive Guide*, 4th ed. Wiley: Hoboken, NJ, 2020.

Brown, M. and L. Trevino. 'Ethical Leadership: A Review and Future Directions.' *The Leadership Quarterly*, 17, no. 6 (2006): 595–616.

Clarke, J. 'Elon Musk's Leadership at DOGE Under Scrutiny After Financial Losses.' *BBC News*, 2025, https://www.bbc.com/news/articles/c23vkd57471o.

Clarke, N. 'Emotional Intelligence and its Relationship to Transformational Leadership and Key Project Manager Competences.' *Project Management Journal*, 41, no. 2 (2010): 5–20, https://journals.sagepub.com/doi/10.1002/pmj.20162.

Cropanzano, R., E. Anthony, S. Daniels, and A. Hall. 'Social Exchange Theory: A Critical Review with Theoretical Remedies.' *Academy of Management Annals*, 11, no. 1 (2017): 1–38, https://doi.org/10.5465/annals.2015.0099.

Davenport, T. H. and L. Prusak. *Working Knowledge: How Organizations Manage What They Know*, 2nd ed. Harvard Business School Press: Boston, MA, 2000.

Edmondson, A. C. and Z. Lei. 'Psychological Safety: The History, Renaissance, and Future of an Interpersonal Construct.' *Annual Review of Organizational Psychology and Organizational Behavior*, 1 (2014): 23–43.

Fortune, J. and D. White. 'Framing of Project Critical Success Factors by a System Model.' *International Journal of Project Management*, 24, no. 1 (2006): 53–65, https://doi.org/10.1016/j.ijproman.2005.07.004.

Foss, N. J., T. Pedersen, J. Pyndt, and M. Schultz. *Innovating Organization and Management: New Sources of Competitive Advantage*. Cambridge University Press: Cambridge, UK, 2012.

Goleman, D. *Emotional Intelligence: Why It Can Matter More Than IQ*. Bantam Books: New York, NY, 1995.

Goleman, D. *Working with Emotional Intelligence*. Bantam Books: New York, NY, 1998.

Goleman, D., R. Boyatzis, and A. McKee. *Primal Leadership: Unleashing the Power of Emotional Intelligence*. Harvard Business Review Press: Boston, MA, 2016.

Greenwood, R., C. R. Hinings and J. Brown. 'Global Professional Service Firms and Institutional Change.' *Organization Studies*, 39, no. 5-6 (2018): 655–675, https://doi.org/10.1177/0170840617717090.

Horton, A. ''Absolutely shocking': Netflix Documentary Examines How the Titan Sub Disaster Happened.' *The Guardian*, 2025, https://www.theguardian.com/film/2025/jun/11/titan-sub-disaster-netflix-documentary.

Kellerman, B. *Bad Leadership: What It Is, How It Happens, Why It Matters*. Harvard Business School Press: Boston, MA, 2004.

Klotz, A. C. and M. C. Bolino. 'When Quiet Quitting is Worse Than the Real Thing.' Harvard Business School Case No. H078L0-PDF-ENG. Harvard Business School Publishing: Boston, MA, 2022, https://hbsp.harvard.edu/product/H078L0-PDF-ENG.

Lange, D., P. Lee, and Y. Dai. 'Organizational Reputation: A Review.' *Journal of Management*, 37, no. 1 (2011): 153–184.

Lipman-Blumen, J. *The Allure of Toxic Leaders: Why We Follow Destructive Bosses and Corrupt Politicians-and How We Can Survive Them*. Oxford University Press: Oxford, UK, 2023.

Lucescu, L., S. Avasilcăi, and N. Bagiu. 'Critical Roles in Balancing Customer Expectations and Software Product Development: A Business Perspective.' *Annals of the University of Oradea: Facsicle of Management & Technological Engineering*, 1 (2023).

Maccoby, M. 'Narcissistic Leaders: The Incredible Pros, the Inevitable Cons.' *Harvard Business Review*, 78, no. 1 (2000): 68–77.

Mackey, J. D., R. E. Frieder, J. R. Brees, and M. J. Martinko. 'Abusive Supervision: A Meta-Analysis and Empirical Review.' *Journal of Management*, 43, no. 6 (2017): 1940–1965, https://doi.org/10.1177/0149206315573997.

Maister, D. H. *Managing the Professional Service Firm*. Free Press: New York, NY, 2003.

Mayer, J. D., P. Salovey, and D. R. Caruso. 'Emotional Intelligence: New Ability or Eclectic Traits?' *American Psychologist*, 63, no. 6 (2008): 503–517, https://doi.org/10.1037/0003-066X.63.6.503.

Merlo, T. R. 'Factors Influencing Knowledge Management Use in Technology Enterprises in Southern United States.' *Procedia Computer Science*, 99 (2016): 15–35, https://doi.org/10.1016/j.procs.2016.09.098.

Monroe, M. (Director). *Titan: The OceanGate Disaster* [Film]. Netflix, 2025.

Müller, R., S. Sankaran, and N. Drouin. *A Theory Framework for Project Governance*. Routledge: Groningen, Netherlands, 2022.

Müller, R., S. Sankaran, N. Drouin, A. Vaagaasar, M. C. Bekker, and K. Jain. 'A Theory Framework for Balancing Vertical and Horizontal Leadership in Projects.' *International Journal of Project Management*, 36, no. 1 (2018): 83–94.

Musumeci, N. 'A former OceanGate submersible pilot was worried CEO Stockton Rush would get himself and others killed in a "quest to boost his ego".' *Business Insider*, 2023, https://www.businessinsider.com/former-oceangate-pilot-worried-stockton-rush-people-killed-ego-email-2023-7.

Nicolaides, V. C., K. A. LaPort, T. R. Chen, A. J. Tomassetti, E. J. Weis, S. J. Zaccaro, and J. M. Cortina. 'The Shared Leadership of Teams: A Meta-Analysis of Proximal, Distal, and Moderating Relationships.' *The Leadership Quarterly*, 25, no. 5 (2014): 923–942, https://doi.org/10.1016/j.leaqua.2014.06.006.

Nonaka, I. and H. Takeuchi. *The Knowledge-Creating Company: How Japanese Companies Create the Dynamics of Innovation*. Oxford University Press: New York, NY, 1995.

Northouse, P. G. *Leadership: Theory and Practice*, 9th ed. Sage Publications: Thousand Oaks, CA, 2022.

Project Management Institute. *A Guide to the Project Management Body of Knowledge (PMBOK® Guide)*, 2021, https://www.pmi.org/standards/pmbok.

Randel, A. E., B. M. Galvin, L. M. Shore, K. H. Ehrhart, B. G. Chung, and M. A. Dean. 'Inclusive Leadership: Realizing Positive Outcomes Through Belongingness and Being Valued for Uniqueness.' *Human Resource Management Review*, 28, no. 2 (2018): 190–203.

Rehan, S. A., D. Thorpe and A. Heravi. 'Project Manager's Leadership Behavioural Practices – A Systematic Literature Review.' *Asia Pacific Management Review*, 29, no. 1 (2024): 1–17, https://doi.org/10.1016/j.apmrv.2023.07.002.

Reuters. 'Western Digital Tops Quarterly Profit Estimates on Demand From Cloud Computing Customers.' *Reuters*, 2024, https://www.reuters.com/technology/western-digital-tops-quarterly-profit-estimates-demand-cloud-computing-customers-2024-10-24/.

Riaz, A., M. Tahir and A. Noor. 'Leadership is Vital for Project Managers to Achieve Project Efficacy.' *Research Journal of Recent Sciences*, 2, no. 6 (2013): 99–102.

Rock, D. and H. Grant. 'Why Diverse Teams are Smarter.' *Harvard Business Review*, 4, no. 11 (2016): 2–5, https://hbr.org/2016/11/why-diverse-teams-are-smarter.

Rosenthal, S. A. and T. L. Pittinsky. 'Narcissistic Leadership.' *The Leadership Quarterly*, 17, no. 6 (2006): 617–633, https://doi.org/10.1016/j.leaqua.2006.10.005.

Rosete, D. and J. Ciarrochi. 'Emotional Intelligence and Leadership Effectiveness.' *Leadership & Organization Development Journal*, 26, no. 7 (2005): 388–399.

Rousseau, D. M. *Psychological Contracts in Organizations: Understanding Written and Unwritten Agreements*. Sage: Thousand Oaks, CA, 1995.

Shore, L. M., J. N. Cleveland and D. Sanchez. 'Inclusive Workplaces: A Review and Model.' *Human Resource Management Review*, 28, no. 2 (2018): 176–189.

Sommerville, J., N. Craig and J. Hendry. 'The Role of the Project Manager: All Things to all People?' *Structural Survey*, 28, no. 2 (2010): 132–141.

Stackpole, C. S. *A User's Manual to the PMBOK Guide*. John Wiley & Sons: Hoboken, NJ, 2013.

Stuckenbruck, L. C. 'Project Management Framework (An Overview of the Project Management Body of Knowledge).' *Project Management Journal*, 17, no. 3 (1986): 25–30.

Stumpf, S. A., J. P. Doh and K. D. Clark. 'Professional Services Firms in Transition: Challenges and Opportunities for Improving Performance.' *Organizational Dynamics*, 31, no. 3 (2002): 259–279.

Tong, L. and N. Tang. 'Inclusive Leadership and Innovative Performance: A Multi-Level Mediation Model of Psychological Safety.' *Frontiers in Psychology*, 13 (2022): 934831, https://doi.org/10.3389/fpsyg.2022.934831.

Turner, J. R. 'Five Necessary Conditions for Project Success.' *International Journal of Project Management*, 22, no. 5 (2004): 349–350.

Turner, J. R. and R. Müller. 'The Project Manager's Leadership Style as a Success Factor on Projects: A Literature Review.' *Project Management Journal*, 36, no. 2 (2005): 49–61.

Wallace-Wells, B. 'What Did Elon Musk Accomplish at DOGE?' *The New Yorker*, 2025, https://www.newyorker.com/magazine/2025/06/23/what-did-elon-musk-accomplish-at-doge.

Yukl, G. *Leadership in Organizations*, 8th ed. Pearson: Boston, MA, 2013.

© 2026 World Scientific Publishing Europe Ltd.
https://doi.org/10.1142/9781800617414_0013

Chapter 13

Wisdom and Leadership: The Role of Collaborative Intelligence in an AI Era

Jeff M. Allen[*,§], Amy Rosellini[†], Mariya Gavrilova Aguilar[*], Tara L. Whitson[‡], and Pamela Scott Bracey[*]

[*]*University of North Texas, USA*

[†]*Southern Methodist University, USA*

[‡]*Tarleton State University, USA*

[§]*Jeff.Allen@unt.edu*

Abstract

This chapter explores how wisdom and leadership influence the responsible use of artificial intelligence (AI) within organizations. The authors introduce collaborative intelligence as a framework that blends human judgment with AI capabilities to foster trust, ethical decision-making, and a shared purpose. Drawing on research, case studies, and emerging workplace trends, we examine how leaders can foster motivation, cultivate ethical behaviors, and guide human–AI partnerships. Leadership competencies such as adaptability, empathy, and discernment are emphasized as essential for navigating complexity. The chapter concludes by advocating for wise, human-centered leadership that ensures AI advances organizational goals without compromising ethical responsibility.

Keywords: Collaborative intelligence, ethical leadership, human-centered AI, organizational resilience, wisdom, human-AI collaboration, AI literacy.

13.1 Introduction

Artificial intelligence (AI) has firmly entered our corporate and daily lexicon, gaining traction as a transformative force challenging fundamental aspects of the global workforce. Individuals, organizations, communities, and governments alike are grappling with the uncertain implications of AI's accelerated advancement. Many concerns stem from the rapid adoption of AI used to complete various tasks, the lack of policies and/or guardrails, and its ethical use and societal impact (e.g., job elimination). While its capabilities continue to expand, the more pressing concern lies not in what AI can do but in how human wisdom will guide its integration through responsible and ethical, human-centered leadership that solves organizational and societal problems.

A survey conducted by Gillespie *et al.* (2025) examined the global perceptions of AI adoption among more than 48,000 people from 47 countries. The study offers key insights relevant to this chapter, which will be explored further and are specifically related to the role of leaders in guiding the responsible use of AI. First, while approximately 70% of respondents accept the use of AI, people are more skeptical of its safety, security, and societal impact and more trusting of its technical capabilities. Second, approximately 60% of AI users have no AI training, and about 50% of users report limited knowledge of AI. This reveals a gap in AI literacy that employers and educational partners will have to address. Third, AI regulation and governance have not kept pace with rapid technological innovations. With 90% of respondents stating they want laws and fact-checking to combat AI-generated misinformation, and 71% specifically expecting co-regulation with industry, there is a clear need for improvement. While challenging to implement, this places the onus on organizational leaders to prepare the workforce and collaborate with various governmental agencies and third-party independent bodies to provide oversight. Another important insight from the survey reveals that many respondents report complacent and non-transparent use of AI in their work, resulting in errors and dependency. This represents yet another area where leaders will need to outline acceptable uses of AI and emphasize the importance of providing proper training in an ever-evolving landscape of workplace innovation.

The growing presence of AI in governance, education, organizational leadership, and human development necessitates a reevaluation of distinctly human attributes – such as sound judgment, ethical reasoning, and lived experience – that remain essential to leadership and institutional resilience (Floridi *et al.*, 2018; Allen, 2022). As AI systems become embedded in institutional decision-making infrastructure, our focus will need to shift from passive adoption to proactive, human-centered stewardship of these systems. The intersection of AI and human intelligence demands that scholars, professionals, and civic leaders cultivate an intentional approach to shaping AI's societal role. Without human and wisdom-centered engagement, systems risk becoming mechanisms of surveillance and control rather than tools of empowerment (Crawford, 2021).

The future of AI is not solely a technical issue but also a profound ethical and intellectual challenge. It calls on institutions of higher learning and research to lead in developing the human capacities needed to guide technological power with wisdom and responsibility. The rapid acceleration of these changes, which affect every sector and organization of all sizes, demands proactive rather than reactive leadership and strategies that are broad enough to allow the organization to adapt quickly while addressing its main competitive demands and challenges to its business model. For instance, higher education institutions have been caught in the middle between widespread concerns about original intellectual contributions and the backlash from imperfect detection platforms intended to curb student cheating, which may result in false positives (Aalai, 2025). Many universities continue to operate out of an abundance of caution, specifically regarding generative AI (GenAI) tools such as ChatGPT, which are disrupting how we teach and learn in formal, structured educational settings (Walsh, 2025). Unfortunately, these short-sighted approaches represent reactive responses to an existential crisis in both K-12 and higher education. In an attempt to address public concerns and prepare employees and students to work alongside AI in discovering long-term, practical, and sustainable solutions that enhance learning and innovation, while emphasizing ethical decision-making, we propose a significant shift that aims to reexamine the paradigm through which we view these societal and ethical challenges as stakeholders, participants, consumers, educators, and leaders. One such framework is collaborative intelligence.

Collaborative intelligence is the process of pooling human insight and technological capabilities to share knowledge, build trust, and create more effective and innovative outcomes together. As human and technological systems become increasingly interdependent in the coming decades, both wisdom and leadership will remain essential for fostering individual and organizational growth. These human attributes serve as guiding forces that enable teams to achieve meaningful and sustainable results. In addition, wisdom will guide leaders in ensuring that AI is used to address pressing problems with human outcomes and ethical principles at the forefront, rather than as a by-product of this integration.

Wisdom provides the capacity to synthesize diverse perspectives, anticipate long-term consequences, and navigate complex "wicked" challenges with empathy and discernment – qualities rooted in lived experience. It also fosters an environment of mutual respect and psychological safety, where individuals feel a sense of belonging and are encouraged to share ideas openly, enhancing the overall collaborative potential of the group. When we operate in a space of mutual trust toward a common goal, we can collectively leverage our insights and expertise to solve new problems. Most importantly, unlike machines, humans can consider both the intended and unintended consequences of employing AI to solve problems we encounter and will likely act as a buffer to prevent the widespread use of AI for morally unacceptable purposes that may continue to erode our societal values. Moreover, wisdom has the capacity to question the purpose of such innovation. If humans continue to invest in such tools for the sake of quick popularity and rapid innovation, we may risk compromising our own capabilities, such as creativity, critical thinking, and problem-solving in the process. Through human wisdom, we should anticipate that a wide majority of the complex problems we continue to encounter will have no playbook and no blueprints. Therefore, we cannot rely on vast data sets that can synthesize existing information in seconds. These problems will require a human-centered approach fostered through collaboration, perseverance, and the capacity to lead responsibly during turbulent times.

Leaders should provide a vision, cohesion, and a sense of belonging. A leader with vision fosters group alignment, ensuring that every participant understands their role in achieving shared objectives. Such leaders provide autonomy and support. Leaders should welcome open dialogue and empower others to contribute their strengths while also compensating for their weaknesses as a group member. Leaders mediate conflicts and adversity into opportunities for growth, resilience, and innovation. The leader balances decisiveness with support to guide the team or group. Leaders transform conflicts and challenges into avenues for development, resilience, and innovation. Moreover, we are at a crossroads where leaders are asked to make decisions with imperfect and often insufficient information, despite the proliferation of large data sets of existing information that can be quickly analyzed. Therefore, leaders must have the courage to challenge ideas, ask tough questions, question assumptions, and accept the consequences of unpopular or uncertain decisions. Most importantly, these leaders must demonstrate the courage to chart a course for how far we are willing to allow AI to enhance and/or infiltrate our organizational dynamics and everyday lives as individuals and as a society. Effective leadership involves a balance between decisiveness and support, enabling the group to utilize its collective intelligence. Thus, leaders play a crucial role in driving the next stage of collaborative intelligence between humans and AI while considering the diverse needs of various stakeholders, anticipating potential unintended consequences, and mitigating risk.

13.2 Leading Collaboration

Both leadership and wisdom are key capacities that cultivate trust, a shared vision, and a sense of belonging, forming a foundation for human-centered organizational intelligence. This is particularly critical in environments where AI is shaping human capital development and strategic decision-making. As AI systems become more embedded in knowledge work, the distinctly human attributes of ethical judgment, contextual reasoning, and interpersonal sensitivity will remain essential for a healthy organization that serves numerous stakeholders. In addition, since organizational leaders are facing enormous challenges with AI implementation and the future of work, the onus is on them to make decisions about both people and systems in an ethical, transparent, and responsible way that ensures long-term continuity and innovation without compromising shared values and guiding principles.

Wisdom enables us to navigate ambiguity, synthesize diverse perspectives, and act with discernment in the face of complexity, informed by our lived experiences. It is through human intelligence and wisdom that individuals develop the capacity to weigh long-term consequences, foster mutual understanding, maintain empathy, and create a sense of belonging – critical elements in addressing complex "wicked problems" that lack simple or singular solutions (Allen, 2022). An added layer of complexity arises from the rapid pace of innovation and the adoption of AI in various industries. Fanuc, the leading robot manufacturer, has used AI in its robots for over 20 years. For over 10 years, Amazon has developed and incorporated more than 750,000 robots designed to enhance workplace safety and streamline task completion while maintaining a focus on delivering exceptional customer service through its employees (Greenawalt, 2025). These state-of-the-art robots are being used to handle inventory more efficiently and decrease instances of workplace injuries by moving pick-and-deliver pods of items from the fulfillment center to employees who package customer orders, selecting items from the highest and lowest pods which eliminates the need for humans to climb ladders or bend, and packaging customer orders sustainably by adjusting bag sizes based on the contents of the packages, and placing items on trucks for delivery.

Within collaborative environments (people-to-people and people-to-technology), wisdom contributes to creating psychological safety and a sense of belonging, where individuals feel respected, valued, and empowered to share ideas without fear of reprisal. This supportive atmosphere is vital for unlocking the full potential of group collaboration because it encourages unique and distributed participation in the workflows and collective insights from the lived experiences. At this stage of AI system development, organizations focus on enhancing individual-level productivity and automating mundane tasks with GenAI tools. Those impacts have not been well explored or documented. Humlum and Vestergaard (2025) indicate there is minimal economic impact from using AI chatbots on metrics such as earnings or recorded hours in any occupation. This raises the question of how leaders can effectively assess the long-term benefits of embracing AI technology and its impact on both workplace productivity and organizational culture. These issues also underscore the need to establish processes that will enable human oversight and guidance of responsible AI use that is not led by industry or government alone.

Leadership, when guided by wisdom, enhances the environment by providing strategic direction, structural cohesion, and generational learning. Wise leaders do more than assign tasks or manage people. They clarify the purpose, bring different strengths together, and turn conflicts into opportunities for growth and innovation (Heifetz *et al.*, 2009). Through shared vision and emotional intelligence, leaders effectively share their strategic objectives while honoring the agency of individual team members. Effective leadership fosters open dialogue, empowers contributors, and addresses weaknesses not only through correction but also through collective support and complementary collaboration. The ability to facilitate such dialogue and create an environment where employees feel empowered to speak up and co-create will be paramount to the continuous emphasis on human–AI collaboration.

In high-functioning teams and organizations, the interaction between wisdom and leadership enables the group, as a whole, to become more insightful, adaptive, and capable than any individual member could be alone, through collaborative intelligence. This collaborative teamwork is not accidental; it is cultivated through intentional practice and principled guidance. As organizations confront increasingly "wicked" social and economic conditions, the fusion of wisdom and leadership becomes not only advantageous but also imperative. A human-centered foundation enables organizations to move beyond coordination toward genuine co-creation, marked by trust, shared meaning, and a collaborative commitment to outcomes focused on more than just sales and profits.

For leaders, collaborative intelligence enhances their capacity to lead and innovate by combining diverse human talents with digital tools, facilitating adaptive thinking and faster decision-making, and ultimately yielding sustainable results. As organizations seek to harness both human wisdom and emerging technologies, collaborative intelligence offers a vital framework for integrating both human and technological capabilities (Allen *et al.*, in press). It offers a paradigm shift in understanding and effectively cultivating intelligence, not as a property of individuals or their skill sets alone, but as an emergent value of the well-aligned, collaborative intelligence of the organization as a whole. Collaborative intelligence thrives in environments where people feel empowered to contribute meaningfully and where technological tools amplify and enhance, rather than replace, human judgment and lived experiences. This approach will also predispose leaders to continuously evaluate the ethical implications and intended and unintended consequences of the impact of AI on the workforce and society.

13.3 Collaboration Between Humans and AI

As AI capabilities within organizational workflows continue to evolve at an unprecedented pace, effective collaboration between humans and AI requires restructuring tasks, expectations, and organizational roles.

A survey of 200 global Chief Human Resource Officers, conducted by Salesforce in 2025, revealed that AI agent adoption is expected to increase by 327% over the next two years, leading to a future workforce composed of both humans and intelligent agents (Salesforce, 2025). For leaders, this transformation presents a challenge that extends beyond understanding AI and its capabilities to embedding practices to support, guide, and inspire teams working alongside AI. When AI is integrated ethically and intentionally, it can augment human potential rather than displace it (Allen *et al.*, in press). However, realizing this potential requires that humans, not AI, be the focal point of the integration.

13.3.1 *Understanding the human perspective*

Successful AI integration requires a strategic focus on the human perspective, specifically how employees experience, respond to, and lead change. The human element requires a focus on employees within an organization, recognizing their perspectives and feelings, such as fear and judgment, as well as excitement and uncertainty. As AI becomes capable of performing tasks as well as or better than humans, many employees experience anxiety about job displacement (Wong, 2024). In addition, employees have questions about AI and its impact on their personal value and identity within the workplace. From customer service to data analytics to employee management, nearly every unit within an organization holds potential for AI integration (Zirar *et al.*, 2023). This widespread capability creates a rippling effect of employee concerns about how AI might impact the future of work and one's place within it. Celiktutan *et al.* (2024) found that employees tend to view the use of GenAI for self-inspiration as more acceptable than its use to outsource one's own work, which reveals perceived ethical boundaries. This finding supports AI's integration as a fundamental human process as much as a technical one.

In this evolving landscape, we must examine how AI fits into the decision-making process. "Across industries, the most commonly used form of human-AI collaboration is AI-advised human decision-making, where the inputs of the machine aid the decision of the human, and the machine acts as a tool in making the decision" (Jain *et al.*, 2023, p. 5018). While this approach has potential, it makes a case for the importance of an employee's confidence and empowerment when acting on AI output. Consequently, humans must be prepared through training and development, as well as technical competencies, to dissect, modify, and interpret AI output to make decisions.

Leaders must address the various concerns involving AI through a proactive, human-centered approach that includes empathy and inclusion. This view positions employees as active participants rather than passive recipients of change. When workers understand that AI can support rather than replace their work, anxiety can shift toward curiosity, experimentation, and trust (Varma *et al.*, 2024). Further, organizations that thrive with AI integration are those that listen to employee concerns and provide clear expectations regarding AI's purpose (Huang and Gursoy, 2024).

As a broader concept, technology integration within an organization goes beyond technical resources and funding; it relies on the cognitive and emotional responses of employees, which are influenced by their work environment. In "wicked" environments, where change is rapid, feedback is inconsistent, and roles are confusing, supportive leadership is critical (Allen *et al.*, in press). The introduction of AI often creates a "wicked" learning environment where operations occur with uncertainty, making it difficult for employees to understand or predict outcomes. Conversely, "kind" learning environments provide structure with steady improvement during practice (Allen *et al.*, in press). To navigate "wicked" learning environments, leaders must recognize the value in human traits such as emotional intelligence, resilience, and ethical judgment. These human traits are essential to complement the weaknesses of AI with fairness, transparency, and accountability. This further solidifies the idea that humans should lead this integration.

13.3.2 *Building trust and empowerment with AI*

Research indicates that employees' attitudes toward AI integration can be both positive and negative (Huang and Gursoy, 2024). On one hand, employees may view AI as an opportunity to improve productivity and reduce repetitive tasks. On the other hand, some express concerns that AI may increase job burnout and turnover. To shift employees from anxiety to engagement, leaders must build trust, instill confidence, and foster a shared sense of purpose toward AI integration efforts.

As AI becomes more embedded within the workflow of an organization, the leadership role must evolve from managing tasks to facilitating meaningful collaboration between people and technology (Makarius *et al.*, 2020). While AI enhances task efficiency and consistency, its successful integration depends not only on technical capability but also on prioritizing the human element (Spector and Ma, 2019). This shift requires more than simply providing access to the technology; it calls for an intentional strategy that fosters trust and supports employees throughout the transition.

Trust is a fundamental prerequisite for successful AI integration. When individuals are expected to act on AI-generated outputs without adequate explanation, they often experience reduced trust and increased discomfort (Jain *et al.*, 2023). To earn trust, organizations must focus on creating transparency and accountability with AI-related decisions (Bedué and Fritzsche, 2022). Leaders must set clear expectations to address how AI works and makes decisions. Leaders should frame AI as a tool for augmentation rather than automation (Allen *et al.*, in press). Transparent communication about AI's capabilities and limitations can help reduce fear and resistance (Bedué and Fritzsche, 2022). Leaders need to communicate that AI is unequivocally meant to support human strengths and workplace roles rather than replace them. This is of utmost importance during the early stages of AI adoption, when uncertainty and anxiety tend to peak.

Trust is built through both communication and strategic implementation. Bedué and Fritzsche (2022) emphasize developing onboarding plans that outline goals, measures, timelines, and support resources. These strategic components help employees navigate transitions with clarity and support. When employees understand that AI is designed to complement their work, they are more likely to be supportive and embrace its use (Bedué and Fritzsche, 2022). To facilitate this understanding, organizations should provide resources for employees such as workshops, step-by-step guides, and dedicated technology assistance. To demonstrate the importance of training and support on a larger scale, Finland, which aims to become a world leader in AI, created a government-industry collaboration to train non-technical employees in the basics of AI (Makarius *et al.*, 2020). This further highlights the importance of implementing AI literacy programs across multiple sectors through government and industry partnerships.

With trust in place, leaders can begin empowering employees to engage with AI (Makarius *et al.*, 2020) by clearly outlining the capabilities, expectations, and strengths of employees and AI, as well as identifying opportunities for employee advancement within collaborative roles.

While AI excels at analytical tasks such as processing data and identifying trends, employees bring strengths such as creativity, empathy, and judgment (Makarius *et al.*, 2020). Leaders should provide opportunities for employees to develop new skills to complement AI capabilities and promote effective human-AI collaboration. Bakonyi (2024) interviewed several managers who have implemented AI within large companies; when AI is perceived as optional or when there is a lack of time to experiment or test it, this may lead to employees abandoning the tool. Proactively scheduling dedicated time for employees to use and test AI before its rollout may minimize such shortfalls. Organizations should also create channels where employees can share their feedback and experiences. A telecommunications company had limited opportunities for feedback, which eroded trust within the organization (Bakonyi, 2024). This eventually led to the organization's decision to hold frequent, routine meetings with employees to attempt to rebuild transparency and engagement. If an employee feels heard, they feel valued and are likely to increase their discretionary effort within the organization. These approaches not only foster trust but also contribute to sustained employee motivation, which can falter due to the numerous ongoing and multi-year transformations that contribute to employee change fatigue (Morain and Aykens, 2023).

13.3.3 *Supporting human motivation*

While trust and empowerment aid employees in navigating AI integration, sustaining their internal drive requires an intentional emphasis on human and behavioral motivation. Humans are not machines. Even though we may exert an inordinate amount of effort and follow a workflow, our performance varies throughout the work month, week, and day, even from hour to hour. Often, this can be due to how jobs are designed, as well as personality traits and predispositions. Leaders play a crucial role in inspiring employees. Unlike AI systems, employees require forms of motivation grounded in psychological factors such as purpose, identity, and emotional well-being (Ryan and Deci, 2020). Motivation is apparent when employees feel valued, supported, and actively involved within the organization. As AI lacks emotions or biochemical processes such as dopamine or serotonin, this suggests that sustaining motivation is a human challenge that requires an active response from leaders.

As previously discussed, as AI becomes increasingly integrated within organizational workflows, understanding its impact on employee roles is critical. The discourse surrounding AI in the workplace remains divided, with some recognizing benefits such as enhanced efficiency and productivity, while others have concerns about harmful effects on employees (Bankins *et al.*, 2024). Conventional strategies such as goal setting, performance feedback, recognition programs, salary increases, and opportunities for promotion and advancement continue to meaningfully contribute to employee engagement. To address employee motivation surrounding AI, leaders can foster purpose and well-being, ensure equity and encourage integrity, provide employees with an opportunity to share concerns, and offer open channels of communication about the accuracy level of AI (Eisbach *et al.*, 2023; Bankins *et al.*, 2024). Human motivation is an essential component of overall employee well-being and performance, making it imperative for leaders to support their employees during transformative and disruptive technology implementations, such as AI integration. With this human-centered approach, organizations can realize the benefits of AI while maintaining motivated and engaged teams that can also employ ethical decision-making principles and question the use of these tools. It is important to note that the coexistence of human motivation and AI capability does not automatically lead to effective collaboration; as such, leaders should consider strategic alignment that is applicable to the specific organizational environment (Eisbach *et al.*, 2023).

13.3.4 *Cultivating a culture of collaborative AI*

Beyond strategies that support motivation, leaders must foster an organizational culture where AI is embedded within shared values, transparent practices, and inclusive participation. With trust, motivation, and empowerment in place, the next challenge for leadership is to shape a workplace culture that supports human–AI collaboration. Recent research explores how AI is already transforming productivity and collaboration across industries. For example, Doron *et al.* (2024) project that GenAI applications will accelerate drug discovery, boost research and development productivity, improve efficiency, and accelerate treatment delivery times by enhancing problem-solving and collaboration. While this example focuses on the healthcare field, where medical treatment and patient care dominate, it illustrates how human–AI collaboration can have a significant impact on all aspects of our lives. However, Gillespie *et al.* (2025) caution that these advancements also carry risky, unintended consequences, such as the loss of human interaction and connection, misinformation and manipulation, harmful or inaccurate outcomes, deskilling and dependency, and redefined tasks and job roles. Hence, this makes it even more critical for leaders to create ethical organizational cultures that allow innovation to improve various desired outcomes without compromising our humanity. Otherwise, the potential negative implications can be severe.

Cultivating a culture of collaborative AI begins with shared values, communication, and purpose (Allen *et al.*, in press). As previously noted, such a culture recognizes that humans and AI bring unique but complementary strengths to the workplace. AI can draft content and analyze data, and humans provide value in workplace settings by providing context, ethical judgment, and emotional intelligence in decision-making and teamwork. Leaders embed these strengths within the workflow and the mindset of their teams. Employees are trained not only in how to use AI tools but also in the continuous development of digital literacy and ethical awareness (Makarius *et al.*, 2020; Allen *et al.*, in press).

Leaders are also responsible for ensuring that the organizational culture is inclusive. When employees feel informed and involved in technology integration, they are more likely to adapt to change (Bedué and Fritzsche, 2022). This idea extends to the necessity of sharing feedback and providing an avenue for employees to be active co-creators of change (Bakonyi, 2024). Ultimately, creating a culture of collaborative AI is about elevating human potential through ethical and transparent use of AI tools. Only with a mindset grounded in values, trust, and inclusion can AI integration evolve from a source of disruption into a catalyst for collaborative intelligence toward the future of work.

13.4 Understanding Collaborative Intelligence in AI

Collaborative intelligence reconceptualizes intelligence as not solely an individual attribute but as a collective phenomenon emerging at the group level. Pierre Lévy characterized the advent of the internet as the foundation for a new form of universally distributed intelligence (Lévy, 1997). With its roots in both philosophical and digital traditions, the concept of collaborative intelligence has evolved into a strategic imperative for contemporary knowledge work. Jarrahi *et al.* (2023) conceptualized the synergistic partnership between humans and artificial intelligence for knowledge creation, storage and retrieval, sharing, and application.

Through an organizational design lens, Puranam (2021) offered several typologies for dividing labor in human–AI collaborative decision-making, with the primary goal of producing a decision. The author proposed dividing the task along two dimensions: "the nature of interdependence whether the decisions of the human and algorithm are related sequentially (only one of their outputs matters directly for final output) or can occur in parallel (human and algorithm outputs both directly matter for final output), and the nature of specialization – whether they engage in different or identical decision tasks." (Puranam, 2021, p. 77).

Nearly 80% of small and medium businesses (SMBs) using AI report that it is improving their business, and 40% of workers will need new job skills within three years (Vora and Stauber, 2025). AI literacy is needed to upskill managers and workers who will interact with AI systems (Jarrahi *et al.*, 2023). Without proper AI literacy, businesses risk inefficiencies, compliance issues, and missed opportunities. AI literacy refers to the ability to understand AI's capabilities, interact with AI systems, and critically evaluate its applications across different contexts. Suggested learning outcomes of an AI literacy program include understanding core AI concepts and operations, demonstrating proficiency with AI tools, and considering the ethical and societal implications of AI use (Cetindamar *et al.*, 2024). As leaders plan to implement AI within organizations, they should consider how to integrate AI literacy development into professional learning programs. These may include offering structured training and/or workshops using AI tools and offering certification upon successful completion. Several recommendations by Gartner (2025) highlight a multi-phased strategy for building AI literacy: Establish structured learning paths of formal courses and short-form content, encourage hands-on learning with AI in day-to-day tasks, tailor learning opportunities by role-specific needs through gap analyses, and maintain a continuous agile model that evolves alongside organizational goals. By fostering AI literacy within an organization, leaders can ensure that their teams understand how AI works and are empowered to use it responsibly.

An example of human–AI collaboration is emerging within the coaching sector, where Saulny (2025) emphasizes empathetic connection, active listening, tailored guidance, and compassionate accountability as key traits of human coaches. Despite limitations such as a lack of emotional intelligence, inability to navigate complexity, and rapport that feels inauthentic, AI coaching can offer scalability, accessibility, real-time feedback, and cost-effectiveness. Potential synergies between humans and AI tools that can enhance the coach's ability to serve their clients efficiently may include providing more relevant resources, tracking client progress, and scheduling sessions. Saulny's main contribution rests in evaluating the purpose of coaching – if it is intended to be a transformational process that relies on emotional connection and holistic development, AI, on its own, will not accomplish this purpose.

As leaders explore the application of AI tools, they should clearly evaluate the purpose behind such implementations. What would make sense for their organization, team, and project at that moment, given the existing time and budgetary constraints and contextual factors? When an individual works with a coach who can help them navigate complex interpersonal dynamics on a cross-functional and global team, will that employee better appreciate having a conversation with a human coach who can see how upsetting and impactful that situation may be on a personal level versus an automated response that lacks empathy and may miss multiple non-verbal cues? In addition, leaders will have to consider and counteract other looming concerns related to the use of AI, such as cybersecurity risks, loss of privacy or intellectual property, and the disadvantages of unequal access to AI, which were reported as harms being observed or experienced by respondents in the global survey conducted by Gillespie *et al.* (2025).

13.5 Core Leadership Competencies in the Age of Collaborative Intelligence in AI

The next evolution in collaborative intelligence complicates the already complex people-to-people interactions to include people-to-AI interactions. This evolution of collaborative intelligence disrupts an already volatile environment. In the VUCA (volatility, uncertainty, complexity, and ambiguity) environment, academics have developed several leadership models that point to the soft skills of leadership, including servant, ethical, authentic, and inclusive leadership (Chee and Zainal, 2022).

VUCA 2.0 was developed by Bill George in 2017 to reflect the rapid changes in the environment and require new leadership competencies. VUCA 2.0 includes the leadership competencies of vision, understanding, courage, and adaptability. Vision is the leader's ability to define a clear purpose for existing that guides the company (George, 2017). When leading as a visionary, leaders know when to lean into change and when change will take the company off course. Second, the leader needs an understanding of the organization's strengths and capabilities and should be aware of creating an echo chamber when new or better ideas are not heard. Third, George describes courage as the competency of leaders to be bold and take risks when necessary. Last and most notably, George identifies adaptability as the skill of staying focused on a vision while being open to change and flexible with contingency plans and new courses of action. While VUCA 2.0 addressed the leadership competencies required in a time of rapid change, it did not yet address the further complexity created by AI and, more recently, GenAI. The development of AI has sparked an evolution of collaborative intelligence that includes not only human and team interactions but also interactions between individuals, teams, and AI.

13.5.1 *The case for new leadership competencies*

Large language models (LLMs) are a type of AI that mirrors human language, masking associations and assumptions based on complex patterns and relationships within text. A study involving the use of LLM search engines versus conventional search found that the AI model was more likely to serve as an echo chamber, affirming users' existing beliefs and limiting exposure to opposing viewpoints (Nikhil *et al.*, 2024). In a study from Canada researching algorithm bias in social media, Li *et al.* (2019) found that algorithmic filtering exposes users to fewer results and accounts over time, limiting their exposure to diverse opinions. Pariser (2011) founds that users visit fewer accounts over time and also view less content that challenges their beliefs, also known as a "filter bubble." In a review of research regarding the impact of AI algorithms, Kaluža (2021), a researcher from Slovenia, found that the filter bubble alone is not enough to show the need for wisdom and discernment when using AI. In fact, he found that current research limitations regarding filter bubbles, with many studies disproving their existence, often ignore the need for discernment when using AI-powered technology. The inability of users to understand how AI is gatekeeping information calls for new leadership competencies within organizations to ensure collaborative intelligence benefits from a complete understanding and diversity of thought to improve knowledge work. Moore (2024) identified technical literacy, ethical considerations, change management, and effective communication as essential competencies for AI integration.

The prevalence of fake data, also known as hallucination, occurs when ChatGPT (or other similar tools) provides false information. This has been seen through research primarily in the medical field, where the cost of disinformation is highest for patients and providers, depending on the information to heal and diagnose (Elali and Rachid, 2023; Mehul *et al.*, 2023; Kedia *et al.*, 2024). In addition, all three publications discuss that the incentive for humans to use this fake data lies in personal gain, career promotion, resume building, and recognition within the medical community. Another concern regarding AI hallucinations is when the user does not understand the limitations of AI and does not know the information is a hallucination of the technology. These errors may be promulgated by the desire to provide information rapidly, but they continue to exacerbate problems regarding the slow but ongoing deterioration of critical-thinking skills. In addition, AI tools reflect the perceptions, beliefs, and attitudes, as well as the existing biases, of their creators. The ability of AI to hallucinate, minimize diversity of thought, limit exposure to what is already known, and drive users to duplicate content calls for new leadership competencies to develop greater understanding in the workplace and among individuals as companies increasingly integrate with AI.

13.5.2 *Leadership competencies to meet the wicked challenges of AI and collaborative intelligence*

Given both the benefits and challenges of AI, leaders must adapt to meet the changes in the workplace. The leadership competencies call on wisdom and adaptation of previous models to ensure that empathy and understanding continue to innovate in a responsible manner. Adapting two leadership competencies from VUCA 2.0, we emphasize that understanding and adaptability are key competencies for the future of collaborative intelligence. Additional relevant leadership competencies are also discussed.

The competency of understanding enables leaders to understand AI for its gifts – efficiency, speed, and accuracy – as well as its limitations – bias, hallucination, and the creation of echo chambers. Understanding is critical to collaborative intelligence because AI can synthesize information, but understanding the individual is a key component to using AI in a productive and beneficial way to solve organizational problems. Adaptability is the competency that allows leaders to continue to evolve and change as the technology evolves. As AI models grow and develop, new challenges will present themselves. Leaders will need to continue planning for contingencies such as AI hallucinations that may cause distrust or poor decision-making if not appropriately managed.

The ability to weigh consequences is perhaps the most necessary leadership competency and is beyond the capability of a technology such as AI. A leader must know when to use technology to solve problems and when to consider that people, not technology, are best suited to address a particular problem. The decision to employ AI or an employee, or a combination of both (e.g., Puranam, 2021), is one that is best made by a competent leader able to weigh consequences and consider the human and technological impacts.

Embracing diverse viewpoints is a competency required for leadership due to current AI limitations. Diverse perspectives allow leaders to see how outcomes vary based on different experiences and allow them to envision new ways of solving problems. In the case studies covered later in this chapter, leaders explore how to practice diversity through collaborative intelligence, partnering with AI. While diversity of thought is proven to be a limitation of AI with the presence of echo-chamber outcomes, strong leadership overcomes this limitation by creating prompts and building AI tools considerate of diverse ways of thinking.

Finally, empathy is the leadership competency that AI can be trained to mirror but not fully demonstrate. Empathy is the most human competency outlined in this chapter. Great leaders understand that decisions have consequences, information can impact people's lives, and people associate feelings with their jobs, tasks, and work in general. The most human of the leadership competencies required in collaborative intelligence is the ability to understand the impact of work on people's lives, emotions, and behaviors.

13.6 The Ethical Leadership Mandate

In today's continuously evolving landscape, shaped by the rapid integration of AI, ethical leadership emerges not as an afterthought or an option but as an imperative responsibility for leaders. As AI becomes more intricately woven into organizational life, leaders are called to step into the spotlight, guiding the deployment with unwavering integrity, keen discernment, and profound human wisdom (Floridi *et al.*, 2018). While AI possesses remarkable capabilities to automate intricate processes, enhance communication, and analyze vast datasets at astonishing speeds, it ultimately lacks a moral compass to discern what is right, fair, or just. This critical obligation rests firmly on the shoulders of human leaders (Johnson and Verdicchio, 2017), empowering them to shape the future of AI.

At the heart of effective leadership lies ethos, a leader's intrinsic moral compass, which has become an essential competency in this age guided by collaborative intelligence. Leaders must grapple with the profound understanding that harnessing AI for unethical purposes, manipulating data to mislead stakeholders, or permitting technology to inflict harm on individuals or communities fundamentally undermines the foundational trust upon which organizations are built upon. Leaders are tasked with bearing the ethical weight of their decisions in this new paradigm, where humans and technology coexist closely. They can set a constructive tone for developing, deploying, and interpreting AI technologies.

Ethical leadership entails far more than merely complying with regulations or adopting a checklist approach. Ethical leaders should consistently demonstrate integrity, fairness, transparency, and accountability while making decisions that prioritize the well-being of individuals, communities, and the broader impact of their actions (Kirk, 2025; Limbore *et al.*, 2025). It demands conscious, value-driven choices that echo with authenticity. As ethical leaders explore AI, they delve deeper, asking who benefits from its application, who might be overlooked or marginalized, and how integrating such tools will shape their organizations' cultural dynamics and interpersonal relationships over time. They thoroughly examine the multifaceted impacts of algorithms on privacy rights, bias, accessibility, and individual autonomy (Floridi *et al.*, 2018). Their overarching aim extends beyond mere operational efficiency, as they must seek to uphold and honor human dignity while being steadfast in solving problems.

When ethical leaders integrate AI, they do so with a holistic perspective that considers the diverse needs of all stakeholders, not just the relentless pursuit of profitability. They place a premium on transparency, accountability, integrity, and privacy. By fostering human-centered environments where employees feel safe, respected, and integral to the process, such leaders cultivate a flourishing culture. People are far more likely to thrive in workplaces where leadership operates with purpose and principle (Metcalf *et al.*, 2019). Ethical leaders must adopt a systemic mindset, think broadly, and act decisively. When implementing AI in sensitive areas such as hiring practices, performance evaluations, or internal communications, leaders must rigorously assess how these technologies might inadvertently reinforce bias or undermine organizational culture. Ethics cannot be relegated to engineers or compliance officers. Organizations anchoring their operations in wisdom and ethical considerations often experience lower employee turnover, higher morale, and enhanced productivity (Busis *et al.*, 2025; Kirk, 2025).

The influence of ethical leaders extends beyond the confines of their individual organizations as they shape public discourse, contribute to policy formation, and advocate for responsible innovation. The principles that anchor ethical leadership – respect, honesty, service, fairness, and community – remain timeless and enduring. Ethical leaders demonstrate respect by elevating the voices of stakeholders and model honesty when they explain AI's capabilities and limitations with clarity and transparency. They lead with service when pursuing long-term benefits for people, not just profits. Ethical leaders also uphold fairness when addressing algorithmic bias and build community by fostering collaboration and a shared purpose. These values build trust and mutual respect, which are essential to any successful human–AI partnership. When trust is diminished, it negatively impacts the organization's culture.

When employees see their leaders modeling ethical behavior, they engage more openly with innovation and contribute to collective growth. Ethical leadership sustains the integrity and resilience of the workplace far beyond any technological tools or applications adopted to enhance efficiency. As collaborative intelligence evolves, leaders must guide its trajectory with wisdom and conscience. The success of AI in the workplace depends not only on what the technology can do but also on what leaders choose to do with it. Ethical leadership ensures that AI amplifies human potential, protects human worth, and creates a future of work grounded in values that matter.

13.7 Case Studies

The following section overviews several case studies that provide insights from global organizational leaders regarding the use of AI across various functions within organizations. In this section, interviews are conducted with a business owner and leaders from New Zealand, Canada, and the United States (U.S.). The interviews were conducted from January through May 2025, with three companies across the globe. First, Skilitics is a technology company driving innovation in training. Second, Platinum Parking is a company that initially began in Canada, operating parking garages, parking lots, and providing paid parking across major metropolitan areas. Third, the Demo Company is a U.S.-based company that specializes in the demolition of buildings in commercial construction. All interviewees approach AI from different backgrounds and with different intents, but all three leaders demonstrate strong moral, ethical, and relational leadership competencies, which make them ideal candidates for this study. At the same time, a consistent theme of sound judgment, ethical conduct, and relationship building lies at the heart of each leader's experience with AI. In some cases, AI enhances leadership at work by utilizing it to save time on routine tasks, freeing leaders' time to work alongside their employees and customers to enhance relationships and connections. In other cases, the business leaders feel a profound responsibility for how AI is employed in the workplace, encouraging their employees to practice empathy and ethics both in their relationships and products.

13.7.1 *Interview #1*

Glenn Bull, CEO of Skilitics Group in Christchurch, New Zealand, utilizes AI in unexpected ways to enhance his leadership competency. As with any CEO of a tech company, Bull utilizes AI in traditional ways as well. Bull finds benefits in AI when it comes to gaining efficiency but says, "Efficiency issues are time saving but not transformative."

At Skilitics, AI is utilized to improve leadership and communication among peers. Bull shares that when employees use AI tools to deconstruct their communication in order to form emails and messages that come across more positively, it enhances their relationships at work. The time it takes to run professional communication does not provide time savings in the task alone, but it also provides deeper relationships within the organization, which can save workers time in the long run. Bull found that the use of AI to dispel communication issues among employees is one of the superior uses of AI in the workplace.

The unexpected outcome of AI utilization in leadership came from the CEO himself. Bull utilizes AI to vet his decision-making, argue alternatives, and identify problems with his solutions. Unlike AI utilization that gains efficiency or improves communication, Bull uses the technology to point out bias, new perspectives, and reasons why his proposed solutions won't work. "AI can make you aware of your biases more quickly, which allows you to reflect more quickly." When AI is utilized as a way to point out bias, blind spots, and obstacles for decisions, it has the capacity to enhance leadership skills. The ability of AI to enhance leadership skills lies in how users utilize it.

Bull finds that AI improves the emotional intelligence of leaders by helping them understand the perspective of someone with a different background, education, or job role. Rather than taking webinars or training to learn the perspectives of others, AI can quickly analyze a work situation and explain how it is viewed differently by people with different roles or backgrounds.

When considering the biggest obstacles to successful leadership with AI, Bull has concerns about ethics. As a technology company that builds human-assisted AI, Bull is passionate about AI tools that augment human intelligence rather than replace it. Skilitics Group is intentional with its products to build human-assisted AI rather than AI-led technology. Human-assisted AI requires human intervention to guide its actions and outcomes. Bull believes that tech companies have a role to play in developing responsible AI tools that facilitate human interaction: "If we start to cut huge chunks of the population out of work, then the feeling of worth will disappear, and it will be cataclysmic and create major issues."

13.7.2 *Interview #2*

Platinum Parking is a privately held company based in Canada and the U.S. Its president, Matt Adey, shared his experience with AI in the workplace and how it impacts his leadership and the leadership of his employees. Adey sees AI as a tool to create efficiency in the workplace so that leaders have more time to devote to their teams and clients. Adey feels that "AI is a great tool to get a base level of information; then you use your knowledge, experience, and insights to expand on the information."

One of the limitations of leaders is the time they have. Leaders who spend their time learning about AI and how to incorporate it into the workplace are more likely to find the time to think, strategize, and plan for the future. AI is a tool that enables leaders to strategize and think.

When he considers the obstacles with AI, Adey worries about young people who are using AI to do their work and then losing real-world experience. The future of AI lies in its use as a tool to create efficiency and free up time for more meaningful work. "AI is not a replacement for real-world knowledge," says Adey.

13.7.3 *Interview #3*

Dave Boroughs, owner and CEO of The Demo Company in the U.S., sees the use of AI as more information-driven, not as a replacement for leadership or as a way to enhance leadership skills. Boroughs utilizes AI "for hard data and facts" versus more relational methods. While AI can tell him who works at a customer's office, AI does not possess the tacit knowledge to find the decision-maker for a particular job and certainly not the capacity to build a relationship and influence the customer.

Boroughs finds value in the time and capacity available to his leadership as AI tools are introduced. While the efficiency is gained, he does not see AI as a replacement for people within the business. Boroughs explains that "the world is going to be different, but it doesn't change the need for soft skills." While an AI tool can create an estimate for a customer, a person will still need to review the estimate. Boroughs sees AI as a shift where people will be transitioned to different areas of the business where they can build value in relationships and directly with the customer.

In all interviews conducted on leadership, the use of AI made it clear that it was human intervention and collaborative intelligence that enhanced the leader's ability to lead. The types of prompts that the leader inputs into AI require judgment and intent, which will result in strengthened leadership. In all interviews, the leaders identified that poor leadership and a poor moral compass could result in a leader using AI to manipulate others, replace humans, or avoid communication and connection with employees. As the leaders in this study express, human intervention with AI requires discernment and judgment on the part of the leader in how AI is being used so that it enhances their ability to lead. This finding is consistent with existing literature, emphasizing that humans perceive collaboration with autonomous algorithms as unfair when the algorithm leads decision-making (De Cremer and McGuire, 2022). Sound judgment requires the ability to weigh consequences, such as those pointed out by Bull: What happens if humans are replaced to the extent that they no longer have worth in the workplace? Boroughs finds that AI cannot replace the human ability to build relationships and practice empathy to connect with people. The outcome of the interviews confirms that the new competencies required in leadership require adaptability, empathy, and a careful weighing of consequences. At the heart of the collaboration between AI and humans is the inability of AI to handle ethical decision-making and demonstrate wisdom when making decisions that impact people and the company.

13.8 The Wisdom Imperative in Leadership

As AI becomes increasingly prevalent in the workplace, human wisdom and judgment remain vital for leaders to guide their organizations in an ethical and sustainable manner. While AI can handle routine tasks such as generating reports, analyzing data, or tracking results, it lacks the more profound understanding required to align actions with human values. That's where leaders step in. Leadership requires more than technical or managerial skills. It involves a mixture of knowledge, lived experience, an understanding of self, ethics, and an understanding of others (Allen, 2022). Unlike AI, which excels at processing information, human wisdom encompasses empathy, moral reasoning, and the capacity to learn from lived experiences. AI cannot truly replicate these qualities (Allen *et al.*, in press). Wise leadership involves considering diverse perspectives, thinking about long-term consequences, making informed decisions in complex or uncertain situations, and taking responsibility for those decisions.

AI presents multifaceted challenges to organizational culture, including concerns over job displacement and the risk of reinforcing existing biases through algorithmic decision-making. Additional concerns around the purpose behind the use of AI were discussed above. Effective leaders confront these issues by positioning AI as a tool that augments, rather than replaces, human capabilities. Doing so demands emotional intelligence to address employee anxieties associated with its use, ethical discernment to navigate AI's limitations, and strategic foresight to build organizational resilience in an era of rapid transformation.

Collaborative intelligence, which has been explained in this chapter as combining the complementary strengths of humans and AI, is especially effective when addressing ambiguous or rapidly changing problems. Leaders who encourage such partnerships enable teams to delegate routine tasks to AI, freeing human judgment for strategic and ethical decision-making. For example, in interviews, one leader described leveraging AI to speed up writing, gain a different perspective, find more clarity on disciplinary issues in emails, and adjust tone to avoid misunderstandings, thereby aligning communications with organizational values (Interview #1).

Wisdom is vital for leadership in an AI-driven world. It ensures AI is used ethically to enhance human potential, not diminish it. By emphasizing transparency, accountability, and empathy, wise leaders foster environments where employees feel respected and motivated to effectively collaborate with newly implemented AI systems. As workplaces face growing technological changes at an accelerated pace, leaders must rely on wisdom to guide AI integration, creating environments that value trust, inclusion, and human creativity. This human-centered approach drives meaningful innovation and preserves the unique role of leadership in an AI-supported, but not AI-dominated, future.

The course of AI's development hinges on human leadership grounded in wisdom and responsibility. Leaders must harness human wisdom to guide ethical AI development. This approach drives sustainable innovation and preserves the uniquely human essence of leadership in an AI-augmented era. Ultimately, a wisdom imperative in leadership is about grounding organizations with human-centered principles that lead with empathy, ethical discernment, and long-term foresight. By fostering collaborative intelligence, where AI helps augment human creativity, judgment, and emotional insight, leaders can create more adaptive and resilient organizations. Such collaborative leadership ensures that as technology evolves with our collective capacity to lead with integrity, we will cultivate environments where both people and technology contribute meaningfully to shared success, driving positive organizational and societal change.

References

Aalai, A. 'What is lost when students turn to AI.' *Psychology Today*, 2025, https://www.psychologytoday.com/us/blog/the-first-impression/202505/what-is-lost-when-students-turn-to-ai.

Allen, J. *Fostering Wisdom at Work*. Rutledge Taylor & Francis Group: London, UK, 2022, https://doi.org/10.4324/9781003018759.

Allen, J., T. Whitson, M. Gavrilova, and P. Bracey. 'Collaborative Intelligence: Cultivating Human-AI Partnerships.' In *Driven Revolution: Transforming the Business Landscape*, edited by T. Merlo. World Scientific, Singapore (2025), https://doi.org/10.1142/9781800616578_0013.

Bakonyi, Z. 'How can Companies Handle Paradoxes to Enhance Trust in Artificial Intelligence Solutions? A Qualitative Research.' *Journal of Organizational Change Management*, 37, no. 7 (2024): 1405–1426, https://doi.org/10.1108/JOCM-01-2023-0026.

Bankins, S., A. C. Ocampo, M. Marrone, S. L. D. Restubog, and S. E. Woo. 'A Multilevel Review of Artificial Intelligence in Organizations: Implications for Organizational Behavior Research and Practice.' *Journal of Organizational Behavior*, 45, no. 2 (2024): 159–182, https://doi.org/10.1002/job.2735.

Baskin, K. 'How continuous learning keeps leaders relevant in the age of AI.' *MIT Sloan School of Management*, 2023, https://mitsloan.mit.edu/ideas-made-to-matter/how-continuous-learning-keeps-leaders-relevant-age-ai.

Bedué, P. and A. Fritzsche. 'Can We Trust AI? An Empirical Investigation of Trust Requirements and Guide to Successful AI Adoption.' *Journal of Enterprise Information Management*, 35, no. 2 (2022): 530–549, https://doi.org/10.1108/JEIM-06-2020-0233.

Busis, N. A., C. M. Alexander, and J. Castner. *A Path to Improved Health Care Worker Well-Being*. National Academy of Medicine (NAM), 2025, https://nam.edu/wp-content/uploads/2025/04/Improved-Health-Care-Well-being.pdf.

Celiktutan, B., A. K. Klesse, and M. A. Tuk. 'Acceptability Lies in the Eye of the Beholder: Self-Other Biases in GenAI Collaborations.' *International Journal of Research in Marketing*, 41, no. 3 (2024): 496–512.

Cetindamar, D., K. Kitto, M. Wu, Y. Zhang, B. Abedin, and S. Knight. 'Explicating AI Literacy of Employees at Digital Workplaces.' *IEEE Transactions on Engineering Management*, 71 (2024): 810–823, https://doi.org/10.1109/TEM.2021.3138503.

Chee, C. Y. and S. R. M. Zainal. 'An Integrative Review of Past Prominent Leadership Literature: Future Research Directions in Malaysia.' *Global Business and Management Research*, 14, no. 3 (2022): 1605–1620.

Crawford, K. *Atlas of AI: Power, Politics, and the Planetary Costs of Artificial Intelligence*. Yale University Press: New Haven, CT, 2021.

De Cremer, D. and J. McGuire. 'Human–Algorithm Collaboration Works Best If Humans Lead (Because It Is Fair!).' *Social Justice Research*, 35, no. 1 (2022): 33–55, https://doi.org/10.1007/s11211-021-00382-z.

Doron, G., S. Genway, M. Roberts, and S. Jasti. 'Generative AI: Driving Productivity and Scientific Breakthroughs in Pharmaceutical R&D.' *Drug Discovery Today*, (2024): 104272.

Eisbach, S., M. Langer, and G. Hertel. 'Optimizing Human-AI Collaboration: Effects of Motivation and Accuracy Information in AI-Supported Decision-Making.' *Computers in Human Behavior: Artificial Humans*, 1, no. 2 (2023): 100015, https://doi.org/10.1016/j.chbah.2023.100015.

Elali, F. R. and L. N. Rachid. 'AI-Generated Research Paper Fabrication and Plagiarism in the Scientific Community.' *Patterns*, 4, no. 3 (2023): 100706, https://doi.org/10.1016/j.patter.2023.100706.

Floridi, L., J. Cowls, M. Beltrametti, R. Chatila, P. Chazerand, V. Dignum, *et al.* 'AI4People, An Ethical Framework for a Good AI Society: Opportunities, Risks, Principles, and Recommendations.' *Minds and Machines*, 28, no. 4 (2018): 689–707, https://doi.org/10.1007/s11023-018-9482-5.

Gartner. 'AI Literacy.' 2025, https://www.gartner.com/en/articles/ai-literacy.

George, B. 'VUCA 2.0: A strategy for steady leadership in an unsteady world.' *Forbes Magazine*, 2017, https://www.forbes.com/sites/hbsworkingknowledge/2017/02/17/vuca-2-0-a-strategy-for-steady-leadership-in-an-unsteady-world.

Gillespie, N., S. Lockey, T. Ward, A. Macdade, and G. Hassed. *Trust, Attitudes and Use of Artificial Intelligence: A Global Study 2025.* The University of Melbourne and KPMG, 2025, https://doi.org/10.26188/28822919.

Greenawalt, T. 'Amazon has more than 750,000 robots that sort, lift, and carry packages – see them in action.' Amazon, 2025, https://www.aboutamazon.com/news/operations/amazon-robotics-robots-fulfillment-center.

Heifetz, R. A., A. Grashow and M. Linsky. *The Practice of Adaptive Leadership: Tools and Tactics for Changing Your Organization and the World.* Harvard Business Press: Brighton, MA 2009.

Huang, Y. and D. Gursoy. 'How does AI Technology Integration Affect Employees' Proactive Service Behaviors? A Transactional Theory of Stress Perspective.' *Journal of Retailing and Consumer Services*, 77 (2024): 103700, https://doi.org/10.1016/j.jretconser.2023.103700.

Humlum, A. and E. Vestergaard. 'Large Language Models, Small Labor Market Effects.' *National Bureau of Economic Research*, 2025, https://www.nber.org/papers/w33777.

Jain, R., N. Garg, and S. N. Khera. 'Effective Human–AI Work Design for Collaborative Decision-Making.' *Kybernetes*, 52, no. 11 (2023): 5017–5040, https://doi.org/10.1108/K-04-2022-0548.

Jarrahi, M., D. Askay, A. Eshragi, and P. Smith. 'Artificial Intelligence and Knowledge Management: A Partnership Between Human and AI.' *Business Horizons*, (2023): 87–99, https://doi.org/10.1016/j.bushor.2022.03.002.

Johnson, K. and M. Verdicchio. 'AI, Agency and Responsibility: The VW Fraud Case and Beyond.' *AI & Society*, 32, no. 4 (2017): 501–507, https://doi.org/10.1007/s00146-016-0666-7.

Kaluža, J. 'Habitual Generation of Filter Bubbles: Why is Algorithmic Personalisation Problematic for the Democratic Public Sphere?' *Javnost – The Public*, 29, no. 3 (2021): 267–283, https://doi.org/10.1080/13183222.2021.2003052.

Kedia, N., S. Sanjeev, J. Ong, and J. Chhablani. 'ChatGPT and Beyond: An Overview of the Growing Field of Large Language Models and Their

Use in Ophthalmology.' *Eye*, 38, no. 7 (2024): 1252–1261, https://doi.org/10.1038/s41433-023-02915-z.

Kirk, V. 'What is ethical leadership and why is it Important?' *Harvard Division of Continuing Education*, 2025, https://professional.dce.harvard.edu/blog/what-is-ethical-leadership-and-why-is-it-important/.

Lévy, P. *Collective Intelligence: Mankind's Emerging World in Cyberspace*, translated by R. Bononno. Perseus Books: New York, NY, 1997.

Li, G., S. Mithas, Z. Zhang, and K.Y. Tam. 'Does Algorithmic Filtering Create a Filter Bubble? Evidence from Sina Weibo.' *Academy of Management Proceedings*, 2019, no. 1 (2019), https://doi.org/10.5465/AMBPP.2019.14168abstract.

Limbore, N. V., N. Anute, and G. K. Ahluwalia. 'Ethical Leadership and Corporate Responsibility.' In *Strategies for Managing Conflict and Corporate Responsibility*, edited by N. Sharma, 193–218. IGI Global, Hershey, PA 2025, https://www.igi-global.com/chapter/ethical-leadership-and-corporate-responsibility/375145.

Makarius, E. E., D. Mukherjee, J. D. Fox, and A. K. Fox. 'Rising with the Machines: A Sociotechnical Framework for Bringing Artificial Intelligence into the Organization.' *Journal of Business Research*, 120 (2020): 262–273, https://doi.org/10.1016/j.jbusres.2020.07.045.

Mehul, B., V. M. Miller, B. Debjani, and L. E. Miller. 'High Rates of Fabricated and Inaccurate References in ChatGPT-Generated Medical Content.' *Cureus*, 15, no. 5 (2023), https://doi.org/10.7759/cureus.39238.

Metcalf, J., E. Moss and D. boyd. 'Owning Ethics: Corporate Logics, Silicon Valley, and the Institutionalization of Ethics.' *Social Research: An International Quarterly*, 86, no. 2 (2019): 449–476.

Moore, A. 'What Competencies will be Needed to Manage Artificial Intelligence?' *Assessment & Development Matters*, 16, no. 1 (2024): 4–7, https://doi.org/10.53841/bpsadm.2024.16.1.4.

Morain, C. O. and P. Aykens. 'Employees are Losing Patience with Change Initiatives: A Gartner Survey Found that Employees' Willingness to Support Enterprise Change fell from 74% in 2016 to just 43% in 2022.' *Harvard Business Review Digital Articles*, (2023): 1–7.

Nikhil, S., Q. V. Liao, and X. Ziang. 'Generative Echo Chamber? Effects of LLM-Powered Search Systems on Diverse Information Seeking.' *arXiv*, 2024, http://arxiv.org/abs/2402.05880.

Pariser, E. *The Filter Bubble: What the Internet Is Hiding from You*. Penguin Random House, 2011.

Puranam, P. 'Human–AI Collaborative Decision-Making as an Organizational Design Problem.' *Journal of Organization Design*, 10, no. 2 (2021): 75–80.

Ryan, R. M. and E. L. Deci. 'Intrinsic and Extrinsic Motivation From a Self-Determination Theory Perspective: Definitions, Theory, Practices, and

Future Directions.' *Contemporary Educational Psychology*, 61 (2020): 101860, https://doi.org/10.1016/j.cedpsych.2020.101860.

Salesforce. 'HR Leaders to Redeploy a Quarter of Their Workforce as Agentic AI Adoption Expected to Grow 327% by 2027.' 2025, https://www.salesforce.com/news/stories/agentic-ai-impact-on-workforce-research/.

Saulny, C. 'Human Coaching vs. AI Coaching.' *Association for Talent Development*, 2025, https://www.td.org/content/atd-blog/human-coaching-vs-ai-coaching.

Spector, J. M. and S. Ma. 'Inquiry and Critical Thinking Skills for the Next Generation: From Artificial Intelligence Back to Human Intelligence.' *Smart Learning Environment*, 6, no. 1 (2019): 1–11, https://doi.org/10.1186/s40561-019-0088-z.

Varma, A., V. Pereira, and P. Patel. 'Artificial Intelligence and Performance Management.' *Organizational Dynamics*, 53, no. 1 (2024): 101037, https://doi.org/10.1016/j.orgdyn.2024.101037.

Vora, H. and Z. Stauber. 'How AI Literacy Builds a Future-Ready Workforce – And What Agentforce Taught Us.' *Salesforce*, 2025, https://www.salesforce.com/blog/ai-literacy-builds-future-ready-workforce/.

Walsh, J. D. 'Everyone is cheating their way through College. ChatGPT has unraveled the entire academic project.' *New York Magazine*, 2025, https://archive.is/0g82n.

Wong, W. K. O. 'The Sudden Disruptive Rise of Generative Artificial Intelligence? An Evaluation of Their Impact on Higher Education and the Global Workplace.' *Journal of Open Innovation: Technology, Market, and Complexity*, 20 (2024): 1–8, https://doi.org/10.1016/j.joitmc.2024.100278.

Zirar, A., S. I. Ali, and N. Islam. 'Worker and Workplace Artificial Intelligence (AI) Coexistence: Emerging Themes and Research Agenda.' *Technovation*, 124 (2023): 102747, https://doi.org/10.1016/j.technovation.2023.102747.

© 2026 World Scientific Publishing Europe Ltd.
https://doi.org/10.1142/9781800617414_0014

Chapter 14

Inner Development Goals and Sustainable Futures: A Path Toward Regenerative Businesses

Alexandra Augusta Pereira Klen* **and Alex Marson**

Neoliderança Ltda., Santa Catarina, Brazil

*xandaklen@gmail.com

Abstract

In an era shaped by systemic crises – climate change, inequality, technological disruption, and geopolitical tensions – the call for a new leadership paradigm is undeniable. This chapter explores how the convergence of Inner Development Goals (IDGs), artificial intelligence (AI), and regenerative leadership models can empower individuals, organizations, and ecosystems to navigate complexity toward thriving and sustainable futures. It introduces the concept of the "digital mirror," an AI-enabled system designed not merely to automate tasks but to cultivate reflective, conscious, and regenerative leadership. Unlike conventional AI agents, a digital mirror operates as a cognitive infrastructure for transformation, enabling users to engage in self-reflection, ethical inquiry, and conscious decision-making aligned with the Sustainable Development Goals (SDGs). Grounded in the IDGs framework and operationalized through the InEx Project, a Brazilian impact-driven initiative, this solution integrates a curated body of knowledge (BoK), AI ethics, and human-centered design. Importantly, the InEx Project adopts a hybrid AI development strategy. The roadmap begins with general-purpose large language models (LLMs) for rapid prototyping and functional validation, but this represents a transitional stage. The core trajectory aims to create a specialist LLM – purpose-built and ethically aligned – that embodies the role of a digital mirror: capable of reflecting, provoking, and accompanying users in processes of self-discovery, conscious leadership, and regenerative decision-making. By bridging inner development, regenerative leadership, and responsible AI, the InEx Project offers more than a technological tool; it proposes a new socio-technical paradigm where inner transformation becomes strategic infrastructure for sustainable, equitable, and regenerative futures.

Keywords: Inner development goals, regenerative leadership, digital mirror, human-centered ai, sustainability.

Humanity faces an era of unprecedented complexity and systemic risk (World Economic Forum, 2025). Climate change, biodiversity loss, geopolitical instability, and widening social inequalities are no longer isolated challenges; they are deeply interconnected symptoms of a civilization operating beyond both planetary and social boundaries. In this landscape of escalating urgency, solutions grounded solely in technological efficiency, productivity, or structural reform prove insufficient.

Achieving the Sustainable Development Goals (SDGs) requires more than external interventions; it demands a profound inner transformation in the people who lead, design, and implement change. Leadership itself must evolve, both in terms of skills and competencies and as a deeper shift in consciousness, mindset, and ways of engaging with complexity.

This chapter argues that the convergence of Inner Development Goals (IDGs), artificial intelligence (AI), and a new paradigm of regenerative leadership offers a viable, scalable, and urgently needed pathway for addressing today's grand challenges. It introduces the concept of the "digital mirror," an AI-powered system designed not to automate tasks but to foster reflection, inner growth, and regenerative action. Unlike conventional AI agents focused on task execution, a digital mirror functions as a form of cognitive infrastructure for transformation, enabling users to engage in deeper self-awareness, ethical inquiry, and values-driven decision-making.

Grounded in the experience of the Brazilian impact-driven startup Neoliderança, this chapter explores the "InEx Project: Inner Development for Global Sustainability," a pioneering initiative that integrates AI, the IDGs framework, and regenerative business principles. The project also serves as a living case study for how leadership development, knowledge systems, and AI technologies can converge to support the next wave of sustainable industrial transformation – what we refer to as "neoindustrialization."

Through ongoing development of a curated body of knowledge (BoK) and a GPT-based digital mirror, the InEx Project aims to create a technological tool that serves as an entire ecosystem of learning, reflection, and regenerative action. This ecosystem is designed to support leaders, organizations, and value chains in aligning inner development with the pursuit of the SDGs, fostering sustainable and regenerative futures by design.

14.1 Theoretical and Conceptual Foundations: Inner Development Goals as a Compass for Sustainable Futures

The Inner Development Guide (Inner Development Goals, 2025; Figure 14.1) emerges from the growing recognition that achieving the SDGs (United Nations, 2015) is not merely a technical, economic, or

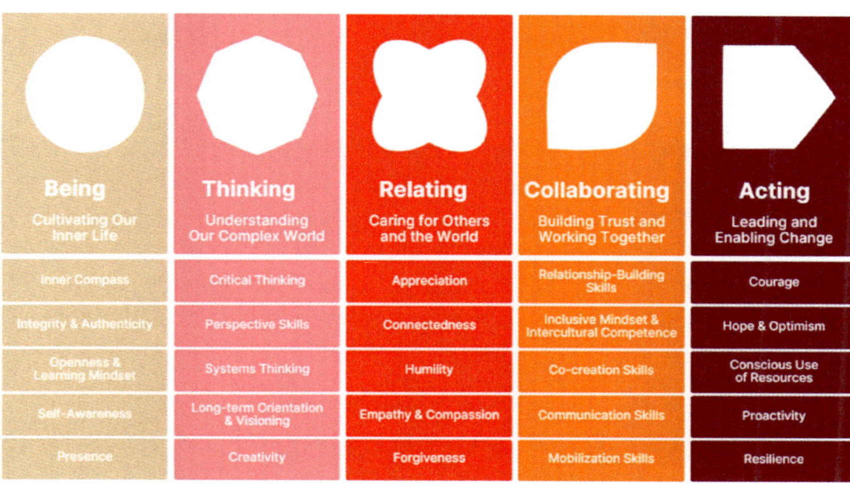

Figure 14.1. Inner Development Guide.

Source: From *Inner Development Guide*, Inner Development Goals (n.d.). https://innerdevelopmentgoals.org/guide/.

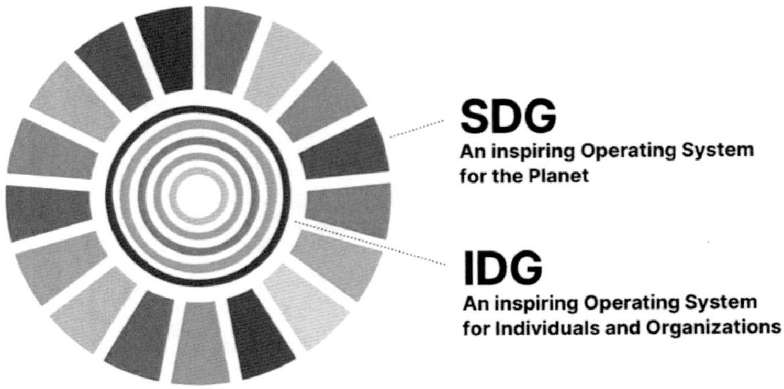

Figure 14.2. IDGs and SDGs.

Source. From *Inner Development Goals Visual Framework,* by The New Division, n.d., https://www.thenewdivision.world/idg. © The New Division.

structural challenge, but fundamentally a human one. The Inner Development Guide articulates five core dimensions – being, thinking, relating, collaborating, and acting – which collectively represent the inner capabilities essential for leading sustainable and regenerative transformation.

These capabilities – including self-awareness, critical thinking, empathy & compassion, co-creation skills, and courage – are not abstract ideals but practical competencies for navigating uncertainty, volatility, and interconnected crises. As such, the Inner Development Guide operates as an invisible yet indispensable form of inner infrastructure, enabling the outer transformations required to meet the SDGs (Figure 14.2).

In this sense, the Inner Development Goals are not peripheral to sustainable development; they are foundational. They provide a developmental compass for leaders, organizations, and ecosystems, aligning inner transformation with systemic change.

14.2 From AI Agents to Digital Mirrors: A Shift in Paradigm

AI has traditionally been deployed as a productivity engine – automating repetitive tasks, optimizing decision-making processes, and scaling information retrieval across domains. These systems, often referred to as

AI agents, are designed to operate efficiently within predefined objectives, producing outputs based on statistical learning and large-scale data patterns. Their function is primarily instrumental: they execute, respond, classify, and predict.

The **digital mirror**, as conceptualized in the InEx Project, signals a paradigmatic departure from this logic. Rather than a task-oriented assistant, a digital mirror functions as a **reflective and generative mentor** – a cognitive and relational interface designed to cultivate awareness, ethical reflection, meaning-making, and inner development. While an AI agent processes queries, a digital mirror reciprocates with deeper questions. Where the agent organizes information, the mirror facilitates the organization of meaning. And where the agent completes functions, the mirror fosters insight, reflection, and transformation.

This reframing from AI agents to digital mirrors is not merely a technical shift; it embodies a deeper philosophical, ethical, and epistemological transformation in how AI can serve human development. Unlike AI agents, which are primarily designed to optimize tasks, process data, and deliver predefined outputs, digital mirrors are structured as cognitive mentors that foster inner inquiry, self-awareness, and regenerative action. They do not simply provide answers; instead, they return better questions, stimulate ethical introspection, and nurture meaning-making processes.

This distinction is not superficial; it permeates every layer of the system, from the curation of the BoK to the architecture of interaction, the epistemological design, and overall user experience.

In AI agents, the BoK is typically functional, technical, and task-oriented – designed to maximize efficiency and optimize outputs. In a digital mirror, however, the BoK is ethically curated, sensitive, and human-centered, organized to support not only information retrieval but deep introspection, ethical inquiry, and capacity-building for sustainable futures.

This contrast is further reflected in how language operates within each system. AI agents prioritize factual, objective, and responsive communication. Digital mirrors, conversely, use language that is metaphorical, reflective, and meaning-generating – a design choice intended to provoke insight rather than merely deliver answers.

Finally, while AI agents operate primarily from data-driven epistemologies, optimizing for efficiency, productivity, and accuracy, digital mirrors are anchored in a more integrative epistemology, combining practical philosophy, subjective experience, and systemic thinking with technical rigor.

Table 14.1. Key distinctions between AI agents and digital mirrors.

Aspect	AI Agent	Digital Mirror
BoK curation	Functional, technical, task-oriented	Ethical, sensitive, focused on consciousness, meaning, and human development
Language style	Factual, objective, responsive	Metaphorical, reflective, meaning-making, provocative
Interaction model	Executes commands, delivers outputs	Reflects, questions, provokes, facilitates sense-making, and accompanies growth
Epistemological base	Data-driven; focused on efficiency and productivity	Integrative knowledge; practical philosophy, subjectivity, ethics, and systems thinking
Primary purpose	Automation, task optimization	Inner development, ethical alignment, sense-making, and regenerative leadership
Relational quality	Transactional, functional	Dialogic, co-evolutionary, consciousness-expanding
Learning dynamic	Output-driven, completion-focused	Insight-driven, transformation-oriented, fosters emergent understanding

Note: This table was created by the authors. It summarizes the conceptual and functional differences between AI agents and digital mirrors. While AI agents are designed primarily for task automation and productivity enhancement, digital mirrors are oriented toward fostering inner development, reflective thinking, and regenerative leadership. The BoK underpinning a digital mirror is curated with ethical sensitivity and human-centric intent, distinguishing it epistemologically and relationally from generic AI systems.

This reframing sets the stage for the development of AI systems that are not merely tools of automation but mentors in conscious leadership and sustainable transformation. Table 14.1 summarizes the key distinctions between an AI agent and a digital mirror.

14.3 LLMs for Humanistic and Transformative Systems

The paradigm shift from AI agents to digital mirrors, as discussed in Section 14.2, has concrete implications for AI architecture, design, and governance. Central to this transformation is the question of how knowledge is structured, curated, and operationalized within the AI system. This leads to a critical design decision: whether to build upon general-purpose LLMs or to develop a specialist LLM tailored to the unique demands of inner development, regenerative leadership, and sustainability transformation.

General-purpose LLMs – such as OpenAI's GPT, Google's Gemini, or Anthropic's Claude – offer scalability, broad informational coverage, and instant accessibility. However, these models are fundamentally designed for generalized problem-solving across diverse domains. They operate predominantly on statistical pattern matching within massive, undifferentiated datasets. This architecture favors surface coherence over epistemic depth, probabilistic accuracy over contextual sensitivity, and task completion over meaning-making.

These limitations become particularly problematic when AI is applied in reflective, developmental, or ethically sensitive contexts. Inner development, regenerative leadership, and systems transformation require data retrieval and also epistemic integrity, psychological safety, ethical alignment, and cultural sensitivity – qualities that general-purpose models were not designed to optimize.

By contrast, specialist LLMs, such as the one envisioned in the InEx Digital Mirror, are fine-tuned with curated knowledge systems anchored in the IDGs, the SDGs, and regenerative leadership principles. These models do not merely serve as information repositories; they function as catalysts for reflective inquiry, meaning-making, and ethical action. They are purpose-built to navigate complexity, facilitate introspection, and support transformational leadership processes.

Importantly, the InEx Project adopts a hybrid strategy. The development roadmap begins with general-purpose LLMs for rapid prototyping and functional validation. However, this represents a transitional stage. The core trajectory moves toward building a specialist LLM that embodies the role of a digital mirror – capable of reflecting, provoking, and accompanying users in processes of self-discovery, conscious leadership, and regenerative decision-making.

This is not simply a technological choice; it is a commitment to epistemological rigor, ethical responsibility (UNESCO, 2021), and transformative potential. A digital mirror cannot emerge from a generic statistical engine alone. It must be intentionally designed, ethically curated, and contextually embedded within a living knowledge ecosystem.

Table 14.2. Comparative characteristics of general-purpose vs. specialist LLMs in the context of digital mirrors.

Criteria	General-Purpose LLM	Specialist LLM (Digital Mirror)
Scope	Broad, general knowledge	Focused on IDGs, regenerative leadership, sustainability, SDGs and inner development
Contextual sensitivity	Limited; culturally generic	High; culturally sensitive, psychologically safe, and context-aware
Ethical alignment	Generic; loosely governed ethics	Purpose-aligned; grounded in IDGs, SDGs, and regenerative leadership
Epistemological depth	Surface-level coherence; pattern matching	Meaning-driven; supports reflective inquiry, sense-making, and epistemic integrity
Interaction purpose	Task execution; information retrieval	Inner development; reflective provocation; regenerative decision support
Adaptability	Highly scalable; general adaptability	Deep contextual relevance; less scalable but highly precise in targeted ecosystems
Development effort	Low; pre-trained and ready for broad use	High; requires curated BoK, ethical governance, and continuous fine-tuning
Transformative potential	Limited; supports tasks more than transformation	High; facilitates inner growth, ethical reflection, systems thinking, and regenerative action

Note: This table was created by the authors. It highlights how general-purpose LLMs, while powerful for broad applications, are not designed for the epistemic rigor, ethical sensitivity, and transformational depth required for digital mirror functions. Specialist LLMs, as developed within the InEx Project, prioritize meaning-making, psychological safety, and inner development – operating as catalysts for conscious leadership rather than task automation.

Table 14.2 summarizes the key differences between general-purpose and specialist LLMs, specifically within the digital mirror framework. It illustrates how these two AI architectures diverge, not only in their technical design but also in their epistemological foundations, ethical commitments, and user impact.

14.4 Knowledge as Strategic Infrastructure: The Role of the BoK

At the heart of the digital mirror lies its BoK – an intentional, curated, and continuously evolving knowledge infrastructure that functions as both the epistemic foundation and the ethical compass for the AI system.

Unlike traditional AI knowledge bases – static, extractive, and task-oriented – the BoK is designed as a **living knowledge ecosystem**, capable of fostering reflection, sense-making, ethical discernment, and regenerative action.

The BoK does not simply feed the AI with information. It encodes intentionality, purpose, and worldview. It embodies the values, heuristics, and epistemologies necessary for an AI to function as a digital mirror. Here, curation transcends being merely a technical step. It becomes an epistemic intervention – a deliberate act of meaning-making that determines how knowledge supports reflection, ethical discernment, and regenerative action (World Economic Forum, n.d.). The AI therefore is not merely designed to compute but to mentor. It supports cognitive tasks as well as existential inquiry, ethical reflection, and systems thinking.

The BoK as a living knowledge ecosystem rests upon a triadic architecture: (1) scientific and technical rigor, (2) ethical and regenerative governance, and (3) aesthetic and experiential intelligence – each inseparable in fostering meaningful, systemic, and conscious transformation.

14.4.1 *Three core knowledge domains*

The BoK integrates and synthesizes three interdependent knowledge domains, each essential to enabling the digital mirror to act as a reflective and generative mentor:

Inner development goals (IDGs): This domain provides the psychological, philosophical, and developmental scaffolding for inner transformation. It draws from frameworks such as the IDGs and also incorporates models of leadership consciousness, developmental psychology, mindfulness, emotional regulation, and cognitive complexity. Beyond cognitive models, this domain acknowledges that transformation also happens through aesthetics, embodiment, and narrative. A poem, a song, or the visceral resonance of a text can become epistemic catalysts – tools for reflection, meaning-making, and perspective-shifting.

Sustainability and the SDGs: This domain connects inner transformation to outer systemic impact. It provides practical knowledge on climate action, circular and regenerative economies, sustainable value chains, and systems change methodologies.

It also embraces the role of ethical imagination, recognizing that technical solutions are insufficient without cultivating ecological consciousness and planetary empathy. Here, the BoK may offer invitations beyond data: Buarque (n.d.); Wenders & Salgado (2014): "Before designing your sustainability roadmap, sit with *The Salt of the Earth* documentary, or contemplate the symbolic ruins and resilience echoed in the music of Chico Buarque."

Applied AI ethics and regenerative leadership: This domain governs how the AI itself operates, ensuring it is aligned with human dignity, ecological integrity, and regenerative futures. It integrates principles of value-sensitive design, AI ethics, responsible innovation, and regenerative leadership.

It also rejects the false binary between rationality and intuition, logic and poetics. The presence of ambiguity, polarities, metaphor, and nonlinear meaning-making – so central to human growth – is explicitly honored in the BoK. Hilst (n.d.): A line from Hilda Hilst or a visual prompt from a contemporary art installation might catalyze a more truthful self-inquiry than any linear checklist could.

14.4.2 *A living, regenerative architecture*

The BoK is not simply a technical backend or a static repository of information. It is a living, regenerative architecture of knowledge, intentionally cultivated to evolve, adapt, and generate continuous value for both the AI system and the humans it serves.

It weaves together three interconnected strands that mirror the dynamics of living ecosystems:

- *Embodied insights and lived experience*: The inner practices, developmental journeys, and lived wisdom of leaders, mentors, and communities.
- *Structured knowledge frameworks*: The conceptual scaffolding that sustains the digital mirror: curated models, heuristics, methodologies, reflective practices, metaphors, narratives, and even artistic and aesthetic references that deepen the quality of sense-making.
- *Relational learning ecosystem*: The dynamic knowledge emerging from co-creation, dialogue, feedback loops, and collective reflection. This includes the ongoing contributions of stakeholders, users, facilitators, and communities engaging with the digital mirror.

This regenerative architecture deliberately moves away from extractive models of knowledge, i.e., approaches that treat knowledge as a commodity to be consumed, extracted, and optimized solely for outputs. Instead, it embodies the logic of ecological systems, where knowledge is nurtured, relational, reciprocal, and continuously renewed. Knowledge in this sense is not owned; it is stewarded. It grows richer the more it circulates, transforms, and regenerates within the system.

By honoring diverse ways of knowing – including rational, intuitive, embodied, and artistic forms – the BoK becomes a **living knowledge ecosystem**, capable of holding complexity, ambiguity, and the plural realities that regenerative leadership requires.

It is this living quality of the BoK that enables the digital mirror to move beyond transactional information exchange and become a reflective, ethical, and transformative companion, supporting inner development while fostering leadership that is aligned with regenerative futures.

14.4.3 *The aesthetic and experiential layer of the BoK: Cultivating a living knowledge ecosystem*

In classical AI systems, knowledge bases function primarily as repositories designed to retrieve facts, generate outputs, or improve predictive accuracy.

In the InEx Digital Mirror, the BoK plays a fundamentally different role:

- It becomes a sense-making infrastructure – a cognitive, ethical, and experiential field that supports reflection, perspective-shifting, and ethical discernment.
- It holds space for plural epistemologies – bridging propositional knowledge (facts), procedural knowledge (skills), and contemplative, poetic, and aesthetic knowing (wisdom).
- It integrates cognitive intelligence with emotional, relational, and aesthetic intelligences, recognizing that transformation happens not only through analysis but also through wonder, resonance, and embodied insight.

Anchoring the AI in this ecosystem transforms it from an answer machine into a mirror for consciousness and regenerative action. It moves beyond data-driven pattern recognition toward a relational technology of meaning-making, from a knowledge repository to a sense-making infrastructure.

In this sense, a distinctive and innovative feature of the InEx BoK is the intentional incorporation of an aesthetic and experiential layer.

This layer recognizes that certain truths cannot be accessed through propositional language alone. Some forms of knowing require metaphor, paradox, rhythm, embodiment, and beauty. As such, a poem, a song, a work of visual art, or an encounter with nature is not merely a reference. Each becomes a form of technology for expanding consciousness, igniting creativity, and cultivating deeper presence.

The digital mirror, drawing from this layer, may offer invitations such as the following:

- Pärt (1978): "Before exploring this leadership challenge, consider listening to Arvo Pärt's '*Spiegel im Spiegel*' to cultivate stillness."
- Buarque (1971): "To accompany your exploration of ethical leadership, I suggest listening to Chico Buarque's song '*Construção*'. As you follow its circular narrative of labor, repetition, and fragility, what parallels do you notice with the systemic patterns in your organization or society?"
- Schwartzberg (2019): "To deepen your reflection on interconnectedness, watch the documentary 'Fantastic Fungi' and contemplate the mycelium as a leadership metaphor."
- "Before engaging with this question about resilience, step outside and observe a tree nearby. Notice how it balances stillness and growth, rootedness and expansion. As you observe, ask yourself: What anchors you when facing uncertainty? Where might you need to prune to allow new growth?"
- Rumi (n.d.): "Read this short poem by Rumi before responding: 'Try not to resist the changes that come your way. Instead, let life live through you.'"
- Barros (1997): "Before we reflect further on resilience, I invite you to read this fragment by Brazilian poet Manoel de Barros: 'I only use words to compose my silences.' What might this teach us about listening as a leadership practice?"
- Hilst (2001): "As you navigate this transition, consider reading Hilda Hilst's reflection: 'I write because I don't know how to act.' Does this resonate with how you currently face complexity and uncertainty?"
- Evaristo (2019): "To deepen your reflection on empathy and social justice, I invite you to spend time with the writings of Conceição

Evaristo, especially her concept of 'escrevivência'—where writing becomes both survival and testimony. How does this inform your understanding of regenerative leadership?"

- "I invite you to step away from this reflection briefly. Visit a local art gallery. Observe one piece that holds your attention. What is it teaching you about impermanence, beauty, or complexity?"
- "To deepen your reflection on complexity and interdependence, spend a few minutes watching the movement of clouds or the flow of water. As you witness how elements shift, dissolve, and reorganize, consider: How do you navigate impermanence in your own life or leadership? What patterns emerge when you surrender control?"

These are not mere prompts. They are portals for self-inquiry, systemic reflection, and the cultivation of regenerative consciousness.

This layer of the BoK is, probably, one of the most profound epistemological and methodological innovations of the InEx Project. It asserts that the cultivation of interiority, depth, aesthetic sensibility, and connection with nature are not an adjunct to sustainability and leadership but serve as the foundation.

Concluding, the BoK as a living knowledge ecosystem integrates scientific and technical rigor, ethical frameworks, and regenerative leadership principles, as well as aesthetic, poetic, and experiential knowledge, as a core epistemic technology for inner growth and systemic transformation. This triadic architecture ensures that the digital mirror transcends the logic of output generation. It becomes a cognitive, ethical, and aesthetic mentor, serving as an instrument of information and also of transformation.

Figure 14.3 illustrates the **Triadic Architecture of the BoK**. The choice of a snowflake is a visual and philosophical metaphor for the epistemic, ethical, and experiential synthesis that constitutes the living knowledge ecosystem of the InEx Digital Mirror.

The snowflake begins with an equilateral triangle, representing the foundational triad of this architecture: Scientific and Technical Rigor, Ethical and Regenerative Governance, and Aesthetic and Experiential Intelligence. As the structure evolves recursively, it mirrors the expansion of knowledge – from simple foundational principles to intricate, adaptive, and interconnected patterns. This fractal growth represents complexity, coherence, and beauty.

Like water itself – which can exist in solid, liquid, and gaseous states – the BoK adapts its form to different contexts and needs. The snowflake, as

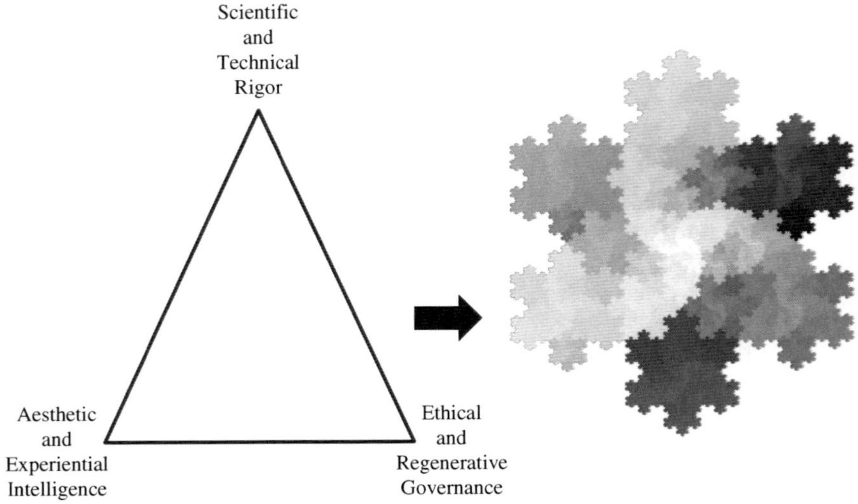

Figure 14.3. Triadic architecture of the BoK.

Source: Adapted from "Koch snowflake" by Wikimedia Commons contributor, n.d., Wikimedia Commons (http://commons.wikimedia.org). Licensed under CC BY-SA 4.0.

crystallized water, symbolizes the solid yet dynamic structure of knowledge when embodied in the digital mirror. And just as no two snowflakes are ever alike – each uniquely shaped by its environment – so too will each user's interaction with the digital mirror produce singular reflections, questions, and pathways of transformation. The same BoK generates different responses, adapted to the context, intention, and consciousness of each user.

This metaphor encapsulates the very nature of the BoK as a regenerative, living knowledge ecosystem: structured yet fluid, rigorous yet poetic, universal in form yet deeply personal in experience.

14.5 Leadership and Neoleadership: A New Paradigm for Complex Futures

In the face of accelerating complexity, traditional models of leadership – rooted in linear thinking, control, and efficiency – are rapidly becoming obsolete. As global systems confront simultaneous environmental, social, technological, and geopolitical disruptions, leadership is being called to evolve beyond its industrial-era origins.

The concept of "Neoleadership," as developed by *Neoliderança*®, emerges as a direct response to this call. It represents a transformative approach that integrates consciousness, responsibility, and regeneration into leadership practices. It transcends traditional paradigms of hierarchical control and linear decision-making, shifting toward a holistic, adaptive, and regenerative approach. In the era of AI, leadership emerges as an evolutionary practice, deeply intertwined with human consciousness, systemic complexity, and the ethical implications of technological advancement.

The AI era presents unprecedented challenges, transforming not only how we work but also how we understand ourselves and our relationship with reality. Leaders are now called upon to navigate contexts marked by profound uncertainty, accelerating change, and novel ethical dilemmas. The traditional tools of planning and prediction, shaped by past experiences, increasingly prove inadequate. Therefore, Neoliderança emphasizes connecting deeply with emergent futures rather than relying solely on historical patterns.

Central to this shift is the often-overlooked capacity to unlearn (Scharmer, 2018), fostering the inner conditions from which transformative solutions can emerge. Neoleadership calls for not only the development of new competencies but also the conscious release of inherited mindsets rooted in control, linearity, and separation. In a culture addicted to speed and accumulation, the act of pausing, emptying, and letting go becomes a radical leadership move. Unlearning creates the inner spaciousness required for new insight to arise – a space where presence, not prescription, guides the way.

From the perspective of Neoliderança, leadership acknowledges the profound importance of slowing down, reflecting, and engaging deeply with complexity rather than rushing toward immediate, superficial solutions. In urgent times, leadership calls for intentionally slowing down, fostering presence, deep reflection, and heightened awareness. In the context of AI, this means leaders must cultivate not only technical proficiency but also a profound sense of ethical reflection, systemic awareness, and humility – the capacity to recognize one's limitations, remain open to continuous learning, and authentically value diverse perspectives.

Neoliderança positions leaders as ecosystem facilitators rather than controllers, emphasizing interdependence, collaboration, and adaptability. Leaders become curators of collective wisdom by fostering environments where diverse perspectives converge, tensions and paradoxes are explored constructively, and innovation is driven by conscious intent. This holistic view extends the role of leadership beyond organizational boundaries, emphasizing social, ecological, and ethical dimensions as equally vital to organizational success.

In practical terms, leadership in the AI era requires cultivating competencies aligned with the IDGs, such as deep self-awareness, emotional intelligence, and the capacity to hold and integrate polarities – balancing innovation with routine, autonomy with control, and global perspectives with local actions. By leveraging the transformative potential of AI ethically and responsibly, leaders can co-create futures that are technologically advanced and profoundly regenerative.

Ultimately, leadership in the AI era, from the Neoliderança perspective, is about humanizing technological evolution. It is a call for leaders to expand their consciousness, embrace complexity, and courageously guide their organizations and communities toward a future marked by sustainability, resilience, and collective well-being.

14.5.1 *Neoleadership in practice: A relational technology for transformation*

Neoleadership, as embodied by the Neoliderança® movement, is not a leadership style. It is a living system of practice designed to meet the challenges of complex, interconnected, and rapidly changing worlds. It transcends conventional leadership models centered on control, linearity, and productivity, offering instead an architecture of consciousness, relationality, and regenerative action. As a living system, Neoleadership continues to evolve through dialogue, experimentation, and collective inquiry – co-created with the very challenges and transformations it seeks to engage.

At its core, Neoleadership cultivates the ability to navigate uncertainty by fostering the inner conditions from which transformative solutions can emerge, rather than by seeking quick answers. It recognizes that some of the most urgent challenges of our time – climate crisis, inequality, and systemic fragmentation – cannot be addressed solely with technical solutions; they require a parallel evolution in how leaders think, feel, relate, and act.

This practice-oriented approach is expressed in three core commitments:

- *Connecting thinking, feeling, sensing, and acting*: Moving beyond intellectualization into embodied and ethical decision-making.
- *Regenerating systems from within*: Supporting the evolution of individuals as the catalyst for transforming teams, organizations, and ecosystems.
- *Bridging purpose and impact*: Aligning inner purpose with practical, systemic outcomes – whether in business, governance, or societal change.

The InEx Digital Mirror is a direct technological manifestation of this philosophy. It serves not as an oracle of answers but as a relational technology that provokes reflection, nurtures ethical inquiry, and supports leaders in designing regenerative futures. Just as Neoleadership itself is a dynamic ecosystem of learning and transformation, the digital mirror becomes an interactive space where knowledge, consciousness, and systemic change intersect.

This is not merely about using AI to solve problems. It is about creating cognitive and relational infrastructure that empowers individuals and collectives to hold complexity, navigate ambiguity, and co-create transitions toward futures that are not only sustainable but also deeply regenerative.

Neoleadership, in practice, asks a profound question: "Are you willing to lead the transformation starting from within?"

14.5.2 *Why Neoleadership matters for sustainable futures*

As we confront the limits of extractive development and seek new models for thriving societies, Neoleadership offers more than just a leadership framework. It embodies a civilizational shift – toward ways of leading rooted in consciousness, interdependence, and regeneration.

It asserts that technological progress, industrial reinvention, and economic development must be fundamentally anchored in human consciousness, ethical responsibility, and ecological regeneration. Any pathway toward sustainable futures that ignores the inner dimension – how we think, how we relate, and how we lead – is destined to reproduce the very problems it seeks to solve.

Neoleadership is both:

- a response to the need to transcend industrial-era leadership paradigms characterized by extractivism, linear thinking, and reductionist problem-solving;
- a proactive architecture for futures in which inner development becomes strategic infrastructure for navigating complexity, fostering innovation, and enabling regenerative transitions.

This paradigm is not an abstraction. It is materially consequential for how organizations design their business models, how value chains are structured, how innovation ecosystems operate, and how technological advancements like AI are deployed.

In the AI era, Neoleadership positions leaders not as controllers of complexity but as stewards of emergence, curators of collective wisdom, and facilitators of systemic coherence. It calls for a leadership practice that integrates inner clarity with outer impact, technological fluency with ethical intentionality, and local accountability with planetary responsibility.

In Brazil, as in many Global South contexts, this approach resonates deeply with the imperative of just transitions, where industrial transformation is a pathway to competitiveness and also a lever for social inclusion, environmental regeneration, and collective flourishing.

Ultimately, Neoleadership matters because it reframes leadership itself, not only as a set of skills for navigating systems but also as a profound practice of transforming self, relationships, and systems simultaneously. It holds that regenerative futures are not designed from the outside in; they are cultivated from the inside out.

14.6 The InEx Project: A Living Laboratory for Regenerative Leadership

The InEx Project – Inner Development for Global Sustainability – is a pioneering initiative developed by the Brazilian impact startup Neoliderança®. It operationalizes the concepts of IDGs, digital mirrors, Neoleadership, and AI ethics into a practical and deeply human model for leadership transformation and systemic regeneration. This vision resonates with global shifts in how AI is seen, not merely as a driver of productivity, but as an enabler of intelligent economies – those capable of combining competitiveness, inclusivity, and regenerative outcomes (World Economic Forum, 2024).

The project is grounded in a dual mission:

- Developing a GPT-based digital mirror, an AI-enabled mentor designed to foster reflective, conscious, and regenerative leadership.
- Building a living knowledge ecosystem (BoK) that curates, evolves, and anchors the epistemic, ethical, and experiential foundations necessary for inner development, regenerative leadership, and the advancement of the SDGs.

14.6.1 *Applied methodology: Co-creation as a design principle*

The InEx Project was conceived not solely as a technological development effort but as a living laboratory of co-creation, where knowledge, technology, and human development are inseparable.

At the heart of this process is an immersive and participatory approach that invites key stakeholders – leaders, educators, sustainability practitioners, and ecosystem innovators – to co-design the future of leadership in the AI era. A diverse community of transformation agents collectively reflects, prototypes, and validates the core functionalities, ethical principles, and design heuristics of the digital mirror. A participatory ethos continues throughout the project in iterative cycles of testing, feedback, and refinement, ensuring that the digital mirror is not a top-down technological imposition but a co-evolved artifact that reflects the needs, values, and aspirations of its user community.

14.6.2 *Strategic response to systemic crises*

The InEx Project positions itself as a strategic response to the intertwined metacrisis of our time. Its design challenges the reductionist, efficiency-driven paradigms that dominate both industry and AI development, proposing instead a regenerative operating system for the future.

This is not simply about creating better AI tools; it is about redefining the purpose of technology itself. The digital mirror is a manifestation of this shift, moving AI from an engine of automation to a catalyst for reflection, inner development, and conscious leadership.

Likewise, the BoK transcends the conventional role of a knowledge base as a static repository. It emerges as a living knowledge ecosystem, capable of evolving, regenerating, and supporting leaders with information, wisdom, discernment, and the relational capacity to navigate complexity.

14.6.3 *The strategic edge of inner development and regenerative AI*

In a world dominated by external solutions – new technologies, policies, and systems – the InEx Project asserts a powerful, often overlooked truth: meaningful systemic change begins from within. Inner development is not a soft skill or a secondary concern; it is a strategic infrastructure for the regenerative futures we urgently need.

This approach reframes both leadership and AI. It challenges the dominant AI narrative centered on task automation and productivity maximization. Instead, it proposes a new paradigm in which AI serves as a partner in sense-making, ethical inquiry, and transformative leadership.

The digital mirror, in this context, is not a replacement for human judgment but an amplifier of self-awareness, relational intelligence, and regenerative decision-making. It becomes a mentor on the leadership journey, provoking deeper questions, surfacing hidden assumptions, and aligning action with purpose and planetary boundaries.

In this sense, the relevance of the InEx Project extends beyond individual transformation. It offers a blueprint for neoindustrialization and for broader global industrial futures in which technology, human development, and sustainability are deeply interwoven.

This model challenges the binary between technological advancement and human flourishing. It proposes that future industries will not be defined solely by automation, efficiency, or digitalization but by their capacity to embed consciousness, ethical reflection, and regenerative principles into their very operating systems.

All this means that the InEx Project is more than a technological prototype. It is a strategic experiment into what it means to lead, organize, and innovate in ways that are truly aligned with the complex realities and regenerative futures our time demands.

14.7 Conclusions

This chapter has explored how the convergence of IDGs, regenerative leadership, and AI – embodied in the concept of the digital mirror – can serve as both a philosophical framework and a practical operating system for organizations, industries, and societies navigating the metacrisis of the 21st century.

At its essence, the InEx Project challenges the dominant narratives that position technology as an end in itself or as a mere driver of efficiency. Instead, it proposes a more radical regenerative proposition: that technological innovation must be in service of inner transformation, ethical leadership, and planetary well-being. It reframes AI not as an agent of automation but as a mirror of consciousness – a mentor that provokes, questions, and invites leaders into deeper reflection, alignment, and regenerative action.

The creation of the digital mirror, supported by a carefully curated living BoK, demonstrates that AI systems, when designed with intention, ethics, and human development at their core, can become powerful catalysts for leadership evolution. The BoK itself transcends static knowledge management, emerging as a living knowledge ecosystem, blending scientific rigor, practical wisdom, artistic sensitivity, and relational intelligence. It becomes a form of regenerative capital, nurturing both the individuals who lead and the systems they inhabit.

A central insight emerges: There is no sustainable outer transformation without a corresponding inner transformation. And at the heart of this transformation lies an inescapable truth: no technology, no system, or AI can substitute the conscious responsibility of a human being. Technology may serve as a catalyst, a mirror, or a guide, but the work of transformation – inner and systemic – remains a fundamentally human endeavor. Without this, the most sophisticated tools risk becoming mirrors of our unconscious biases rather than instruments of regeneration.

Climate breakdown, social fragmentation, and technological disruption are not problems to be solved solely by external interventions. They are invitations – or even urgent calls – for a reconfiguration of how we lead, relate, and create meaning. Inner development is no longer peripheral; it is a strategic infrastructure for regenerative futures.

The InEx approach, rooted in knowledge curation, a hybrid AI development pathway, and stakeholder co-creation, offers a blueprint for a new form of leadership in the AI era. It aligns with the imperatives of neoindustrialization, particularly in the Global South, by demonstrating the possibility of reconciling technological advancement with ecological boundaries, social cohesion, and human flourishing.

Looking forward, the journey does not end here. The continued evolution of the digital mirror will demand technological refinement and a deepening of its epistemological, ethical, and aesthetic foundations. It calls for scalable models of co-creation, stronger mechanisms for cultural contextualization, and ongoing research into the impact of AI-enabled inner development on leadership effectiveness and systemic transformation.

As AI systems become increasingly embedded in how societies work, decide, and reimagine the future, one question becomes paramount: Will AI be another tool for accelerating extraction, disconnection, and fragmentation? Or will it become an amplifier of reflection, care, and regeneration?

In the words of the Neoliderança Manifesto:

> "We are not here merely to predict the future. We are here to co-create it – beginning from within."

This is the ultimate proposition of InEx: that the most profound technologies we can cultivate are those that reconnect us to ourselves, to each other, and to the living systems of which we are a part. And that the most essential technology – now and always – is the conscious, ethical, and courageous responsibility of being human.

Acknowledgments

This project was financially supported by the *Fundação de Amparo à Pesquisa e Inovação do Estado de Santa Catarina (FAPESC)*, under Public Call FAPESC No. 48/2024 – Programa de Apoio à Inovação Social – Negócios Sociais.

We are deeply grateful to *Konvex Jr.*, the junior enterprise from UDESC-SC, for their valuable contribution to the development of the AI system. We would also like to express our sincere thanks to *Jorge Gustavo Sandoval Simão*, who has generously and voluntarily provided technical guidance and mentorship to the Konvex team throughout the project.

References

Barros, M. *Livro sobre nada*. Editora Record: Rio de Janeiro, 1997.

Buarque, C. 'Construção' [Song]. In *Construção* [Album]. Philips, 1971.

Buarque, C. *Music by Chico Buarque* [Music]. Brazil, [n.d.].

Evaristo, C. *Escrevivência: A escrita de nós*. Pallas, 2019.

Hilst, H. *Cantares de perda e predileção*. Globo, 2001.

Hilst, H. *Selected works* [Poetry and prose]. Brazil, [n.d.].

Inner Development Guide. Inner Development Guide [Digital image]. Inner Development Goals, [n.d.], https://innerdevelopmentgoals.org/framework/.

Inner Development Goals. *IDG official website*. 2025, https://www.innerdevelopmentgoals.org/.

Pärt (1978): "Before exploring this leadership challenge, consider listening to Arvo Pärt's 'Spiegel im Spiegel' to cultivate stillness."

Rumi. *Selected poems* [Poetry collection]. [n.d.].

Scharmer, O. *The Essentials of Theory U: Core Principles and Applications*. Berrett-Koehler Publishers: Oakland, CA, USA., 2018.

Schwartzberg, L. (Director). *Fantastic Fungi* [Film]. Moving Art, 2019.

The New Division. *Inner Development Goals visual framework* [Digital image]. The New Division, [n.d.], https://www.thenewdivision.world/idg.

UNESCO. 'Recommendation on the ethics of artificial intelligence.' 2021, https://unesdoc.unesco.org/ark:/48223/pf0000380455.

United Nations. *Transforming our world: The 2030 agenda for sustainable development*. United Nations, 2015, https://sdgs.un.org/2030agenda.

Wenders, W. and J. R. Salgado (Directors). *The Salt of the Earth* [Film]. Decia Films; Amazonas Images, 2014.

Wikimedia Commons contributor. *Koch Snowflake* [Image]. Wikimedia Commons, [n.d.], https://commons.wikimedia.org/wiki/File:Koch_snowflake.png.

World Economic Forum. *Artificial intelligence, curation: Desautels Faculty of Management, McGill University*. World Economic Forum, [n.d.], https://intelligence.weforum.org/topics/a1Gb0000000pTDREA2.

World Economic Forum. *Blueprint for intelligent economies: AI competitiveness through regional collaboration*. World Economic Forum, 2024, https://www.weforum.org/publications/blueprint-for-intelligent-economies/.

World Economic Forum. *The global risks report 2025*. World Economic Forum, 2025, https://www.weforum.org/publications/global-risks-report-2025/.

© 2026 World Scientific Publishing Europe Ltd.
https://doi.org/10.1142/9781800617414_0015

Chapter 15

Algorithmic Leadership: A Bibliometric Analysis of Robot Autonomy's Impact on Hybrid Team Leadership and Effectiveness

Ricardo Pereira, Solange Maria da Silva*, Karla Cristina Rocha Botão, and Cristiano José Castro de Almeida Cunha

Federal University of Santa Catarina, Brazil

**solange.silva@ufsc.br*

Abstract

The integration of autonomous robots into workplaces is reshaping the nature of teamwork and leadership with the emergence of hybrid teams comprising both humans and robots. In this study, we conduct a field mapping through a bibliometric review to examine the impact of robotic autonomy on the power dynamics and effectiveness of these teams, identifying patterns, trends, and gaps in the existing scientific literature. Systematic searches were conducted in Scopus, Web of Science, and IEEE Xplore databases. The keywords used included "robotic autonomy," "leadership," and "hybrid teams," enabling a quantitative and qualitative analysis of academic output on this subject. The analysis identified the following: prominent trends in the literature concerning shared leadership between humans and robots; challenges related to trust, reliability, and communication within these hybrid teams; and the need to adapt leadership styles and develop performance evaluation metrics for this new team structure. This bibliometric review provides a comprehensive overview of research on robotic autonomy and leadership in hybrid teams, highlighting avenues for future investigation and contributing to the development of more effective leadership strategies in these emerging contexts.

Keywords: Robot autonomy, leadership dynamics, team effectiveness, leadership, very vague.

15.1 Introduction

The increasing integration of autonomous robots into organizational environments is driving a substantial reconfiguration of collaborative work dynamics, directly impacting team composition and challenging traditional leadership models. This landscape has led to the emergence of human–robot teams (HRTs), defined as collaborative arrangements in which humans and robotic agents operate interdependently to achieve shared goals, often in complex and dynamic contexts (Johnson *et al.*, 2014; Lewis *et al.*, 2018).

These teams are structured around coordinated tasks, mutual communication, and an adaptive division of roles, requiring robots to be not merely command executors but active participants in decision-making, environmental monitoring, and real-time behavioral adjustment (Donner *et al.*, 2017; Sheng *et al.*, 2015).

One of the most significant consequences of this new configuration is the emergence of algorithmic leadership, a concept describing the increasingly relevant role of artificial intelligence (AI) systems and autonomous robots in coordinating tasks, making decisions, and influencing the social and functional dynamics of mixed teams (Few *et al.*, 2006; Sheng *et al.*, 2015).

Robotic autonomy is a cornerstone of this phenomenon, enabling robots to exhibit intelligent behaviors such as fluidly switching between leadership and follower roles based on inferences about human behavior (Sheng *et al.*, 2015), controlling dynamic formations through reinforcement learning (Knopp *et al.*, 2017), or acting proactively by identifying "capability deltas" – i.e., gaps in capabilities between humans and machines (Mandischer *et al.*, 2024). Furthermore, the establishment of "working agreements" between robots and humans represents a form of collaborative and adaptive self-management tailored to the situational context (Mioch *et al.*, 2017).

From a behavioral perspective, robots have demonstrated the capacity to adopt classic leadership styles, such as transformational leadership, which aims to emotionally engage team members, and transactional leadership, which is centered on rewards and performance. Each style has distinct implications for leadership acceptance and collective performance (Stock-Homburg *et al.*, 2021). However, the acceptance of robots in leadership positions remains a challenge, with evidence of human resistance, particularly in ambiguous or high-cognitive-load contexts (Luo *et al.*, 2024; Wolf and Stock-Homburg, 2021).

Psychosocial factors, such as perceived usefulness, familiarity with technology, perceived empathy, and behavioral similarity, have been shown to be decisive in individuals' willingness to accept robots as "operational leaders", that is, robots, while not holding formal organizational authority or strategic decision-making power, assume tactical coordination and task-specific guidance roles in operational contexts (You and Robert, 2018; Latikka *et al.*, 2021; Wolf and Stock-Homburg, 2021). Additionally, strategies such as facilitative leadership, where the robot leads specific tasks, have proven effective in mitigating mental overload and reducing operational errors (Few *et al.*, 2006; Scheggi *et al.*, 2014).

Furthermore, leadership roles in HRTs tend to be dynamic and negotiable, featuring fluid alternation between robots and humans, often mediated by technologies such as interactive graphs and haptic feedback, which enhance team cohesion and situational awareness (Genovese and Sabatini, 2006; Scheggi *et al.*, 2014).

In light of this emerging landscape, the current study aims to map the field of algorithmic leadership, with an emphasis on the role of robotic autonomy in the leadership and effectiveness of human–robot hybrid teams. We intend to map publication patterns, identify thematic gaps, analyze recurring methodological approaches, and highlight emerging theoretical trends. This analysis seeks to provide a comprehensive overview of an emerging field of study concerning leadership in organizational contexts mediated by autonomous technologies.

15.2 Conceptual Framework

Digital transformation and the advancement of AI have catalyzed the increasing integration of autonomous robots into organizational environments, leading to the emergence of HRTs. These teams represent a collaborative arrangement in which humans and artificial agents operate interdependently to achieve shared goals (Johnson *et al.*, 2014; Philip and Wong, 2024). In this emerging context, the concept of algorithmic leadership gains prominence, understood as the ability of autonomous systems to perform leadership roles and influence the coordination, decision-making, and social dynamics of teams (Harms and Han, 2019; Stock-Homburg *et al.*, 2021).

15.2.1 *The algorithm*

An algorithm is a structured, finite set of encoded instructions designed to solve problems or execute tasks through the logical and sequential processing of data (Cormen *et al.*, 2009). In the organizational context, algorithms cease to be mere invisible computational mechanisms and instead function as autonomous decision-making agents capable of influencing behavior, distributing tasks, evaluating performance, and even leading teams (Harms and Han, 2019; Zuboff, 2019).

Unlike its traditional definition in computer science, the algorithm in this environment not only performs technical functions but also actively participates in social and organizational dynamics. This includes allocating resources based on historical data, determining who leads an action within a mixed team, or adjusting operational strategies in real time based on behavioral patterns detected in humans (Stock-Homburg *et al.*, 2021; Walsh, 2019).

This expansion of the algorithm's role is central to the notion of algorithmic leadership, in which authority and influence emerge not from human hierarchical status but from the algorithmic system's ability to interpret, decide, and act on behalf of the team.

15.2.2 *Robotic autonomy and social robots*

Robotic autonomy refers to the capacity of a robotic system to execute tasks and make decisions independently, without continuous human intervention (Parks and Allison, 2023). This characteristic can be categorized into different levels, ranging from specific tasks controlled by predictable algorithms to highly complex operations involving machine learning, real-time environmental adaptation, and advanced data processing. With advancements in AI, sophisticated sensors, and machine learning algorithms, autonomous robots have become capable of navigating, manipulating objects, identifying environmental patterns, and interacting effectively in dynamic and unpredictable environments. In the context of hybrid teams, robotic autonomy is of fundamental importance in defining power dynamics, intra-team communication, and the effectiveness of joint operations (Wolf and Stock-Homburg, 2021).

Social robots, in turn, represent a subcategory of autonomous robots designed to interact with humans in a socially competent manner, recognizing and responding to emotional, behavioral, and cognitive cues. Interaction modalities involving speech, facial expressions, gestures, and other forms of non-verbal communication are essential for establishing trust and cooperation in mixed teams (Lopes *et al.*, 2021). Theories of emotional intelligence, social learning theory, and models of human–robot interaction have underpinned the development of social robots capable of performing roles as facilitators, leaders, or collaborative partners (Sirintuna *et al.*, 2024).

The operationalization of autonomy in social robots incorporates concepts such as mission autonomy, decision autonomy, and cooperative autonomy, which influence aspects like perceived reliability, social acceptability, and team performance (Sicat *et al.*, 2017). With the growing integration of these robots into organizational settings, understanding how autonomy influences power dynamics, communication, and the effectiveness of hybrid teams is highly relevant for developing more effective and socially acceptable leadership strategies (Lopes *et al.*, 2021).

15.2.3 *Hybrid teams*

HRTs are composed of humans and robots working interdependently to achieve common goals through effective interaction and collaboration (Johnson *et al.*, 2014). Three primary structural configurations are recognized in the literature. In a human-directed robot team, an operator supervises autonomous robots, guiding them in specific tasks (Yazdani *et al.*, 2016). In peer-based mixed teams, humans and robots share physical or cognitive tasks and may hold similar leadership roles, often adapting human capabilities to those of robots to enhance coordination (Wolf and

Stock-Homburg, 2023). In autonomous mixed teams, both agents operate with greater independence, mutually adapting to perform complex tasks cooperatively (Mioch *et al.*, 2018).

The essential characteristics of these teams include continuous interaction, shared goals, and functional interdependence between tasks and team members (Ma *et al.*, 2017; Alboul *et al.*, 2008). Such elements are fundamental for effective performance in dynamic and technologically advanced contexts.

15.2.4 *Leadership*

In its most essential form, leadership can be understood as the process of influencing, motivating, inspiring, and developing individuals to achieve common objectives (Northouse, 2018). Leaders play crucial roles in setting goals, providing appropriate support, valuing individual contributions, and cultivating a sense of belonging and cohesion within teams (Yukl, 2012). Classic literature highlights the importance of leadership for the effectiveness of work groups, showing that clarity of purpose, effective communication, and emotional support are determinants of collective performance (Bass and Bass, 2008).

As organizations become more complex, volatile, and technologically mediated, the concept of leadership is also transforming. More recent models emphasize behavioral flexibility and the management of contradictions, as seen in transformational, servant, and paradoxical leadership (Lopes *et al.*, 2021; Philip and Wong, 2024; Luo *et al.*, 2024). These models recognize that effective leaders not only direct but also negotiate constantly evolving social, emotional, and technological dynamics. In the context of HRTs, there is a clear need to re-evaluate leadership, as authority is no longer restricted to human agents: algorithms and robots can influence behavior, allocate tasks, and even exercise operational command functions (Stock-Homburg *et al.*, 2021). This implies a new way of thinking about the competencies required to lead and promote coordination, trust, and adaptability.

15.2.5 *Algorithmic leadership*

The concept of "algorithmic leadership" has recently emerged in academic literature as a response to the growing use of AI systems in decision-making and task supervision within organizational environments.

Harms and Han (2019) were the first to formalize the term, describing it as the replacement or supplementation of traditionally human leadership functions with algorithms capable of allocating tasks, monitoring performance, providing feedback, and even influencing the emotional state of workers.

In HRTs, algorithmic leadership involves algorithms assuming or sharing leadership roles by delegating decisions, monitoring progress, and adapting roles within the team. To optimize coordination, algorithms structure situational hierarchies between humans and robots using models such as leadership graphs and ensure contextual responsiveness that improves fluidity in executing complex tasks, such as search and rescue missions (Natarajan *et al.*, 2023).

Beyond task-related functions, algorithms are increasingly capable of handling relational aspects of leadership, such as motivating, supporting, and developing workers, and even predicting emotional well-being and implementing therapeutic interventions (Harms and Han, 2019). Algorithmic leadership can also be dynamic and negotiated, with autonomous agents assuming leader and supporter roles based on "capability deltas," which quantify the capability gaps between team members to optimize performance (Mandischer *et al.*, 2024).

15.2.6 *Robotic leadership*

Still undergoing theoretical consolidation and sometimes treated as synonymous with algorithmic leadership, this term was initially addressed by Stock-Homburg *et al.* (2021) who classified robots as leaders in experimental scenarios, analyzing their effectiveness in styles such as transformational, transactional, and *laissez-faire* leadership.

The theoretical origins of robotic leadership are tied to the evolution of robotic autonomy and advancements in social artificial intelligence. A key milestone was the proposal by Few, Fong, and Nourbakhsh (2006), who introduced the concept of "dynamic leadership" in HRTs, suggesting that robots could alternate between leader and follower roles depending on the task context. The adoption of classic leadership styles, such as transformational and transactional, by social robots to influence the acceptance and performance of human teams expands the relational, emotional, and cognitive perception of leadership and alters interpersonal dynamics that require adaptation within automated contexts.

15.2.7 *Paradoxical leadership*

The term "paradoxical leadership" was formally articulated by (Philip and Wong, 2024) as a leadership style that integrates opposing behaviors to meet the conflicting expectations of subordinate performance and development. Their empirical study demonstrated that leaders who reconcile autonomy with clear direction and consistency with flexibility achieve better outcomes in terms of team innovation and trust.

Paradoxical leadership has emerged as a particularly effective model in contexts characterized by cultural diversity, VUCA (volatile, uncertain, complex, and ambiguous) environments, and hybrid organizations, owing to the importance of the leader's paradoxical mindset – that is, their cognitive ability to accept and integrate contradictions – as a determining factor of their effectiveness (Miron-Spektor *et al.*, 2018). In the specific context of HRTs, where the interaction between biological and technological agents poses ontological and operational dilemmas, this form of leadership becomes even more strategic. The coexistence of algorithmic rationality and human judgment intensifies organizational tensions and requires leaders to exhibit high interpretive and behavioral flexibility to sustain cohesion and collective performance (Philip and Wong, 2024).

15.3 Methodological Procedures

The method employed in this research was a bibliometric review, a systematic approach to analyzing the evolution and structure of a scientific field of study. The primary objective of this method is to identify trends, the most significant topics (motor themes), and the relationships between different topics over time within a research area (Sott *et al.*, 2020). Its two main techniques are performance analysis and science mapping (Pereira *et al.*, 2023).

Performance analysis evaluates the output of different authors, organizations, and countries based on their publications and citation data. The relative contribution of each actor to the knowledge area is assessed and used to identify the most productive and impactful contributors. In this article, the following bibliometric performance indicators were used: number of published articles, number of citations, and keywords (Pereira *et al.*, 2023).

Science mapping is an advanced bibliometric technique that visually and structurally represents the organization, dynamics, and evolution of knowledge within a specific scientific field. This approach emphasizes the connections and relationships between authors, institutions, documents, and concepts, enabling the identification of thematic clusters, emerging trends, and research gaps (Cobo *et al.*, 2011). This technique uses bibliographic data to construct graphical representations that aid in understanding the development and intellectual structure of a scientific domain. The mapping of the selected articles for this study was performed using the VOSviewer tool (Van Eck and Waltman, 2017).

The bibliographic search that supported the bibliometric analysis was conducted in Scopus, Web of Science, and IEEE Xplore databases, which are considered primary reference sources for scientific journal articles related to the researched topic. Two criteria were adopted for selecting these databases: the breadth of coverage and the level of data structuring and exportability.

The search strategy utilized the string presented in Figure 15.1 and filtered for articles and reviews based on title, abstract, and keywords. The search was limited to publications in the English language, with no time constraints, including all publications up to the date of data extraction as of June 9, 2025.

The search across the databases retrieved 87 bibliographic references. In a subsequent step, an initial screening was conducted, and 29 duplicate articles were discarded. The data were then organized in a matrix, and articles were selected if they aligned with the research objective and/or addressed the intersection of the core constructs: hybrid teams composed of humans and robots, their collaboration, and their subjection to a leadership process.

Following the full-text evaluation, a final set of 24 articles was deemed eligible for the bibliometric analyses. This process is detailed in the flowchart presented in Figure 15.2.

TITLE-ABS-KEY ("hybrid teams") OR TITLE-ABS-KEY ("human-robot teams") OR TITLE-ABS-KEY ("human and robot collaboration") AND TITLE-ABS-KEY (leader) AND (LIMIT-TO (LANGUAGE, "English"))*

Figure 15.1. Search string.

Source: Research data (2025).

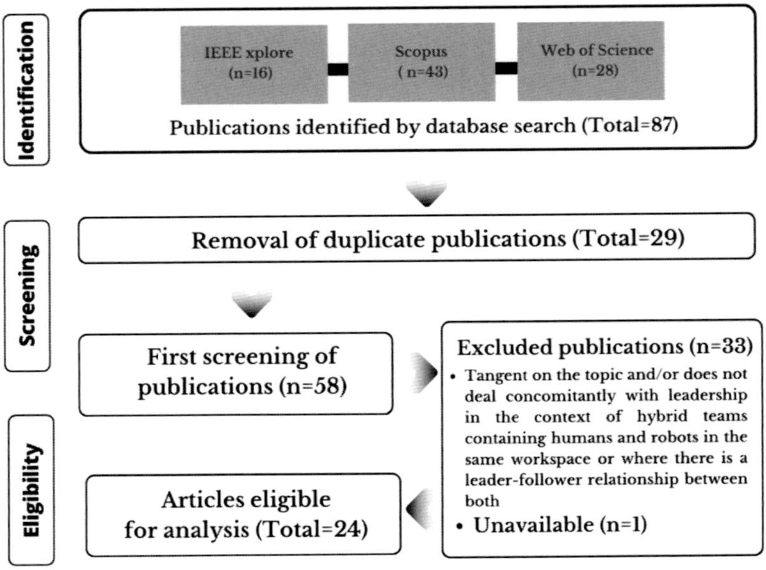

Figure 15.2. Flowchart of the article selection process for bibliometric analysis.

The 24 selected articles were analyzed using the two previously mentioned bibliometric techniques: performance analysis and science mapping. In the performance analysis, the following variables were examined: (a) the number of articles per year; and (b) the most productive countries, institutions, journals, and authors; the methods used; and the most cited articles.

Subsequently, the science mapping was conducted. Bibliographic data were exported from the databases into a metadata file. This file was processed using the VOSviewer software to generate graphs representing the network of relationships among keywords, which enabled the creation of a co-occurrence map of those keywords within the selected works.

A network "is a set of items, which we call vertices (nodes), with links between them, called connections (edges)" (Castro, 2007, p. 45). In this network, the larger the size of a node, the greater its importance. The more central a node's position in a network, the greater the number of links (connections) it establishes with other nodes (centrality). In this type of analysis, it is important to consider clusters – that is, groupings of nodes that exhibit stronger and more numerous links among themselves (proximity) (Pereira *et al.*, 2020; Pereira, Rosa and Cunha, 2023).

15.4 Bibliometric Analysis

The results of the bibliometric analysis are presented in the following two sections. The first section presents the performance analysis, detailing the results based on traditional indicators such as the number of published documents, the most productive authors, countries, and journals, the methods used, and the most cited publications. The second subsection covers field mapping (qualitative analysis) and the categorization derived from the cluster analysis performed using the VOSviewer tool.

15.4.1 *Performance analysis* (*quantitative analysis*)

Traditional bibliometric studies involve the quantification of scientific output in a specific field, based on established indicators and following specific scientometric laws, such as Lotka's Law (to assess the concentration of author productivity), Bradford's Law (to identify core journals by topic), and Zipf's Law (to study the frequency of keywords in abstracts and titles), to describe patterns of productivity, dissemination, and use of scientific information (Guedes and Borschiver, 2005).

The performance analysis conducted in this study applies these laws to identify the most prominent authors, journals, higher education institutions, and countries within the research area.

The first aspect of the analysis concerns the evolution of scientific output on the topic over time. The earliest identified study on hybrid teams composed of humans and robots was conducted by Few *et al.* in 2006, affiliated with the Idaho National Laboratory (USA). At that time, due to the early stage of technological development, the studies were more prospective in nature, conducted in laboratory settings through simulations. Nevertheless, this study explored the concept of Standard Shared Mode - SSM, anticipating what would later be formalized as the concept of algorithmic leadership.

The graph in Figure 15.3 illustrates the historical evolution of research on algorithmic leadership in HRTs. The analysis is based on the year each article was first made available. Some articles were

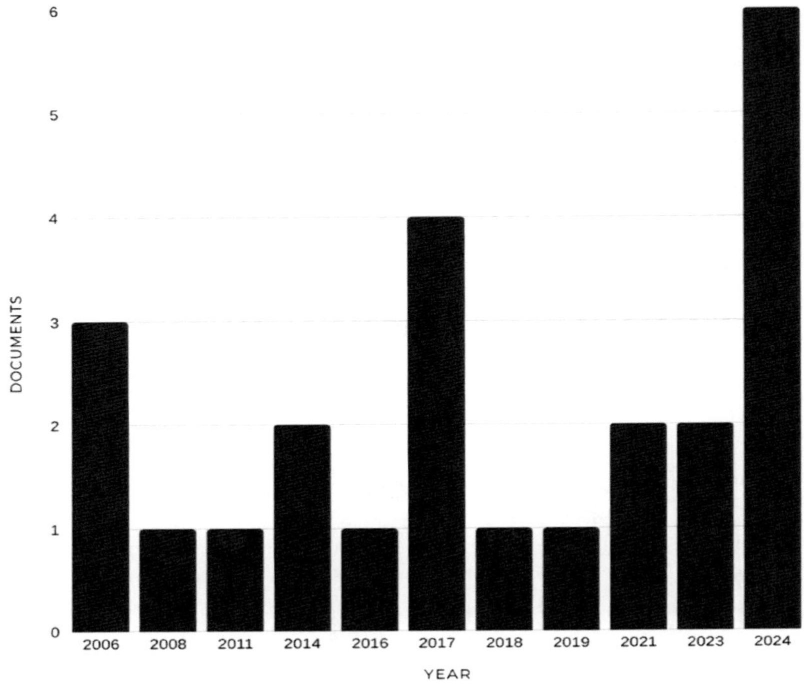

Figure 15.3. Evolution of scientific output on the topic.

Source: Research data (2025).

subsequently revised, potentially resulting in a discrepancy with their final publication dates.

Conceptual and technological milestones can be highlighted throughout this period:

Phase 1: Robotic Initiative and Technical Leadership (2006–2011). Focus: Shared control, navigation, supervision.

- 2006 – Few *et al.*: Facilitative leadership with collaborative control mode (CTM).
- 2006 – Genovese & Sabatini: Leader-follower coordination via a differential compass.
- 2006 – Few *et al.*: Cognitive load reduction and increased control in HRTs; an expanded version of the previous study.
- 2008 – Alboul *et al.*: First mentions of mutual robotic leadership.
- 2011 – Nizette *et al.*: Adaptation of human leadership styles in robots.

Phase 2: Leadership Styles and Adaptive Interfaces (2014–2017). Focus: Social interaction, haptic feedback, role-switching.

- 2014 – Scheggi *et al.*: Leadership via haptic feedback in formation.
- 2015 – Sheng *et al.*: Leadership switching through predictive learning.
- 2016 – Yazdani *et al.*: Cognitive control for robots in rescue missions.
- 2017 – Knopp *et al.*: Utilized GQ(λ) reinforcement learning.
- 2017 – Donner *et al.*: Cooperative manipulation with haptic leadership.
- 2017 – Sicat *et al.*: Human reaction to robotic leadership attempts.
- 2017 – Yazdani *et al.*: "Working Agreements" for autonomy within agreed-upon limits.

Phase 3: Organizational Leadership and the Psychology of Acceptance (2018–2025). Focus: Real robotic leadership, social acceptance, paradoxes.

- 2018 – Mioch *et al.*: Value-Based "Working Agreements" for adaptive coordination in HRTs.
- 2021 – Kwon *et al.*: Mathematical modeling of leadership relations for robotic influence in human teams.
- 2021 – Wolf & Stock-Homburg: Hiring decisions for leader robots.
- 2021 – Lopes *et al.*: Comparison of transformational and transactional styles.
- 2023 – Parks & Allison: Adaptive autonomy as a countermeasure to fatigue in HRTs.
- 2023 – Wolf & Stock-Homburg: Characterization of HRTs over 30 years.
- 2024 – Philip & Wong: Paradoxical leadership in HRTs.
- 2025 – Wolf & Stock-Homburg: Robot managers and relational resistance.
- 2024 – Luo *et al.*: Impact of non-intervention and leadership ambiguity.
- 2024 – Mandischer *et al.*: Proposed "capability deltas" for negotiated leadership.
- 2024 – Sirintuna *et al.*: Multimodal haptic feedback for situational awareness in human-robot co-transport.
- 2024 – Walker *et al.*: Mixed reality and leadership perception.

The chart in Figure 15.4 shows the nine countries with the highest scientific output. The list comprises five European countries, two North American countries, one from Oceania, and one from Asia.

Figure 15.4. Publications by country.

Source: Research data (2025).

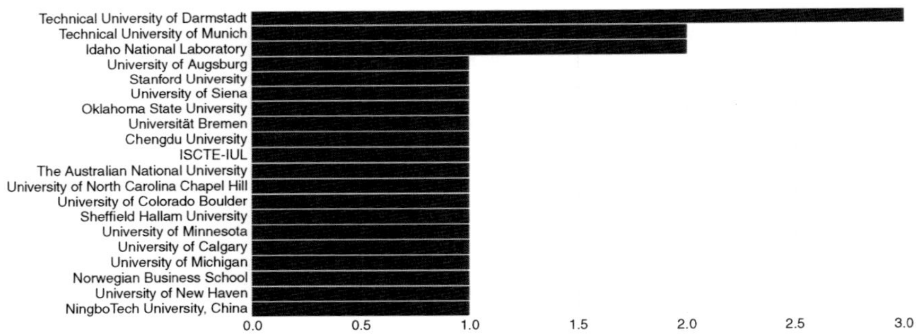

Figure 15.5. Publications by institution.

Source: Research data (2025).

Figure 15.4 reveals a concentration of studies on algorithmic leadership in Europe, with Germany being one of the most productive countries, followed by the United States with seven publications and Italy with three articles. It is important to note that since an article can be co-authored by researchers from different countries, the sum of publications per country may exceed the total number of articles selected for analysis. The authors' countries of origin were determined by the nationality of the institutions to which they are affiliated.

Figure 15.5 presents the 20 most productive institutions. Of these, eight are in the United States, four in Germany, and two in China. The top-ranked institution is the Technical University of Darmstadt (GER), with three articles. In second place is the Technical University of Munich

(GER), followed by the Idaho National Laboratory (USA), both with two articles. For each article, the institution of the primary author was counted.

Table 15.1 presents the most productive authors in the field and the results of the triangular analysis involving the most productive countries, institutions, and authors. The criterion used to define author productivity was the number of published articles.

Table 15.2 presents the articles that constitute the analytical portfolio of this study.

Table 15.1. Most productive authors.

No.	Author(s)	Institution/Country	Number of Publications on the Topic
1	Wolf, F.D.	Technical University of Darmstadt/Germany	3
2	Stock-Homburg, R.M.	Technical University of Darmstadt/Germany	3
3	Few, D. A.	Idaho National Laboratory/USA	2
4	Bruemmer, D. J.	Idaho National Laboratory/USA	2
5	Walton, M. C.	Idaho National Laboratory/USA	2

Source: Research data (2025).

Table 15.2. Articles comprising the analysis portfolio.

No.	Year	Author(s)	Title
1	2024	Philip, J. and Wong, S. I.	The paradoxical leader, crafting human worker, and robot teammate: A commentary on the future of leader behaviors
2	2025	Franziska D. Wolf and Ruth M. Stock-Homburg.	One size does not fit all: Mechanisms of employees' acceptance of robotic lower-level managers
3	2016	Fereshta Yazdani, Benjamin Brieber, and Michael Beetz	Cognition-enabled robot control for mixed human–robot rescue teams
4	2023	Max Parks and Mark Allison	Autonomy and fatigue in human–robot teams
5	2021	Franziska D. Wolf and Ruth M. Stock-Homburg.	Making the first step towards robotic leadership – Hiring decisions for robotic team leader candidates

(*Continued*)

Table 15.2. (*Continued*)

No.	Year	Author(s)	Title
6	2006	Vincenzo Genovese and Angelo Maria Sabatini	Differential compassing helps human–robot teams navigate in magnetically disturbed environments
7	2024	Jia Luo, Xinyan Mu and Qianyou Zhang	Is non-intervention feasible? How laissez-faire leadership moderates the relationship between AI usage and service employee empathetic creativity
8	2023	Franziska Doris Wolf and Ruth Maria Stock-Homburg	How and when can robots be team members? Three decades of research on human–robot teams
9	2015	Weihua Sheng, Anand Thobbi, and Ye Gu	An integrated framework for human–robot collaborative manipulation
10	2017	Martin Knopp, Can Aykın, Johannes Feldmaier, and Hao Shen	Formation control using GQ(λ) reinforcement learning
11	2006	Douglas A. Few, David J. Bruemmer, and Miles C. Walton	Dynamic leadership for human–robot teams
12	2024	Nils Mandischer, Marcel Usai, Frank Flemisch, and Lars Mikelsons	Exploring capability-based control distributions of human–robot teams through capability deltas: Formalization and implications
13	2014	Stefano Scheggi, Fabio Morbidi, and Domenico Prattichizzo	Human–robot formation control via visual and vibrotactile haptic feedback
14	2021	Minae Kwon, Mengxi Li, Alexandre Bucquet, and Dorsa Sadigh	Influencing leading and following in human–robot teams
15	2024	Doganay Sirintuna, Theodora Kastritsi, Idil Ozdamar, Juan M. Gandarias, and Arash Ajoudani	Enhancing human–robot collaborative transportation through obstacle-aware vibrotactile warning and virtual fixtures
16	2021	Sara L. Lopes, José Bernardo Rocha, Aristides I. Ferreira, and Rui Prada	Social robots as leaders: Leadership styles in human–robot teams
17	2017	Philine Donner, Franz Christange, Jing Lu, and Martin Buss	Cooperative dynamic manipulation of unknown flexible objects: Joint energy injection based on simple pendulum fundamental dynamics

Table 15.2. (*Continued*)

No.	Year	Author(s)	Title
18	2011	Ben E. Nizette and Changbin Yu	Human leadership approaches to hybrid human/robot teams
19	2024	Michael E. Walker, Maitrey Gramopadhye, Bryce Ikeda, Jack Burns, and Daniel Szafir	The cyber-physical control room: A mixed reality interface for mobile robot teleoperation and human–robot teaming
20	2006	Douglas A. Few, David J. Bruemmer, and Miles C. Walton	Improved human–robot teaming through facilitated initiative
21	2017	Shelly Sicat, Shreya Chopra, Nico Li, and Ehud Sharlin	Playing the mirror game with a humanoid: Probing the social aspects of switching interaction roles
22	2008	Lyuba Alboul, Joan Saez-Pons, and Jacques Penders	Mixed human–robot team navigation in the guardians project
23	2018	Tina Mioch, Marieke M. M. Peeters, and Mark A. Neerincx	Improving adaptive human–robot cooperation through work agreements
24	2017	Fereshta Yazdani, Matthias Scheutz, and Michael Beetz	Guidelines for improving task-based natural language understanding in human–robot rescue teams

Source: Research data (2025).

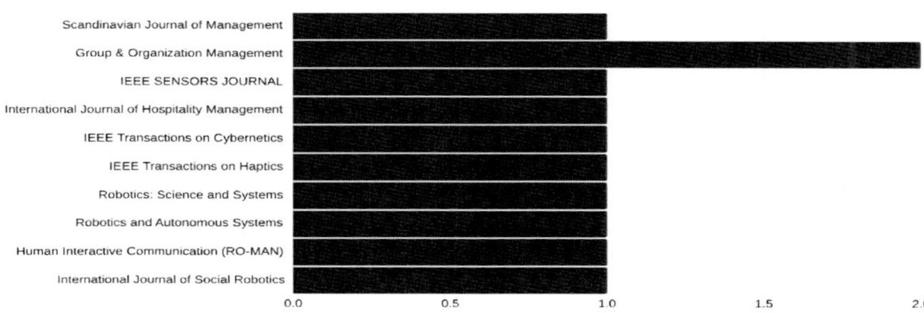

Figure 15.6. Most productive journals.

Source: Research data (2025).

Figure 15.6 lists the 10 journals that have published on algorithmic leadership and hybrid teams composed of humans and robots.

The journal *Group & Organization Management* has the highest number of publications among the studies in the analytical bibliographic portfolio. It is important to note that of the 24 selected studies, only 10 were published in journals; the remainder are from conference or symposium proceedings or are book chapters. Information regarding the most productive journals is relevant for researchers to identify the most suitable or interested publication outlets for the topic under investigation.

15.4.2 *Field mapping (qualitative analysis)*

Keyword co-occurrence analysis is a technique that uses words from documents to establish relationships and construct the conceptual structure of a knowledge domain (Pereira *et al.*, 2023). The underlying premise is that when keywords frequently co-occur in documents, the concepts behind them are related. This analysis uses the actual content of the documents to build a similarity measure. The result is a network of themes whose relationships represent the conceptual space of a field (Zupic and Cater, 2015).

The graph presented in Figure 15.7 shows the network of the most frequently occurring keywords in the set of articles. The network is subdivided into six main clusters, represented by the colors red, yellow, green, purple, blue, and turquoise.

Each cluster aggregates keywords that exhibit similarities and interactions among related authors and themes. For example, if a set of

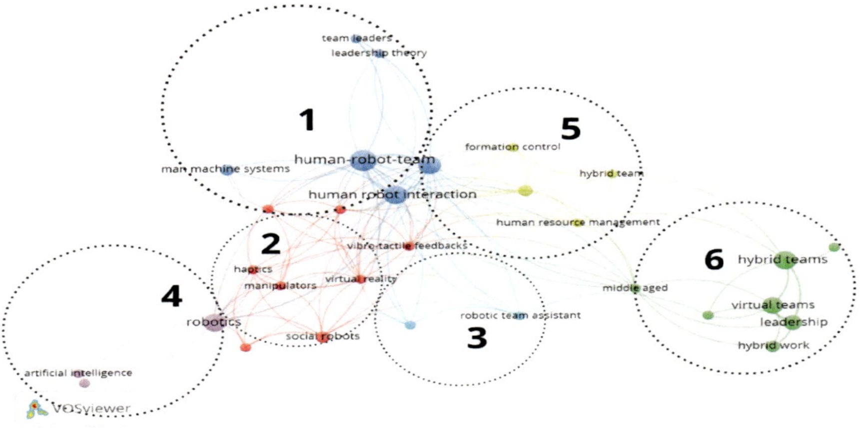

Figure 15.7. Keyword co-occurrence map.

Source: Created by the authors using the VOSviewer tool (2025).

articles addresses a specific theme, those documents will show structural connections, represented by linking lines. The stronger this line, the greater the interaction between these themes (Pereira *et al.*, 2023).

Cluster 1, the blue cluster, aggregates keywords related to HRTs and human–robot interaction. The most prominent nodes ("human-robot team" and "human-robot interaction") are at the center, connected to terms such as "team leaders" and "leadership theory". This confirms that team structure and leadership dynamics are the central concepts unifying the literature. The centrality and size of these nodes indicate that much of the research revolves around how HRTs are formed and led. The subtheme of "Control and Role Dynamics" is visible through the direct connection to the term "formation control" (yellow cluster), showing that formation control is a key practical application of this leadership dynamic.

Cluster 2, the red cluster, groups the technologies and modalities that enable interaction: "robotics", "social robots", "haptics", "virtual reality", "manipulators", and "vibro-tactile feedbacks". **Cluster 3**, the turquoise cluster with the "robotic team assistant" node, points to a specific role for the robot as a collaboration mechanism. The strong links between Cluster 2 (red) and Cluster 1 (blue) demonstrate that the study of leadership in HRTs is inextricably linked to the technologies that mediate it. The "artificial intelligence" node (**Cluster 4**, the purple cluster) acts as the foundational basis for this entire field.

The term "human resource management" (**Cluster 5**) connects directly to team and management dynamics, highlighting the organizational and psychosocial impacts of robot adoption.

The presence of the "middle-aged" node (**Cluster 6**) is particularly revealing. It suggests that research is beginning to consider human demographic factors (such as workforce age) in the acceptance and effectiveness of HRTs, a key component of psychosocial factors.

The co-occurrence map shows that human factors are not studied in isolation but rather within the context of management ("human resource management"), team types ("hybrid teams"), and the interaction itself. All research areas represented on the map (leadership, interaction mechanisms, and human factors) ultimately aim to understand or improve effectiveness and performance, which is a core theme in **Cluster 6** (green). For example, "formation control" (**Cluster 5**, yellow) is studied to improve navigational efficiency. "Virtual teams" and "hybrid teams" (green cluster) are investigated to understand their performance outcomes. The entire map is a visual representation of the academic pursuit to optimize the outcomes of these teams. This theme represents the "why" behind the existence of the entire network.

Table 15.3 describes the clusters and their respective themes and related works, allowing for an analysis of the theoretical trends in the area.

Table 15.3. Clusters, themes, and related works.

Cluster No.	Cluster Color	Cluster Themes	Keywords	Related Works
1	Blue	Configurations and dynamics of leadership in HRTs	Human–robot interaction and human–robot teams	Philip and Wong, 2024; Wolf and Stock-Homburg, 2025; Wolf and Stock-Homburg, 2021; Wolf and Stock, 2023-Homburg; Kwon *et al.*, 2021; Lopes *et al.*, 2021, Few *et al.*, 2006
2	Red	Mechanisms of interaction and collaboration	Robotics, social robots, haptics, virtual reality manipulators; vibro-tactile feedbacks	Yazdani *et al.*, 2016; Sheng *et al.*, 2015; Scheggi *et al.*, 2014; Sirintuna *et al.*, 2024; Donner *et al.*, 2017; Walker *et al.*, 2024; Yazdani *et al.*, 2017; Mandischer *et al.*, 2024; Wolf and Stock-Homburg, 2023
3	Turquoise		Robotic team assistant	
4	Purple		Artificial intelligence	
5	Yellow	Human factors and psychosocial impact	Human resource management; hybrid team; formation control (strongly connected to the 'human–robot interaction' node in the blue cluster)	Genovese and Sabatini, 2006; Knopp *et al.*, 2017; Alboul *et al.*, 2008; Mioch *et al.*, 2018
6	Green	Team effectiveness and performance outcomes	Hybrid teams; hybrid work; leadership	Parks and Allison, 2023; Luo *et al.*, 2024; Few *et al.*, 2006; Sicat *et al.*, 2017

From the analysis of the co-occurrence map, it can be inferred that there is a central core (the blue cluster) focused on the dynamics of leadership and interaction. This core is enabled by a set of technologies (the red and purple clusters) and is studied within different organizational contexts (the green and yellow clusters). The interaction among these clusters aims to understand the psychosocial impact (a distributed theme) with the ultimate, implicit goal of optimizing performance.

15.5 Concluding Remarks

Bibliometric studies play a crucial role in introducing a specific subject or field to interested readers or researchers. The current study went beyond traditional bibliometrics by providing both a quantitative (performance analysis) and a qualitative (field mapping) analysis of research on algorithmic leadership and hybrid teams composed of humans and robots.

The performance analysis (the quantitative perspective of the study) of bibliometric data on algorithmic leadership in HRTs reveals a field undergoing expansion and thematic diversification. The scientific output has clearly evolved through three distinct phases. Between 2006 and 2011, the initial studies focused on robotic initiatives and technical leadership, emphasizing shared control and navigation and highlighting the proposal of facilitative leadership as an alternative to exclusive human control (Few *et al.*, 2006). From 2014 to 2017, the works began to address leadership styles and adaptive interfaces, incorporating technologies such as haptic feedback, reinforcement learning, and cognitive control, reflecting a growing concern with social interaction and role-switching between humans and robots (Scheggi *et al.*, 2014; Sheng *et al.*, 2015; Yazdani *et al.*, 2016). Since 2018, a transition toward organizational and psychosocial themes has been observed, with studies on the acceptance of robot leaders, the paradoxes of algorithmic leadership, and the impacts of autonomy in real-world work scenarios (Wolf and Stock-Homburg, 2021; Philip and Wong, 2024).

Publications are distributed across international conferences and journals in robotics, human–machine interaction, and intelligent systems. Prominent outlets include *IEEE Transactions on Human-Machine Systems* and *Frontiers in Robotics and AI*. Among the most recurrent authors, Wolf and Stock-Homburg (TU Darmstadt) have established themselves as leading voices in discussions on robots in managerial roles and acceptance factors, while Few, Bruemmer, and Walton (Idaho

National Laboratory) authored one of the earliest experimental studies on facilitative leadership, which has been widely cited in subsequent work.

Methodologically, experimental studies conducted in simulated or laboratory environments prevail, with samples predominantly composed of students and controlled tasks. Only recently have studies emerged that address robotic leadership in real organizational settings. The most recurrent themes include: the dynamic switching of leadership and follower roles between humans and robots; the application of classic leadership styles (transformational and transactional) in social robots; the psychosocial factors affecting the acceptance of robotic leadership; the technologies and algorithms that underpin the exercise of leadership; and the effects of these approaches on team performance and safety.

The quantitative analysis reveals a maturing interdisciplinary field that is transitioning from initial technical concerns to the incorporation of more complex organizational, cognitive, and social dimensions. The consolidation of thematic lines and the emergence of gaps, such as the scarcity of validation in real-world scenarios and the need for unified theories on HRTs, point to promising directions for future research.

Based on the field mapping of studies on algorithmic leadership in HRTs, a qualitative evolution is observed, revealing the progressive complexification of the topic and a notable diversification of methodological, theoretical, and contextual approaches. The analyzed studies show a significant advancement in conceptualizing leadership, not only as a function exercised by humans but also as a delegable or emergent capability in robotic systems. This new perspective implies a redefinition of traditional roles, allowing the robot to take initiative based on situational parameters, competence, or task optimization. Models such as "facilitative leadership" (Few *et al.*, 2006) and negotiated leadership based on "capability deltas" (Mandischer *et al.*, 2024) exemplify this trend.

Recent literature has begun to address in-depth the subjective barriers to the acceptance of robot leaders. It is evident that familiarity with technology, perceived usefulness, trust, and perceived empathy are decisive factors in the social legitimization of algorithmic authority. However, there is also significant resistance in contexts requiring moral judgment or relational empathy, suggesting that robotic leadership encounters social and emotional limitations that are not yet fully understood (Wolf and Stock-Homburg, 2021, 2025).

The qualitative analysis (field mapping), in turn, revealed a rapidly evolving and interdisciplinary research field. The four themes that emerged from the science mapping analysis are interconnected: Configurations and Dynamics of Leadership (Theme 1) are implemented through Mechanisms of Interaction (Theme 2). Both profoundly influence Human Factors and Psychosocial Impact (Theme 3), such as trust and acceptance. Finally, the effectiveness of this entire interaction is measured by Performance Outcomes (Theme 4).

The thematic and co-occurrence analysis also allowed for the identification of several trends:

1. *Dominance of simulations:* Many studies, particularly those of a more technical nature, are based on controlled laboratory experiments or simulations (e.g., MTurk). There is a clear need for more longitudinal field studies to understand how these dynamics unfold in real organizational contexts over time.
2. *Theoretical fragmentation:* Although there are attempts to apply classic leadership theories, the field still appears fragmented. Paradoxical leadership (Article 2) and facilitative leadership (Articles 12 and 22) emerge as theoretical approaches that are particularly well-suited to the dynamic and, at times, contradictory nature of HRTs.
3. *The tension between the technical and the social:* The research is clearly divided between a more technical approach, focused on control, algorithms, and interfaces (Themes 1 and 2), and a more psychosocial approach focused on human perception and acceptance (Theme 3). The true frontier lies in the holistic integration of these two worlds.

The qualitative mapping confirms that algorithmic leadership is emerging as an interdisciplinary research field at the intersection of computer science, organizational psychology, and systems engineering. Despite significant advances, important gaps persist, especially concerning long-term (longitudinal) studies, analyses in real organizational contexts, and investigations into the ethical and cultural impacts of this new form of authority. Research opportunities exist for developing unified theoretical models and research methodologies to capture the complexity and ambiguity of leadership in hybrid environments where humans and algorithms co-inhabit and co-decide.

Acknowledgments

During the preparation of this work, the author(s) utilized the tools and services SciSpace and NotebookLM to support data extraction and the evaluation of selected articles. Additionally, the Gemini tool was used to assist in the translation of the manuscript. After using these resources, the author(s) thoroughly reviewed and edited the content as necessary and assume full responsibility for the accuracy and integrity of the publication.

References

Alboul, L., J. Saez-Pons, and J. Penders. 'Mixed Human-Robot Team Navigation in the Guardians Project.' In *2008 IEEE International Workshop on Safety, Security and Rescue Robotics*. IEEE, 2008, 95–101, https://doi.org/10.1109/SSRR.2008.4745884.

Bass, B. M. and R. Bass. *The Bass Handbook of Leadership: Theory, Research, and Managerial Applications*, 4th ed. Free Press New York, NY, 2008.

Castro, P. A. 'Rede Complexa e Criticalidade Auto-Organizada: Modelos e Aplicações.' Doctoral Dissertation, Universidade de São Paulo, 2007.

Cobo, M. J., A. G. López-Herrera, E. Herrera-Viedma, and F. Herrera. 'An Approach for Detecting, Quantifying, and Visualizing the Evolution of a Research Field: A Practical Application to the Fuzzy Sets Theory Field.' *Journal of Informetrics*, 5, no. 1 (2011): 146–166.

Cormen, T. H., C. E. Leiserson, R. L. Rivest, and C. Stein. *Introduction to Algorithms*, 3rd ed. MIT Press, The MIT Press: Cambridge, MA, London, 2009.

Donner, P., F. Christange, J. Lu, *et al.* 'Cooperative Dynamic Manipulation of Unknown Flexible Objects.' *International Journal of Social Robotics*, 9, no. 4 (2017): 575–599, https://doi.org/10.1007/s12369-017-0415-x.

Few, D., D. Bruemmer, and M. C. Walton. 'Improved Human-Robot Teaming Through Facilitated Initiative.' In *2006 IEEE International Symposium on Robot and Human Interactive Communication*. IEEE, 2006, 171–176, Hatfield, Hertfordshire, United Kingdom https://doi.org/10.1109/ROMAN.2006.314413.

Few, D., T. Fong, and I. Nourbakhsh. 'Dynamic Leadership for Human-Robot Teams.' In *ACM/IEEE International Conference on Human-Robot Interaction*. IEEE, 2006, 24–31.

Genovese, V. and A. M. Sabatini. 'Differential Compassing Helps Human–Robot Teams Navigate in Indoor Environments.' In *IEEE International Symposium on Robot and Human Interactive Communication*. IEEE, 2006, 128–133.

Guedes, V. L. and S. Borschiver. 'Bibliometria: Uma Ferramenta Estatística Para a Gestão Da Informação e Do Conhecimento, em Sistemas de Informação, de Comunicação e de Avaliação Científica e Tecnológica.' *Encontro Nacional de Ciência da Informação*, 6, no. 1 (2005): 18.

Harms, P. D. and G. Han. 'Algorithmic Leadership: The Future Is Now.' *Journal of Leadership Studies*, 12, no. 4 (2019): 74–75, https://doi.org/10.1002/jls.21615.

Johnson, M., J. Bradshaw, P. J. Feltovich, C. Jonker, M. van Riemsdijk, and M. Sierhuis. 'Coactive design: Designing Support for Interdependence in Joint Activity.' *Journal of Human-Robot Interaction*, 3, no. 1 (2014), https://doi.org/10.5898/JHRI.3.1.Johnson.

Knopp, J., A. Hentout, and M. Aouache. 'Formation Control Using GQ(λ) Reinforcement Learning.' *Procedia Computer Science*, 109 (2017): 1023–1028.

Latikka, R., T. Turja, and A. Oksanen. 'Self-efficacy and Acceptance of Robotic Assistance Among Older Adults.' *International Journal of Social Robotics*, 13, no. 4 (2021): 701–710.

Lewis, M., K. Sycara, and P. Walker. 'The Role of Trust in Human-Robot Interaction.' In *Foundations of Trusted Autonomy*. Springer, 2018, 135–159.

Li, M., M. Kwon, and D. Sadigh. 'Influencing Leading and Following in Human–Robot Teams.' *Autonomous Robots*, 45, no. 8 (2021): 959–978, https://doi.org/10.1007/s10514-021-10016-7.

Lopes, S. L., J. B. Rocha, A. I. Ferreira and R. Prada. 'Social Robots as Leaders: Leadership Styles in Human-Robot Teams.' In *2021 30th IEEE International Conference on Robot and Human Interactive Communication (RO-MAN)*. IEEE, 2021, 258–263, https://doi.org/10.1109/RO-MAN50785.2021.9515464.

Luo, X., Y. Xie, and L. Ye. 'Is non-intervention feasible? The Impact of Laissez-Faire Leadership on Human-AI Service Collaboration.' *International Journal of Hospitality Management*, 117 (2024): 104074.

Ma, L., T. Fong, M. Micire, Y. Kim, and K. Feigh. 'Human-Robot Teaming: Concepts and Components for Design.' In *Cognitive Robotics*. Springer, Cham, Switzerland, 2017, 649–663, https://doi.org/10.1007/978-3-319-67361-5_42.

Mandischer, N., A. Hinz, and S. Mütze-Niewöhner. 'Exploring Capability-Based Control Distributions of Human-Robot Teams through Capability Deltas: Formalization and Implications.' *ACM Transactions on Human-Robot Interaction*, 13, no. 1 (2024): Article 4.

Mioch, T., N. Smets, and M. Neerincx. 'Improving Adaptive Human-Robot Cooperation Through Work Agreements.' In *Engineering Psychology and Cognitive Ergonomics. Performance, Emotion and Situation Awareness*, edited by D. Harris. Springer, Nanjing, China, 2017, 192–203.

Miron-Spektor, E., A. Ingram, J. Keller, W. K. Smith, and M. W. Lewis. 'Microfoundations Of Organizational Paradox: The Problem Is How We

Think About the Problem.' *Academy of Management Journal*, 61, no. 1 (2018): 26–45, https://doi.org/10.5465/amj.2016.0594.

Natarajan, M., E. Seraj, B. Altundas, R. Paleja, S. Ye, L. Chen, R. Jensen, K. Chestnut Chang, and M. Gombolay. 'Human–Robot Teaming: Grand Challenges.' *Current Robotics Reports*, 4, no. 3 (2023): 69–83.

Nizette, B. E. and C. Yu. 'Human Leadership Approaches to Hybrid Human/ Robot Teams.' In *2011 Chinese Control and Decision Conference (CCDC)*. IEEE, 2011, 4028–4032, Mianyang, China. https://doi.org/10.1109/ CCDC.2011.5968928.

Northouse, P. G. *Leadership: Theory and Practice*, 8th ed. SAGE Publications, 2018. Thousand Oaks, California, United States: SAGE Publications, Inc

Parks, M. and M. Allison. 'Autonomy and fatigue in human-robot teams.' In *2023 IEEE International Performance, Computing, and Communications Conference (IPCCC)*. IEEE, 2023, 158–159, Anaheim, California, United States. https://doi.org/10.1109/IPCCC59175.2023.10253851.

Pereira, R., D. de Oliveira Massad, F. L. do Canto, and G. A. Dandolini. 'The Interrelationship Between Sustainable Development and Social Innovation: A Bibliometric Study.' In *Proceedings of IDEAS 2019*, edited by L. Pereira, J. Carvalho, P. Krus, M. Klofsten and V. De Negri. Springer, Cham, Switzerland (published by Springer Nature Switzerland AG 2020, 525–539, https://doi.org/10.1007/978-3-030-55374-6_47.

Pereira, R., K. C. M. Rosa, and C. J. C. de Almeida Cunha. 'Teoria Implícita da Liderança: Uma Revisão Bibliométrica e Mapeamento Científico.' *Revista Pretexto*, 24, no. 3 (2023): 1–20.

Philip, J. and S. I. Wong. 'The Paradoxical Leader Crafting Human Worker and Robot Teammate: Exploring Hybrid Team Management Through Paradox Theory.' *Scandinavian Journal of Management*, 40, no. 1 (2024): 101371, https://doi.org/10.1016/j.scaman.2024.101371.

Scheggi, S., M. Aggravi, and D. Prattichizzo. 'Human-Robot Formation Control Via Visual and Vibrotactile Haptic Feedback.' *ACM Transactions on Interactive Intelligent Systems*, 4, no. 1 (2014): Article 4.

Sheng, W., A. Kazi, N. Xi, and Y. Chen. 'An Integrated Framework for Human–Robot Collaborative Manipulation.' *IEEE/ASME Transactions on Mechatronics*, 20, no. 4 (2015): 1905–1916.

Sicat, S., S. Chopra, N. Li, and E. Sharlin. 'Playing the Mirror Game With a Humanoid: Probing the Social Aspects of Switching Interaction Roles.' In *2017 26th IEEE International Symposium on Robot and Human Interactive Communication (RO-MAN)*. IEEE, 2017, 1078–1083.

Sirintuna, D., T. Kastritsi, I. Ozdamar, J. M. Gandarias, and A. Ajoudani. 'Enhancing Human–Robot Collaborative Transportation Through Obstacle-Aware Vibrotactile Warning and Virtual Fixtures.' *Robotics and*

Autonomous Systems, 178 (2024): 104725, https://doi.org/10.1016/j.robot.2024.104725.

Smith, W. K. and M. W. Lewis. 'Toward a theory of paradox: A Dynamic Equilibrium Model of Organizing.' *Academy of Management Review*, 36, no. 2 (2011): 381–403, https://doi.org/10.5465/amr.2009.0223.

Sott, M. K., M. S. Bender, L. B. Furstenau, L. M. Machado, M. J. Cobo, and N. L. Bragazzi. '100 Years Of Scientific Evolution of Work and Organizational Psychology: A Bibliometric Network Analysis From 1919 To 2019.' *Frontiers in Psychology*, 11 (2020): Article 598676, https://doi.org/10.3389/fpsyg.2020.598676.

Van Eck, N. and L. Waltman. 'Citation-Based Clustering of Publications Using CitNetExplorer and VOSviewer.' *Scientometrics*, 111, no. 2 (2017): 1053–1070.

Walker, M. E., M. Gramopadhye, B. Ikeda, J. Burns, and D. Szafir. 'The Cyber-Physical Control Room: A Mixed Reality Interface for Mobile Robot Teleoperation And Human-Robot Teaming.' In *2024 ACM/IEEE International Conference on Human-Robot Interaction*. ACM, 2024, 762–770, Colorado, United States, https://doi.org/10.1145/3610977.3634981.

Walsh, T. *2062: The World That AI Made*. La Trobe University Press, Carlton, Victoria, Australia, 2019.

Wolf, F. D. and R. M. Stock-Homburg. 'Making the First Step Towards Robotic Leadership – Hiring Decisions for Robotic Team Leader Candidates.' In *42nd International Conference on Information Systems (ICIS)*. Association for Information Systems, 2021, https://aisel.aisnet.org/icis2021/hci_robot/hci_robot/2.

Wolf, F. D. and R. M. Stock-Homburg. 'How and When Can Robots Be Team Members? Three Decades of Research on Human–Robot Teams.' *Group & Organization Management*, 48, no. 6 (2023): 1666–1744, https://doi.org/10.1177/10596011221076636.

Wolf, F. D. and R. M. Stock-Homburg. 'One Size Does Not Fit All: Mechanisms of Employees' Acceptance of Robotic Lower-Level Managers.' *Group & Organization Management*, (2025), https://doi.org/10.1177/10596011251313568.

Yazdani, F., B. Brieber, and M. Beetz. 'Cognition-Enabled Robot Control for Mixed Human-Robot Rescue Teams.' In *Intelligent Autonomous Systems 13*, edited by E. Menegatti, N. Michael, K. Berns and H. Yamaguchi. Springer, 2016, 1171–1182, Debrecen, Hungary, https://doi.org/10.1007/978-3-319-08338-4_98.

Yazdani, F., M. Scheutz, and M. Beetz. 'Guidelines for Improving Task-Based Natural Language Understanding in Human-Robot Rescue Teams.' In *8th IEEE International Conference on Cognitive Infocommunications (CogInfoCom 2017)*. IEEE, 2017, 000203–000208, Debrecen, Hungary https://doi.org/10.1109/CogInfoCom.2017.8268243.

Yukl, G. *Leadership in Organizations*, 8th ed. Pearson: Boston, Massachusetts, United States, 2012.

You, S. and L. P. Robert. 'Human-Robot Similarity and Willingness to Work with a Robotic Co-Worker.' *Proceedings of the ACM on Human-Computer Interaction*, 2, no. CSCW (2018): 1–19.

Zhang, Y., D. A. Waldman, and Y. Wang. 'A Multilevel Investigation of Leader–Member Exchange, Informal Leader Emergence, and Individual Performance.' *Academy of Management Journal*, 58, no. 2 (2015): 608–628, https://doi.org/10.5465/amj.2013.0713.

Zuboff, S. *The Age of Surveillance Capitalism: The Fight for a Human Future at the New Frontier of Power*. PublicAffairs: New York, NY, 2019.

Zupic, I. and T. Čater. 'Bibliometric Methods in Management and Organization.' *Organizational Research Methods*, 18, no. 3 (2015): 429–472.

© 2026 World Scientific Publishing Europe Ltd.
https://doi.org/10.1142/9781800617414_bmatter

Index

Made in the USA
Las Vegas, NV
23 August 2026

b8e4650a-93a7-473b-adbb-6f2c9a9f5075R02